Criminal Law for Legal Professionals

Michael Gulycz

Mary Ann Kelly

emond

Toronto, Canada
2014

Emond Montgomery Publications Limited
60 Shaftesbury Avenue
Toronto ON M4T 1A3
http://www.emond.ca/highered

Printed in Canada.
Reprinted November 2015.

We acknowledge the financial support of the Government of Canada.
Nous reconnaissons l'appui financier du gouvernement du Canada.   Canada

The events and characters depicted in this book are fictitious. Any similarity to actual persons, living or dead, is purely coincidental.

Publisher, higher education: Mike Thompson
Senior developmental editor: Sarah Gleadow
Director, editorial and production: Jim Lyons
Copy editor: Cindy Fujimoto
Production editor: Andrew Gordon
Proofreader: David Handelsman
Indexer: Paula Pike
Cover and text designer: Tara Wells
Cover image: Duncan Walker/iStockphotography.com

Library and Archives Canada Cataloguing in Publication

Gulycz, Michael, 1958-
    Criminal law for legal professionals / Michael Gulycz,
Mary Ann Kelly.

Includes index.
ISBN 978-1-55239-324-6

    1. Criminal law—Canada—Textbooks.
I. Kelly, Mary Ann, 1948-   II. Title.

KE8809.G85 2012   345.71   C2012-900798-6
KF9220.ZA2G85 2012

*To Veronica, for her continuing support and encouragement, and to Sarah,
who has taught me that true joy does not exist without challenge.*

— M.G.

*To the memory of Eliz Thoms, my friend and colleague
of many years at Seneca College.*

— M.A.K.

Contents

CRIMINAL PROCEDURE

PART IV
YOUNG PERSONS AND CRIMINAL LAW

PART V
OFFICE PROCEDURES FOR CRIMINAL LAW

Preface

There have been many books written about criminal law and one may very well wonder "why another?" One answer is that criminal law is fascinating. It has been the subject of many novels, texts, articles, television programs, and movies. Criminal law is studied in elementary school, high school, college, and university, and at the post-graduate level. Not a single day passes without several media reports about crime. It is, in short, an area in which there is an abundance of interest.

Criminal Law for Legal Professionals was written with several purposes in mind. First and foremost, it was written for the college student studying law, including paralegal students. A major objective of the text is to focus on satisfying the Law Society of Upper Canada's educational requirements for paralegal licensees. In a broader sense, this book fills a void by dealing with both substantive law and procedural law. It is also intended to bridge the gap between a theoretical analysis of criminal law and the practical realities of working as a legal professional. In short, it is hoped that this text will provide a comprehensive presentation for the college student studying law in any program.

This text will, however, find other uses. It can be a resource for legal professionals at all levels including lawyers, paralegals, law clerks, and others employed in the criminal justice field. The text can also be used by other students studying law, either at university or in law school. Finally, it is hoped that the text will be read by anyone with an interest in criminal law.

Criminal Law for Legal Professionals starts with an introduction and overview of criminal law in Canada in Part I. Part II focuses on substantive law and includes chapters on the elements of an offence, common defences, and corporate criminal liability. Part III covers criminal procedure from the investigative process, through the laying of an information and all subsequent procedures, right up to trials and appeals. Part IV is dedicated to young persons and criminal law and comprehensively covers the *Youth Criminal Justice Act*. Part V provides a practical overview of the unique considerations of working in a law office and includes sections on correspondence, privilege, billing, retainer agreements, legal aid, and common legal forms and documents.

A distinctive and practical feature of this text is the Appendix, which contains the most commonly used criminal forms, including forms under the *Criminal Code* and those under the *Criminal Rules of the Ontario Court of Justice*. A key feature of this text is the inclusion of practical step-by-step checklists and information-gathering forms found in the Appendix. These checklists and forms set out clearly the various steps that should be considered in gathering initial information from a client and a prospective surety, and in preparing for a bail hearing or trial.

In preparing the questions and exercises for review and discussion that follow each chapter, we relied on *Martin's Annual Criminal Code*, an annotated version of the *Criminal Code* authored by Greenspan, Rosenberg, and Henein and published by Canada Law Book. It is recommended that students use an annotated version of the *Criminal Code* when working through the problems posed in the questions and exercises.

As the reader progresses through this book it will become clear that criminal law is constantly evolving as legislators and courts respond to societal needs and pressures. As a result, the reader is cautioned that the text is current to the date of printing and it is good practice to update and confirm the current status of the material covered in this book before relying on it.

Michael Gulycz
Mary Ann Kelly
June 2013

About the Authors

Michael Gulycz

Michael holds a B.A. from York University and both an LL.B. and LL.M. from Osgoode Hall Law School. Michael is currently a full-time professor at Seneca College in the School of Legal and Public Administration. He is also a member of the Law Society of Upper Canada and started practising law in 1987. Before joining Seneca College in 2002, Michael practised first as a partner in a small firm and then as a sole practitioner. His professional experience as a lawyer includes civil and criminal litigation, administrative law, alternative dispute resolution, and wills and estates. Michael also co-authored the text *Rules of Evidence: A Practical Approach*.

Mary Ann Kelly

Mary Ann Kelly retired after having taught for 14 years in Seneca College's School of Legal and Public Administration in Toronto. She is a lawyer and a member in good standing of the Law Society of Upper Canada, holding a B.A. from the University of Toronto and a J.D. from Osgoode Hall Law School. She has also studied international law at The Hague Academy at the International Court of Justice in the Netherlands.

Mary Ann practised law as a partner in a small law firm before moving to the Ontario Ministry of the Attorney General, where she acted as Reciprocity Counsel from 1990 to 1997. In that role she managed the ministry's obligations under the *Hague Convention on the Civil Aspects of International Child Abduction* and the *Reciprocity Act*. From 1997 to 2000 Mary Ann acted as a legal policy consultant to the federal Department of Justice working on drafting and implementing policy and legislation. She has also taught in the faculties of Business and Continuing Education at Ryerson University.

PART I

Introduction and Overview

Criminal Law in Canada

1

LEARNING OUTCOMES

After completing this chapter, you should be able to:

- Differentiate between public and private law and how the distinction applies to criminal law.

- Identify the differences between criminal and civil law.

- Differentiate between substantive and procedural law.

- Demonstrate an understanding of the purpose of criminal law.

- List the sources of criminal law.

- Discuss statute law and common law in relation to their roles as sources of criminal law.

Introduction

Before embarking on a more in-depth study of criminal law, it is important to place it within the general context of Canadian law. In this chapter we provide an overview of the nature and purpose of criminal law. We also discuss the differences between criminal and non-criminal or civil law and look at the major sources of criminal law in Canada.

The overview is not meant to be an in-depth study, but rather is intended to provide an introduction or short review of topics that may already be familiar. It is necessary to understand some basic concepts and principles before embarking on a more concentrated study of criminal law.

The Nature of Criminal Law

criminal law
body of law that deals with wrongs or harm caused to society as a whole that is prosecuted by the state or government rather than the person who is harmed by the wrongdoing

In Canada, as in many other countries, **criminal law** is one of the most commonly discussed areas of law. It has political implications and repercussions and regularly forms the basis for news headlines, television series, and movies. Most people have an opinion on various aspects or principles of criminal law. A large part of what forms people's opinions may be founded on information they have gathered from the popular media. However, to study criminal law, we must look at it much more closely. First off, we have to examine where criminal law fits into the Canadian legal system.

When we talk about "the law" we mean the entire body of law laid down by the courts or the government to control the behaviour of the people under their authority. Another way of talking about people under the authority of lawmakers and law-making bodies is to say that those people are "within their jurisdiction."

The Categorization of Law

The entire body of law of a jurisdiction can be broken down into various areas of law, such as criminal law, family law, property law, tax law, immigration law, contract law, and tort law. Within each area of law there are specific rules or laws. It is most often the specific rule or law within an area of law that changes, rather than a whole body of law. When we are talking about law changing, it is important to note that law tends to change in response to circumstances in society that have already changed rather than the other way around. The law therefore tends to be more responsive than proactive. In the normal course of legal development, the law does not tend to modify society; rather, once society has changed, the law tends to adjust to reflect that societal change.

There are a number of different ways to categorize, type, or classify law and we are now going to examine some of those categorizations, types, and classifications and discuss where criminal law fits into the structure of the law.

Public Law and Private Law

One of the major ways to divide law into classes is to make the distinction between public law and private law.

Public Law

Public law relates to the relationship between an individual or business and the government. Criminal law is primarily public law. It is not principally focused on righting the harm or wrong done to an individual; rather, its main purpose is to ensure that wrongdoers are found guilty and dealt with appropriately in the justice system. Criminal law is established to maintain social order. A criminal offence is viewed chiefly as a wrong against society and it is the government, for the most part, that enforces and prosecutes the wrongdoer rather than the individual who has been harmed. The parties, meaning the legally recognized participants in the court case, are the government and the person who has been charged with the offence. The person charged is usually referred to as the accused. The victim of a criminal offence is not a party to the criminal case. He is only a witness. We will more closely examine the roles of the various players in criminal cases in Chapter 4.

Lawyers who prosecute criminal cases in Canada are either government employees or people retained by the government to represent it. They are called Crown attorneys because they represent the head of government, who in Canada is the Queen of England, otherwise known as the Crown. In addition, criminal cases are prosecuted in the name of the British monarch, not in the name of the victim. If Mr. Ali is assaulted by Ms. Jones and Ms. Jones is charged by the police with an offence, the name of the criminal case against Ms. Jones will be *R. v. Jones*. The *R.* stands for "*Regina*," which is Latin for "queen." In older cases, when the present Queen's father was the monarch, the *R.* stood for "*Rex*" or "king" and will stand for *Rex* again in the event that the Queen's son or grandson replaces her on the throne as the head of the Government of Canada. In our example, Mr. Ali, the victim, is not a party to the legal proceeding.

Other areas of public law are:

- constitutional law—law that is concerned with the protection of the rights of individuals in dealing with the government and the government's agents;
- administrative law—law that deals with the regulations made by government and enforced by agencies, boards, or tribunals that are set up by government;
- tax law—law that deals with both individual and business obligations to pay taxes and the penalties for failure to do so.

Public law also involves what we call "quasi-criminal" offences, examples of which would be provincial statutes governing traffic and liquor offences.

public law
body of law that deals with the relationship between the government and individuals or businesses—criminal law is an example

Private Law

Private law, on the other hand, involves areas of law where the interests of individuals or businesses and the interaction between them are the focus. Contract law and tort law are both examples of private law:

- **Contract law** focuses on the making of legally enforceable agreements between people or businesses and the consequences for breaking such an agreement.
- **Tort law** deals with harm caused to people or their property by others.

In that tort law focuses on harm, there is a connection between it and criminal law, but not all torts involve criminal harm. For instance, a homeowner might be careless in not shovelling the snow from her walkway and a passerby might suffer an injury when he slips and falls. This is likely not a criminal action on the homeowner's part, so the state is not necessarily interested in prosecuting her, but if the law says she caused the harm, then the homeowner will be required by the court to pay the injured passerby money to compensate him for any financial losses he suffered and any pain he experienced as a result of being injured. In order to seek compensation for the injury, the victim would sue the homeowner. For instance, if Mr. Ali slipped on Ms. Jones' icy walkway, the formal name of the case would be *Ali v. Jones* to represent the fact that Mr. Ali, a private individual, is suing Ms. Jones, another private individual.

This does not mean that a private individual who is the victim of criminal harm cannot sue an offender. If Ms. Jones, one of the characters in the examples we have been using, assaulted Mr. Ali, the criminal case against Ms. Jones would be conducted by the government against the accused with a view to holding Ms. Jones criminally responsible and punishing her for her wrongdoing. As we have discussed, the criminal law is not focused on compensating Mr. Ali for the harm caused to him.

However, if Mr. Ali was injured in the assault and, as a result, lost wages, had pain and suffering, or suffered other harm or loss, he may wish to sue Ms. Jones in tort law for monetary compensation, which is called damages.

Usually, the criminal case would be heard first. The reason is that the **standard of proof** is different. In a criminal case, the individual faces the power and resources of the state or government and, therefore, in an attempt to place the parties on a more equal footing, the justice system requires the Crown to bear the responsibility (or onus) of proving the case to a very high level of proof, beyond a reasonable doubt.

In the tort case example above, the parties are both private individuals, so they are on a more level playing field, and although Mr. Ali, who in the private law case is called a plaintiff, must still prove his case against Ms. Jones, who is the defendant, the level of proof required is much lower. The level or standard of proof required in a tort case is on the balance of probabilities. Standards and burdens of proof will be discussed more fully in a later section.

---

private law
the body of law that deals with relationships between individuals or individuals and businesses—contract law is an example

contract law
the body of law that deals with legally enforceable agreements made between parties that spell out their rights and obligations in relation to each other in a particular transaction

tort law
the body of law that deals with harm caused to a person by another for which the injured person may sue the wrongdoer for monetary compensation for the harm caused

standard of proof
the legal level of proof that must be established in a court case before the case may be won; the standard of proof in a criminal case is beyond a reasonable doubt and in a non-criminal case it is the lower standard of the balance of probabilities

civil law
the body of law in the Canadian legal system that is non-criminal; the term may also be used to describe world legal systems that are based on foundations other than British common law; most countries in Europe have civil law systems, as does the province of Quebec in its provincial law

The Distinctions Between Criminal Law and Civil Law		
	Criminal Law	**Civil Law**
What is it?	• A legal action, started by the state (government) against an individual	• A legal action started by private citizens, one against the other

Parties	• The Crown (government) v. an accused
	  – *R. v. Smith*
		• One private citizen v. another
		  – *Plaintiff v. Defendant* (e.g., *Jones v. Smith*)

Purpose	• To punish and deter criminals, and to protect society	• To compensate a person who has been physically or financially harmed
End result of case	• Determines guilt, fine, and imprisonment	• Finding of liability and payment of damages
Standard of proof	• Beyond a reasonable doubt	• On the balance of probabilities

When private individuals or businesses begin a court action against other private individuals or businesses, we say they have begun a civil action. We might also say that civil law principles govern the case to distinguish it from a case where criminal law principles apply. Sometimes the two areas of law are discussed as criminal law and **civil law**, to differentiate them.

Substantive and Procedural Law

Another manner of categorizing law is to differentiate between **substantive law** and **procedural law**. All areas of law, including criminal law, consist of both substantive and procedural law.

Substantive law is often described in general terms as the law that sets out the rights and duties of individuals. When we talk about a substantive right, we are talking about a right that can be enforced by law. In criminal law, the substantive law is the part of the law that prohibits certain behaviour or conduct from which we have the right to be protected. It is the area of the criminal law that establishes and defines all the very specific elements of each offence and defence.

Procedural law provides details of the particular steps or processes that are required to be followed in order to enforce the substantive law. Procedural law deals with the rules that govern many aspects of criminal law, including the powers of the police to conduct an investigation, the charging of the accused, bail procedures, and modes of trial and **adjudication**.

In this text, we will deal first with some aspects of substantive criminal law when we examine a number of offences and defences in Part II, Substantive Criminal Law. In Part III, Criminal Procedure, we will look at criminal procedure from the investigative stages through to the adjudication of the charge before the court.

substantive law
the part of an area of law that defines the rights and responsibilities in that area of law; in criminal law, it is the part of the law that deals with the creation of criminal offences, the defences that may apply, and the penalties for breaking the law

procedural law
the body of law that sets out the rules for a case that is making its way through the court to completion; in criminal law, it begins with the police investigation and the laying of the charge and goes through to the end of the trial

adjudication
the process that leads to the making of a legal decision

The Purpose of Criminal Law

As previously discussed, criminal law deals with harm. Often the harm is directed toward a person who is the victim of a crime. However, criminal law is viewed not simply as a matter between the perpetrator of a crime and the victim; criminal law, rather, is regarded as a wrong against society as a whole. When a crime is committed, the social order or social fabric is affected. When someone is the victim of a crime, all of the people in the area where the crime took place feel less safe. The crime is a potential threat to them all. That is why the government takes a leading role in creating laws with an aim to protect the social order and to prosecute or bring to justice those who commit criminal offences. That is also why criminal law can play a major role in politics.

If people feel unsafe in their communities, politicians may want to try to convince them that a particular political party has a solution to the issue. Politicians often claim that they will be "tough on crime," and such a claim often plays well with voters, even when crime rates might be dropping. The average person may not feel safe in their own home or neighbourhood, even though statistics suggest that they are.

Ultimately, criminal law and the criminal justice system must determine the guilt or non-guilt of a person charged with an offence. It is important to note that the court is not determining the guilt or factual innocence of a person, but rather whether a person can be found guilty under the law. As we have discussed, because the accused person is facing the weight of the state or government that is prosecuting the case, in an effort to even out the odds, the individual is guaranteed certain rights at law to try to ensure that they are not the victim of a powerful state using its resources against a powerless individual. One of these rights is the right to be presumed innocent until the Crown proves guilt beyond a reasonable doubt. Therefore, under Canadian law, the accused does not have to prove her innocence. She starts from the legal presumption that she is innocent until the Crown prosecutor meets a high standard in proving otherwise. We will look more closely at these rights in Chapter 2, The Constitution and Criminal Law.

When an accused person is found guilty of an offence, the principles of sentencing attempt to directly address the protection of society and the preservation of social order as the purposes of criminal law. While one of the major principles of sentencing is the punishment of the offender, the punishment in itself is not random, but is set so that it deters not only the offender before the court but also anyone else who might be tempted to commit the offence in the future. Punishment, however, is not the only purpose of sentencing. In addition to deterrence, s. 718 of the *Criminal Code* sets out the other main purposes of sentencing. They are:

1. to denounce unlawful conduct;
2. to deter the offender and other persons from committing offences;
3. to separate offenders from society, where necessary;
4. to assist in the rehabilitation of offenders;
5. to provide reparation for harm done to victims and/or the community; and

6. to promote a sense of responsibility in offenders and acknowledgment of the harm done by them to victims and the community.

The principles and purposes of sentencing are dealt with at some length in Part III, Criminal Procedure.

Sources of Criminal Law

Canadian criminal law is provided through two major sources:

1. statute law and
2. common law.

We will briefly examine both of these sources. A deeper examination of the sources of law can be found in texts that deal with general introductions to Canadian law. See Further Reading at the end of this chapter for some suggestions.

Statute Law

Alternative names for statute law are legislation, act, or code. Statute law is law made by the federal government in Parliament in Ottawa, or by the elected legislature in one of the provinces. The Canadian Constitution divides the authority to make statutes in various areas of law between the federal government and the provinces. If either the federal or provincial government attempts to make or pass law in a subject area that is not within its constitutional authority, the law is **ultra vires**, Latin for "outside their power," and the law is invalid. If a law is properly made within the law-making authority, then the law is **intra vires**, or "within their power."

ultra vires
a Latin term meaning that a law has been made outside the authority of the law-making body

The Constitution is the supreme law of the land. All other statutes, whether federal or provincial, must comply with the Constitution, which includes the *Canadian Charter of Rights and Freedoms*. Furthermore, the Constitution, unlike a normal statute, may only be amended through an extremely complicated set of rules and procedures set out in the Constitution itself.

intra vires
a Latin term meaning that a law has been made within the authority of the law-making body

The actual law-making process is very similar at both levels of government. More may be learned both about this process and Canada's Constitution by reading any text on an introduction to Canadian law; some suggestions can be found at the end of this chapter.

The power to make criminal law is given to the federal government pursuant to s. 91 of the *Constitution Act, 1867*; therefore, only the federal government can make what might be referred to as "true criminal law."

Provincial governments may not make any criminal law. However, they do have the constitutional power to make laws to regulate and enforce laws that they have made that are within their law-making authority. For instance, provincial governments may pass statute law that relates to highways situated within their province.[1]

---

1. Provincial powers are enumerated in s. 92 of the *Constitution Act, 1867* (U.K.), 30 & 31 Vict., c. 3.

All provinces have such statutes and they all include speed limits for various roadways. It would be senseless to give provinces the power to make laws pertaining to speed limits and then not allow them to enforce those laws with penalties. The provinces do have the power to pass statutes that enforce their laws through the creation of offences that have legal consequences. These provincial laws may be referred to as "**provincial offences**," or "**quasi-criminal offences**." They are not true criminal law and any conviction for a breach of a provincial offence does not result in a criminal record. This text does not deal with provincial offences other than in passing. For more information on this topic you may wish to refer to a text that deals specifically with this area of law.

The primary statute that creates and deals with criminal law is the *Criminal Code*. The Code contains a major portion of both the substantive and procedural criminal law of Canada, but is not the only statute in the country that is a source of criminal law. Some other federal statutes that create criminal law are the *Youth Criminal Justice Act* (YCJA), which addresses the criminal law and justice system as it applies to persons under eighteen years of age; the *Controlled Drugs and Substances Act*, which deals with drug and narcotics control; and the *Crimes Against Humanity and War Crimes Act*, which criminalizes genocide, crimes against humanity, and other war crimes based on international law and treaties. While these statutes contain most of the body of Canadian criminal law, they do not form an exhaustive list. Even the *Income Tax Act* creates a number of offences that are criminal in nature.

This text deals primarily with the *Criminal Code*, and to a lesser extent, the *Youth Criminal Justice Act*. Chapters 3 and 23 deal specifically with the history and organization of the Code and the YCJA.

Common Law

Common law, often called case law, is law made by judges. It is the oldest source of law in Canada and dates from centuries-old British common law, which was incorporated into the law of Canada at the time of Confederation in 1867. The common law continues to change and develop over time and is not the same as it was in 1867.

The body of case law builds up over time as judges apply the law in court decisions. In very simple terms, common-law (or case law) principles require judges who make decisions in the lower courts in the legal structure to follow the previous decisions of higher court judges when they are dealing with a legal issue that is based on substantially the same facts as the prior, higher court decisions. When making decisions, judges in the common-law system, particularly those at the higher level, give reasons for their judgments. These reasons are called "precedent." The rule that requires judges to follow the precedent set in earlier, higher court cases is called ***stare decisis***. Over time, sometimes over hundreds of years, a body of law grows and sets of rules develop from the following of precedent.

The earliest source of criminal law in Britain was common law. All of the original offences and defences were developed through judge-made law, not through statute law.

Historically, the common law dates back centuries to a time when there was no Parliament in Britain to make statute laws. The source of all law was the king. There-

---

provincial offences
offences created by provincial legislatures to enforce certain regulatory laws that are within their constitutional law-making authority; they are not criminal offences

quasi-criminal offences
offences created to enforce regulatory laws—they are not criminal offences but they have a number of the features of criminal law; provincial offences are an example

stare decisis
the legal principle used in the common law by which the lower courts must follow the decisions, or precedents, set by the higher courts when the facts of a case are generally the same

fore, common law is an earlier form of law than statute law. Once Parliament was established, the elected officials became the supreme lawmakers, not the king or the courts. Courts continued to make law and it was good and valid law, but if Parliament did not approve of the law, it could change it.

Statute law can change case law. The elected government can enact statutes that modify or overturn judge-made law, and this remains true in Canada today. Parliament and the provincial legislatures are supreme and can alter common law through the passing of statutes. Their only major limitation in this regard is that all statute law must comply with Canada's constitutional principles and must not violate the *Charter of Rights and Freedoms*.

Other Systems of Law

It is important to note that common law is not the only system of law in the world. For instance, much of the law of continental European countries has developed through a totally different process from the common law. Dating back to Roman times and law, this system is called "civil law." The term "civil law" can be quite confusing because it is used in two very different ways within the Canadian legal system. For instance, we talked about civil law earlier when we were examining the differences between private law and public law, and criminal law and non-criminal law. In the context of comparing criminal law and non-criminal law, non-criminal law is called civil law. But, we can also compare common law, which developed in early Britain, with a totally different system of law called civil law. This latter system of civil law developed from early Roman law and is used in most European countries. In this context, the term "civil law" means a system of law with many rules and principles that are different from those of the common law.

To complicate matters further, in Canada, federally and in all provinces other than Quebec, the common-law system is followed, but because the earliest law of Quebec was established when Quebec was a colony of France, the provincial law of Quebec still follows the civil law system used in France. This means that when the Quebec legislature makes law that is within the constitutional power of the province and when Quebec courts apply that law, they follow the principles of the civil law system, not the common-law system. However, since criminal law is federally made law, the criminal law in Quebec is the same as the criminal law in the rest of Canada.

As discussed earlier in this chapter, criminal law in Canada is primarily established by statute law, in particular the *Criminal Code*. This does not mean that the common law does not play a major role in current Canadian criminal law. Judges must apply statutes, including the *Criminal Code*, but a statute must be interpreted to be applied. When judges interpret statutes or particular provisions in them, they are making case law. Therefore, the common law and statute law have a close, interactive relationship as sources of criminal law in Canada.

Basic Principles of Canadian Criminal Law

There are a number of basic principles that form the framework of the Canadian criminal justice system and they must be kept in mind when examining the creation, structure, and procedure of the law. These principles are:

1. All persons charged with a criminal offence are presumed to be not guilty.
2. To establish guilt, the Crown must prove guilt beyond a reasonable doubt.
3. The proof must be presented in a fair and public hearing.

onus of proof
the prosecutor in a criminal case or the plaintiff in a civil case has the burden or onus to present enough evidence to win their case beyond a reasonable doubt or on the balance of probabilities, respectively

Our system of law does not require the accused to prove his innocence to the court. In fact, the accused does not have to say anything in a criminal trial. Moreover, the Crown has the burden of presenting evidence of the accused's guilt to the level of "proof beyond a reasonable doubt" and the proof must be made in a trial that is open to the public and not in a secret hearing. We call the Crown's burden the "**onus of proof**" and the level of proof to be met the "standard of proof." The presumption of innocence accompanied by the evidentiary burden and standard placed on the Crown and the procedure of a fair and open trial are principles that attempt to create a more even, legal playing field for the person charged. Otherwise, one individual might be overwhelmed by the power and resources of the state and might face the prospect of being wrongfully convicted.

The presumption of innocence is a significant common-law principle that forms the major foundation of the criminal justice system. Although the principle has existed for centuries, it is now a right enshrined in s. 11(d) of the Charter. The fact that the principle is now a Charter right means that the remedies available for a Charter violation apply. The remedies available under the Charter are addressed more fully in Chapter 2.

CHAPTER SUMMARY

This chapter gives students a brief overview of the nature of criminal law and an explanation of some topics, such as the classification of offences and the purpose of criminal law in sentencing offenders, which will be covered in more depth later in the text. The various ways of differentiating between areas of law are discussed, such as the distinction between public and private law, criminal and civil law, and substantive and procedural law, as well as how Canadian criminal law fits into the general structure of Canadian law.

We examine the sources of criminal law and discuss the role of both statute and common law in the development and ongoing application of this area of the law.

The purpose of criminal law is also discussed both within the context of societal harm and in relation to findings of guilt and sentencing in the criminal justice system. In addition, the fundamental principles of Canadian criminal law and the Canadian criminal justice system are examined.

KEY TERMS

adjudication, 7
civil law, 6
contract law, 6
criminal law, 4
intra vires, 9
onus of proof, 12

private law, 6
procedural law, 7
provincial offences, 10
public law, 5
quasi-criminal offences, 10
standard of proof, 6

stare decisis, 10
substantive law, 7
tort law, 6
ultra vires, 9

FURTHER READING

Laurence Olivo, ed., *Introduction to Law in Canada* (Concord, ON: Captus Press, 2013).
Philip Sworden, *An Introduction to Canadian Law*, 2nd ed. (Toronto: Emond Montgomery, 2006).

REVIEW QUESTIONS

1. What are the differences between private law and public law and, of the two, where does criminal law belong?
2. How do we name criminal cases and why do we name them this way?
3. What is a civil action?
4. How would you generally describe substantive law?
5. What is procedural law?
6. What is the purpose of criminal law?
7. Name the two sources of criminal law and describe each.
8. Which statute is the supreme law of the land?
9. Which level of government has the authority to make criminal law and where is that authority found?
10. What are the three basic principles of criminal law?
11. Describe each of the three basic principles of criminal law.

EXERCISES

1. Why do you think criminal law is an area of law that most people have opinions about? Do you believe that the general public is well informed about criminal law? Do you think the media has a good perspective on criminal law? What role, if any, do you think the media has in shaping Canadian attitudes toward criminal law?

2. The Parliament of Canada in Ottawa has the power to create and change the *Criminal Code* and other criminal law statutes. Judges have the power to shape and apply criminal law through the common law. Discuss whether or not you think judges should have the power to create criminal law through the interpretation of the criminal statutes.

3. Fahid was the victim of an attack by Donald. The police have charged Donald with a criminal offence. Fahid also plans to sue Donald in tort law for the damages that he suffered. Discuss the differences between these two potential court cases.

The Constitution and Criminal Law

2

LEARNING OUTCOMES

After completing this chapter, you should be able to:

- Demonstrate an understanding of the nature of the division of powers under the Canadian Constitution.

- Demonstrate an understanding that criminal law is a federal law-making power.

- Explain how the Charter applies to criminal law.

- Give a brief description of the rights enshrined in the Charter.

- Describe the two remedies under the Charter that a court may prescribe when it finds there has been a Charter violation.

Introduction

In this chapter we will review the interaction of the Constitution and criminal law. Canada's Constitution is a complex series of statutes and unwritten principles, or conventions, that are derived from British law. The primary purpose of a constitution is to establish rules about the structure of government and what powers, including law-making powers, it may and may not exercise.

The first written constitution in Canada was the *British North America Act, 1867*, a statute passed by the British Parliament that established the country of Canada, which up until then had been a colony of Great Britain.

In 1982, the Constitution was repatriated to Canada, which means that it was enacted, at that time, as a statute of Canada rather than of Britain. The *Constitution Act, 1982* kept and amended the *British North America Act, 1867* and renamed it the *Constitution Act, 1867*. In addition, the 1982 Act created the *Canadian Charter of Rights and Freedoms*.

It is important when reading this chapter to keep in mind that the Canadian Constitution consists of both the statute that sets out the structure of government and the division of law-making powers between the provinces and the federal government, and the *Charter of Rights and Freedoms*, which grants and protects certain rights given to individuals.

The Division of Powers and Criminal Law

federal state
a country in which the constitution provides for more than one level of government—Canada is a federal state

Constitutionally, Canada is what is called a **federal state**. This means that the constitution provides for more than one level of government. In Canada, these levels are the federal government in Ottawa and the provincial governments in each province. Canada's three territories, the Northwest Territories, Yukon Territory, and Nunavut, do not have the same constitutional authority as a province. They have only those powers that are given to them by the federal government. Likewise, a municipal government has no constitutional authority of its own because it is the creation of a province and therefore has only those powers given to it by the province.

Not all countries are federal states. Some are what we call unitary states, in that they have a central government that holds the sole authority to make laws and carry out other governing functions. Examples of federal states are the United States, Germany, Australia, India, and Mexico; examples of unitary states are France, Italy, New Zealand, Colombia, and the United Kingdom.

Under the Canadian Constitution, both levels of government have authority to make laws in the areas listed in the *Constitution Act, 1867*. Section 91 of that Act sets out the areas in which the federal government has the power to make law and s. 92 lists the provincial government law-making powers. Each level of government has the authority to make laws only in its specified areas.[1] Any law made outside the

---

1. Although there are overlapping powers in some areas, which are referred to as concurrent jurisdiction, and the doctrine of paramountcy applies when there are valid laws. In such cases, it is the federal law that applies. Considerably more information and discussion on Canadian constitutional law can be found in any introductory textbook on Canadian law. A good source is Sworden, *An Introduction to Canadian Law*, 2nd ed. (Toronto: Emond Montgomery, 2006).

confines of the constitutional authority is said to be *ultra vires*. A law that is *ultra vires* is invalid.

Section 91(27) of the *Constitution Act* provides that criminal law, including criminal procedure, falls within the **federal law-making power**; therefore, only Parliament in Ottawa can pass law that is criminal in nature. However, s. 92(15) gives the provincial governments the authority to create laws that relate to the "imposition of punishment by fine, penalty or imprisonment for enforcing any law of the province … ." It would make little sense to have a constitution that provided provinces with the powers to make laws within certain defined areas but did not give them the power to enforce them. Therefore the provincial legislatures may pass statutes that create offences for failure to abide by the laws that they have the constitutional authority to make. For instance, there is no question that the provinces have the jurisdiction to make laws related to highways in the province. Such laws include speed limits. The legislature of each province also has the power, pursuant to s. 92(15), to create offences and punishments for failure to obey set speed limits.

Although at first glance these provincially created offences may appear to be criminal in nature, they are not true criminal law. We call these offences "**provincial offences**" or refer to them as "**quasi-criminal offences**" in order to distinguish them from true criminal law. This text will deal only with true criminal law and not with the area of provincial offences, which warrants an entire body of material on its own.

As we have discussed, laws that are outside the constitutional authority of a level of government are said to be *ultra vires*. Laws passed by a level of government that are within the proper constitutional power are *intra vires*. On occasion, the Supreme Court of Canada has ruled that a provincial legislature has passed a law related to provincial offences that has crossed the line into the area of criminal law, which is *ultra vires*. Laws that are outside a level of government's constitutional authority to pass will be struck down by the courts under s. 52 of the *Constitution Act* and cannot be applied. The power in s. 52 to strike down unconstitutional law also applies to the Charter and is discussed in more detail in the following section.

federal law-making power
the authority given by the Constitution to the federal government to make laws in certain areas—criminal law is made only by the federal government

provincial offences
offences created by provincial legislatures to enforce certain regulatory laws that are within their constitutional law-making authority; they are not criminal offences

quasi-criminal offences
offences created to enforce regulatory laws—they are not criminal offences but they have a number of the features of criminal law; provincial offences are an example

The Charter of Rights and Freedoms and Criminal Law

The Constitution as the Supreme Statute

The *Charter of Rights and Freedoms* became part of the Canadian Constitution in 1982. For the most part, the rights enshrined in the Charter were not new rights. The majority were rights and freedoms that existed at common law and which had been included in the *Canadian Bill of Rights*, a statute passed by Parliament in 1960. However, the inclusion of these rights and freedoms in the Charter meant that they now became part of the constitutional law of Canada. The Constitution is unlike other statutes in that it is the **supreme statute** and all other statutes must be consistent with it. In other words, both federal and provincial legislation must comply with the Constitution, including the Charter. If a piece of either provincial or federal legislation violates the rights set out in the Charter, the offending legislation

supreme statute
a statute with which all other statutes must comply; the Constitution is a supreme statute

potentially will be struck down by the courts. Legislation that is struck down is of no force or effect.

Section 52 of the *Constitution Act, 1982* provides:

> 52(1) The Constitution of Canada is the supreme law of Canada, and any law that is inconsistent with the provisions of the Constitution is, to the extent of the inconsistency, of no force or effect.

It is important to note that the Charter applies only in the interaction between the individual and the state. It does not apply between individuals. Violation of rights between individuals is dealt with by human rights legislation.[2]

Even when the Charter does apply, the rights and freedoms set out are not absolute in nature. The Charter places some significant limitations on them.

First of all, s. 1 states:

> 1. The *Canadian Charter of Rights and Freedoms* guarantees the rights and freedoms set out in it subject only to such reasonable limits prescribed by law as can be demonstrably justified in a free and democratic society.

infringement of rights
action by governments or their agents that violates a right granted under the *Charter of Rights and Freedoms*

In other words, the Charter allows **infringements of rights** and freedoms if it can be shown to the court that the infringement is reasonable and can be justified. Usually this sort of infringement arises when the government is attempting to balance various interests. For instance, s. 9 of the Charter guarantees the right to be free from **arbitrary detention**. This means that the police may not stop people or vehicles at will. They must have reasonable and probable grounds for believing that an offence has been committed before they can stop and detain someone.

arbitrary detention
action in which the police improperly and unlawfully stop and hold a person in their custody for even a few minutes

However, in the *Hufsky* case, the Supreme Court of Canada upheld the use of programs operated by many police forces that involve the arbitrary stopping of vehicles. Under these programs, drivers are stopped at random to determine whether they have been drinking. The Court ruled that the stops by the police under these programs were a Charter violation, but that their use could be upheld under s. 1 on the basis that their purpose was to curb the impaired driving that kills many people every year on Canadian roadways.

The Notwithstanding Clause

In addition to s. 1, s. 33 of the Charter also provides for a limitation on guaranteed rights and freedoms. This section is usually referred to as the "**notwithstanding clause**." It provides as follows:

notwithstanding clause
a rarely used controversial provision in the *Charter of Rights and Freedoms* that allows the federal government or a provincial legislature to override certain portions of the Charter

> 33(1) Parliament or the legislature of a province may expressly declare in an Act of Parliament or of the legislature, as the case may be, that the Act or a provision thereof shall operate notwithstanding a provision included in section 2 or sections 7 to 15 of this Charter.

---

2. For example, *Canadian Human Rights Act*, R.S.C. 1985, c. H-6; British Columbia *Human Rights Code*, R.S.B.C. 1996, c. 210; Ontario *Human Rights Code*, R.S.O. 1990, c. H.19.

(2) An Act or a provision of an Act in respect of which a declaration made under this section is in effect shall have such operation as it would have but for the provision of this Charter referred to in the declaration.

(3) A declaration made under subsection (1) shall cease to have effect five years after it comes into force or on such earlier date as may be specified in the declaration.

(4) Parliament or the legislature of a province may re-enact a declaration made under subsection (1).

(5) Subsection (3) applies in respect of a re-enactment made under subsection (4).

This section allows Parliament or a provincial legislature to override the Charter and declare a particular piece of legislation valid despite the fact that it infringes on a Charter right or freedom. Any such validation of infringing legislation would last for only five years, although there is no stated minimum on the number of times infringing legislation may be re-enacted.

This notwithstanding clause, which was added to the Charter as a compromise, permits the government to override a number of guaranteed rights or freedoms, knowing that the legislation is an infringement on those rights and freedoms. The section, although rarely used, has been employed in the province of Quebec. The Supreme Court of Canada found that sections of the Quebec language law regarding the use of French were a violation of the Charter. In 1989, the provincial legislature used s. 33 to save the legislation despite the Charter infringement. Since then, the language law has been rewritten and the notwithstanding clause that applied to it is no longer in effect.

The section is used sparingly largely because its use by any level of government tends to raise significant political concern in its opponents. It would essentially amount to the government saying, "We know this statute will deprive individuals of a particular right but we are doing it anyway." To put it mildly, that would likely be an extremely controversial position to take and is not in keeping with government commitment to the Charter.

Section 33 applies to only the rights and freedoms set out in s. 2 (fundamental rights) or ss. 7 to 15 (legal and equality rights) of the Charter. Other rights, such as democratic rights or mobility rights, cannot be overridden.

Rights and Freedoms Set Out in the Charter

A number of different types of rights are set out in the Charter:

Section 2 sets out fundamental rights such as freedom of conscience and religion; freedom of thought, belief, opinion, and expression, including freedom of the media; freedom of peaceful assembly; and freedom of association.

Sections 3 to 5 set out democratic rights such as the right of citizens to vote.

Section 6 sets out mobility rights such as the right of citizens to enter, remain in, and leave Canada; and the right to live and work in any province.

Sections 7 to 14 set out legal rights: Section 7 provides a general statement that grants the right to life, liberty, and security of the person and the right not to be deprived of these rights except in accordance with fundamental justice.

Section 8 provides the right to be secure against unreasonable search and seizure. It is the interpretation of this section by the Supreme Court that requires police to obtain search warrants, other than in exceptional circumstances.

Section 9 provides that everyone has the right not to be arbitrarily detained or imprisoned. **Section 10** grants the right upon arrest or detention to be advised of the reason, to be informed of the right to have a lawyer, and to be afforded the right to retain one without delay.

In both of these sections, the courts have given the term "detention" a broad definition. A person can be either physically detained, for instance, in the back of a police car, or psychologically detained. A psychological detention occurs when a person is not legally required to comply with the demands of a police officer, but is unaware of that fact and believes that he has no choice but to comply.

Section 11, one of the most important Charter sections for the purposes of criminal law, sets out the rights in criminal matters and proceedings. It states:

11. Any person charged with an offence has the right
(a) to be informed without unreasonable delay of the specific offence;
(b) to be tried within a reasonable time;
(c) not to be compelled to be a witness in proceedings against that person in respect of the offence;
(d) to be presumed innocent until proven guilty according to law in a fair and public hearing by an independent and impartial tribunal;
(e) not to be denied reasonable bail without just cause;
(f) except in the case of an offence under military law tried before a military tribunal, to the benefit of trial by jury where the maximum punishment for the offence is imprisonment for five years or a more severe punishment;
(g) not to be found guilty on account of any act or omission unless, at the time of the act or omission, it constituted an offence under Canadian or international law or was criminal according to the general principles of law recognized by the community of nations;
(h) if finally acquitted of the offence, not to be tried for it again and, if finally found guilty and punished for the offence, not to be tried or punished for it again; and
(i) if found guilty of the offence and if the punishment for the offence has been varied between the time of commission and the time of sentencing, to the benefit of the lesser punishment.

Sections 12 and 13 provide for the right to not be subjected to cruel and unusual punishment and the right against self-incrimination, respectively.

Section 14 grants the right to an interpreter to a party or a witness in proceedings.

Section 15 sets out the equality rights that provide equality before the law and the right not to be discriminated against on the basis of race, national or ethnic origins, colour, religion, sex, age, or mental or physical disability. This section also protects any affirmative action programs set up in an attempt to create a level playing field for those who are disadvantaged on any of the above-mentioned grounds.

Section 16 prescribes language rights in relation to the two official languages, English and French.

Remedies for Charter Violations

As discussed above, s. 52 of the *Constitution Act, 1982* provides for the striking down of any law that is found by the court to infringe upon the Constitution, including the Charter. Once a **law is struck down**, we say that it is of **no force or effect**. The court may strike down the entire piece of legislation or only the portion of the statute that offends. Courts are reluctant to strike down a piece of legislation in its entirety, and are more likely to want to sever the offending parts. For example, in 1988 the Supreme Court of Canada found that s. 287 of the *Criminal Code*, the section that relates to procuring a miscarriage, violated s. 7 of the Charter.[3] Section 287 was struck down and is no longer law in Canada.

In addition to the remedy of striking down the offending legislation, s. 24 of the Charter offers a second remedy for a Charter violation.

The section reads as follows:

> 24(1) Anyone whose rights or freedoms, as guaranteed by this Charter, have been infringed or denied may apply to a court of competent jurisdiction to obtain such remedy as the court considers appropriate and just in the circumstances.
>
> (2) Where, in proceedings under subsection (1), a court concludes that evidence was obtained in a manner that infringed or denied any rights or freedoms guaranteed by this Charter, the evidence shall be excluded if it is established that, having regard to all the circumstances, the admission of it in the proceedings would bring the administration of justice into disrepute.

The first thing to note about s. 24 is that s. 24(1) provides a remedy that is "appropriate and just" to anyone whose rights or freedoms, as guaranteed by the Charter, have been infringed or denied while s. 24(2) provides a remedy in cases where evidence was obtained in a manner that infringed or denied any rights or freedoms guaranteed by the Charter. Clearly there are two separate remedies contained in s. 24, a general remedy under s. 24(1) and, in s. 24(2), a remedy for evidence that was obtained in a manner that infringed a person's rights.

In relation to the first subsection, it provides a broad remedy of what is "appropriate and just" in the circumstances. Although "appropriate and just" remedies might include damages and injunctions, the usual remedy in a criminal or quasi-criminal context would be a stay of proceedings. When proceedings are stayed, the Crown is prevented from continuing the tainted prosecution. This may be an

striking down a law
power given to the courts under the *Charter of Rights and Freedoms* to make a law inoperable because the law violates the Charter

no force or effect
a law that is struck down by the courts is said to be of no force or effect because it is inoperable

---

3. *R. v. Morgentaler*, [1988] 1 S.C.R. 30, 37 C.C.C. (3d) 449.

Bringing the Administration of Justice into Disrepute

R. v. Grant, 2009 SCC 32, [2009] 2 S.C.R. 353

Facts

In late 2003, three police officers were conducting a daytime patrol in the east end of Toronto. There were four schools in the area and there had been a history of violence in the area. Two of the officers were in plain clothes and one was in uniform.

The two plainclothes officers noticed the accused, Donnohue Grant, an 18-year-old man, walking up the street and decided to ask the uniformed officer to stop and question him on the basis that he was "acting suspiciously" by adjusting his clothing. All three officers ended up standing in front of Mr. Grant, blocking his way and questioning him.

During the questioning they asked him if he had anything that he shouldn't have and Mr. Grant answered that he had a small bag of marijuana and a loaded firearm. The officers seized the drugs and the gun, read Mr. Grant his rights, and arrested him. He was charged with several serious firearm offences.

Issues

There were a number of issues in this case, including whether or not Mr. Grant had been illegally detained contrary to s. 9 of the Charter and whether his right to counsel had been violated by the police questioning him without first advising him of his right to counsel, contrary to s. 10(b) of the Charter.

Secondly, if his Charter rights were violated, should the evidence of the gun be admissible under s. 24 of the Charter?

The Decision

At trial, the gun evidence was admitted and Mr. Grant was convicted of the gun offences. The case eventually wound its way through the appeal courts to the Supreme Court of Canada.

The Supreme Court of Canada found that Mr. Grant had been detained illegally on a psychological rather than a physical basis, and that his right to counsel had been violated by the police questioning prior to him being advised of his right to counsel.

Given the violations of ss. 9 and 10(b) of the Charter, the Court was then required to determine whether the gun

evidence was admissible against Mr. Grant. If the gun was not admissible, there was no case against him. In determining the admissibility, the Court set out a new test for admissibility of illegally obtained evidence under s. 24(2).

After applying the revised test, the Court concluded that the gun evidence was admissible against Mr. Grant and that his conviction should stand.

The Test

The Supreme Court revised the existing test for the admissibility of evidence obtained as a result of Charter violations. The test is a balancing of a number of factors to be considered in determining whether the admission of the evidence would bring the administration of justice into disrepute.

The test consists of three parts and is to be applied by all courts in weighing factors and analyzing the admissibility of illegally obtained evidence under s. 24(2). Under the test, courts must consider the following factors:

1. **The Seriousness of the Charter Breach**

    The court must assess whether the admission of the evidence would bring the administration of justice into disrepute. The admission of evidence obtained by deliberate and flagrant violations of the Charter by the police will likely bring the administration of justice into disrepute whereas more minor breaches, conducted in good faith by the police, will not necessarily do so.

2. **The Impact of the Charter Breach on the Interests of the Accused**

    The court must determine whether the Charter infringement had the effect of being profoundly intrusive on the accused rights or whether it was more, in the words of the Court, "fleeting and technical" in nature. If the impact on the accused was more fleeting and technical, the Charter infringement will not necessarily bring the administration of justice into disrepute. An example of a profoundly intrusive violation of rights might be an illegal strip search of an accused.

3. **Society's Interest in a Trial on the Merits**

    The Canadian public has a strong interest in bringing those who have broken the law to a fair and just trial that is based on reliable findings of the truth. Therefore, a court faced with a Charter breach affecting the accused must determine whether the breach compromised the reliability of the evidence and affected its ability to help find the truth. Admitting unreliable evidence would undermine the truth-finding function expected of the courts and would bring the adminis-tration of justice into disrepute. For instance, if the accused was held by the police in oppressive circumstances that bordered on torture, was not advised of his right to counsel, and in order to simply end the torture-like conditions, the accused confessed to a crime, such a confession would not likely be regarded as reliable.

---

appropriate remedy where there has been a breach of an accused's right to be tried within a reasonable period of time pursuant to s. 11(b)[4] or where the Crown has failed to provide complete disclosure to the accused.[5]

The words "appropriate and just" provide a wide range of other possible remedies. Clearly there can be no exhaustive list and the possibility exists for novel approaches in appropriate cases. For example, s. 24(1) has been used to return property seized in violation of s. 8 of the Charter to the lawful owner.[6]

The primary Charter provisions with regard to **wrongfully obtained evidence** are contained in s. 24(2). When the remedies provided in s. 24(2) are combined with Charter protections such as s. 7 (life, liberty, and security of the person), s. 8 (unreasonable search and seizure), s. 9 (arbitrary detention), s. 10 (rights on arrest and detention), and s. 12 (cruel and unusual treatment or punishment), evidence seized as a result of the Charter violation may be excluded by the court. This acts as a deterrent to police in the conduct of their investigation. If the courts rule that strip-searching a prisoner in public is contrary to the individual's right to be secure from unreasonable search and seizure and they exclude the cocaine found during the illegal search, the police will very quickly stop that practice and conduct such searches in private. The process of excluding evidence is not so much punitive as an attempt to reform substandard practices and educate or retrain law enforcement personnel with regard to the proper Charter standard that applies to their dealings with the public.

There are a number of purposes that have been identified for excluding evidence that is wrongfully obtained.[7] These include:

- restoring parties to the position they were in before the Charter breach;
- stopping the police from engaging in improper practices;
- educating the police and the public;
- ensuring that the courts continue to be held in high regard; and
- recognizing and protecting a core group of basic human rights.

wrongfully obtained evidence
evidence that is obtained as a result of a violation of a person's rights under the *Charter of Rights and Freedoms*

---

4. *R. v. Askov*, [1990] 2 S.C.R. 1199.

5. *R. v. Stinchcombe*, [1991] 3 S.C.R. 326.

6. *Lagiorgia v. Canada*, [1987] 3 F.C. 28 (C.A.), leave to appeal to Supreme Court of Canada refused (1988), 43 C.C.C. (3d) vi (note) (S.C.C.).

7. For an in-depth discussion of evidence law, see Cochran, Gulycz, and Kelly, *Rules of Evidence: A Practical Approach* (Toronto: Emond Montgomery, 2008).

The two subsections of s. 24 work together. Before there is even a consideration of whether or not the evidence should be excluded, there has to be a "proceeding" under s. 24(1) to determine whether there in fact has been an infringement of an individual's right or freedom.

Therefore, when you read the subsections in terms of their interrelationship, the exclusionary remedy operates as follows:

1. Anyone
2. whose rights and freedoms, as guaranteed by this Charter, have been infringed or denied
3. may apply to a court of competent jurisdiction.
4. Where a court concludes that evidence was obtained in a manner that infringed or denied any rights or freedoms guaranteed by this Charter
5. the evidence shall be excluded if it is established that, having regard to all the circumstances, the admission of it in the proceedings would bring the administration of justice into disrepute.

exclusionary remedy
power given to the courts under s. 24 of the Charter to prevent the admission of wrongfully obtained evidence at an accused person's trial

Evidence that meets all of the other components of the **exclusionary remedy** will still be admissible unless its admission would bring the administration of justice into disrepute. The expression "would bring the administration of justice into disrepute" is a bit of a mouthful, so another way of saying it is that the public would lose respect for the justice system if such evidence were admitted. For example, a confession that was obtained by torture, or evidence obtained by police officers who searched people because of their skin colour or the way that they dress, would cause the public to have less respect for, or even lose respect for, the system of justice.

R. v. Grant[8] is a Charter case in which the Supreme Court of Canada considered, among other issues, the test that courts are to apply in determining whether the administration of justice will be brought into disrepute should evidence be admitted. This case refined the previous test for determining the admissibility of evidence that had been laid out by the Supreme Court in the earlier case of *R. v. Collins*.[9] The Case in Point feature on pages 22 and 23 in this chapter outlines the *Grant* case and the test.

---

8. 2009 SCC 32, [2009] 2 S.C.R. 353.

9. [1987] 1 S.C.R. 265, 33 C.C.C. (3d) 1.

CHAPTER SUMMARY

This chapter gives an overview of the Canadian Constitution that includes the division of law-making powers between the federal and provincial governments. Criminal law is a law-making power that is expressly granted to the federal government and, therefore, only that level of government can pass true criminal law. Provinces may, however, pass laws to enforce the law-making powers given to them under the Constitution. Such provincial laws are often referred to as provincial offences, or quasi-criminal offences. They are not true criminal law. Speeding is an example of such an offence. Should a level of government pass a law that is outside its constitutional authority, the law will be struck down by the courts.

The chapter then goes on to examine the Charter in terms of its content and its operation. The Charter applies only to the interaction of the government and individuals. All laws of the land must comply with the Constitution, including the Charter, and those that fail to do so may be struck down by the courts pursuant to s. 52 of the *Constitution Act, 1982*. Any law that is struck down is not operational and cannot be applied.

Charter rights are not absolute, however, and a law that violates the Charter may be saved by the court under s. 1, which provides that the infringement of the right must be one that is "demonstrably justified in a free and democratic society." If the court finds no such justification for the infringement, it will strike the law down under s. 52. The law is then of no force or effect. Parliament or the legislature of a province may save a law that has been struck down by the courts by using the "notwithstanding clause" in s. 33 of the Charter. Lawmakers are reluctant to use such power because it would mean that they were upholding a law that the courts found unconstitutional.

Section 24 of the Charter provides a second remedy for a violation or infringement. Sections of a statute such as the *Criminal Code* might not, in their wording, violate a right or freedom, but the manner in which they are applied by the government or its agents, such as the police, may violate the Charter. After determining that a violation has occurred, the court may apply a remedy that is "appropriate and just." Section 24(2) provides that illegally obtained evidence may be excluded if the court finds that it would bring the administration of justice into disrepute; in other words, that it would diminish respect for the justice system. The chapter concludes with a look at the *Grant* Test, which sets out the factors that courts must consider when determining whether the admission of evidence would bring the administration of justice into disrepute.

KEY TERMS

arbitrary detention, 18
exclusionary remedy, 24
federal law-making power, 17
federal state, 16

infringement of rights, 18
no force or effect, 21
notwithstanding clause, 18
provincial offences, 17

quasi-criminal offences, 17
striking down a law, 21
supreme statute, 17
wrongfully obtained evidence, 23

REVIEW QUESTIONS

1. What do we mean when we say Canada is a federal state?

2. Which level of government has the power to make criminal law and how do we know this?

3. Explain why we say the Constitution is the supreme law of Canada.

4. When does the *Charter of Rights and Freedoms* apply?

5. Are the rights and freedoms under the Charter absolute? Explain your answer.

6. What is the *Grant* Test?

EXERCISES

1. Discuss why the application of the Charter plays a major role in the criminal justice system.

2. What are the two remedies for Charter violations? Discuss each remedy and when and how it applies. Note the differences in the two remedies.

3. List the legal rights that are granted by the Charter. Discuss whether or not some of these rights and freedoms are more important to you than others.

The Criminal Code

3

LEARNING OUTCOMES

After completing this chapter, you should be able to:

- Give a brief explanation of the history of criminal law in Canada and the development of the *Criminal Code* of Canada.

- Demonstrate a basic understanding of the structure of the *Criminal Code*.

- Describe the general classification of offences in the *Criminal Code* and give simple examples.

- Explain the limits of a paralegal practice in the representation of clients charged with criminal offences.

Introduction

In this chapter we briefly examine some of the history and structure of Canada's major statutory source of criminal law, the *Criminal Code*. The Code is a very complicated statute and it is not possible to fully embark on a study of this area of law without understanding the basics of its structure and numbering system.

In addition, we take an initial look at the classifications of offences within the Code. It is this classification system that dictates the procedure a criminal case will follow as it winds its way through the court system. We will study this classification system in more depth in Chapter 11.

History of the Code

Originally, as it developed in England, criminal law was common law, also known as judge-made law. There was no statute law pertaining to criminal offences. By the 1800s, the English government was gradually codifying the common law in relation to crime. This meant that the common law was being written into legislation and passed as statute law by the British Parliament. There were a number of statutes at that time dealing with various crimes and aspects of criminal law. By the latter part of that century, there was a concerted effort in Britain to unify all the various statutes relating to criminal law and codify them into a single statute. The purpose of codification was to make the law more open and accessible both to those who were legally trained and to the average person; the principle was that if all criminal law were in one statute, it would not only make it easier to do legal research, but also make the law better known to citizens. However, efforts to create a single, consolidated English criminal code have not been successful and, to date, England has no comprehensive criminal code. A portion of its criminal law is still common law, although most offences are now codified and can be found in a number of different statutes.

We know that Canadian law derived from the English common law. At the time of Confederation in 1867, the first prime minister of Canada, Sir John A. Macdonald, who was a lawyer, was determined to avoid the difficulties that England was struggling with due to its disparate criminal law. He was adamant that the new country should have a unified criminal law statute as soon as possible. The *Criminal Code, 1892* was passed by Parliament in Ottawa and was the first comprehensive code of criminal law in Canada. It was based on the proposed English code that was drafted by the British Parliament, but never passed.

The entirety of criminal law in Canada was not codified into the first *Criminal Code* and it was still necessary in many instances to rely on the common law, but the Code did provide an orderly approach to Canadian criminal law right from its beginning.

The *Criminal Code* has not remained static since 1892—far from it. As society changes, the *Criminal Code* very often also changes to reflect new social thought, mores, and policy. In 1955, there was a major revision to the Code. One of the significant amendments was the elimination of all common-law criminal offences except contempt of court in s. 9. Contempt of court is the only remaining common-law criminal offence because all other Canadian criminal *offences* now exist only in statute law, but s. 8(3) preserves all the existing common-law *defences*. As a result, there are some defences that are codified and some that are found in the common law. There is more information on this in Chapter 10, which deals with defences.

Structure of the Code

The *Criminal Code* is one of the longest and most complex statutes in Canada. It contains both substantive criminal law and procedural law. In order to be able to work effectively with the Code, it is important to understand how it is structured and how changes to the criminal law, made by Parliament, are included in the existing structure.

The statute comprises over 800 sections that are grouped together according to subject matter under numerous Parts. The Parts are numbered in Roman numerals and the sections in ordinary numbers (Arabic numberals). For example, Part III is entitled "Firearms and Other Weapons," and contains the substantive criminal offences related to guns and other types of weapons. There are more than 20 sections in that Part—for example, s. 87, which provides that it is an offence to point a firearm at another person without a lawful excuse, and s. 104, which makes it an offence, without lawful excuse, to import or export a firearm or a component or part designed exclusively for use in the manufacture of an automatic weapon. Part VIII contains offences against the person, such as s. 265, assault, and ss. 229 and 231, murder. This Part also contains offences that have the potential to cause harm to a person, such as s. 253, operating a motor vehicle while impaired, or s. 249, dangerous operation of a motor vehicle, most commonly known as dangerous driving.

The criminal law is regularly revised, and when new offences are created the drafters of the Code attempt to place them within a Part that contains similar offences. For instance, a few years ago, due to a growing problem that was causing widespread public concern and was covered extensively in the media, an amendment was made to the Code to create a specific new offence of "fleeing the police in a motor vehicle, while the police are in pursuit." Fleeing vehicles had injured and killed a number of innocent people, so Parliament created a stronger deterrent in this new offence, which carries a higher penalty than the offence of dangerous driving.

Since this new offence deals with an offence against the person, it made the most sense to place it in Part VIII, Offences Against the Person and Reputation. Moreover, it is a very specific type of dangerous driving, so this new offence needed to be placed logically not only within Part VIII, but also close to the existing offence of dangerous driving.

When new offences are added, it creates problems for the numbering structure in the Code. It was necessary to assign a section number to this new offence. If the new offence were placed close to s. 249, the offence of dangerous driving, it might be given the next number in the sequence, for example, s. 250; however, if that method were used, it would necessitate the renumbering of all the hundreds of following sections. Because that approach is very unwieldy, a different system is used to add new sections. The new section is placed near any existing offence to which it relates and is given the same section number as the existing offence, followed by a decimal point and an additional number. Following this scheme, the new offence of "fleeing the police in a motor vehicle" was given the section number 249.1. Additional offences were added to the statute to create specific offences related to street racing, which are also associated with dangerous driving, and they were given the same section number as dangerous driving, followed by decimal points and succeeding numbers to indicate that they are new sections: for example, ss. 249.2, 249.3, and 249.4. There are numerous other examples of amendments, both to substantive law and procedural law in the Code, that follow this numbering format.

Sometimes, however, a new amendment is too cumbersome to be accommodated by simply adding new sections to the Code, and an entire new Part will have to be created. As with new sections, the new Part is placed near any existing Part to which it relates. For example, a great number of new offences were created by Parliament to deal with terrorism, and they were put together in a separate Part following Part II, Offences Against Public Order. The new Part was numbered Part II.1, Terrorism.

To make the most effective use of this text, the reader should keep a copy of the *Criminal Code* close by for easy reference. It would be useful to use an annotated copy of the Code. An annotated copy contains not only the wording of the statute, but also short summaries of related criminal cases, common wording synopses, and other helpful information. Annotated versions of the *Criminal Code* are available through a number of legal publishers. In the alternative, there is a copy of the Code available online at the Government of Canada website at http://laws-lois.justice.gc .ca/eng/acts/C-46, but this version of the statute contains only the Code itself and may be less helpful than an annotated version.

Classification of Offences

All of the substantive criminal offences can be classified as one of three types of offences:

1. **indictable offences**,
2. **summary conviction offences**, and
3. **hybrid offences**.

Indictable offences are the most serious and carry the highest penalties. Murder (ss. 229, 230, and 231) is an indictable offence, and carries a penalty of imprisonment for life (s. 235). Summary conviction offences are the least serious offences. Disturbing a religious service (s. 176(2)) is a summary conviction offence and carries a maximum penalty of $5,000 or six months' imprisonment, or both (s. 787). Indictable offences follow a different procedural stream from summary conviction offences. Hybrid offences are those that can be treated as either summary conviction or indictable at the election of the Crown. In other words, the prosecutor decides

indictable offences
offences that are the more serious offences in the *Criminal Code* and that follow the indictable procedure in the Code

summary conviction offences
offences that are the least serious offences in the *Criminal Code* and that follow the summary conviction procedure in the Code

hybrid or Crown option offences
offences that may be prosecuted as either summary conviction offences or indictable offences, at the choice or election of the Crown

whether the offence will proceed as either an indictable offence or a summary conviction offence. These offences carry two different potential penalties depending on whether the Crown proceeds by indictment or summarily. Section 265, the offence of simple assault, is an example of a hybrid offence.

In those provinces in which paralegals are licensed to practise, such as Ontario, s. 802.1 permits agents or paralegals to represent only those persons charged with summary conviction offences when the offence has a maximum potential jail sentence of no more than six months. The exception to this is if the lieutenant governor in council of a province has authorized them to do so under an approved program. To date, no such approved program exists, including in Ontario, so paralegals and agents are limited in their practice of criminal law.

The classification of offences is dealt with in considerable depth in Chapter 11 in Part III, Criminal Procedure.

CHAPTER SUMMARY

In this chapter we take a brief look at the history of the development of criminal law in Canada. Emphasis is placed on the codification of criminal law and the creation of a comprehensive *Criminal Code* and how that sets Canadian criminal law apart from British criminal law.

We also examine the basic structure of the *Criminal Code*, with emphasis on the numbering system used in that statute.

It is essential that the numbering of Parts and sections be understood in order to make effective use of the Code in study and in practice.

Finally, we give an overview of the classification of offences in the *Criminal Code*, with examples of each. This topic will be discussed in more detail in Chapter 11.

KEY TERMS

hybrid or Crown option offences, 30
indictable offences, 30
summary conviction offences, 30

REVIEW QUESTIONS

1. What is a comprehensive criminal code?
2. Explain briefly the history of the *Criminal Code* of Canada.
3. How has the *Criminal Code* changed over the years?
4. Briefly describe the general organization of the *Criminal Code*.
5. What are the major classifications of offences in the *Criminal Code*? Briefly describe each type of major classification.

EXERCISES

1. What do you think might be the advantages and disadvantages of a comprehensive criminal statute over a collection of different criminal statutes based on specific topics or based primarily on the common law?
2. Locate in the *Criminal Code* examples of each type of offence classification. Find different examples from those given in the chapter.
3. Using the *Criminal Code*, answer the following questions:
   a. Is suicide against the law? Explain.
   b. Is prostitution a crime? Explain.
   c. Is it a crime to leave a nine-year-old child alone in a car with the windows closed on a hot July day? Would your answer be the same if the child were 10 years old?
   d. Johnny went ice fishing (i.e., he was trying to catch fish by drilling a hole in the ice—he was not fishing for ice!). He caught his limit and left. Later, Murray, after consuming 12 bottles of beer in 90 minutes, went for a snowmobile ride on the lake. It was dark and Murray was quite drunk. Unfortunately he did not see the hole in the ice. Murray went through the hole and into the freezing water, but was saved because he was wearing a survival suit. What criminal offences have been committed?

The Canadian Criminal Process

4

LEARNING OUTCOMES

After completing this chapter, you should be able to:

- Understand the adversarial nature of the Canadian judicial process.

- Explain the role of the police in the criminal justice system.

- Demonstrate an understanding of the roles of the judge and jury in the criminal justice system.

- Describe the role and duties of the Crown prosecutor in the criminal justice system.

- Describe the role and duties of the defence legal representative in the criminal justice system.

- Demonstrate an understanding of the role of and limitations on the licensed paralegal or agent in the criminal justice system.

- Describe the basic court structure in Canada.

Introduction

Canada's legal system is adversarial in nature and is the type of judicial process used in most countries that base their system on the British common-law system. In the adversarial model, each party is represented by a skilled advocate, with legal knowledge and training. One party's legal representative presents his or her party's case in the best possible light within well-established ethical rules. The opposing party's legal representative then has the right to challenge the other side's case through questioning witnesses and calling their own evidence. The judge is unbiased and impartial, taking a passive role in the proceedings in the sense that the judge does not actively question witnesses. The premise is that when each party presents his or her case in the most favourable light, and has an opportunity to vigorously challenge the opposing party's case, the truth will emerge. There are a number of players in the process, and each has a particular role.

The Role of the Police

In the area of criminal law, we start with the police because they are duty-bound in the system with the responsibility to protect the public by investigating possible breaches of the law, apprehending and charging persons who are accused of breaches, and bringing the accused before the court. Historically, these duties in early criminal law were performed by members of the community, but as society became more complex, a specific group was hired to perform these tasks. In Canada and many other countries, although not in the United Kingdom, front-line police officers are armed and patrol their communities to keep order and enforce the law. In the United Kingdom, an ordinary police officer is not armed.

Canada is a democracy and, to protect against any potential drift toward a police state where the police have unreasonable power over citizens, its citizens are guaranteed rights that the police and judicial system must recognize. The rights of the individual are enshrined in the *Canadian Charter of Rights and Freedoms*, which was discussed in Chapters 1 and 2. As a result, there are limitations on police powers, and a violation of a person's Charter rights by the police can result in a case being thrown out of court.

There are limitations on the ways that police can investigate crime. For instance, they are required to obtain a search warrant before they can search a suspect's home, unless there are exceptional circumstances. The law of search and seizure is discussed at length in Chapter 13, Investigatory Powers.

In addition, police officers are expected to obtain an arrest warrant and there is a duty on them to not arrest a person without a warrant, except in very specific circumstances that are outlined in s. 495 of the *Criminal Code*. The powers of arrest are examined in detail in subsequent chapters, particularly in Chapter 14, Bringing the Accused Before Court.

If a person is detained or arrested, the police must ensure that the person is advised of the reason for the arrest and of his or her rights to retain counsel without delay. The police and the accused do not always agree as to when particular detention begins, and the courts have ruled that whether or not a detention occurred is a factual determination. The court will examine the circumstances and decide whether or not the person was actually detained. It is important to note that detention need not be solely physical in nature, but can be psychological. The court may find that a psychological detention has occurred when a person has an interaction with the police in which they mistakenly believe that they cannot walk away from the police, even on an open street. In such instances, the police are obligated to inform the person of their rights in the same way that they would be required to do so if they placed the person in handcuffs and put them in the back of a police car.

Finally, while police officers are allowed to use reasonable force in making an arrest, an officer who is found to have used excessive force may be charged criminally under s. 26 of the Code.

The Role of the Judge and Jury

The judge in the adversarial system must be both impartial and unbiased and must not descend into the fray of the trial. For instance, the judge must not engage in any questioning of witnesses that resembles **cross-examination**. Such action by a judge can result in a decision being overturned on appeal. The restriction does not mean that the judge cannot ask any questions. A judge can certainly seek clarification of what a witness is saying by asking questions, but any type of questioning by a judge that can be seen as adversarial is not permitted. It is the lawyers and legal representatives who are adversarial in the process. Any behaviour by a judge that appears to be adversarial endangers the impartiality and unbiased nature of the proceedings.

In a trial, two types of decisions must be made: (1) the facts must be decided and (2) the law that applies to those facts must be determined. If an accused is tried by a judge and jury, the jury determines the facts and the judge advises them on how to apply the law. In such instances, we say that the jury is the **trier of fact** and the judge is the **trier of law**. When a judge sits alone, without a jury, the judge fulfills both decision-making roles. Since all summary conviction matters are tried by judge alone, in those cases it is the judge who is both the *trier of fact* and the *trier of law*.

In addition, the judge ensures that the trial is conducted fairly and that the rules, including the rules of evidence, are properly applied. If an accused is unrepresented by counsel or another legal representative, the judge has a duty in a criminal case to ensure that the rights of the accused are protected.

The Role of the Prosecutor

Duties of the Prosecutor

In Canada, criminal prosecutors prosecute cases on behalf of the state and prosecutions are conducted in the name of Her Majesty the Queen, who is the head of state in Canada. Criminal prosecutors are therefore referred to as Crown attorneys. Usually, there is one Crown attorney in each judicial district and there are a number of assistant Crown attorneys working under their supervision.

cross-examination
principle of the adversarial system in which one side in a legal proceeding is given an opportunity to question the witnesses for the opposing party in order to challenge their evidence and the entire case

trier of fact
person or persons who must determine the credible facts in a case; this can be a jury, or if there is no jury, the judge who hears the evidence

trier of law
the judge who determines the law that applies to the facts of a case and who, in a trial with a jury, instructs the jury on the application of the law

Unlike in the United States, where the chief prosecutor is often an elected official, Canadian prosecutors are employees of the government and are therefore public servants. All Crown attorneys are lawyers. They are not agents for the police, do not attend at crime scenes, and have a role that does not centre on winning a conviction. Rather, the Crown attorney is expected to assist the court in arriving at the truth, even if the truth is that the accused is not guilty of the offence charged. The Supreme Court of Canada has clearly set out Crown prosecutors' responsibilities. The Court has pointed out their duty to the truth and to fairness.[1]

These duties of the Crown arise out of the fact that the state has far greater resources than those available to the accused. The state has the assistance of the police in investigating and gathering evidence. It has the availability of forensic experts to test the evidence. It has financial resources significantly greater than those of most accused persons. This imbalance could lead to considerable unfairness to the accused without the special duties placed on the prosecution.

The Crown prosecutor should not be seen as either trying to win or trying to lose a case. One of the Crown prosecutor's major roles is to assist the court in arriving at the truth. In fulfilling that duty, the Crown must be fair and should avoid tunnel vision. He or she must not ignore evidence that points to a conclusion other than the guilt of the accused. In circumstances where the accused is not aware of a potential or possible defence, the Crown should bring the matter to the attention of the court. If there is no reasonable prospect of conviction or if prosecution is not in the public interest, the Crown should withdraw the charge.

Of course, the above duty does not mean that the prosecutor should not strongly advocate his or her case. On cross-examination, the prosecutor must vigorously test the evidence presented by the defence because it is this testing that assists in the adversarial process that results in the truth emerging from the court.

Disclosure

In relation to its duties to seek the truth and be fair, the Crown has a responsibility to disclose to the defence all relevant evidence. In the leading case of *R. v. Stinchcombe*,[2] the Supreme Court of Canada held that there was a duty on the Crown to disclose all relevant evidence, whether or not it was to be presented at trial by the prosecution. Although *Stinchcombe* applied to indictable offences, this principle has been extended by policy to all criminal matters, including summary conviction proceedings. Disclosure is discussed in detail in Chapter 17, Pretrial Procedure.

Most Crown attorneys or Crown prosecutors are employees of the provincial government. The reason for this is that although the Constitution gives authority to the federal government to make criminal law, it gives responsibility for the administration of justice, including criminal justice, to the provinces. Crown prosecutors report to their provincial Attorney General's department or ministry.

---

1. There are a number of cases in which the Supreme Court of Canada talks about the role of the Crown; two, for example, are *Boucher v. The Queen*, [1955] S.C.R. 16 and *R. v. Gruenke*, [1991] 3 S.C.R. 263, at 295.

2. [1991] 3 S.C.R. 326.

However, criminal prosecutions under federal statutes other than the *Criminal Code*, such as those that fall under the *Controlled Drugs and Substances Act*, the *Income Tax Act*, and so on, are conducted by Crown attorneys who are either employees of the federal government or counsel in private practice who are retained by the federal government to prosecute particular cases on behalf of that level of government. They are often referred to as federal Crowns to distinguish them from their provincial employee counterparts.

The Role of the Defence

The role of the legal representative for the defence is to represent and protect his client's interests to the best of his ability within the ethical boundaries set out by the rules or codes of professional conduct.

Misunderstanding the Role of the Defence

The role of the defence is often the most misunderstood in the justice system. Many people who do not understand the structure of the system wonder how someone could represent the interests of a person charged with a heinous offence. They do not understand that the Canadian criminal justice system cannot function without defence representatives. As noted above, our justice system is adversarial. This means that it operates on the principle that the truth is disclosed to the court through each party having the opportunity to present its best case to an unbiased and impartial judge, and to vigorously test the case put forward by the opposing party. Without skilled legal representation, this would be very hard to do. Even an accused charged with the worst criminal offence cannot go to trial and be judged by the system if he wants legal representation and cannot obtain it. Section 10 of the *Charter of Rights and Freedoms* guarantees the right to counsel and that right cannot be exercised if no one is willing to represent the accused. Presumably, if the accused were left without representation in court, the charges against him would eventually have to be withdrawn or stayed because no trial could be held, let alone be held within a reasonable time, as guaranteed by the Charter. Therefore, the defence plays an integral role in the criminal justice system.

Duties and Ethical Responsibilities of the Defence

It is not the role of the legal representative for the defence to judge her client. That is the role of the judge and jury and the defence representative should not ever usurp that role. Rather she is to perform her professional duties in a competent and ethical manner. Even if the client were to admit his guilt to the representative, this in itself does not preclude the representative from going to trial and requiring that the Crown prove the elements of the offence beyond a reasonable doubt. There is a Charter right to be presumed innocent until proven guilty and a plea of not guilty does not indicate a plea of absolute factual innocence but is rather a requirement that the Crown fulfill the obligation they are given under the Charter. However, the

Duties and Responsibilities of the Defence Representative

Duty to the Court

- Do not misrepresent the facts of the case, the evidence, or the statutory or case law. If you know of leading precedents that are not helpful to your case, you still must disclose them to the court.

- Do not criticize or mock the judicial system, the court process, the decision of the justice, or any witnesses or the prosecution outside the court or to the media. If you or your client are dissatisfied with the court's decision, the correct route to challenge it is through the appeal court.

- Follow through on all undertakings (personal promises) to the court or the prosecution. Do not make an undertaking unless you are able to fulfill it.

Duty to Your Client

- Your job is not to judge your client—that is the role of the justice system. Your job is to defend your client's rights. Remember that the justice system cannot properly function unless there is a strong advocate for the defence.

- The decision on how to plead to the charge is the client's, not the legal representative's, but you must advise your client fully and honestly in helping him or her decide how to plead. If your client has no real defence, a plea of guilty may be in his or her best interests, but a plea of guilty should not be seen as the easy way out if there is a proper legal defence available.

- You must fearlessly defend your client's rights and present every available defence within the limit of the law and professional ethics.

- Even if your client has confessed to you in confidence, he or she may still wish to plead "not guilty" because the Canadian criminal justice system requires the Crown to prove the case beyond a reasonable doubt. A "not guilty" plea is not a declaration of factual innocence in our system; rather, it is a statement made to the court that requires the Crown to meet their obligation to prove the matter. This is the absolute right of all people who are charged with a criminal offence. What you may not do is call your client or witnesses to give false evidence to the court.

- Best practice involves giving written information to the client about timelines, cost, etc., and getting the client's instructions in writing.

- In jurisdictions that permit licensed paralegals, the client must be made aware that the representative is not a lawyer.

- Once you have appeared in court for a client, you are now "on the record" as the legal representative and cannot simply quit without the court's permission. Permission will not be given by the court if the withdrawal will result in prejudice to the client, or inconvenience to the court or any witnesses; for example, if the trial is to begin soon and a delay will be required for a new representative to get up to speed, permission may be denied.

- If you have reasonable grounds to believe that your client is obstructing or distorting the truth you must ask them to stop and if they do not, you should ask the court for permission to withdraw. However, you must be discreet in explaining to the court your reasons for seeking to withdraw. Only minimal reasons should be given because anything more would prejudice your client. The justice is alert to these situations and will usually accept a minimal reason such as "the relationship has broken down."

Duty to Be Competent

- While a considerable amount of competency is built up through experience, you must not take on a case that you do not have sufficient knowledge or skill to handle. If you need advice from a more skilled advocate, refer the case or ask the more skilled person if he or she will act as a mentor.
- Keep up to date in the law and methods of legal research.
- Be fully prepared for every court date. Cases can be won on the basis of proper preparation alone.

Duty to Witnesses

- It is improper to harass or humiliate a witness who is giving evidence in the courtroom.
- Do not try to coach your witnesses about what evidence to give. You should, however, rehearse a witness so that he or she understands the questions you will be asking and the pressure they may be under in cross-examination; what you do not want to do in the rehearsal is to suggest possible answers to the questions. Always advise a witness to tell the truth.

representative, in fulfilling her duty to her client, must also advise the client of her professional opinion as to the outcome of the case. It might be in the client's interests to plead guilty in many instances, but it must be the client's decision, not that of the legal representative.

Generally speaking, if an accused pleads guilty to an offence, they will receive a lesser sentence than if they went to trial and were convicted. This is based on the principle that in pleading guilty the accused is taking responsibility for his or her actions. It would, however, be improper to advise a client who is claiming innocence to plead guilty for the sole purpose of receiving a more lenient sentence.

After a representative is advised in confidence by her client of his guilt, she cannot do anything unethical in presenting the case. For instance, she cannot put her client on the witness stand to lie or distort the truth. Nor can she call a witness to give evidence that she knows is false. Such actions are the most grievous forms of professional misconduct.

If a client is instructing a representative to do something unethical, there is a duty on the representative to attempt to persuade them to stop or, if that is unsuccessful, the representative should withdraw from the case. Once the case has started and the representative has appeared in court or filed formal legal documents in the court on behalf of her client, she cannot withdraw without the permission of the court. In legal terms, once the case is under way or formal documents have been filed, a representative is regarded as being "on the record." This means that she is listed on the court record as the formal legal representative.

When asking the court for permission to withdraw from a case for a valid reason, such as the client instructing unethical behaviour, the representative must be very discreet and give only minimal reasons, such as saying that the relationship with the client has broken down. The judge will not normally press a representative for more information because he will be aware that there is a serious problem and that the representative is bound by the principle of confidentiality.

In circumstances in which the client has confessed his guilt to his legal representative, the representative cannot ethically claim that her client did not factually commit the offence, nor can she call factual evidence that promotes anything other than her client's admissions. For example, in the face of her client's confidential admissions, she could not call on the client's girlfriend to give evidence that the client was with her, at home, at the time the offence was committed. However, the representative can raise any legal issue, such as the jurisdiction of the court, the constitutional validity of the law, the admissibility of any evidence the Crown might wish to call, and any other technical defences that the case presents.

The legal representative might also want to investigate the possibility of a **plea agreement** with the Crown if her client has no clear defence to a charge and the client is not insisting on his innocence. These agreements are often called plea bargains and the media or the public are sometimes highly critical of the process. However, the criminal justice system could not properly function without such arrangements.

As we know, the Crown has the legal burden of proving the case against the accused beyond a reasonable doubt. The Crown may have some concern about one or more elements of the offence and being able to meet the standard of proof. In such circumstances, the Crown may be willing to look favourably on the accused pleading guilty to a lesser charge or receiving a lesser penalty upon a plea of guilty. In addition, the Crown may be willing to lower a charge against an accused if the accused has evidence against a more serious offender who cannot be charged without the accused's evidence.

> **plea agreement**
> an arrangement between the prosecution and the defence in which the accused agrees to plead guilty to the charge in exchange for a lesser penalty or to plead guilty to a lesser charge; the justice must agree to the arrangement before it can be put into place

Paralegals

The phrase "legal representative" has been used so far in our discussion of the role of the defence. In the case of serious criminal charges, the legal representative will always be a lawyer. The common term used in the *Criminal Code* to refer to a lawyer is "counsel." However, ss. 800(2) and 802(2) make reference to the fact that the accused may be represented by an "agent" in a summary conviction matter, although there are significant limitations placed on who will be recognized by the court as an "agent" for the defence, and even if the agent is recognized by the court as being generally qualified, the types of charges on which an agent may appear are restricted.

Section 802.1 of the Code reads as follows:

> 802.1 Despite subsections 800(2) and 802(2), a defendant may not appear or examine or cross-examine witnesses by agent if he or she is liable, on summary conviction, to imprisonment for a term of more than six months, unless the defendant is a corporation or the agent is authorized to do so under a program approved by the lieutenant governor in council of the province.

To date, the only province that has a program "approved by the lieutenant governor in council of the province" is Ontario. That province has a properly approved program for the licensing of paralegals by the Law Society of Upper Canada, the governing body for members of the legal profession within the province. Paralegals who meet licensing requirements may appear in summary conviction courts to represent an accused on a summary conviction charge that carries a potential jail term of no more than six months. Paralegals may not appear on any indictable offence. The licensing requirements for paralegals involve specified educational qualifications and the writing of an entrance examination set by the Law Society.

The classification of offences, including summary conviction offences, is discussed more thoroughly in Part III of this text in Chapter 11, but generally speaking, summary conviction offences are the least serious. The most serious offences fall within a classification called indictable offences. Indictable offences are prosecuted by a different procedure from that used for summary conviction offences.

There is a third classification: hybrid offences or Crown election offences. The offences that fall within this category can be prosecuted by either the indictable procedure or the summary conviction procedure. The Crown attorney makes the choice on how to proceed, and if the indictable procedure is chosen, it opens up higher penalties if the accused is convicted. These hybrid offences are regarded as indictable unless the Crown chooses to proceed summarily. A paralegal may not appear on a hybrid offence unless and until the Crown advises the court that he wishes to proceed by way of summary conviction.

In some instances, the Crown may be willing to advise a paralegal on how he wishes to proceed before the court date. If it is going to be by way of summary conviction, the paralegal can attend court with the client. Once the Crown has advised the judge that he wishes to proceed summarily, the paralegal can rise and inform the court that she is representing the client. Of course, even before requesting advance information from the Crown, the paralegal must ensure that the potential penalty under the Code will not be more than six months' imprisonment. This can be determined by reading the statute and referring to the further discussion of this topic in Part III of this text.

Trial and Appeal Courts

Basic Court Structure

Basic Court Structure
Supreme Court of Canada
Court of Appeal (for each province)
Superior or Supreme Court (for each province)
Provincial Court (for each province)

The Supreme Court of Canada is the highest court in Canada and any ruling or decision made by this court is law throughout the entire country. Constitutionally, the authority to set up this court is given to the federal government under s. 101 of the *Constitution Act, 1867*.[3]

We know that the power to make criminal law constitutionally falls within the power of the federal government; however, s. 92(14) of the *Constitution Act, 1867* gives the provinces the authority to set up, name, and administer the court system within their geographical area. That power includes setting up courts to hear criminal law cases. All the provinces and territories of Canada basically have the same court structure, with the exception of Nunavut, which has only one level of court, the Nunavut Court of Justice.[4]

Specific Names of the Superior or Supreme Court in Each Province or Territory

- Court of Queen's Bench for Saskatchewan
- Court of Queen's Bench of Alberta
- Court of Queen's Bench of Manitoba
- Court of Queen's Bench of New Brunswick
- Nunavut Court of Justice
- Ontario Superior Court of Justice
- Quebec Superior Court
- Supreme Court of British Columbia
- Supreme Court of Newfoundland and Labrador (Trial Division)
- Supreme Court of Nova Scotia
- Supreme Court of Prince Edward Island
- Supreme Court of the Northwest Territories
- Supreme Court of the Yukon Territory

---

3. This section of the *Constitution Act, 1867* (U.K.), 30 & 31 Vict., c. 3 also gives the federal government the authority to set up the federal courts, which are specialized courts that deal with tax law, immigration matters, admiralty cases, and intellectual property cases. There are two federal courts: the Federal Court of Appeal and the Federal Court, but neither court deals with criminal law and so the federal courts are therefore not dealt with in any further detail in this text.

4. The Nunavut Court of Justice is a superior court composed of federally appointed judges. It has the jurisdiction to hear all matters, including those that would be heard at a lower level court in the other provinces and territories.

The courts of each province and the other territories can be divided into higher level and lower level courts. The higher court judges are appointed by the federal government and the lower court judges by the province or territory.[5] The higher levels of courts within a province include the Court of Appeal for the province, which is the highest court in the province, and the superior or supreme court of the province.

The names of the superior or supreme level of court may vary from province to province or territory to territory, but they have the same role in the justice system. They are trial courts and also hear appeals from the lower courts.

The lower level courts are also trial courts but because these courts were created by statute they do not have the authority to hear the same broad span of cases as the superior courts. In most provinces they are called provincial courts, although in Ontario the name is the Ontario Court of Justice and in Quebec, the Court of Quebec.

Specific Names of Lower Level Courts in Each Province or Territory

- Court of Quebec
- Ontario Court of Justice
- Provincial Court of Alberta
- Provincial Court of British Columbia
- Provincial Court of Manitoba
- Provincial Court of New Brunswick
- Provincial Court of Newfoundland and Labrador
- Provincial Court of Nova Scotia
- Provincial Court of Prince Edward Island
- Provincial Court of Saskatchewan
- Territorial Court of the Northwest Territories
- Territorial Court of the Yukon

Trial and Appeal Court Structure

The court structure and how it relates to criminal law can be quite complex, and a much more detailed discussion of courts and court jurisdiction can be found in Part III, Chapter 12 of this text. At this point, we will briefly examine the difference between the roles of a trial court and an appeal court.

Trial courts are those in which criminal cases are heard, witnesses are called, evidence is presented, facts are determined, and the law is applied to those facts to

---

5. *Constitution Act, 1867* s. 96.

decide whether an accused is guilty or not guilty. Summary conviction trials always occur in the provincial or lower level court of a province or territory. There are no juries at this level of court, so both the facts and the law are determined by the judges who hear the cases.

More serious indictable offences are usually heard in the superior or supreme court of a province by a judge who has been appointed by the federal government. There may or may not be a jury involved in hearing cases at this court level. More information about trials for more serious charges that are conducted by judge alone or by judge and jury can be found in Part III, Chapter 13 of this text.

As with provincial court trials, in superior or supreme court trials evidence is called, witnesses are heard, and the facts of the case are determined and the law is then applied to those facts to determine the guilt or non-guilt of the accused.

In criminal matters, the superior or supreme court of a province also acts as a first level of appeal court from the decisions of the provincial court.

transcript
a word-for-word, written record of everything said in court; it is prepared by a court reporter

The primary role of courts hearing appeals is to determine whether or not the trial court made a legal mistake or a legal error. In most instances, the court hearing an appeal does not hear evidence. Instead, it relies on a transcript taken during the trial. A **transcript** is a word-by-word record of the trial proceeding.

panel of judges
appeals in the higher courts are often heard by more than one judge; the judges form a panel

Normally, more than one judge hears an appeal. The judges together form what is called a **panel**, and, in order to avoid a tie, there is never an even number of judges sitting on an appeal panel. For the most part, during an appeal, the judges on the panel hear the legal arguments of the lawyers; they do not, except in the most unusual cases, hear evidence.

The function of appellate courts and judges and the right to appeal are addressed in depth later in this text in Chapter 21, Appeals.

CHAPTER SUMMARY

In this chapter we examine the roles of the major players in the criminal justice system: the judge, jury, Crown prosecutor, and defence legal representative. Particular attention is paid to the role of licensed paralegals in Ontario. We also discuss the ethical duties of both the defence representative and the Crown.

We then review the general court structure for trials and appeals in each province and territory.

KEY TERMS

cross-examination, 35
panel of judges, 44
plea agreement, 40

transcript, 44
trier of fact, 35
trier of law, 35

REVIEW QUESTIONS

1. What do we mean when we say that the justice system in Canada is adversarial?

2. What is the general role of the police in the criminal justice system?

3. What are the limitations on the role of the police and what could happen if the police step beyond their limitations?

4. What is the difference between the role of the judge and the role of the jury?

5. What is the primary duty of the Crown prosecutor in a criminal case?

6. What is the primary role of the legal representative for the defence?

7. Why is the role of the defence legal representative extremely important in an adversarial system like Canada's?

8. When may an accused person be represented by someone other than a lawyer?

9. In what circumstances may an agent or paralegal appear on a hybrid offence?

10. What are trial courts?

11. What is the function of an appeal court?

EXERCISES

1. Do you think that judges in Canada should be elected, rather than appointed?

2. Do you think the general public has a higher opinion of prosecutors than they do of defence representatives? Discuss what you believe is the reason for this.

3. What do you think might be some of the advantages and disadvantages of licensing paralegals?

PART II

Substantive Criminal Law

The Elements of an Offence 5

LEARNING OUTCOMES

After completing this chapter, you should be able to:

- Identify and understand the elements of an offence.

- Distinguish between the different types of *actus reus*.

- Distinguish between the different types of *mens rea*.

- Demonstrate an understanding of the role of voluntariness in the *actus reus* of an offence.

- Explain the difference between objective and subjective *mens rea*.

Introduction

reasonable doubt
very high standard of
proof that the Crown must
meet to prove the guilt
of the accused person

We know that the prosecution must prove a criminal offence beyond a **reasonable doubt**. But what is it exactly that the Crown must prove? He or she must prove the elements of the offence beyond a reasonable doubt.

An offence is made up of two separate elements. The first element is the **actus reus**. The *actus reus* comprises the physical elements of the offence that describe the wrongful conduct or actions or physical circumstances in which the offence was committed. The second element is the **mens rea**, which comprises the mental aspects of the offence.

actus reus
Latin term that is often
translated as "the guilty
act"; it involves the
physical elements of
a criminal offence

Actus Reus

mens rea
Latin term that is commonly
translated as "the guilty
mind"; it involves the
mental or fault elements
of a criminal offence

Actus reus is a Latin term that is often translated as "the guilty act."

Despite the term "guilty act," not all offences have an *actus reus* that involves an action or a behaviour. Some offences involve the accused being found in certain *circumstances*. Others entail a *failure* to act. In short, the types of *actus reus* may be broken down into the following categories:

1. offences that require an action, conduct, or certain behaviour;
2. offences that involve the accused being found in certain prescribed circumstances;
3. offences that involve the failure of the accused to act (omissions); and
4. offences that cause certain consequences to occur.

These categories are discussed in the following sections and examples.

Offences Requiring Action, Conduct, or Behaviour

Section 372(2) creates the summary conviction offence of making an indecent telephone call. It reads:

> 372(2) Every one who, with intent to alarm or annoy any person, makes any indecent telephone call to that person is guilty of an offence punishable on summary conviction.

This offence requires the accused to perform a certain action. They must make a telephone call that is indecent.

Offences Requiring the Accused to Be in Specific Circumstances

Section 201(2)(a) makes it an offence to be found in a common gaming or betting house,[1] without a lawful excuse for being there. The section reads:

---

1. Section 197(1) of the *Criminal Code*, R.S.C. 1985, c. C-46 provides definitions of "common gaming house" and "common betting house."

201(2) Every one who

   (a) is found, without lawful excuse, in a common gaming house or common betting house, …

is guilty of an offence punishable on summary conviction.

To be charged with this offence, the accused need only be in the house without a lawful reason. (Lawful reasons for being there, for example, might be to read the electric meter or make a pizza delivery.) Being there is enough to meet the test of completing the *actus reus* of this offence. The accused need not actually be engaged in the illegal gambling that is occurring there.

Possession offences involving various items or substances are other examples of this type of offence relating to circumstances. According to ss. 354(1)(a) and (b):

354(1) Every one commits an offence who has in his possession any property or thing or any proceeds of any property or thing knowing that all or part of the property or thing or of the proceeds was obtained by or derived directly or indirectly from

   (a) the commission in Canada of an offence punishable by indictment; or

   (b) an act or omission anywhere that, if it had occurred in Canada, would have constituted an offence punishable by indictment.

For example, a person who stores property in her garage, knowing it is stolen, need not have committed or even been involved in stealing the property; merely having it in her possession is sufficient in terms of establishing the *actus reus*.

Offences Involving Failure to Act: Omissions

There are a number of offences in the *Criminal Code* that have an *actus reus* for a failure to do something, which is known as an **omission**. However, no one can be convicted of any offence involving a failure to act, unless she has a legal duty to act. The duty can be one created by the *Criminal Code* or by another statute. For instance, s. 215 creates a legal duty for a specific person, such as a parent or guardian, to supply a child with the necessaries of life. Failure to meet this duty is a criminal offence. It is regularly charged in cases of child neglect. Sections 215(1) and (2) state:

omission
a type of *actus reus* in which the accused person fails to do something that he is legally required to do

215(1) Every one is under a legal duty

   (a)   as a parent, foster parent, guardian or head of a family, to provide necessaries of life for a child under the age of sixteen years;

   (b) to provide necessaries of life to their spouse or common-law partner; and

   (c) to provide necessaries of life to a person under his charge if that person

      (i) is unable, by reason of detention, age, illness, mental disorder or other cause, to withdraw himself from that charge, and

      (ii) is unable to provide himself with necessaries of life.

   (2) Every one commits an offence who, being under a legal duty within the meaning of subsection (1), fails without lawful excuse, the proof of which lies on him, to perform that duty, if

(a) with respect to a duty imposed by paragraph (1)(a) or (b),

(i) the person to whom the duty is owed is in destitute or necessitous circumstances, or

(ii) the failure to perform the duty endangers the life of the person to whom the duty is owed, or causes or is likely to cause the health of that person to be endangered permanently; or

(b) with respect to a duty imposed by paragraph (1)(c), the failure to perform the duty endangers the life of the person to whom the duty is owed or causes or is likely to cause the health of that person to be injured permanently.[2]

The breakdown of the *actus reus* into the above categories is done to assist us in analyzing various offences and identifying the *actus reus* required. However, not all offences in the Code fall neatly into one type of *actus reus*. Many offences have an *actus reus* that involves conduct, action, or behaviour that must occur within a set of certain circumstances. For instance, s. 265 creates the offence of assault. Section 265(1)(a) reads as follows:

265(1) A person commits an assault when

(a) without the consent of another person, he applies force intentionally to that other person, directly or indirectly; ... .

The *actus reus* of this offence is applying force to another person, directly or indirectly. Applying force involves an action. However, to meet the complete *actus reus* for the offence, the force must have been applied without the consent of the person to whom the force was applied. The element of consent is a circumstance that frames the required action.

Offences That Cause Certain Consequences and Causation

There are a number of offences in the *Criminal Code* that require a consequence as part of the *actus reus*. An example of an offence that has a consequence is the offence of causing a disturbance in s. 175.

175(1) Every one who

(a) not being in a dwelling-house, causes a disturbance in or near a public place,

(i) by fighting, screaming, shouting, swearing, singing or using insulting or obscene language,

(ii) by being drunk, or

(iii) by impeding or molesting other persons, ...

is guilty of an offence punishable on summary conviction.

---

2. It should be noted that the wording in s. 215(2) "the proof of which lies on him" has been struck down by the Ontario Court of Appeal as a violation of s. 11(d) of the Charter because it places an onus of proof on the accused that cannot be justified under s. 1. Therefore, the section must now be read as though those words do not form a part of it. The Crown must now prove beyond a reasonable doubt that the accused did not have a lawful excuse for his or her failure to act. *R. v. Curtis* (1998), 123 C.C.C. (3d) 178 (Ont. C.A.).

To prove the *actus reus* of this offence, the Crown must prove not only that the accused acted in one of the proscribed ways, while not being in a dwelling house (circumstances), but also that the actions of the accused caused a disturbance. A disturbance in or near a public place must be proved to have been the consequence of the accused's actions, behaviour, or conduct. For instance, if the accused was quietly staggering home drunk down a deserted street, the Crown might have significant difficulty in securing a conviction.

In these offences that require a consequence, the Crown must prove beyond a reasonable doubt that the conduct of the accused caused the particular consequence. In other words, the Crown must prove **causation**. This causal link can usually be proved fairly easily. For instance, if the drunk in our above scenario was rolling home down the street, singing and yelling, and woke up all the neighbours, it would not be difficult to show a direct link between the behaviour of the accused and the disturbance caused to the neighbours.

causation
part of the *actus reus* of some criminal offences where the Crown is required to prove that the actions or behaviour of the accused resulted in or caused a specified consequence

Voluntariness of the Actus Reus

The actions of the accused in committing the *actus reus* of the offence must be conscious and voluntary. There is no criminal responsibility in Canadian law for actions that are illegal if the accused did not act consciously and voluntarily. Some defences that might go to the voluntariness of the defendant's conduct are necessity, duress, and automatism. For example, if the accused can successfully raise the defence of duress, let's say that she can establish that she was forced at gunpoint to commit the offence, she may be acquitted of the offence on the basis of her actions not being voluntary. Likewise, if the defence could prove that the accused was sleepwalking while committing the offence, she may be acquitted on the basis that she was acting as an automaton in an unconscious manner.

Mens Rea

Mens rea is a Latin term that is commonly translated as "the guilty mind." We do not apply criminal sanctions to a person on the basis of their actions only. A person may perform the same actions with entirely different intent. Before a person can be found criminally responsible for her actions, the courts must be satisfied that she had a state of mind that was blameworthy, that there was a level of fault. It is the *mens rea* that establishes the fault element of the offence.

For instance, earlier we looked at s. 265 of the *Criminal Code*, the offence of assault. We learned that the *actus reus* necessary for that offence is that force must be applied to another person without that person's consent. However, there is a difference between someone getting angry and pushing the person with whom they are angry and someone pushing another person on a crowded subway car in an attempt to keep their balance when the train stops suddenly. In both cases the actions are the same, the application of force to another without consent. We are all likely to agree that the latter situation, pushing someone inadvertently on a crowded subway train, is not one in which we would apply criminal consequences, whereas pushing someone in anger may very well be criminal in nature. The difference is the mental element involved in the application of force. In the first scenario, the application of force is morally blameworthy, and in the second, it is not.

Subjective and Objective Mens Rea

The law recognizes several types of *mens rea*. In the 1993 Supreme Court of Canada case *R. v. Creighton*, the court made a clear distinction between subjective and objective *mens rea*.

Subjective *mens rea* is concerned with the actual intention or knowledge of the accused. It is concerned with "what was actually going on in the mind of this particular accused at the time in question." Subjective *mens rea* requires proof that the accused "intended the consequences of his or her acts, or that knowing of the probable consequences of those acts, the accused … proceeded recklessly in the face of the risk."[3]

Objective *mens rea* is not concerned with what was happening in the mind of the accused. It is not established by proving what the particular accused intended or knew, but rather by applying the **reasonable person test**. What would a reasonable person, in the same circumstances as the accused, have understood to be the risk of his or her actions? In the words of the Court in the *Creighton* case, "Objective *mens rea* is not concerned with what was actually in the accused's mind, but with what should have been there, had the accused proceeded reasonably."

In order to clearly distinguish the criminal test for objective *mens rea* from the non-criminal test for mere negligence, the Supreme Court has determined that the correct standard in criminal law is that the accused's conduct was a "marked departure" from the standard of care that a reasonable person would have applied in the circumstances.[4]

While any accused with sufficient *mens rea* to be found guilty of an offence is morally blameworthy, those accused who commit the *actus reus* with a subjective *mens rea* are generally regarded as being more blameworthy than those who have an objective *mens rea*. Those with subjective *mens rea* have deliberately made a choice to engage in wrongful behaviour. The courts therefore recognize various levels of fault, with the most serious levels being those offences that require proof of subjective intent. Subjective intent may involve intention, knowledge, **recklessness**, or **wilful blindness** on the part of the particular accused.

In addition to the levels of *mens rea* required for true criminal offences, there are also regulatory, quasi-criminal, and/or provincial offences that are less serious in nature and that may therefore involve less serious levels of fault-finding. These less serious levels of fault-finding are referred to as strict liability offences and absolute liability offences.

The common-law presumption is that subjective *mens rea* is required for true criminal offences unless the wording of the federal statute that creates the offence clearly contemplates an objective level of fault or *mens rea*.[5]

reasonable person test
an objective test for *mens rea* in which the court does not look at what was in the mind of the actual accused person before the court, but rather at what an ordinary person of normal capabilities, in the same circumstances as the accused, would have understood to be the risk of his or her actions

recklessness
a type of *mens rea* in which the accused fully understands the risk of harm associated with his behaviour or actions and engages in the behaviour despite the risk

wilful blindness
a type of *mens rea* in which the accused person intentionally closes his eyes to obvious criminal actions in an attempt to claim that he did not know that the actions were criminal

---

3. *R. v. Creighton*, [1993] 3 S.C.R. 3, 83 C.C.C. (3d) 346.

4. *R. v. Hundal*, [1993] 1 S.C.R. 867, 79 C.C.C. (3d) 97, at 108.

5. *R. v. Sault Ste. Marie (City)* (1978), 40 C.C.C. (2d) 353 (S.C.C.).

In relation to regulatory or provincial offences there is a presumption that the offence is strict liability, but some of these quasi-criminal offences contain wording that clearly requires a higher level of fault such as intention, knowledge, wilful blindness, or recklessness. In addition, some of these offences also contemplate a conviction without any level of fault.

We may therefore break down the levels of fault or the level of *mens rea* required for various offences as shown below.

We will examine each level of *mens rea* in detail.

Levels of Mens Rea

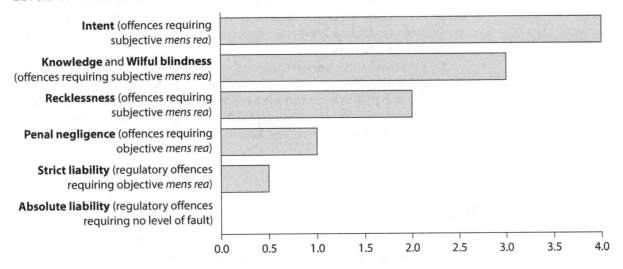

Intention

Some offences require the Crown to prove that the accused actually meant to perform the *actus reus*; that she purposely went about causing the consequences of her actions. For example, we have already examined s. 265 of the *Criminal Code*, which states that an assault is committed when someone, without the consent of another person, applies force intentionally to that other person.

It is the intentional nature of the conduct that distinguishes an assault from an accidental push when the crowded subway train comes to a sudden halt.

In some sections of the Code, the words "intention" or "intentionally" will actually be used to identify this level of *mens rea*, but in other sections the wording used may involve terms such as "wilful," "wilfully," "purposely," or something similar. Courts have interpreted these words referring to a deliberate action to mean the same as the words "intention" or "intentionally."

In other sections of the Code, no specific wording is used to describe the intention at all. Rather, it must be inferred from the conduct of the accused. For instance, s. 343 lays out the requirements for the offence of robbery:

> 343. Every one commits robbery who ...
> (d) steals from any person while armed with an offensive weapon or imitation thereof.

There is no mention of the words "intention," "intentionally," or anything similar, but if a person goes into a bank armed with a sawed-off shotgun and demands money from a teller, it can be inferred that she intended to rob the bank.

> ### Intention Versus Motive
>
> When looking at the issue of intention, it is important to differentiate between intention and motive. Motive is the reason that the accused may have committed the offence. It may be of some help to the police as an investigative tool in finding the person who committed the offence or it may even be presented as evidence in a trial where it helps to implicate the accused as the person who committed the offence, but a person can be, and often is, convicted of an offence without any motive having been established. There is no requirement that the Crown prove any motive for the offence whatsoever.
>
> On the other hand, a person may have a very good motive for committing an offence. A woman arrested for theft of food from a store may have stolen the food to feed her hungry children, but if she intended to steal the food, she will be found guilty of the offence. The court may deal with a situation of this type in sentencing, but the intention does not have anything to do with the guilt or non-guilt of the accused.

Knowledge

For many offences, it is necessary for the Crown to establish *mens rea* by proving beyond a reasonable doubt that the accused had knowledge of certain facts. Section 201(2)(b) of the *Criminal Code* states:

> 201(2) Every one who ...
>   (b) as owner, landlord, lessor, tenant, occupier or agent, knowingly permits a place to be let or used for the purposes of a common gaming house or common betting house,
> is guilty of an offence punishable on summary conviction.

In order to be convicted of this offence, the owner, landlord, lessor, tenant, occupier, or agent must actually know that the premises are being used in the proscribed manner.

Wilful Blindness

Knowledge is often the level of *mens rea* required in offences involving possession. For instance, s. 354 of the *Criminal Code* lays out the offence of possession of stolen property:

> 354(1) Every one commits an offence who has in his possession any property or thing or any proceeds of any property or thing knowing that all or part of the property or thing or of the proceeds was obtained by or derived directly or indirectly from

(a) the commission in Canada of an offence punishable by indictment; or

(b) an act or omission anywhere that, if it had occurred in Canada, would have constituted an offence punishable by indictment.

For an accused to be found guilty of this offence, the Crown must prove beyond a reasonable doubt that he or she knew that the property was stolen. However, what if the accused is observed by the police buying from the back of a van outside the local pub a brand new, big-screen television for $50? Will it be a satisfactory defence for the accused to claim that he did not know that the goods were stolen?

He may not have asked the seller where she obtained the goods, and so may not "know," in the usual sense of the word, that the goods were stolen, but it is obvious that a brand new, big-screen television costs much more than $50 and that if someone is selling such an item for that price out of the back of a van, outside a pub, it was not obtained by the seller in a legal fashion. In these circumstances, claiming that he didn't know the goods were stolen amounts to purposely closing his eyes to the obvious. That is wilful blindness.

Recklessness

Recklessness and wilful blindness are very closely related. Recklessness can be defined as gross carelessness or negligence. In the context of criminal law, it is carelessness that is so extreme that it amounts to criminal fault. When we are talking about recklessness, we are not talking about a situation where the accused meant or intended the wrongful consequences of his or her actions, we are talking about a situation in which he or she, even while able to foresee the risk that wrongful consequences could result from his or her actions, engaged in the actions anyway. In other words, the accused was grossly careless as to whether the wrongful consequences occurred or not.

For example, let's say that a student in a crowded classroom becomes frustrated and throws an empty glass bottle of juice at a wall with considerable force. The bottle breaks on impact and the pieces fly all over, striking the people nearby. The angry student did not intend to hit people with broken glass shards, but knew that throwing a breakable object like a glass bottle at a wall in a crowded room could result in people being struck by broken bits of glass.

In the case of *Sansregret*, the Supreme Court of Canada determined that recklessness must involve a subjective foresight to meet the test for criminal fault or *mens rea*. The reasonable person standard is not sufficient for criminal recklessness. Rather, the accused must actually have foreseen the risk of harm arising from his or her actions and then taken the risk that harm will not result. The accused must be aware of the wrongful consequences that his or her actions could cause. If the accused was not aware of the potential risk of harm, then the Crown will be unable to prove recklessness.

In addition, the risk taken must be unjustifiable. In some instances, taking a risk may be totally justifiable. For example, a surgeon may perform emergency brain surgery on an unconscious accident victim to try to reduce bleeding in the brain. The surgery may carry a risk of the patient dying, but that risk can be justified as an attempt to save the victim's life.

There are a number of sections in the Code that actually use the words "reckless" and "recklessly." For example, the offence of criminal harassment provides as follows:

> 264(1) No person shall, without lawful authority and knowing that another person is harassed or recklessly as to whether the other person is harassed, engage in conduct referred to in subsection (2) that causes that other person reasonably, in all the circumstances, to fear for their safety or the safety of anyone known to them.

However, even where the words are not expressly set out in the section creating the offence, the test for the *mens rea* of recklessness may be met if the Crown can prove that the accused subjectively foresaw the risk of his actions and took the risk anyway.

Penal Negligence

penal negligence
a type of *mens rea* in which an objective standard is applied to determine the mental element of some offences

Although the Supreme Court of Canada has determined that there is a presumption that criminal *mens rea* must involve a subjective standard, there are offences in which the wording created by Parliament in the *Criminal Code* creates a primarily objective test for *mens rea*. The Court has referred to this standard as "**penal negligence**."[6] It applies to offences such as criminal negligence, under s. 219 of the Code.

The test the courts must apply in determining penal negligence is whether a reasonable person with the capabilities of the accused would have made himself aware of the likely consequences of the unlawful conduct and the resulting risk. This is primarily an objective test that has a subjective aspect because it takes into account the abilities of the actual accused person. A person with limited capacity may not be aware of the potential consequences of his conduct and therefore may not be convicted depending on the charge and the circumstances.

Strict Liability

strict liability
a regulatory offence (non-criminal) that requires the Crown to prove only the *actus reus* and not the *mens rea* of the offence—the accused may raise the defence of due diligence

absolute liability
a regulatory offence (non-criminal) that has no fault element—the Crown need only prove the *actus reus* of the offence and the accused may not raise any defence as to his intention

due diligence
a defence to a strict liability offence in which the accused attempts to establish that he or she took every reasonable precaution to avoid committing a regulatory offence

Strict liability, like **absolute liability**, is a standard that applies primarily in regulatory offences, including provincial offences. In fact, as noted above, there is a presumption that most regulatory offences are strict liability offences. The purpose of these offences is to regulate some sort of conduct and they are not viewed as serious criminal offences, even though some of them may result in the imposition of a jail term.

If an offence is a strict liability offence, the Crown is required to prove beyond a reasonable doubt the *actus reus* of the offence. Once the *actus reus* has been properly proved, the Crown need not prove a *mens rea*. Due to the regulatory nature of an offence based on simple negligence, the fault element of the offence is presumed to exist once the *actus reus* has been proved. However, the defendant then has the opportunity to raise the defence of **due diligence** and to prove it on the balance of probabilities. Due diligence involves the defendant proving lack of negligence. For instance, in an environmental offence, the defendant corporation may attempt to

---

6. Supra footnote 3, at 381-82.

establish that it took all reasonable precautions to prevent the chemical pollutant it was using in its manufacturing process from escaping into the air.

To successfully raise due diligence, the defendant must prove on the balance of probabilities that it

- took reasonable care not to commit the illegal act, or
- made a reasonable mistake of fact (not of law), which, if true, would have made the act legal.

Absolute Liability

Absolute liability is a standard that can only apply in relation to some regulatory offences. The standard does not involve a concept of fault. The Crown must prove the *actus reus* beyond a reasonable doubt and the defendant has no recourse to the defence of due diligence. In other words, the defendant will be held responsible for his or her actions whether or not he or she was at fault.

Offences involving absolute liability have resulted in a number of Charter challenges on the basis that people who were morally innocent could be punished. However, the Supreme Court of Canada has established that an absolute liability offence does not violate the Charter as long as it does not involve a possible jail term as punishment.[7] If there is no potential for incarceration, even though a morally innocent person may be convicted, his or her s. 7 Charter rights have not been violated because the penalty does not place their liberty at stake.

---

7. *Re B.C. Motor Vehicle Act*, [1985] 2 S.C.R. 486 and *R. v. Pontes*, [1995] 3 S.C.R. 44, 100 C.C.C. (3d) 353.

CHAPTER SUMMARY

In this chapter we examine, in some detail, the elements of an offence, the *actus reus*, and the *mens rea*. Actus reus is generally translated from Latin as "the guilty act," and *mens rea* is translated as "the guilty mind." However, the terms encompass more than that simple, general definition. We look at both the *actus reus* and the *mens rea* to identify different types of *actus reus* and *mens rea* that might be found in an offence and look at examples of each. We discuss the role of voluntariness required for the commission of the *actus reus* and the important difference between a subjective and an objective *mens rea*.

KEY TERMS

absolute liability, 58
actus reus, 50
causation, 53
due diligence, 58

mens rea, 50
omission, 51
penal negligence, 58
reasonable doubt, 50

reasonable person test, 54
recklessness, 54
strict liability, 58
wilful blindness, 54

REVIEW QUESTIONS

1. What are the two elements of an offence and what does each Latin term generally mean?

2. How can the *actus reus* be broken down into different types?

3. Under what circumstances can a person be convicted for failing to do something?

4. What role does voluntariness play in determining whether or not the *actus reus* has been committed?

5. What is the difference between a subjective *mens rea* and an objective *mens rea*?

6. What are the different types of *mens rea*?

7. Explain how the Crown may prove the *mens rea* of an offence by establishing wilful blindness.

8. Can an accused person be convicted of an offence on the basis of recklessness even if the wording of the section creating the offence does not include the words "reckless" or "recklessly"?

9. What is the difference between a *mens rea* involving recklessness and one involving penal negligence?

10. Can there be any true criminal offences that involve absolute liability?

EXERCISES

1. Bonnie and Asha, two college students, are in a restaurant. They get into a heated argument about their criminal law examination. Bonnie sweeps her arm across the table in anger, purposely knocking the glasses and dishes off the table and onto the floor, where they shatter. One of the shards of glass flies up and makes a small cut on Asha's leg. Can Bonnie be convicted of assault under s. 265(1)(a) of the Code?

2. The accused, named Thomas, was a former drug addict who had contracted hepatitis C, an extremely serious medical infection, from a dirty needle. He was very well aware that he was suffering from hepatitis C and also knew that the infection could be transmitted to others through blood. Despite this, he decided to donate blood. Fortunately, all collected blood was tested for various transmittable diseases, including hepatitis C, and during testing it was discovered that Thomas's blood donation was infected. The blood was never given to anyone and was eventually destroyed.

   Following the discovery of the hepatitis C in his blood donation and the fact that Thomas knew he had the disease when he donated it, he was charged under the *Criminal Code* with being a common nuisance. Do you think he will be convicted? Explain your answer.

3. Marty and Farah are a married couple who live together with their two-year-old child. Marty is taking care of Farah and their child because Farah was severely injured in a car accident a month ago. She broke both of her legs and one arm, and her broken limbs are in large casts. She cannot get out of bed, feed herself, or even hold her child. One evening, when he was feeling very stressed out, Marty left his wife and child alone in the house and went out for a very long walk. When he got back several hours later, he found that his wife and child had been severely injured in a fire caused by the child playing with matches. Can Marty be convicted of any offence?

4. Stephen was in a restaurant in Toronto with his friends. A group of American tourists came in and one of Stephen's friends decided to have some fun. He had a toy badge in his pocket that he had bought for his six-year-old brother to use as part of his police officer Halloween costume. He gave Stephen the badge and convinced him that it would be hilarious to play a practical joke on the Americans. Stephen went over to the Americans' table, flashed the fake badge, and told them that he was an FBI agent who had them under surveillance. He said they were all under arrest for suspected terrorist activity. At first the tourists became quite frightened. However, once they realized they had been the victims of a silly prank, they called the Toronto police and the police arrested Stephen for impersonating a peace officer.

   Do you think Stephen will be convicted of this offence? Explain your answer.

Parties to an Offence

6

LEARNING OUTCOMES

After completing this chapter, you should be able to:

- Explain the various ways a person may become a party to an offence.

- Identify the difference between aiding and abetting.

- Identify and apply the offence of counselling.

- Identify and apply the offence of being an accessory after the fact.

Introduction

A party to an offence is a person who can be charged with the offence. We know that the person who has the required intention (*mens rea*) to commit the offence and who actually performs the *actus reus* can be charged with the offence, but what about those who help him or her in some way? This chapter examines ss. 21, 22, 23, and 23.1 of the *Criminal Code*. These sections deal with charges that may be laid against the helpers, advisers, or protectors of the accused. Section 21 describes the offence of aiding and abetting; s. 22 the offence of counselling; and s. 23 the offence of being an accessory after the fact. Section 23.1 permits conviction of a person even though the person that he or she helped, advised, or protected cannot be convicted of the offence.

principal offender
the person who actually commits the offence

The person who actually commits the offence is the **principal offender**. The *mens rea* and *actus reus* can be committed by more than one person—for instance, a group of people who all physically assault a victim by each punching and kicking him. Because there can be more than one principal offender, the people who take part in actively assaulting the victim are all principal offenders. But people can be involved in an offence by helping the principal offender(s) to commit the offence even though the helpers themselves do not commit the *actus reus*. Those who in some way assist the principal offender(s) to commit an offence may also be held criminally responsible for the offence and will be liable to the same penalty as the principal offender. Along with the principal offender, they are regarded as **parties to the offence**. The assistance may have been given before (s. 22), during (s. 21), or after the commission of the main offence (s. 23).

party to the offence
anyone who helps, encourages, advises, or protects the principal offender may also be a party to the offence and can be charged with that offence even though they did not actually commit it

Aiding and Abetting, s. 21

Sections 21(1)(b) and (c) of the *Criminal Code* define **aiding** and **abetting**:

> 21(1) Every one is a party to an offence who
> (a) actually commits it;
> (b) does or omits to do anything for the purpose of aiding any person to commit it; or
> (c) abets any person in committing it.

aiding
helping or assisting the principal offender to commit the offence, knowing that an offence is being committed

"Aiding in the commission of an offence" is assisting or helping the principal offender carry out an offence. For example, if the accused acts as a lookout while the principal offender shoplifts, he is aiding in the commission of the offence. "Abetting" is encouraging the principal offender to commit an offence. An example would be an assault situation where the principal offender is pushing the victim and his friends are standing around yelling, "Get him!" "Hit him!" The friends are abetting the offence.

abetting
encouraging the principal offender to commit the offence, knowing that an offence is being committed

A person who aids or abets in the commission of a particular offence may be charged with either aiding or abetting or with the offence itself. The aider or abettor may also receive the same sentence as the principal offender. For instance, the lookout in the shoplifting example above may be charged with aiding or with the offence of theft. If convicted, he may receive the same sentence as the principal offender.

The Crown must prove that the accused knew that the principal was committing or intended to commit an offence and that the accused intentionally aided or assisted, helped, or encouraged the offender. Merely being present at the scene of a crime is not sufficient for a conviction. The accused must actually have intended to help or encourage the principal offender in some way. If the accused was tricked or duped into helping the offender, he will not be held responsible for aiding or abetting. We call a person who is tricked in this manner to participate in the offence an "**innocent agent**." For example, if a person is asked to deliver a package to a home and he is told that the package contains a computer printer but it actually contains drugs, the delivery person is an innocent agent, someone who is used to commit an offence but has no knowledge that there is an offence being committed.

Section 21(2) of the *Criminal Code* deals with the issue of common intention in the commission of an offence. It reads:

> 21(2) Where two or more persons form an intention in common to carry out an unlawful purpose and to assist each other therein and any one of them, in carrying out the common purpose, commits an offence, each of them who knew or ought to have known that the commission of the offence would be a probable consequence of carrying out the common purpose is a party to that offence.

If a number of people form the same intention to carry out an offence and to assist each other during the commission of the offence and one of them commits an offence in addition to the one originally intended, then, generally, everyone involved in the commission of the intended offence will be convicted of any additional offences as long as the Crown can prove that each of them knew or *ought to have known* that the second offence was a probable consequence of the first unlawful action. For example, let's say that Joe and his friends decide to "key" Tim's car; Tim is someone whom they all dislike. They go to Tim's house and while in the process of damaging the car, they are caught by Tim's sister. Joe panics, attacks her with a rock, breaks her nose and cheekbone, and disfigures her. None of the others touches Tim's sister. Joe is convicted of mischief to property and aggravated assault. The friends who joined him in damaging the car will also be charged with mischief to property and aggravated assault. They will be convicted of the second offence if the Crown can prove that each of them knew or *ought to have known* that the aggravated assault was a probable consequence of the mischief they engaged in.

The phrase "ought to have known," which is contained in the section, involves a level of **objective *mens rea***; that is, the *mens rea* of the accused would be determined, not on the basis of what he actually knew, which is **subjective *mens rea***, but on what a reasonable person in the accused's circumstances should have known.[1] The Supreme Court of Canada has ruled that it must be presumed that *mens rea* should be subjective for very serious criminal offences unless Parliament has made it very clear in the wording that creates the offence that the *mens rea* should be objective.

innocent agent
a person who helps the principal offender commit the offence, without realizing that an offence is being committed

objective *mens rea*
proving criminal intention by determining what a reasonable person would have had in his or her mind

subjective *mens rea*
determining criminal intention by looking at what was actually in the mind of the accused before the court

---

1. See pages 54-59 in Chapter 5 for a discussion of the concepts of objective and subjective *mens rea*.

The words "ought to have known" have been challenged under the *Charter of Rights and Freedoms* in relation to a charge of murder. In the case of *R. v. Logan*, the Supreme Court of Canada declared that to convict an accused person of murder or attempted murder on the basis of what he "ought to have known" would be a violation of s. 7 of the Charter because a conviction for murder or attempted murder requires a level of subjective *mens rea*. Therefore, what the accused ought to have known is irrelevant in these instances. In a case of murder or attempted murder, the Crown must prove that the accused actually knew or actually could foresee that the principal offender would kill someone during the commission of the offence.

Counselling, s. 22

counselling
instructing, recruiting, or advising a person to commit a criminal offence, knowing that the person is likely to commit the offence

Section 22 applies only when the accused has counselled an offence that has been committed. **Counselling** an offence that has not been committed is dealt with in s. 464 and is discussed in Chapter 7, Inchoate Offences.

In order to be found guilty of counselling, a person must "procure, solicit or incite" someone else to commit an offence. The definition of counselling is in s. 22(3).

Section 22 provides that someone who counsels an offence is a party to the offence. If convicted, the counsellor may receive the same sentence as the person who committed the offence. It doesn't matter if the offence was actually committed differently from what was counselled. It also doesn't matter if a different offence was committed as long as the offence that was committed was reasonably foreseeable as a result of the counselling. The counsellor of the offence will be found guilty as long as the Crown can prove that he "knew or ought to have known" that the offence committed was likely to be committed.

However, if the principal offender committed the offence of murder or attempted murder while committing the offence that was counselled, the person counselling could not be found guilty of murder or attempted murder on the basis that he or she "ought to have known" that murder could be a consequence of the principal offender's actions. In the case of *R. v. Logan*, mentioned above, this would be a Charter violation in relation to the offences of murder or attempted murder because the Supreme Court of Canada has determined that these offences require a subjective, rather than an objective, *mens rea*. In other words, if one person counselled another on how to commit an armed robbery and during the robbery a bank clerk was shot to death by the principal offender, the counsellor of the bank robbery could only be charged with counselling robbery, not murder. The only way to convict a person of counselling murder or attempted murder is if the counsellor actually counselled murder and not another offence that led to murder.

Accessory After the Fact, s. 23

A person may also be held criminally liable for an offence if they know that an offence has been committed and they offer assistance to the offender for the purpose of helping him to escape detention or capture. Providing food, shelter, and/or clothing to an offender after the commission of an offence is considered sufficient for conviction as an **accessory after the fact**.

It is not enough to offer assistance that *results* in an offender escaping the police. In order to be convicted of this offence, the accused must actually have offered assistance with the purpose of *enabling* the offender to escape.

The penalty for this offence is the same as the penalty for attempting to commit an offence. Section 463 sets out the penalty for an offender convicted of an attempt when the law does not apply any other specific penalty.

> **accessory after the fact**
> a person who, knowing that an offence has been committed, offers assistance to the offender for the purpose of helping him to escape detention or capture by the police

- If convicted of attempting to commit or being an accessory after the fact to an offence that carries a maximum sentence of life imprisonment, the offender will be found guilty of an indictable offence and may be sentenced to a prison term not exceeding 14 years.

- If convicted of attempting to commit or being an accessory after the fact to an offence that carries a sentence of up to 14 years, the offender will be found guilty of an indictable offence and will be liable to imprisonment for a term up to but not exceeding one half of the maximum term of imprisonment for the complete commission of the offence.

- If convicted of attempting to commit or being an accessory after the fact to a summary conviction offence, the offender will be found guilty of a summary conviction offence.

- If found guilty of attempting to commit or being an accessory after the fact to a hybrid offence, the offender will be liable for a prison term up to but not exceeding one half of the maximum term of imprisonment for the complete commission of the offence if the Crown proceeds by indictment and for a summary conviction offence if the Crown proceeds summarily.[2]

When the Principal Offender Is Not Convicted of the Offence, s. 23.1

In the event that the principal offender is not convicted of the offence, a person aiding and abetting, counselling, or being an accessory after the fact may still be convicted of the offence. At first glance it may seem strange that someone can be found guilty of aiding in or counselling an offence that legally has not resulted in a conviction for the person who committed it. However, this section is intended to deal with situations such as an adult counselling an 11-year-old to steal goods from a local store. The 11-year-old cannot be convicted of, or even charged with, a criminal offence because he is under 12 years old, the minimum age for being criminally charged. The adult can still be charged with counselling the offence. If this section were not in force, an adult could recruit a gang of very young thieves and avoid any criminal responsibility for their wrongdoing.

---

2. See Chapter 11, pages 129-130 for information on Crown elections for hybrid offences.

CHAPTER SUMMARY

This chapter examines the sections of the *Criminal Code* that provide for the laying of criminal charges against people who help, advise, or protect the person who actually committed the offence and who is called the principal offender. The assistance given to the principal offender may be given before, during, or after the offence has been committed.

Section 21 makes it an offence to help or encourage the principal offender during the commission of an offence by aiding or abetting him in his actions. Section 22 makes it an offence to advise or counsel the principal offender on how to commit an offence. This section is applicable in situations where an offence has actually been committed, even if it was committed in a different way than the person counselling advised. Section 23 creates the offence of being an accessory after the fact by intentionally helping the principal offender to escape, knowing that he has committed an offence.

KEY TERMS

abetting, 64
accessory after the fact, 67
aiding, 64
counselling, 66
innocent agent, 65

objective *mens rea*, 65
party to the offence, 64
principal offender, 64
subjective *mens rea*, 65

REVIEW QUESTIONS

1. Who is regarded as the principal offender?

2. What does it mean to be a party to an offence?

3. What is the difference between aiding and abetting? What section of the Code applies?

4. What is an innocent agent?

5. What is counselling an offence?

6. What would the Crown need to prove to have a person found guilty of being an accessory after the fact?

7. What is the purpose of s. 23.1, which permits a person who aids, abets, counsels, or acts as an accessory after the offence to be convicted even if the principal offender is not convicted?

EXERCISES

1. Curly, Larry, and Moe were really angry with Groucho because Groucho had reported them to the police for serving alcohol at a party where most of the guests were only 18 years old. They hated him.

   One Friday night, the three of them went to the Good Times coffee shop to get some take-away coffee. As they walked up to the door of the coffee shop, they saw Groucho coming out. Larry said, "Come on guys, let's get Groucho."

   Larry ran up to Groucho and started pushing and shoving him. Curly didn't touch Groucho, but he kept urging Larry to keep pushing Groucho. He said things like, "Push him harder, Larry! Push him down and kick him!" Moe really didn't want to get involved and he stayed back. He didn't help Groucho in any way, but he didn't walk away from the scene or call the police either.

   While this was going on, Donald, a customer in the coffee shop, came out and saw what was happening. He didn't know Groucho, but could see that he was being attacked by a larger man and so Donald decided to try to help Groucho. He ran over and tried to pull Larry away so that Groucho could run away. At that point, Curly grabbed Donald, shoved him up against a wall and forcibly held him there so that he couldn't help Groucho.

When people driving by saw what was happening, they called 911.

When Curly, Larry, and Moe heard the police siren, they started running across the parking lot. They jumped a fence and continued running through people's backyards. Moe suddenly realized that his cousin, Bingo, lived just a couple of houses away. Moe ran to Bingo's place and started hammering on the back door. When Bingo answered, Moe said, "Bing, you have to let us in and hide us. The cops are after us for pounding a guy." Bingo let all three of them in.

For each of the people in the scenario, determine whether they can be charged with anything. Explain your answers. Give the sections of the *Criminal Code* that apply.

2. Mickey was a drug dealer. One of his customers asked for a delivery of his weekly supply of cocaine. Mickey was worried that the police might have been watching his customer's place so he went upstairs to his neighbour's apartment and asked the neighbour's 17-year-old son, Arun, to deliver the drugs to the customer for a fee of $100. Arun was a regular courier for Mickey's drug business and knew that drugs were in the package. However, Arun's cousin Kinto was visiting him and so he asked him to come along. When they got to the customer's house, Arun asked Kinto to take the package inside while Arun sent a text to his girlfriend.

   As Kinto turned the drugs over to the customer, the police burst in. The police then went to Mickey's place to try to arrest him for trafficking, but Mickey had a gun and got into a shootout with the police and was killed.

   What kind of charges might be laid here?

3. Rita Dogood is a very upstanding person, but, unfortunately, one of her sons has fallen in with a bad group of friends. She is very worried about this situation and has consulted several community agencies to see what help she might be able to get for him.

   Unfortunately, she may be a bit late. Tonight, her son came running into the house looking very frightened and distressed. Rita questioned him and although, at first, he was reluctant to say anything to his mother, he eventually told her the whole story. He said that he had been out with some of the friends she was worried about and they had robbed a local convenience store. One of the group had a gun and he shot the store owner in the arm when he wouldn't hand over the money from the till quickly enough.

   Neighbours heard the shot and called the police, who soon arrived outside the store. Rita's son was able to run out the back door of the store and make it home before the police surrounded the place. He wants Rita to hide him because he thinks the police will be looking for him.

   Rita is frantic with worry. She doesn't want to turn her son in to the police, but she doesn't know what to do. She tells him to try to get some rest. While he's sleeping, she decides that the best thing to do is to try to get him to turn himself in to the police in the morning.

   About an hour later, the police, who have a search warrant, break down Rita's door and arrest both her and her son. Rita's son is charged with robbery. Rita is charged with being an accessory after the fact. Does she have a defence?

Inchoate Offences

7

LEARNING OUTCOMES

After completing this chapter, you should be able to:

- Explain the meaning of an inchoate offence.
- Understand the reason for the creation of inchoate offences.
- Apply the elements of an attempt to commit an offence to a fact situation.
- Explain the offence of conspiracy.
- Explain the offence of counselling an offence that is not committed.

Introduction

inchoate offence
an offence in which the *mens rea* is present but the *actus reus* may not be complete

As we discussed in Chapter 5, the elements of a criminal offence are the *actus reus* and the *mens rea*. The Crown is usually required to prove both elements of an offence beyond a reasonable doubt. **Inchoate offences** are different in that although the Crown must prove the *mens rea* beyond a reasonable doubt (because criminal blame or fault cannot be attached unless a person has the necessary intent to commit a criminal offence), it does not have to prove that the *actus reus* of the offence is complete. Examples of inchoate offences are attempts to commit an offence, a conspiracy in which a criminal offence is planned but not necessarily carried out, and counselling an offence that was not committed.

beyond mere preparation
a legal test applied by a judge to determine whether the accused has taken enough significant steps toward the commission of an offence to be found guilty of an attempt

The criminal law punishes inchoate offences because although the accused has not committed the completed *actus reus*, he or she has taken steps **beyond merely preparing** for the offence and is actually trying to commit it. The law recognizes that society has an interest in granting police the ability to prevent the completion of an offence before it causes criminal harm and potentially endangers innocent bystanders. In addition, if more than one person is involved in planning an offence and only some of them commit the offence, the law must be capable of punishing all of the planners, not just those who completed the *actus reus*, because they all had the intent to commit the offence.

Attempted Offences, s. 24

A person may be found guilty of an offence even if he does not complete the entire *actus reus*. Section 24 of the *Criminal Code* provides:

> 24(1) Every one who, having an intent to commit an offence, does or omits to do anything for the purpose of carrying out the intention is guilty of an attempt to commit the offence whether or not it was possible under the circumstances to commit the offence.
>
> (2) The question whether an act or omission by a person who has an intent to commit an offence is or is not mere preparation to commit the offence, and too remote to constitute an attempt to commit the offence, is a question of law.

This section, like most sections in Part I of the Code (the General part), applies to offences throughout the Code, although some offences may have specific wording in relation to attempts that apply to that particular offence.[1]

It obviously makes sense that provision is made to charge and prosecute people who are caught before they have the opportunity to complete an entire offence. Without such a provision, police, sent to a scene by a 911 caller reporting that his brother and brother's friend had just left the house with guns and masks and were on their way to rob a local bank branch, would be unable to stop the suspects en route and arrest them. The police would be forced to wait until the men had entered

---

1. For example, see *Criminal Code*, R.S.C. 1985, c. C-46, s. 265(1)(b).

the bank, threatened the occupants with their guns, and left with the money. The public would be placed at major risk and the perpetrators might even be given an opportunity to escape.

An examination of s. 24 indicates that there are several elements of the offence of attempting to commit a crime:

- the accused must have had the intent (*mens rea*) to commit the offence that he is charged with attempting to commit (the required *mens rea* can be found by looking at the section that creates the offence that was attempted),
- the accused must have done something or omitted to do something to carry out his intention, and
- the actions or omissions of the accused must have gone beyond mere preparation toward committing the offence.

Beyond Mere Preparation

The *actus reus* of an attempt does not occur until the accused has taken a step beyond mere preparation. This is not a factual test but a legal question to be determined by a judge. A person who is preparing to commit an offence has not yet done anything criminal, but once a judge finds that the accused's acts or omissions have gone beyond merely preparing to commit a crime, the person may be found guilty of an attempt to commit an offence.

There is no clear rule that may be applied in every case to distinguish between mere preparation and taking a step beyond that preparation, but the Supreme Court of Canada has stated that in making the determination the court must consider both the nature and quality of the accused's actions and the proximity of those actions to the completed offence with regard to time, location, and acts that remain to be completed.[2] In other words, the major factors to be considered are the importance of the actions and how close they took the accused to actually completing the offence. It is a commonsense judgment.

For instance, if prospective bank robbers make preparations to rob a bank and they put guns and masks in their car and drive to the bank but do not stop or get out of the car because they see a police car parked next door to the bank, they will still likely be found guilty of attempted robbery. They took major steps toward committing the offence by putting the guns and masks in the car and driving to the bank. They were extremely close, both in terms of time and place, to commencing the offence. All that stood between them and entering the bank was the parked police car. In cases such as this, it does not matter that the accused changes his or her mind after he or she has gone beyond mere preparation because the offence of attempt has already been committed at that point.

---

2. *R. v. Deutsch*, [1986] 2 S.C.R. 2, 27 C.C.C. (3d) 385.

Impossibility

Section 24(1) makes it clear that even if it is impossible to commit the offence, an accused may still be convicted of an attempt. If the bank robbers went to the bank with the intent to rob it and upon arriving they discovered that the bank had a power failure that day and was closed and therefore impossible to rob, they could still be convicted of attempted robbery. Another example would be that of an employee who despised his boss and decided to kill him. The employee bought a gun and on the day he intended to kill his boss, took the gun to work. Once there, he learned his boss had gone on vacation and would not be at work again for three weeks. Even though it was impossible to kill his boss that day, the employee could still be charged and convicted of attempted murder.

Penalties for Attempts

Section 463[3] sets out the penalty for an offender convicted of an attempt when the law does not apply any other specific penalty.

- If convicted of attempting to commit an offence that carries a maximum sentence of life imprisonment, the offender will be found guilty of an indictable offence and may be sentenced to a prison term not exceeding fourteen years.
- If convicted of attempting to commit an offence that carries a sentence of up to fourteen years, the offender will be found guilty of an indictable offence and will be liable to imprisonment for a term up to but not exceeding one half of the maximum term of imprisonment for the complete commission of the offence.
- If convicted of attempting to commit a summary conviction offence, the offender will be found guilty of a summary conviction offence.
- If found guilty of attempting to commit a hybrid offence, the offender will be liable for a prison term up to but not exceeding one half of the maximum term of imprisonment for the complete commission of the offence if the Crown proceeds by indictment and for a summary conviction offence if the Crown proceeds summarily.[4]

Conspiracy Offences, s. 465

conspiracy
a serious indictable offence in which two or more persons make an agreement to commit an offence and intend to commit the planned offence

A **conspiracy** is an agreement between two or more people to carry out an indictable criminal offence. Conspiracy itself is a serious criminal offence. The *mens rea* of this offence has two aspects. In order to prove a conspiracy, the Crown must prove (1) that the people involved had a serious intention to carry out the proposed unlawful act and (2) that they intended to and did make an agreement to do so. Since a conspiracy must involve at least two people, a person cannot be convicted of

---

3. This section also sets out the penalty for the offence of "accessory after the fact."

4. See Chapter 11, pages 129-130 for information on Crown elections for hybrid offences.

conspiracy by making an agreement with an undercover police officer to commit an offence because the officer was not actually planning the offence.

The prosecution need not prove that the *actus reus* of the planned offence was carried out by anyone or that any further steps beyond the agreement were taken toward the commission of that offence. In other words, it is possible that the accused could be convicted of conspiracy even if there were no steps taken to actually commit the planned offence. The *actus reus* of a conspiracy is the agreement to commit the planned offence. The *actus reus* is complete once the agreement is made.

However, if the *actus reus* was actually completed by some members of the planning group and not others, the planners who took no part in the completion of the *actus reus* can still be convicted of conspiracy. Conspiracy is often used in drug offences and in charges laid against those involved in organized crime.

The penalty imposed upon a conviction for conspiracy is the same penalty that would be given if the offence were fully carried out.

Counselling an Offence That Is Not Committed, s. 464

We know from our earlier examination of parties to an offence that s. 22 makes it an offence to **counsel** someone to commit a crime. In order to be found guilty of counselling, a person must procure, solicit, or incite someone else to commit an offence. However, s. 22 deals with offences that are actually committed.

Under s. 464, it is also an offence to counsel another person to commit an offence even when the offence is not committed. This charge would be laid in circumstances where the person who is being counselled has absolutely no intention of committing the offence—for instance, an undercover police officer or someone working for the police. The Crown need only prove that only the person doing the counselling intended that the offence be committed.

counselling
instructing, recruiting, or advising a person to commit a criminal offence, knowing that the person is likely to commit the offence

CHAPTER SUMMARY

In this chapter we examine inchoate offences or offences in which the *actus reus* may not be complete. We discuss the types of inchoate offences, attempts, conspiracies, and counselling offences that have not been committed.

We pay particular attention to the elements of an attempted offence laid out in s. 24 of the *Criminal Code*,

including that it is not a defence to a charge of attempt that the offence was impossible to commit. In addition, we discuss the penalties for attempts.

KEY TERMS

beyond mere preparation, 72
conspiracy, 74
counselling, 75
inchoate offence, 72

REVIEW QUESTIONS

1. What is an inchoate offence?

2. What must the Crown always prove in relation to an inchoate offence and why must the Crown prove it?

3. What are the elements of an attempt that the Crown must prove?

4. What does it mean when we say that to commit an offence, the accused must have gone beyond mere preparation?

5. Does it matter if circumstances make it impossible for the offence to be committed that day?

6. What is a conspiracy?

7. What is "counselling an offence that is not committed"?

EXERCISES

1. George is a pickpocket who regularly goes into crowded places with the intention of finding people whom he can approach and steal from. He intends to put his hand in their pockets, bags, or purses, in order to take wallets or other valuable items, such as smart phones, from them.

    One Saturday, he sets off on his trip to the local shopping mall, which is typically very crowded with shoppers on the weekends. He looks around and spots Parminder, who is window-shopping with her friend. Parminder has a purse over her shoulder, and it

is open and slung around her back. She and her friend are stopping regularly in front of stores and examining their displays.

George is really pleased because he regards Parminder as his ideal "hit," a person who isn't paying attention and who has made it easy for him to reach into her purse and steal her property before she even realizes it is gone. He approaches and reaches into her purse just as the mall's plainclothes security guards, who have been looking for pickpockets, grab him and call the police, who charge George with attempted theft.

By chance, Parminder had accidentally picked up the wrong purse when she left home. The purse she was carrying was one that had nothing in it.

Do you think that George will be convicted of attempted theft?

2. Sonja, Jacques, and Ramon made a plan to rob the local bank. The three agreed that Ramon would carry an empty gun in the event that he was seen and needed to threaten someone. The money was to be split three ways.

    On the day the plan was to be carried out, Jacques got cold feet and after the three had entered the bank, he shouted, "Watch out, they are going to try to rob you! Call the cops." The police were called and arrested all three.

    What offences did they commit?

Corporate Liability

8

LEARNING OUTCOMES

After completing this chapter, you should be able to:

- Understand how the concept of corporate criminal liability emerged.

- Discuss the various theories of corporate criminal liability.

- Understand the identification theory of corporate criminal liability.

- Define the concept of the directing mind of a corporation.

- Understand the impact of Bill C-45 on corporate criminal liability in Canada.

- Discuss how corporations can be parties to a criminal offence.

Introduction

A corporation is a legal entity that is created under either federal or provincial law. It is treated as an entity separate and apart from its owners and those who manage its affairs. For the most part, the law recognizes corporations as having the rights and obligations of natural persons. Corporations can pay taxes, own property, enter into contracts, maintain or defend lawsuits, hire employees, and conduct commercial and business transactions. However, for all of the rights and obligations that are conferred on a corporation, it is not a living, breathing entity. A corporation is a legal fiction that is designed to facilitate business, trade, and commerce. One of the major features of a corporation is the concept of the "limited liability" of its shareholders/owners. Under this concept, the owners of a corporation are not responsible for the actions of the company because it is treated as a separate entity in law. Those involved in the affairs of a corporation have the capacity to commit crimes (for example, when a shareholder defrauds or steals from the company), but is it possible for the company to commit a crime?

Corporations are clearly subject to the *Criminal Code*. Section 2 defines "every one," "person," "owner," and similar expressions to include an "organization." The definition of an "organization" includes a "body corporate." Thus, a corporation is clearly caught by the language whenever the *Criminal Code* uses words such as "person" or "any one" in creating an offence. However, the more difficult task is in determining how a fictitious entity can commit a prohibited act or have the requisite *mens rea* to be held criminally responsible.

Theories of Corporate Criminal Liability

At common law a corporation can be found liable in tort based on the concepts of agency and vicarious liability. The actions and intentions of the corporation's agents and employees can be imputed to the company. This means that the corporation is responsible for the tortious conduct of those who work for it or act on its behalf. However, a corporation *per se* cannot form *mens rea*, which is needed for establishing **criminal liability**. There is also the pragmatic problem that a corporation, being a legal fiction, cannot be imprisoned. This can result in a situation where a corporation could face civil liability for wrongful acts committed by those who work for it, but might not be held criminally responsible for the same acts.

There are three possible ways that criminal intent can be found to reside in a corporation:[1]

criminal liability
liability for committing
a criminal act

1. A corporation could be held vicariously liable for the criminal acts of any agent or employee acting within the scope of their duty.

2. Liability could arise if criminal acts were directed or authorized by the board of directors.

---

1. *Canadian Dredge & Dock Co. v. The Queen*, [1985] 1 S.C.R. 662, at 675.

3. The criminal conduct, including state of mind, of an employee or agent of a corporation could be attributed to the corporation.

Directing Mind

In England, the leading case that first attributed *mens rea* to a corporation was a civil case. In *Lennard's Carrying Co. v. Asiatic Petroleum Co.*, the House of Lords dealt with a corporation's civil liability under a statute that provided for a defence that was based on lack of fault. The issue in the case was whether the fault of a director of the company was in law the fault of the corporation. The decision established the following principle of corporate liability:

> [A] corporation is an abstraction. It has no mind of its own any more than it has a body of its own; its active and directing will must consequently be sought in the person of somebody who for some purposes may be called an agent, but who is really the directing mind and will of the corporation, the very ego and centre of the personality of the corporation.[2]

Following this case, the courts of England started imposing criminal liability on corporations on the basis of the behaviour of the "directing mind and will" of the company. An individual must have a certain level of authority to be the **directing mind** and will of a corporation. The courts have used the terms "alter ego" and sometimes "soul" of the corporation when identifying the directing mind and will. The determination of who is the directing mind and will is made on a case-by-case basis and it would normally be a person who has the authority to set policy for the corporation.

The principle of looking at the directing mind and will to impose criminal liability on corporations was soon followed by Canadian courts.[3] Canadian courts have, over time, refined their approach to corporate criminal liability, and the Supreme Court of Canada decision in *Canadian Dredge & Dock Co. v. The Queen* became the leading case on this issue.

Canadian Dredge & Dock involved various bid-rigging charges against several different corporations. It was alleged that the corporations colluded and acted in concert with one another when bidding on contracts, which is contrary to the provisions of the *Criminal Code*. Four corporations were convicted and they appealed to the Supreme Court of Canada. The appellant corporations argued that the managers who were responsible for the bidding were acting in fraud of their employers, were acting for their own benefit, and were acting outside of the scope of their employment. Some of the corporations challenged the very existence of corporate criminal liability for *mens rea* offences.

The Supreme Court noted that in the case of absolute and strict liability offences where the Crown does not have to prove *mens rea*, a corporation is treated as a

directing mind
the person within a corporation who has the power to exercise decision-making authority on matters of corporate policy

---

2. *Lennard's Carrying Co. v. Asiatic Petroleum Co.*, [1915] A.C. 705, at 713-14.

3. For example, see *R. v. Fane Robinson Ltd.*, [1941] 3 D.L.R. 409 (Alta. C.A.) and *R. v. Ash-Temple Co.* (1949), 93 C.C.C. 267 (Ont. C.A.).

natural person and there is no need to establish a rule or rationale for corporate liability. Simply put, absolute and strict liability offences are made out upon proof that the corporation performed the prohibited act—only in traditional criminal offences is there an issue of finding criminal intent.

Identification Theory

identification theory
the theory that establishes
mens rea in a corporation by reference to
the directing mind

The Supreme Court, in following the English cases and earlier Canadian cases, adopted the "**identification theory**" of corporate criminal liability. This theory is legal fiction that produces the element of *mens rea* in a corporation, when in reality it can exist only in a natural person. The identification theory establishes the identity of the corporation by reference to the directing mind. Criminal liability is attributed primarily to the corporation rather than vicariously through the acts of its agents and employees. The essence of this principle is that the identity of the directing mind and the corporation are viewed as one, with the result that the corporation is found guilty of the act of the natural person. The Court concluded:

> In order to trigger its operation and through it corporate liability for the actions of the employee (who must generally be liable himself), the actor-employee who physically committed the offence must be the "*ego*," the "centre" of the corporate personality, the "vital organ" of the body corporate, the "*alter ego*" of the corporation or its directing mind.[4]

The defences put forth by the appellants in *Canadian Dredge & Dock* centred on the premise that a corporation cannot be held criminally responsible for the unauthorized and unlawful acts of a directing mind. In particular, it was argued that those responsible for the bidding were acting in fraud of their employers, were acting for their own benefit, and were acting outside of the scope of their employment. While dismissing these arguments on the facts of the case, the Supreme Court did, however, recognize that there are limits to the responsibility of corporations for the acts of their employees or agents, irrespective of whether they are the operating mind or not:

> [T]he identification doctrine only operates where the Crown demonstrates that the action taken by the directing mind (a) was within the field of operation assigned to him; (b) was not totally in fraud of the corporation; and (c) was by design or result partly for the benefit of the company.[5]

Clarification of Directing Mind

The Supreme Court of Canada clarified the meaning of "directing mind" in a 1993 decision in the following terms:

---

4. Supra footnote 1, at 682.

5. Ibid., at 713-14.

The key factor which distinguishes directing minds from normal employees is the capacity to exercise decision-making authority on matters of corporate policy, rather than merely to give effect to such policy on an operational basis.[6]

This means that a day-to-day manager who does not have the power to implement policy would not, under normal circumstances, qualify as a directing mind. For example, the manager of a bank or trust company would not be operating as a directing mind if a loan were authorized to a friend or relative without the usual precautions. On the other hand, a vice-president or regional manager of a bank might very well qualify as a directing mind if he or she devised a scheme to advance mortgages based on overinflated property values.

More Than One Directing Mind

Interestingly, it is possible for a corporation to have several directing minds. This applies especially in the case of large companies. The law says that a company is responsible for the actions of an employee who is in the control of a particular sphere of its operations, where that employee is essentially the company's will and mind in that sphere. Most large companies have a complex management structure with several divisions, each with its own sphere of responsibility. Although part of the same corporate structure, each division normally has autonomy within its sphere of influence. If the autonomy includes policy-making power, one would expect to find a directing mind in the division, notwithstanding that, ultimately, the directing mind would report to more senior management or to the board of directors. This was the case in *Canadian Dredge & Dock* where in some instances a directing mind was found to reside in a general manager and vice-president of a division.

Major Defences to the Identification Theory

Under *Canadian Dredge & Dock*, a company facing criminal liability would have two major defences. First, the company would escape criminal liability if the individual within the company who committed the act was not a directing mind. The Crown must prove that the wrong was committed by a person of sufficient authority to have policy-making powers. This is usually reserved for officers, directors, and executive employees. Second, a company would not be convicted if the directing mind operated wholly in fraud of the company or if the company received no benefit at all from the acts.

Criticism of the Identification Theory

There are a number of criticisms of the identification theory of corporate criminal liability. Many have criticized the approach as too narrow because only the actions of high-level employees can trigger criminal liability. For example, why should a company escape liability where there exists a corporate culture that encourages lower-level managers and supervisors to cut corners on health and safety issues,

---

6. *Rhône (The) v. Peter A.B. Widener (The)*, [1993] 1 S.C.R. 497, at 526.

even if contrary to stated corporate policy? Others, however, have argued that the approach is too broad in that it automatically imputes to a corporation the actions of one employee in isolation, irrespective of the company's conduct as a whole, and without regard to efforts to prevent illegal activity. Many companies expend considerable resources in becoming good corporate citizens. Why should an otherwise model corporation be convicted for the actions of a single rogue employee when it has implemented measures to ensure that employees behave appropriately?

In addition, the concept of *mens rea* does not always apply well to corporations. For example, while technically available, it is difficult to see how the defence of mental disorder could apply to a corporation or how a corporation could be unfit to stand trial.

Statutory Provisions

The Westray Report

The law relating to corporate criminal liability underwent significant changes on March 31, 2004 when the *Criminal Code* was amended by Bill C-45. Bill C-45 was enacted partly in response to the findings of the Westray Mine disaster public inquiry (the "Westray Report").[7]

The Westray coal mine opened in Nova Scotia on September 11, 1991. Concerns about the safety of the mine were expressed before it even opened, and these concerns continued after operations began. On May 19, 1992, a massive methane explosion trapped and killed 26 miners at the Westray Mine. The company that operated the mine, Curragh Resources Inc., was charged with 52 non-criminal counts of operating an unsafe mine. All of these charges were subsequently stayed. Two managers were charged with criminal negligence and manslaughter. All of these charges were eventually withdrawn by the Crown for lack of evidence. Mounting pressure from organized labour and other interest groups following the mining disaster eventually led to the passage of Bill C-45.

The Westray Report found that there were numerous problems with the mine. Workers were not adequately trained and basic safety measures were not always taken. The many factors that led to the cause of the explosion were all avoidable. The Honourable Mr. Justice K. Peter Richard, commissioner of the Inquiry, summarized the situation that preceded the explosion in the following manner:

> It is a story of incompetence, of mismanagement, of bureaucratic bungling, of deceit, of ruthlessness, of cover-up, of apathy, of expediency and of cynical indifference.[8]

The Westray Report made a number of recommendations based on the findings of the Inquiry. A key recommendation addressed the issue of corporate criminal liability as follows:

---

7. K. Peter Richard, *The Westray Story: A Predictable Path to Disaster—Report of the Westray Mine Public Inquiry* (Halifax: Province of Nova Scotia, 1997).

8. Ibid., from the executive summary.

The Government of Canada, through the Department of Justice, should institute a study of the accountability of corporate executives and directors for the wrongful or negligent acts of the corporation and should introduce in the Parliament of Canada such amendments to legislation as are necessary to ensure that corporate executives and directors are held properly accountable for workplace safety.[9]

On April 23, 1999, a private member's motion was introduced recommending that the *Criminal Code* be amended in accordance with the recommendations set out in the Westray Report. The motion was successful and resulted in the Standing Committee on Justice and Human Rights issuing a discussion paper on corporate criminal liability. In response, Bill C-45 was introduced on June 12, 2003 and eventually proclaimed into force on March 31, 2004.

Bill C-45

The first point to note about Bill C-45 is that it did not result in any changes being made to any of the common-law rules that deal with the personal liability of directors, officers, and employees of corporations. These individuals remain liable for all crimes that they commit. The purpose of Bill C-45 was to revise the law to better deal with the way modern corporations are structured. There is no question that, as corporations have grown larger, the concept of a directing mind has become increasingly more difficult to rationalize with corporate criminal liability. It is increasingly more challenging to identify the specific acts or decisions necessary under the common law to find criminal responsibility in a modern corporation. The reality is that rarely in large modern corporations do high-level employees personally commit acts or make decisions that attract criminal liability. The conduct of these employees, may, however, encourage or permit a corporate culture of cutting corners and putting productivity before health and safety concerns.

One purpose of Bill C-45 is to ensure that the same rules for attributing criminal liability apply to *all* "bodies" that engage in criminal conduct. Prior to March 31, 2004, the *Criminal Code* defined "every one," "person," and "owner" to include "public bodies," "bodies corporate," "societies," and "companies." However, there are other forms of enterprise that individuals can participate in when conducting business or other affairs. Before the passage of Bill C-45, the legislature dealt with this challenge by developing new definitions in the *Criminal Code* as it became necessary. For example, 1997 amendments created the ability to prosecute *Criminal Code* offences committed by "criminal organizations." A "criminal organization" was defined as "a group, however organized" of three or more persons for the purpose of committing a serious criminal offence. The definition is wide enough to include gangs, telemarketers, and organized crime. In 2001, in response to the terror attacks in the United States, the *Criminal Code* was amended to create terrorism offences committed by an "entity." Criminal organizations and terrorist entities may not be corporations, but they can resemble corporations in the way they are structured and carry out their activities.

---

9. Ibid., recommendation 73.

Current Provisions of the Criminal Code

Definition of Organization

Section 2 of the *Criminal Code*[10] now defines "every one," "person," and "owner" as including an "organization." The definition of "organization" in s. 2 of the *Criminal Code* now reads as follows:

> "Organization" means
>> (a) a public body, body corporate, society, company, firm, partnership, trade union or municipality, or
>> (b) an association of persons that
>>> (i) is created for a common purpose,
>>> (ii) has an operational structure, and
>>> (iii) holds itself out to the public as an association of persons.

These provisions make it clear that liability for criminal acts is based not only on the form, but also on the nature, of the organization.

Level of Mens Rea: Negligence Versus Intent or Recklessness

In addition to expanding the types of enterprises that can attract criminal sanctions, Bill C-45 changed the common-law approach to corporate criminal liability in two fundamental ways:

1. Where the offence is criminal negligence, liability is based on the broader actions and moral fault of the corporation.[11]

2. For crimes that require recklessness or *mens rea*, the class of persons capable of triggering corporate liability has been expanded.[12]

Section 22.1 of the *Criminal Code* applies to offences where the Crown is required to prove negligence. The section provides as follows:

> 22.1 In respect of an offence that requires the prosecution to prove negligence, an organization is a party to the offence if
>> (a) acting within the scope of their authority
>>> (i) one of its representatives is a party to the offence, or
>>> (ii) two or more of its representatives engage in conduct, whether by act or omission, such that, if it had been the conduct of only one representative, that representative would have been a party to the offence; and
>> (b) the senior officer who is responsible for the aspect of the organization's activities that is relevant to the offence departs—or the senior officers, collec-

---

10. *Criminal Code*, R.S.C. 1985, c. C-46.

11. *Criminal Code* s. 22.1.

12. *Criminal Code* s. 22.2.

tively, depart—markedly from the standard of care that, in the circumstances, could reasonably be expected to prevent a representative of the organization from being a party to the offence.

A **representative** is defined as a director, partner, employee, member, agent, or contractor of an organization.[13] A representative could be anyone who is employed or otherwise affiliated with a corporation. A **senior officer** is a representative who plays an important role in the establishment of an organization's policies, or is responsible for managing an important aspect of an organization's activities and includes a director, chief executive officer, or chief financial officer.[14] A senior officer would include the common-law directing mind as a representative who plays an important role in establishing policy, but would also include those who manage an important aspect of an organization's activities. In other words, in addition to a person who sets policy, a senior officer can also be a manager with no policy-making power.

Considering what we have said above, under s. 22.1 the concept of a directing mind is not really relevant to crimes that involve negligence. Instead, liability is based on the behaviour of representatives and senior officers. The *actus reus* and *mens rea* no longer need to be derived from the same individual. The physical element can be committed by one or more representatives (any employees) while the mental element can be found in one or more senior officers (managers). Essentially, criminal negligence liability for corporations and other organizations can now be established through the combined acts, omissions, and state of mind of representatives and senior officers.

Liability for non-negligent crimes that involve intent and recklessness is found in s. 22.2 of the *Criminal Code*, which reads as follows:

> 22.2 In respect of an offence that requires the prosecution to prove fault—other than negligence—an organization is a party to the offence if, with the intent at least in part to benefit the organization, one of its senior officers
>
> (a) acting within the scope of their authority, is a party to the offence;
>
> (b) having the mental state required to be a party to the offence and acting within the scope of their authority, directs the work of other representatives of the organization so that they do the act or make the omission specified in the offence; or
>
> (c) knowing that a representative of the organization is or is about to be a party to the offence, does not take all reasonable measures to stop them from being a party to the offence.

Again, criminal liability does not depend on the conduct of a directing mind. Rather, the relevant individuals are representatives and senior officers. For criminal liability to exist, the requisite *mens rea* must be found in a senior officer. The physical act may be committed by the senior officer or by any representative under his or her direction. In addition, criminal liability arises in situations where a senior officer

representative
any director, partner, employee, member, agent, or contractor of an organization

senior officer
a representative who plays an important role in the establishment of an organization's policies, or is responsible for managing an important aspect of an organization's activities

---

13. *Criminal Code* s. 2.
14. Ibid.

fails to take reasonable measures to prevent an offence from being committed by a representative when he or she knows that the representative is committing, or is about to commit, an offence.

A key feature of Bill C-45 is that it amended the *Criminal Code* to clarify that its criminal negligence provisions apply to a workplace setting. Section 217.1 imposes a legal duty on those who direct others in their work to take reasonable steps to prevent bodily harm to that person, or any other person, arising from that work. The existence of this duty confirms that the criminal negligence provisions of the *Criminal Code* apply to corporations and other organizations.

As with all offenders, a corporation that has been convicted of a criminal offence will be sentenced. A senior officer or representative who has committed an offence is subject to the same penalties as any other individual offender, with penalties ranging from an absolute or conditional discharge to jail. However, a corporation cannot be imprisoned. Other than the imposition of a fine, the traditional sentencing options in the *Criminal Code* are not really appropriate in the case of an entity that is a legal fiction. Therefore, a monetary fine has been the usual sentence that is imposed on a corporation. The maximum permitted fine is much higher in the case of a corporation than it is for an individual. A corporation that has been convicted of an offence punishable by summary conviction is liable to a maximum fine of $100,000 while an individual would normally be subject to a maximum fine of $5,000. There is no maximum fine where a corporation is convicted of an indictable offence.[15]

Sentencing Provisions

One purpose of Bill C-45 was to introduce new sentencing principles designed specifically for corporations. The new principles supplement, rather than replace, general sentencing principles. This means, for example, that a sentence must be proportionate to the seriousness of the offence and the degree of responsibility of the offender.[16] The new provisions are found in s. 718.21, which directs the court to consider the following factors when sentencing an organization:

> 718.21 A court that imposes a sentence on an organization shall also take into consideration the following factors:
> (a) any advantage realized by the organization as a result of the offence;
> (b) the degree of planning involved in carrying out the offence and the duration and complexity of the offence;
> (c) whether the organization has attempted to conceal its assets, or convert them, in order to show that it is not able to pay a fine or make restitution;
> (d) the impact that the sentence would have on the economic viability of the organization and the continued employment of its employees;
> (e) the cost to public authorities of the investigation and prosecution of the offence;

---

15. *Criminal Code* s. 735.
16. *Criminal Code* s. 718.1.

(f) any regulatory penalty imposed on the organization or one of its representatives in respect of the conduct that formed the basis of the offence;

(g) whether the organization was—or any of its representatives who were involved in the commission of the offence were—convicted of a similar offence or sanctioned by a regulatory body for similar conduct;

(h) any penalty imposed by the organization on a representative for their role in the commission of the offence;

(i) any restitution that the organization is ordered to make or any amount that the organization has paid to a victim of the offence; and

(j) any measures that the organization has taken to reduce the likelihood of it committing a subsequent offence.

In addition to setting out these new sentencing principles, Bill C-45 also amended the *Criminal Code* to provide new probation conditions for organizations. This is an important feature that can be used to help rehabilitate an organization and deter it from engaging in unlawful acts in the future. It can also be used to deter other organizations from engaging in similar criminal conduct where general deterrence is a sentencing objective. Section 732.1(3.1) of the *Criminal Code* sets out the following additional conditions that a court may impose on an organization:

732.1(3.1) The court may prescribe, as additional conditions of a probation order made in respect of an organization, that the offender do one or more of the following:

(a) make restitution to a person for any loss or damage that they suffered as a result of the offence;

(b) establish policies, standards and procedures to reduce the likelihood of the organization committing a subsequent offence;

(c) communicate those policies, standards and procedures to its representatives;

(d) report to the court on the implementation of those policies, standards and procedures;

(e) identify the senior officer who is responsible for compliance with those policies, standards and procedures;

(f) provide, in the manner specified by the court, the following information to the public, namely,

(i) the offence of which the organization was convicted,

(ii) the sentence imposed by the court, and

(iii) any measures that the organization is taking—including any policies, standards and procedures established under paragraph (b)—to reduce the likelihood of it committing a subsequent offence; and

(g) comply with any other reasonable conditions that the court considers desirable to prevent the organization from committing subsequent offences or to remedy the harm caused by the offence.

Summary of Key Features of Bill C-45 Amendments to the Criminal Code

While the conduct of the directing mind, as a senior officer, is still an important factor in attaching criminal liability to a corporation, Bill C-45 has significantly affected the law with regard to when and how corporations commit crime. The Legislative Summary[17] of Bill C-45 summarizes the *Criminal Code* amendments in the following manner:

- Criminal liability is not dependent on a directing mind having committed the offence.
- It is no longer necessary to derive the *actus reus* and *mens rea* necessary to commit an offence from a single individual.
- The class of individuals who can supply the *actus reus* of an offence has been expanded to include all employees, members, agents, and contractors.
- For negligence-based crimes, *mens rea* is attributed to the aggregate fault of senior officers.
- For crimes requiring intent or recklessness, *mens rea* exists where a senior officer is party to the offence, or when a senior officer has knowledge of the commission of the offence by another representative and fails to take all reasonable measures to stop them from committing the offence.
- There are no special rules of criminal liability for corporate executives.
- Special sentencing provisions have been adopted.
- A legal duty has been established for those who direct the work of others, to take reasonable steps to prevent bodily harm from arising from that work.

17. David Goetz, *Bill C-45: An Act to Amend the Criminal Code (Criminal Liability of Organizations)* (Ottawa: Law and Government Division, Parliamentary Research Branch, 2003), Legislative Summary LS-457E, http://www.parl.gc.ca/Content/LOP/LegislativeSummaries/37/2/c45-e.pdf.

CHAPTER SUMMARY

It is logical that if corporations are afforded the rights and privileges attributable to natural persons, then corporations should also be subject to criminal liability in the same manner as are natural persons. This is especially true in modern times when corporations are, for the most part, the economic engine that powers the economy. The decisions made on behalf of corporations and the acts of corporations have a profound impact on daily lives. The case can easily be made that controlling the actions of corporations has a greater societal impact than does imposing criminal sanctions on living entities for criminal conduct.

KEY TERMS

criminal liability, 78
directing mind, 79
identification theory, 80

representative, 85
senior officer, 85

REVIEW QUESTIONS

1. What is the identification theory of corporate liability? How does this theory attach criminal liability to corporations?

2. What major defences are available to corporations under *Canadian Dredge & Dock*?

3. What was responsible for the change in the way corporations were prosecuted under the *Criminal Code*?

4. What is an "organization" under the *Criminal Code*?

5. Who is a "representative" under the *Criminal Code*? Who is a "senior officer"?

6. What is the significance of the distinction between a representative and a senior officer?

EXERCISES

1. Do you think that the Westray Mine disaster would result in criminal liability under the current provisions of the *Criminal Code*?

2. Beta Consulting Ltd. is a corporation that provides various consulting services for managing computer and data management systems. Beta's clients include several large municipalities. One of Beta's sales managers made a series of "friendly" payments totalling over $10,000 to several municipal officials of Beta's largest client. The sales manager and Beta Consulting Ltd. have both been charged with various bribery offences. Do you think that Beta will be convicted? Do you think that Beta would have been convicted under the law as it existed before Bill C-45? Explain your answer.

3. Power Corporation is an incorporated company that operates several small hydroelectric generating plants in the province. Power has a centrally located head office and several smaller regional offices. Each regional office operates independently and is headed by a regional vice-president. Each regional vice-president reports directly to the president of the company. All of the regional offices are profitable except for the northern office, which has been losing money for several years. The northern office also happens to be the only office with a unionized workforce. Power's head office has been exerting pressure on the northern office to cut costs so that it too can be profitable. As a result of this pressure, the vice-president of the northern office laid off several employees in the health and safety department to cut overall labour costs. Some time later a worker was caught in a malfunctioning turbine and seriously injured. The defective turbine had been regularly inspected, but was no longer inspected following the layoffs. Has the company committed any criminal offences? Explain your answer.

Some Specific Offences

9

LEARNING OUTCOMES

After completing this chapter, you should be able to:

- Demonstrate a general understanding of some specific offences in the *Criminal Code*.
- Demonstrate a more in-depth understanding of the offence of common or simple assault, s. 265.
- Understand the concept of a lesser and included offence.
- Demonstrate a general understanding of the *Controlled Drugs and Substances Act*.
- Understand the limited role of licensed paralegals and agents in defending charges under the *Controlled Drugs and Substances Act*.

Introduction

In this chapter we look at examples of some offences. It is important when reading to keep in mind the *actus reus* and *mens rea* and to try to identify these elements in each offence discussed. Properly identifying the full *actus reus* and *mens rea* of an offence is essential to building either a prosecution or a defence case. The first consideration in planning any defence strategy would be whether or not it can be argued that the accused did not commit the *actus reus* or have the necessary *mens rea*.

In addition, we also examine some controversial offences. While most rational people would agree that murder should be a criminal offence, some offences, such as the controversial ones discussed in this chapter, are not always agreed upon in terms of their criminalization, and because of this, we enter into the realm of justice policy. Controversial offences also often give rise to Charter arguments.

Violent Offences

Homicide

Homicide is defined in s. 222 of the *Criminal Code*. A person commits homicide when, directly or indirectly, by any means, he causes the death of another person. Homicide is either culpable or non-culpable or, in simpler terms, criminally blameworthy or non-blameworthy. Non-culpable homicide is not an offence and would include situations such as a soldier killing an enemy during a war or a death resulting from a traffic accident where the victim failed to stop at a red light and the other driver could not avoid hitting the victim's car.

Culpable homicide is an offence, and the person causing death is held criminally accountable. According to ss. 222(5)(a) to (d), a person commits culpable homicide when he causes the death of another person

(a) by means of an unlawful act;
(b) by criminal negligence;
(c) by causing that human being, by threats or fear of violence or by deception, to do anything that causes his death; or
(d) by wilfully frightening that human being, in the case of a child or sick person.

There are three forms of culpable homicide: murder, manslaughter, and infanticide.

Murder

Murder is the most serious type of culpable homicide. Section 229 sets out the circumstances when culpable homicide is murder, and these are:

- When the person who causes the death means to do so.

- When the person who causes the death means to cause bodily harm and knows the act is likely to cause death.

- When the person causes the death while committing a criminal act, whether the death is caused accidentally or not.

In other words, the accused must voluntarily do something to cause the death of the victim (the *actus reus*) and one of the required mental elements listed above (the *mens rea*) must be present. However, if the accused tries to kill a particular person but instead accidentally kills someone else, she will still be guilty of murder even though she did not intend to kill the person who died.[1]

Section 230, which provides that a person could be convicted of murder where she caused the death of another during the commission of certain offences listed in the section, even when the death was caused unintentionally, has been struck down as being a violation of the *Charter of Rights and Freedoms*. The section is no longer of any force or effect.

Section 231 classifies murder into two types for the purpose of determining what sentence should be applied upon conviction. This section does not create an offence, but deals only with the nature of the punishment that will be meted out. Murder is either first-degree or second-degree. Murder is first-degree when the victim's death "is planned and deliberate." In addition, if the victim is a police officer or any other law enforcement agent listed in s. 231(4), or if the death occurs during the commission of, or attempt to commit, any of the offences listed in s. 231(5), including a hijacking of a plane, a sexual assault, or a kidnapping, then the offence is first-degree murder.

Murder that is not first-degree is considered to be second-degree. In other words, if the Crown can prove that the accused committed murder in accordance with s. 229, but cannot prove beyond a reasonable doubt that the murder was planned and deliberate, then the accused will be convicted of second-degree murder and sentenced accordingly.

There is a mandatory sentence of life imprisonment for murder. The minimum penalty for first-degree murder is life imprisonment without eligibility for parole for 25 years. For second-degree murder, the minimum time to be served in prison without parole eligibility is 10 years, and can be as high as 25 years.

Manslaughter

Manslaughter is a culpable homicide that is not murder or infanticide.[2] This means that once it has been proved that a death is culpable homicide under s. 222(5), it must be determined whether it is murder, manslaughter, or infanticide. If the death does not meet the requirements of murder, s. 229, or infanticide, s. 233, it will be manslaughter under s. 234. The Crown may be able to prove beyond a reasonable doubt that the death of the victim was culpable homicide but cannot prove beyond a reasonable doubt that the accused had the *mens rea* for murder. In such a case, the judge might find the accused guilty of manslaughter or instruct the jury to consider manslaughter as a verdict.

---

1. *Criminal Code*, R.S.C. 1985, c. C-46, s. 229(b).

2. *Criminal Code* s. 234.

The sentence for manslaughter is provided in s. 236. The maximum sentence is life imprisonment, and if a firearm is used in the commission of the offence, there is a minimum sentence of four years in prison. This is a different sentence from that for murder. The minimum sentence for murder is life imprisonment.

Infanticide

Infanticide, the final type of culpable homicide, is defined in s. 233. It occurs when a mother, suffering from the effects of giving birth so that her mind is disturbed, causes the death of her newly born child by a wilful act or omission. "Newly-born child" is defined in s. 2 as a child under one year old. Under s. 237, the sentence is up to five years' imprisonment.

Assault

There are several criminal offences involving assault. The basic offence and the definition of assault are contained in s. 265.

> 265(1) A person commits an assault when
>   (a) without the consent of another person, he applies force intentionally to that other person, directly or indirectly;
>   (b) he attempts or threatens, by an act or a gesture, to apply force to another person, if he has, or causes that other person to believe on reasonable grounds that he has, present ability to effect his purpose; or
>   (c) while openly wearing or carrying a weapon or an imitation thereof, he accosts or impedes another person or begs.
> (2) This section applies to all forms of assault, including sexual assault, sexual assault with a weapon, threats to a third party or causing bodily harm and aggravated sexual assault.
> (3) For the purposes of this section, no consent is obtained where the complainant submits or does not resist by reason of
>   (a) the application of force to the complainant or to a person other than the complainant;
>   (b) threats or fear of the application of force to the complainant or to a person other than the complainant;
>   (c) fraud; or
>   (d) the exercise of authority.
> (4) Where an accused alleges that he believed that the complainant consented to the conduct that is the subject-matter of the charge, a judge, if satisfied that there is sufficient evidence and that, if believed by the jury, the evidence would constitute a defence, shall instruct the jury, when reviewing all the evidence relating to the determination of the honesty of the accused's belief, to consider the presence or absence of reasonable grounds for that belief.

This offence, sometimes referred to as simple assault or common assault, requires the intentional application of force, directly or indirectly, to another person without consent. Assault may also occur when there is an attempt or threat to apply force. The attempt or threat may occur by an act or a gesture. However, the potential victim of the attempt or threat must have reasonable grounds for believing that the accused is able to carry out the assault. Therefore, someone joking that he will punch out his friend if the friend gets an A in his criminal law examination is unlikely to be charged or convicted of assault unless the friend actually believes that an assault will occur.

The final manner of committing assault provided in the section requires proof that the accused physically confronted, stopped, or begged from the victim while openly wearing or carrying a weapon. The wearing of a weapon while engaged in the described activities involves an implied threat.

The application of the force in violation of s. 265(1)(a) does not need to involve any strength or power. Any unwanted touching of the victim could lead to a conviction under this section. The lack of consent is a crucial element of the *actus reus* of this offence, not the level of force used.

Consent

Consent must be informed and freely given under s. 265(3). To be freely given, the consent must not simply be the result of submission or failure to resist or protest the touching due to fear, fraud, or the exercise of authority. The exercise of authority encompasses both those circumstances in which someone gives consent as a result of being ordered to do so by someone who has obvious power over them, and those situations in which there is an imbalance of power in the relationship, such as between a psychiatrist and his patient.[3] Informed consent involves an understanding of the risks of consent. For instance, a doctor must properly explain the dangers or risks of medical treatment to a patient to make the patient's consent valid.

Issues of consent most often arise in the context of consensual fights or sporting activities that involve physical contact. The consent may be implied in these circumstances. For instance, two people in a bar begin to argue. One says to the other, "You want to take this outside?" This is generally regarded as an invitation to fight and if the other person takes up the challenge and goes outside to engage in a fight, he will likely be viewed as having implied his consent. Likewise, hockey often involves a lot of physical contact between players. Players are giving implied consent to this contact when they participate in a game.

However, when the consent is implied in a fight or sporting activity, the courts have placed limits on the level of force to which the victim consented. If the force used in a situation is excessive, the courts will likely find that the victim did not consent to that extent of bodily contact. For example, in a hockey game, if a player takes off his gloves and hits another player over the head from behind, the courts have determined that the victim did not consent to that level of force. Generally speaking, if the physical force is outside the rules of a game and beyond the risks normally associated with the manner in which the game is played, the courts will find that there was no consent.

---

3. In the case of *R. v. Saint-Laurent* (1993), 90 C.C.C. (3d) 291, the Court determined that a patient did not freely consent to having a sexual relationship with her psychiatrist because of the overwhelming imbalance of power in the relationship.

In cases that involve a consensual fight, in addition to s. 265, the courts apply a common-law rule that the consent of an adult to engage in such a fight is vitiated or negated when the accused has applied force that was intended to cause serious harm or injury to the victim.

It is important to note that s. 265(2) provides that the definitions of assault in the section apply to all forms of assault, including sexual assault, assault causing bodily harm, etc.[4]

Penalties for Common Assault

The penalty for the offence of common assault is not found in s. 265, but rather in s. 266. This is a **hybrid offence**, which means that the Crown may elect, or choose, the procedure to be followed in prosecuting the offence. (See Chapter 11 of this text for a discussion of the procedure for prosecuting various classifications of offences.) If the Crown chooses to use the procedure for prosecuting a more serious offence, the maximum penalty is five years in prison. On the other hand, if the Crown decides to proceed by way of summary conviction procedure, the method used for the prosecution of a less serious offence, the penalty is the general penalty for summary conviction offences: a fine of up to $5,000 or a maximum of six months in prison, or both.

> **hybrid or Crown option offences**
> offences that may be prosecuted as either summary conviction offences or indictable offences, at the choice or election of the Crown

Property Offences

Offences involving property make up the vast majority of offences listed in the *Criminal Code*. In this section we will focus on theft and break and enter.

Theft

Section 322 states:

> 322(1) Every one commits theft who fraudulently and without colour of right takes, or fraudulently and without colour of right converts to his use or to the use of another person, anything, whether animate or inanimate, with intent
>
>   (a) to deprive, temporarily or absolutely, the owner of it, or a person who has a special property or interest in it, of the thing or of his property or interest in it;
>
>   (b) to pledge it or deposit it as security;
>
>   (c) to part with it under a condition with respect to its return that the person who parts with it may be unable to perform; or
>
>   (d) to deal with it in such a manner that it cannot be restored in the condition in which it was at the time it was taken or converted.
>
>   (2) A person commits theft when, with intent to steal anything, he moves it or causes it to move or to be moved, or begins to cause it to become movable.
>
>   (3) A taking or conversion of anything may be fraudulent notwithstanding that it is effected without secrecy or attempt at concealment.

---

4. See *Criminal Code* ss. 267, 268, 270, 271, 272, and 273 for other forms of assault.

(4) For the purposes of this Act, the question whether anything that is converted is taken for the purpose of conversion, or whether it is, at the time it is converted, in the lawful possession of the person who converts it is not material.

(5) For the purposes of this section, a person who has a wild living creature in captivity shall be deemed to have a special property or interest in it while it is in captivity and after it has escaped from captivity.

Theft is one of the most commonly charged property offences. The *actus reus* of the offence requires taking or fraudulently converting someone else's property. A person converts property when she uses another person's property for her own purposes as though she were the true legal owner, thereby depriving the rightful owner of his use of the property. The act of converting is called conversion. An example of converting or conversion would be the borrowing of a friend's stereo while the friend was away on holiday, setting it up, and then refusing to return it to the friend at the end of the loan period. The initial borrowing does not involve conversion or theft because it was done with the rightful owner's permission. The act of borrowing was entirely legal. The conversion occurs when the borrower refuses to give the stereo back. However, "borrowing" someone else's property without permission may be illegal and may be regarded as theft.

The *mens rea* of theft or conversion must involve the intention to fraudulently deprive another person of his property. It need not be an intention to permanently deprive the other person of use of the property. A temporary deprivation would be enough. The person who is deprived of use of the property also need not be the legal owner. A person who has a "special interest" in the property, while not the legal owner, may also be a victim of theft. A "special interest" might be held by a renter of property.

In addition, the person taking or converting the property to her own use must do so without **colour of right**. The term "colour of right" refers to a situation in which a person honestly believes that they have a legal right to the property. For the accused to be convicted of theft, the Crown must prove that the accused knew, or should have known, that he had no legal right to the property in question. For instance, if the accused found a used leather chair on the side of the road, he might believe that the chair had been abandoned and take it home to use in his family room. He would be acting under "colour of right" if it were reasonable to believe that the chair actually had been abandoned, even if it had not and had fallen off the back of a moving van and the true owner was searching for it. On the other hand, if the bank made an error and incorrectly deposited $60,000 in the accused's account and he withdrew it before the bank realized the mistake it had made, he would be convicted of conversion unless he could establish that he had some legitimate reason for believing that the money was his, which would be unlikely in such circumstances.

colour of right
a person honestly believes that they have a legal right to the property in question

Section 334 provides different penalties depending on whether the value of the property taken or converted exceeds a value of $5,000. Theft of property valued at over $5,000 is an indictable offence, liable for punishment for a term of up to 10 years. Theft of property valued at $5,000 or less is a hybrid offence, subject to Crown election to be prosecuted as either an indictable offence or a summary conviction offence. See Chapter 11, pages 127 to 130 for a discussion of the classification of offences and various modes of prosecuting. Theft of property worth over $5,000 is commonly referred to as "theft over" and theft of $5,000 or less as "theft under."

Taking a Motor Vehicle Without Consent

Section 335 presents the offence of taking a motor vehicle without consent. This offence is often referred to as joyriding and it is included in the *Criminal Code* along with other offences that resemble theft.

> 335(1) Subject to subsection (1.1), every one who, without the consent of the owner, takes a motor vehicle or vessel with intent to drive, use, navigate or operate it or cause it to be driven, used, navigated or operated, or is an occupant of a motor vehicle or vessel knowing that it was taken without the consent of the owner, is guilty of an offence punishable on summary conviction.
>
> (1.1) Subsection (1) does not apply to an occupant of a motor vehicle or vessel who, on becoming aware that it was taken without the consent of the owner, attempted to leave the motor vehicle or vessel, to the extent that it was feasible to do so, or actually left the motor vehicle or vessel.
>
> (2) For the purposes of subsection (1), "vessel" has the meaning assigned by section 214.

This is an offence that often involves accused who are young persons. The *actus reus* must involve taking the vehicle "without the consent of the owner." Occupants of the vehicle may also be charged under this section if they knew it was taken without the owner's consent or did not try to leave the vehicle when they became aware that it was taken without permission.

The *mens rea* does not require the intent to keep the car or vessel or to deprive the rightful owner of its use. Rather, the intent must be to drive, use, navigate, or operate it or to cause any of these actions to happen.

Under many circumstances, the offence of taking a car would amount to theft over, but this section allows the police to lay a more minor charge when circumstances warrant. Such circumstances might involve a group of teenagers taking one of their parents' cars and driving around for fun. The parent discovers the car missing and calls the police, who apprehend the teens in the car before they cause any damage. Since s. 335 creates a summary conviction offence, which carries a much less harsh sentence than a more serious indictable offence, the police may, in circumstances such as these, choose to lay a charge under this section. (An in-depth discussion of the differences between summary conviction offences and indictable offences can be found in Chapter 11 of this text.) Joyriding is not the same as theft because the intent is different. A person who takes a vehicle without consent is not intending to deprive the rightful owner of the vehicle. With joyriding, the intent is merely to drive or use the vehicle for a period of time.

Lesser and Included Offences

lesser and included offence
an offence that includes all the elements of a less serious offence

A **lesser and included offence** is not an offence on its own, but is an offence for which the *actus reus* and *mens rea* are included in a more serious offence. In other words, an "included" offence is part of a more serious offence. The more serious offence must contain all the elements of the less serious offence.

There are several ways in which a lesser offence may be included in a more serious offence. First of all, the *Criminal Code* may specifically provide that certain offences are lesser and included offences. For example, s. 662(3) of the *Criminal Code* includes manslaughter or infanticide as a lesser and included offence of the offence of murder.

Another way for an offence to be an included offence is where the *Criminal Code* section that creates the offence is worded in such a manner that it includes the commission of another, less serious offence. For example, assault in s. 265 is a lesser and included offence within the offence of assault causing bodily harm created by s. 267 of the Code:

> 267. Every one who, in committing an assault, …
>   (b) causes bodily harm to the complainant, …

In order for the accused to be convicted of assault causing bodily harm, the Crown must prove beyond a reasonable doubt that she committed all the elements of an assault, as defined in s. 265. She must have intentionally applied force to another person without their consent. Then, to prove assault causing bodily harm, the Crown must establish beyond a reasonable doubt that she caused bodily harm to the victim while committing the assault. Bodily harm has a very specific meaning within s. 2 of the Code, and if the Crown cannot prove that the harm suffered by the victim meets that precise definition, then the accused may only be convicted of the lesser and included offence of common assault. The latter carries a much less serious penalty than does assault causing bodily harm.

Finally, s. 660 provides that the offence of attempt is an included offence in the complete offence that was charged. If, at trial, the Crown can prove all the elements of an attempt, but not that the offence was fully completed, then the accused may be convicted of an attempt even though she was charged with the fully completed offence and not an attempt.

Section 606(4) of the *Criminal Code* provides that an accused may plead not guilty to the offence with which she is charged, but guilty to any other offence arising out of the same transaction, whether or not it is an included offence. This can only be done with the consent of the prosecutor. For instance, using the charge of assault causing bodily harm as an example, during plea discussions, an accused who has been charged with assault causing bodily harm may offer to plead guilty to common assault. If the prosecutor agrees, the guilty plea to the lesser included charge will go before the court.

Controversial Offences

Most people would agree that murder, assault, and theft should be criminal offences, but there are a number of offences or potential offences that create considerable debate or disagreement in relation to whether or not these behaviours should be regarded as criminal and attract criminal penalties and consequences. Some of these controversial offences result in challenges under the *Charter of Rights and*

Freedoms, as with charges relating to abortion, obscenity, and some prostitution-related offences. We will now examine some of these offences.

Abortion

The relationship between abortion and criminal law is an extremely controversial issue that involves differing religious, moral, and social policy viewpoints. Pro-choice groups believe that the decision to have an abortion should be between a woman and her doctor and that the government of Canada and criminal law should have no role in that decision. Anti-abortion groups take the position that abortion should result in a criminal conviction for both the woman and the doctor.

Section 287 provided that a legal abortion could only be obtained if the woman applied to and received permission from a "therapeutic abortion committee" set up by an "approved hospital." The committee, composed primarily of doctors, considered the applicant's medical information and the recommendations of her personal doctor and decided whether an abortion would be performed. The criteria for making the decision was to be based on a medical finding that continuing the pregnancy would endanger the woman's health and well-being. However, not all hospitals in Canada had these committees and, in some areas of the country, abortions were unavailable because there was no hospital with a committee.

In 1988, in the case of *R. v. Morgentaler*,[5] the Supreme Court of Canada ruled that s. 287 of the *Criminal Code* was a violation of s. 7 of the *Charter of Rights and Freedoms* in that it restricted approval of abortion to these hospital committees. The three accused in this case were medical doctors who were charged with performing abortions in clinics outside of hospitals, without committee approval. The Supreme Court examined a number of Charter issues and, among other things, determined that "security of the person" within the meaning of s. 7 of the Charter must include a right of access to medical treatment for a condition representing a danger to life or health without fear of criminal sanction. The Court then deemed s. 287 of the Code to be of no force or effect because of its unconstitutionality.

As a result, although s. 287 remains in the *Criminal Code*, it cannot be enforced and Canada has no law that prohibits abortions.

Obscenity

Obscenity is another issue that often generates public and legal debate as to what types of behaviours and material should be regarded as warranting criminal consequences. Section 2 of the *Charter of Rights and Freedoms* guarantees freedom of expression. The issue then arises as to what kind of writing, photographs, films, etc. constitute obscenity and how freedom of expression interacts with the criminal law in this regard. Just how far can the criminal law go in attaching penal consequences to some forms of expression without violating the Charter? Can some material be art

---

5. [1988] 1 S.C.R. 30, 37 C.C.C. (3d) 449.

in the eyes of some individuals while being obscene in the view of others? These are the questions that courts are asked to examine when deliberating obscenity offences.

Section 163 of the *Criminal Code* provides:

163(1) Every one commits an offence who

(a) makes, prints, publishes, distributes, circulates, or has in his possession for the purpose of publication, distribution or circulation any obscene written matter, picture, model, phonograph record or other thing whatever; or

(b) makes, prints, publishes, distributes, sells or has in his possession for the purpose of publication, distribution or circulation a crime comic.

(2) Every one commits an offence who knowingly, without lawful justification or excuse,

(a) sells, exposes to public view or has in his possession for such a purpose any obscene written matter, picture, model, phonograph record or other thing whatever;

(b) publicly exhibits a disgusting object or an indecent show;

(c) offers to sell, advertises or publishes an advertisement of, or has for sale or disposal, any means, instructions, medicine, drug or article intended or represented as a method of causing abortion or miscarriage; or

(d) advertises or publishes an advertisement of any means, instructions, medicine, drug or article intended or represented as a method for restoring sexual virility or curing venereal diseases or diseases of the generative organs.

(3) No person shall be convicted of an offence under this section if the public good was served by the acts that are alleged to constitute the offence and if the acts alleged did not extend beyond what served the public good.

(4) For the purposes of this section, it is a question of law whether an act served the public good and whether there is evidence that the act alleged went beyond what served the public good, but it is a question of fact whether the acts did or did not extend beyond what served the public good.

. . .

(8) For the purposes of this Act, any publication a dominant characteristic of which is the undue exploitation of sex, or of sex and any one or more of the following subjects, namely, crime, horror, cruelty and violence, shall be deemed to be obscene.

Section 164 authorizes a judge, who is satisfied by sworn information that there is material that may violate s. 163, to issue a warrant allowing the police to seize any material deemed to be obscene. The person found with the material will be charged and, if convicted, will be liable for up to two years' imprisonment.

The only definition of what constitutes obscenity appears to be very broadly drawn in s. 163(8). A dominant characteristic of the publication must be "the undue exploitation of sex" or a combination of sex and any one or more of crime, horror, cruelty, and violence.

The defences available to this charge include challenging the allegation that the "dominant characteristic" of the material is sexual, or that there is an "undue exploitation of sex."

Section 163 was challenged under s. 2(b) of the Charter in the case of *R. v. Butler*. The Supreme Court of Canada found that s. 163 was a violation of the Charter but that it could be saved under s. 1 of the Charter as a reasonable limit "prescribed by law as can be demonstrably justified in a free and democratic society." In making this determination, the Court turned its mind to the issue of harm, particularly harm caused to society and women by unfettered publication or distribution of obscenity.

Prostitution

Prostitution itself is not a criminal offence in Canada; however, many of the activities surrounding prostitution do have criminal consequences. Rather than making prostitution itself illegal, the federal government has attempted to curtail it by criminalizing related activities. Communicating for the purpose of prostitution in a public place is a criminal offence,[6] as are keeping or being found in a common bawdy house[7] and procuring a prostitute or living on the avails of prostitution.[8] The *Criminal Code* defines "procuring" as an attempt to obtain a female person for sexual intercourse with another person, or living wholly or in part on the avails of prostitution of another person. A prostitute cannot be convicted of living on the money she makes herself, but someone who relies on the prostitute's earnings to support himself may be convicted.

Communicating involves stopping or attempting to stop another person in a public place for the purpose of asking them to engage in prostitution. Both the prostitute and/or the client may be charged with this offence. It is a summary conviction offence.

There are those who argue that prostitution is more of a nuisance problem than a criminal activity and that it would be better to set up "red-light districts" where prostitutes are licensed and regulated by the government. Advocates of this position argue that rounding up street prostitutes and putting them in jail overnight does little to stop them and that the next night they will be out on the same streets again. Instead, they propose that the sex trade be regulated and confined to a particular district, away from residential neighbourhoods, to a place where prostitutes can be protected from pimps through government licensing.

Those opposed to this approach argue that licensing prostitutes is not a proper activity for governments and that prostitution is very closely linked with other offences, such as the drug trade, and that decriminalizing prostitution would create opportunities for organized crime. In addition, there are concerns about the trafficking in women from poorer countries, who may be enticed into prostitution unwittingly.

---

6. *Criminal Code* s. 213.

7. *Criminal Code* s. 210.

8. *Criminal Code* s. 212.

In 2010, several Ontario women involved in the sex trade challenged the constitutionality of the prostitution-related laws. They argued that their lives were put in danger because they were unable to work inside, in the safety of their homes, without risking being charged with bawdy house offences and that they cannot hire security or drivers to protect them because this could amount to the guards and drivers being charged with living on the avails of prostitution.

A judge of the Ontario Superior Court agreed with their argument and found the communicating, procuring, bawdy house, and living on the avails sections of the Code to be a violation of s. 7 of the *Charter of Rights and Freedoms* because they are too broad in their wording and thus infringe the rights to security of the person. At the date of publication, this decision is under appeal by the federal government and is currently awaiting a date before the Supreme Court of Canada.[9]

Possession of Marijuana for Personal Use

There has been an ongoing legal discussion about the decriminalization of marijuana possession laws. At one point, the federal government tabled a bill[10] to amend the *Controlled Drugs and Substances Act*, but there was an election called before the proposed legislation could be dealt with and the current government has indicated that it has no intention to bring any similar legislation before Parliament.

Those advocating for change in the legislation propose the decriminalization of the possession of small amounts of marijuana, for personal use. Decriminalization is different from making something legal. Decriminalization means that marijuana will remain an illegal substance but that a conviction for possession of small amounts would result in a fine without any criminal record. However, conviction for possession for the purposes of trafficking, growing marijuana, and other related offences would still result in criminal prosecution.

People in support of decriminalization take the position that the use of marijuana is not addictive and there is no evidence that it leads to the use of harder drugs. It is recognized that large numbers of people in Canada have used or experimented with marijuana and many believe it is unfair that a person who is caught with a small amount of the substance should be followed throughout their lives by a criminal record.

However, others are strongly opposed to decriminalization, including the Canadian Association of Chiefs of Police, which is concerned that marijuana use can lead to involvement with more serious drugs and that decriminalization does not give the police a range of escalating options for dealing with the offence. Police are also concerned about the potential increase in smuggling of marijuana into and out of Canada and its connection, in some instances, to organized crime.

---

9. *Bedford v. Canada*, 2010 ONSC 4264; 2012 ONCA 186.

10. Bill C-38, *An Act to Amend the Controlled Drugs and Substances Act*, Second Session, Thirty-seventh Parliament, 51-52 Elizabeth II, 2002-2003.

Controlled Drugs and Substances Act

As we have already discussed, criminal law may be made only by the federal government. Most Canadian criminal law is contained in the *Criminal Code*, but there are a number of other federal statutes that contain criminal law, such as the *Youth Criminal Justice Act*, dealt with later in this text in Chapter 23, and the *Controlled Drugs and Substances Act* (CDSA).

Classification Schedules and Offences

The CDSA is federal legislation that controls and regulates drug use in Canada. Drugs are classified and categorized into a number of different schedules included in the Act. In addition, the statute establishes five main offences in relation to drugs and controlled substances. They are:

1. possession, which can be broken down into possession for personal use and possession for the purpose of trafficking,
2. trafficking itself,
3. importing,
4. exporting, and
5. drug production.

Schedules

The type of activity in relation to the drug combined with the type of drug according to its place on a particular schedule will determine the seriousness of the offence and the ultimate penalty available on conviction for the offence.

The schedules group and classify the drugs and substances as follows:

- Schedule I lists many of the most dangerous drugs, including narcotics such as heroin and cocaine. The most serious penalties are provided for offences relating to Schedule I substances, since they present the greatest health and social problems.

- Schedule II lists marijuana and other forms of cannabis, such as hashish. There are normally less serious penalties for possession of small amounts of marijuana and other forms of cannabis. There is also a lighter penalty for trafficking in and possession for the purpose of trafficking in a small amount of the substances listed in this schedule.

- Schedule III lists drugs such as amphetamines, often referred to in street terms as "uppers," MDA, and LSD.

- Schedule IV includes drugs such as tranquilizers, referred to on the street as "downers," barbiturates, and anabolic steroids. Schedule IV substances are not illegal to possess with a prescription from a doctor or otherwise authorized health professional. It is illegal, however, to import, export, or traffic in such drugs.

Sentencing

In relation to sentences, almost all the offences created in the CDSA are hybrid (dual) or indictable.[11] The vast majority of CDSA offences carry a minimum sentence of at least a fine of $5,000 and/or at least a year in jail. The maximum sentence for some offences is life imprisonment. Therefore, licensed paralegals in Ontario cannot represent an accused person on most CDSA offences.

The least serious offence in the Act is the possession of a Schedule II drug (cannabis) in an amount of 30 grams[12] or less of marijuana or 1 gram of hashish. These small amounts of cannabis are considered to be possession for personal use. The offence is summary conviction in nature, and is therefore automatically treated as less serious. It carries a maximum sentence of six months in jail and/or a $1,000 fine. Licensed paralegals may represent someone charged with this offence.

First offences involving possession for personal use of substances other than the limited amount of marijuana or hashish previously discussed above may also result in a possible maximum sentence of six months in jail and/or a fine of up to $1,000. However, an agent may only appear on such a charge after the Crown has advised the court that he or she is proceeding by way of the less serious summary conviction route.

It is important to note that, for the most part, the procedural law that governs cases under the CDSA is set out in the *Criminal Code* and is the same as for most prosecutions for offences under the Code.

11. Classification of offences as summary conviction, hybrid (dual), or indictable is dealt with at some length in Part III of this text in Chapter 11, Classification of Offences. Generally, the classification of the offence determines which procedure it will follow through the courts and the potential sentence upon conviction. Summary conviction offences carry the least serious penalties and indictable offences the highest. Hybrid (dual) offences can follow either the summary conviction procedure or the indictable procedure at the choice of the Crown and carry a higher or lower sentence depending upon the procedure used.

12. This amount is set out in Schedule VIII of the *Controlled Drugs and Substances Act*.

CHAPTER SUMMARY

This chapter examines a number of different offences. Included are some examples of violent offences such as homicide and assault, and property offences such as theft and taking a motor vehicle without consent, along with their penalties. Controversial offences such as abortion, obscenity, and prostitution are covered, and the concept of a lesser and included offence is studied. Also provided is an overview of the *Controlled Drugs and Substances Act* that discusses classification schedules, offences, and sentencing relating to drug offences.

KEY TERMS

colour of right, 97
hybrid or Crown option offences, 96
lesser and included offence, 98

REVIEW QUESTIONS

1. What is culpable homicide?
2. What are three types of culpable homicide?
3. What is a common or simple assault?
4. How can someone consent to an assault?
5. What is the difference between theft and taking a motor vehicle without consent?
6. What is a lesser and included offence?
7. What is the *Controlled Drugs and Substances Act*?
8. What is the purpose of the schedules in the *Controlled Drugs and Substances Act*?
9. On what types of offences may an agent or paralegal represent an accused charged under the *Controlled Drugs and Substances Act*?

EXERCISES

1. Janelle was in the mall and saw Kyla walking ahead of her looking in store windows. Janelle saw Kyla using her smart phone and watched her put it in her purse when she had finished her call. Janelle came up behind Kyla and grabbed her purse. Kyla and some witnesses say that Janelle wrestled Kyla for her purse, finally tearing it out of Kyla's hands.

   Other witnesses say that Janelle totally surprised Kyla, who didn't try in any way to hold onto her bag—she just let it go.

   In any event, Janelle was caught before she could escape from the mall, the purse was recovered, and she was charged with robbery.

   The defence is looking at options for a defence and is considering whether there may be a lesser and included offence involved. Is there such an offence? Discuss your answer in detail.

2. Do you think that some offences should be (1) decriminalized and regulated, (2) legalized and regulated, or (3) left as criminal offences? What criteria should be applied to a decision of this nature? Discuss these questions above in relation to

   a. communicating for the purposes of prostitution and related offences

   b. possession of marijuana for personal use.

Major Defences

10

LEARNING OUTCOMES

After completing this chapter, you should be able to:

- Demonstrate an understanding of the sources of defences in the common law and statute.

- Identify and understand a number of major defences to criminal charges.

- Demonstrate an ability to apply some major defences to simple fact situations.

Introduction

Canadian criminal law developed from British common law in which all the offences and defences were based on case law. However, Canada has had a statute-based criminal law since the late 19th century. Today, there are no common-law offences in Canadian law with the exception of criminal contempt of court. The only other offences for which a person may be charged and convicted are proscribed by the *Criminal Code* or another federal statute that creates criminal law. However, s. 8(3) of the Code specifically preserves existing common-law defences.[1] This means that some defences are based on the common law and others are specifically set out in the Code or other federal legislation.

We will now take a look at some of the major defences available in Canadian criminal law.

Mental Disorder

mental disorder
a disease of the mind that legally makes a person incapable of appreciating the nature or quality of his or her act, or of knowing it is wrong

The defence of **mental disorder** has replaced the old defence of insanity. Section 16 provides:

16(1) No person is criminally responsible for an act committed or an omission made while suffering from a mental disorder that rendered the person incapable of appreciating the nature and quality of the act or omission or of knowing that it was wrong.

(2) Every person is presumed not to suffer from a mental disorder so as to be exempt from criminal responsibility by virtue of subsection (1), until the contrary is proved on the balance of probabilities.

(3) The burden of proof that an accused was suffering from a mental disorder so as to be exempt from criminal responsibility is on the party that raises the issue.

Several elements must be proved in order to establish the defence. First, the court must be satisfied that an accused is suffering from a recognized mental disorder. A mental disorder is defined in s. 2 of the Code as a "disease of the mind." In determining what constitutes a disease of the mind, courts must apply a legal test and not simply a factual medical test. A psychiatrist or psychologist may give evidence as to the accused's mental health, but it is up to the judge to determine whether the legal definition has been met.

Second, once the disease of the mind has been established, one of two tests must be met. It must be proved that due to the disease of the mind, the accused is

know
to be merely aware of one's actions

1. incapable of appreciating the nature and quality of his act, or

2. incapable of knowing it is wrong.

appreciate
to have an awareness and understanding of the consequences of one's actions

Courts have drawn a distinction between "**knowing**" and "**appreciating**." To "know" means to merely be aware of one's physical actions. To "appreciate" involves

---

1. *Criminal Code*, R.S.C. 1985, c. C-46, s. 8(3).

a higher awareness and understanding of the consequences of one's actions. The courts have interpreted "wrong" to mean legally wrong as opposed to morally wrong.

Every person is presumed not to suffer from a mental disorder exempting him of criminal responsibility unless it is proved to the contrary on the balance of probabilities. The party raising the defence bears the onus of proof.

This defence is unusual in that either the Crown or the defence may raise it; however, the right of the Crown to raise the defence has been constitutionally challenged and, as a result, has been limited by the Supreme Court. The Court's concern was that the accused has a fundamental legal right to have control over the defence that they wish to raise. In the case of *R. v. Swain*,[2] the Court ruled that the prosecution may only raise the defence in two situations:

1. the accused has, in the opinion of the trial judge, already raised a defence that puts at issue the question of his mental capacity to form the criminal intent of the offence charged, or
2. the accused has been found guilty of the offence by the trier of fact.

In a case where the Crown raises the defence of mental disorder after a finding of guilt there will be a second part to the trial where it must be determined whether the accused should be relieved of that criminal responsibility by virtue of her mental disorder.

A person found not criminally responsible by reason of a mental disorder is not automatically set free into the community. There must be a disposition hearing at which the accused faces court-ordered detention in a mental health facility for an indeterminate period of time.

Intoxication

Before examining the issue of **intoxication** as a defence, we must first make a distinction between voluntary and involuntary intoxication. Involuntary intoxication would involve a situation where a person had consumed an intoxicant without being aware they were doing so. This might occur where a person's non-alcoholic drink was spiked when she was not looking, she was tricked into eating baked goods that contained hashish, or she had an adverse reaction to a prescribed medication. In such circumstances, the accused may be successful in raising involuntary intoxication as a defence. She would argue that due to the intoxication, she was unable to form the intent required to be found at fault or that she did not perform the *actus reus* of the offence voluntarily.

However, if the accused voluntarily became intoxicated, the situation is quite different. Voluntary intoxication is often referred to as self-induced intoxication. In order to examine the issue we must first recognize the difference between the common-law concepts of **general intent** and **specific intent** offences.

---

2. [1991] 1 S.C.R. 933.

intoxication
to have an impaired consciousness of one's actions due to the use of alcohol or drugs

general intent
a basic level of *mens rea* in which the Crown must prove that the accused had the intent to commit the *actus reus* of the offence

specific intent
a *mens rea* that has two levels in that the Crown must prove that the accused had the intent to perform the *actus reus* for a specific purpose or ulterior motive

In the vast majority of criminal offences, the Crown need only prove that the accused committed the *actus reus* intentionally, knowingly, or recklessly, etc., as the case may be. These offences are general intent offences. A defence of intoxication is not normally available for these offences.

Specific intent offences, on the other hand, are offences requiring a special or ulterior intent. There are essentially two levels of intent to be proven. The Crown must prove not only that the accused intentionally committed the *actus reus*, but that they also intended some further consequence. This concept can be difficult to understand without looking at examples. The offence of theft is a specific intent offence, as outlined in s. 322 of the Code:

> 322(1) Every one commits theft who fraudulently and without colour of right takes, or fraudulently and without colour of right converts to his use or to the use of another person, anything, whether animate or inanimate, with intent
>   (a) to deprive, temporarily or absolutely, the owner of it, or a person who has a special property or interest in it, of the thing or of his property or interest in it; …

The offence requires that the Crown prove beyond a reasonable doubt, not only that the accused intended to take the other person's property, but that she did so **with the additional intent** to deprive the rightful owner of that property on a temporary or permanent basis. A person can have the intent to take something but there is no additional intent to deprive the rightful owner of it. For example, I may pick up a copy of the *Criminal Code* that was left behind in the classroom. My intention is to take the book. This can be inferred from the fact that I picked it up and carried it out of the room, but unless the Crown can prove that I intended to keep it, sell it, or otherwise deprive the rightful owner of it, I will not be convicted. I may raise a reasonable doubt by arguing that my intention was to find the book's owner and return it to him.

Another type of specific intent offence is breaking and entering. Section 348(1) says:

> 348(1) Every one who
>   (a) breaks and enters a place with intent to commit an indictable offence therein, …

The prosecution must prove not only that the accused intended to break and enter the premises but also that they did so with the intention to commit an indictable offence within those premises. A person who smashes a window to save a child in danger inside a house certainly intends to break the window and enter the premises, but they don't intend to commit an indictable offence once they are inside.

Other examples of specific intent offences are murder, robbery, and assault with intent to resist arrest.

Up until the mid-1990s, the *Criminal Code* did not deal with the defence of intoxication. It was an entirely common-law defence. The general common-law principle was that intoxication could not be used as a defence to a general intent offence, but it could be a partial defence to a specific intent offence. It can be used to establish that the accused was too impaired to form the necessary second level of intent required for a specific intent offence.

In the 1994 case of *R. v. Daviault*,[3] the Supreme Court of Canada altered the long-standing common-law in relation to the availability of intoxication as a defence to a general intent offence. The Court ruled that intoxication could be a defence to a general intent offence if the level of intoxication was so extreme that it produced a state in the accused akin to a mental disorder or automatism. This case was widely criticized, particularly because it involved a violent sexual assault on a helpless victim by the extremely drunk accused. In response to public outcry, the federal Parliament added s. 33.1 to the *Criminal Code* in 1995.

Section 33.1 overrides the case law in *Daviault* and precludes the use of self-induced, voluntary intoxication as a defence to a general intent offence that involves any element of assault or interference with the bodily integrity of another:

> 33.1(1) It is not a defence to an offence referred to in subsection (3) that the accused, by reason of self-induced intoxication, lacked the general intent or the voluntariness required to commit the offence, where the accused departed markedly from the standard of care as described in subsection (2).
>
> (2) For the purposes of this section, a person departs markedly from the standard of reasonable care generally recognized in Canadian society and is thereby criminally at fault where the person, while in a state of self-induced intoxication that renders the person unaware of, or incapable of consciously controlling, their behaviour, voluntarily or involuntarily interferes or threatens to interfere with the bodily integrity of another person.
>
> (3) This section applies in respect of an offence under this Act or any other Act of Parliament that includes as an element an assault or any other interference or threat of interference by a person with the bodily integrity of another person.

The current application of the defence of voluntary or self-induced intoxication can be summarized as follows:

1. Self-induced intoxication **may be** a defence to a specific intent offence if the accused was intoxicated to the extent that he could not form the specific intent required as an element of that offence (traditional common-law rule).

2. Self-induced intoxication **cannot** be a defence to a general intent offence involving assault or violence (s. 33.1 of the *Criminal Code*).

3. Self-induced intoxication **may be** a defence to a general intent offence when

   a. the voluntary intoxication is so severe that the accused is in a state similar to insanity or automatism and thereby unable to form the intent to commit the offence

   AND

   b. the general intent offence does not involve assault or physical violence as part of the *actus reus* of the offence (common-law rule established in the *Daviault* case in 1994).

It should also be noted that the above application applies only to those offences requiring a subjective *mens rea*. Self-induced intoxication is not a defence to an

---

3. [1994] 3 S.C.R. 63.

offence requiring an objective *mens rea*, such as criminal negligence, because the objective test involves the reasonable person test. The reasonable person can never be an intoxicated person. See Chapter 5 for more on the reasonable person test.

Automatism

Automatism is a common-law defence. The term refers to behaviour or actions that a person performs while in a state of impaired consciousness. There are two types of automatism: (1) automatism caused by a mental disorder or extreme self-induced intoxication, often referred to as insane automatism, and (2) automatism caused by something other than a mental disorder or extreme intoxication, often referred to as non-insane automatism.

Insane Automatism

If the defence of insane automatism is established because the accused was suffering from a mental disorder at the time the offence was committed, the accused will be dealt with in the same manner as any other accused who meets the requirements of the defence of mental disorder. He or she will be found not criminally responsible by reason of a mental disorder and, following a disposition hearing, the person will most often be detained in a mental health facility, possibly indefinitely. A person suffering from such extreme self-induced intoxication that he or she is in a state similar to mental disorder will also be treated as having insane automatism.

Non-Insane Automatism

Non-insane automatism is dealt with differently from a mental disorder. An accused that successfully raises this defence will be acquitted and immediately released by the courts.

In order to successfully raise this type of automatism defence, it must be established that the impaired consciousness was caused by something other than a mental disorder or self-induced intoxication. Automatism may be caused by a physical condition that produces impaired consciousness, a blow to the head, or even by involuntary intoxication, such as unknowingly drinking a spiked beverage. The most common example of a state of automatism is a person who is sleepwalking. Sleepwalking is not a disease of the mind. It is caused by various factors other than mental illness.[4]

The defence is very difficult to establish. The Supreme Court of Canada has ruled[5] that an accused raising the non-mental disorder defence of automatism must prove on the balance of probabilities that his or her state of consciousness was impaired to the degree that the actions were not voluntary. Usually, much of the evidence of automatism would be medical, but other factors that would be considered are the

---

4. See *R. v. Parks*, [1992] 2 S.C.R. 871.

5. *R. v. Stone*, [1999] 2 S.C.R. 290, 134 C.C.C (3d) 353.

evidence of witnesses, a past history of impaired consciousness in the accused, and the nature of the trigger of the automatism.

Provocation

Provocation can only be used as a defence to a charge of murder (see s. 232 of the *Criminal Code*). It is not applicable to any other offence. If the defence is established, the conviction for murder will be reduced to manslaughter. It is therefore only a partial defence, not a complete defence, because the accused is not acquitted but instead convicted of a lesser offence.

The concept is that the accused was so inflamed that he could not control his violent impulses and, in the throes of passionate feeling, he lashed out and killed someone. Provocation may involve blows, words, or gestures that cause a person to lose their self-control: the loss of control must be sudden and the reaction of the accused must be immediate. The accused must not have had any time at all to consider the consequences of his actions.

The standard for establishing provocation is an objective one. The provocation must have been of such magnitude that it would have caused an ordinary person to lose control. If an accused has little self-control and is liable to fly off the handle at minor slights, he will likely have considerable difficulty establishing this defence.

Duress

Duress is a very complicated defence with both statutory and common-law aspects.

Section 17 of the *Criminal Code* provides the statutory defence:

> 17. A person who commits an offence under compulsion by threats of immediate death or bodily harm from a person who is present when the offence is committed is excused for committing the offence if the person believes that the threats will be carried out and if the person is not a party to a conspiracy or association whereby the person is subject to compulsion, but this section does not apply where the offence that is committed is high treason or treason, murder, piracy, attempted murder, sexual assault, sexual assault with a weapon, threats to a third party or causing bodily harm, aggravated sexual assault, forcible abduction, hostage taking, robbery, assault with a weapon or causing bodily harm, aggravated assault, unlawfully causing bodily harm, arson or an offence under sections 280 to 283 (abduction and detention of young persons).

The section requires that, first, in order for this defence to be established, the accused must act under the threat of imminent bodily harm or death, to herself or members of her family. Second, the person making the threats must be present when the offence is committed and finally, the defence is not available for the offences excluded by s. 17, which include most of the serious offences such as murder, assault causing bodily harm, arson, and sexual assault. The rationale for these restrictions is that if the accused has a period of time when he is not under the direct watch of the person making the threats, then he should go to the police.

Section 17 has been constitutionally challenged. In the case of *R. v. Ruzic*,[6] the Supreme Court of Canada found s. 17 to be in violation of s. 7 of the Charter to the extent that it allows individuals who acted involuntarily to be found guilty of a criminal offence. It is a principle of criminal law that the *actus reus* must be performed voluntarily. If a person is forced to act by a threat to her own well-being or that of her loved ones, the required voluntary aspect of her actions is removed.

The constitutional issue is created by the requirement in s. 17 that the person issuing the threat be present during the commission of the offence, coupled with the necessity of the threat being immediate. There are circumstances where the threat may not be immediate from a person present at the scene of the offence being committed, and yet the act may still not be voluntary in the sense that the accused person had no realistic choice other than to break the law to avoid the implementation of the threat; for example, the accused is threatened that his children will be harmed by someone he has reason to believe has the capability to do so, unless the accused commits the offence. The Court decided that this was too restrictive, and it struck down the two requirements of "presence of the person making the threat" and "immediacy of the threat," but it did not strike down the entire section.

The section as reformulated by the Supreme Court would still exclude the use of the defence for all of the offences listed, but now seems to apply to those who commit an offence under compulsion of death or bodily harm if they believe that the threats will be carried out. There is no longer a need for the person making the threats to be present or for the threats to be immediate. The defence could still not be used by any accused who had been part of a conspiracy to commit the offence.

There is also a common-law defence of duress. It applies, by virtue of s. 8(3), as a defence in all those situations where the s. 17 statutory defence does not apply.

The common-law version of the defence does not include any requirement that the person doing the threatening be present for the commission of the offence or that the threat be immediate. It also does not exclude any offences. It does not apply to the principal offender but rather only to other parties to the offence such as those who may aid or abet. However, in the *Hibbert*[7] case, the Supreme Court ruled that the common-law defence of duress does not apply to any accused who had an obvious and safe avenue of escape.

Necessity

Necessity is a common-law defence that traditionally has been very difficult to prove. It is similar in its early roots to duress, but can be distinguished from that defence. In its most basic form, the accused arguing the defence of necessity is claiming that she had no choice but to break the law to prevent a greater harm and therefore her actions were not voluntary in any true sense. As we have discussed

---

6. *R. v. Ruzic*, 2001 SCC 24, [2001] 1 S.C.R. 687.

7. *R. v. Hibbert*, [1995] 2 S.C.R. 973.

previously, to establish the *actus reus* of an offence, it must be proved that the accused acted voluntarily. The most-used example of necessity is driving in an unsafe manner in an attempt to get an injured or ill person to the hospital.

In the 1984 case of *Perka*,[8] the Supreme Court of Canada clearly set out the specific elements of the defence of necessity. In order for the defence to be successful, the following must be established:

1. The accused must have been facing a situation of clear and imminent peril or danger.

2. There must have been no avenue of escape from the danger or other reasonable legal way to avoid it.

3. The potential harm caused by committing the offence must be less than the harm that would have been caused by doing nothing and allowing the dangerous situation to continue.

The third part of the test is a test of proportionality. This means that the harm of committing the criminal offence and the harm caused by the danger the person is trying to avoid or escape must be in proper relationship to one other. For instance, if the accused killed four people while racing to the hospital, the issue would be whether his actions in trying to save one person were proportional to the loss of four other lives.

Necessity was raised as a defence in the *Latimer*[9] case. In that case, a Saskatchewan farmer killed his severely disabled, 12-year-old daughter and argued in court that he did it to prevent her from horrible suffering. The Court did not accept the defence.

In applying the test set out in the *Perka* case, the Court found that:

1. There was no imminent danger to the child.

2. There were many legal avenues open to Latimer other than killing his daughter. He could have worked with doctors and other caregivers to help alleviate her pain.

3. There was no proportionality of harm. The harm he inflicted on his daughter by ending her life was far greater than the harm of her suffering because there was a possibility that different medical treatments might have alleviated her suffering.

Self-Defence

The law permits a person to use reasonable force to protect himself, herself, or others from an unlawful assault. In addition, in some limited circumstances, a person may also use a measure of force to protect property. The basic principle involved in all self-defence is that an assault was taking place or that the accused reasonably

---

8. *Perka v. The Queen*, [1984] 2 S.C.R. 232.

9. *R. v. Latimer*, 2001 SCC 1, [2001] 1 S.C.R. 3.

believed an assault was about to take place and used force to either end the assault or stop it from taking place.

Until March 2013, there were a number of provisions in the Code that dealt with self-defence and they tended to be fairly complex and complicated. However, these provisions were replaced in the Code by one self-defence provision, a new s. 34, which attempts to clarify self-defence.

Section 34 reads as follows:

> 34(1) A person is not guilty of an offence if
>   (a) they believe on reasonable grounds that force is being used against them or another person or that a threat of force is being made against them or another person;
>   (b) the act that constitutes the offence is committed for the purpose of defending or protecting themselves or the other person from that use or threat of force; and
>   (c) the act committed is reasonable in the circumstances.
> (2) In determining whether the act committed is reasonable in the circumstances, the court shall consider the relevant circumstances of the person, the other parties and the act, including, but not limited to, the following factors:
>   (a) the nature of the force or threat;
>   (b) the extent to which the use of force was imminent and whether there were other means available to respond to the potential use of force;
>   (c) the person's role in the incident;
>   (d) whether any party to the incident used or threatened to use a weapon;
>   (e) the size, age, gender and physical capabilities of the parties to the incident;
>   (f) the nature, duration and history of any relationship between the parties to the incident, including any prior use or threat of force and the nature of that force or threat;
>   (f.1) any history of interaction or communication between the parties to the incident;
>   (g) the nature and proportionality of the person's response to the use or threat of force; and
>   (h) whether the act committed was in response to a use or threat of force that the person knew was lawful.
> (3) Subsection (1) does not apply if the force is used or threatened by another person for the purpose of doing something that they are required or authorized by law to do in the administration or enforcement of the law, unless the person who commits the act that constitutes the offence believes on reasonable grounds that the other person is acting unlawfully.

Under the new provision, a person may successfully raise self-defence to an offence, usually a charge of assault, if they can establish that they have reasonable grounds for believing that force or a threat of force is being used against them or another person, and the actions they take are for the purpose of defending or protecting themselves or the other person against that force. However, any actions taken to defend or protect must be reasonable in the circumstances. This test is both subjective, in that the person claiming self-defence must believe that they are being assaulted or being threatened with assault, and objective in that the belief must be reasonable.

In addition, the new s. 34 sets out a list of factors the courts must take into consideration in determining whether the actions taken by the person claiming self-defence are reasonable in the circumstances. These factors are:

- the nature of the force or threat;
- the extent to which the use of force was imminent and whether there were other means available to respond to the potential use of force;
- the person's role in the incident;
- whether any party to the incident used or threatened to use a weapon;
- the size, age, gender, and physical capabilities of the parties to the incident;
- the nature, duration, and history of any relationship between the parties, including any prior use or threat of force and the nature of that force or threat;
- any history of interaction or communication between the parties to the incident;
- the nature and proportionality of the person's response to the use or threat of force; and
- whether the act committed was in response to a use or threat of force that the person knew was lawful.

This list is non-exhaustive in that these are not the only factors that the court may consider. The court may also look at other relevant circumstances in deciding the reasonableness of the actions.

The defence will not apply in cases involving claims of self-defence against police or other law enforcement officials unless the person had reasonable grounds to believe that the law enforcement officer was acting in an unlawful manner.

As with the law relating to self-defence of a person, the law on defence of property (as of 2013) has also changed. Section 35 is the new provision and it replaces several former, more complex sections that dealt with protecting property.

Section 35 reads as follows:

35(1) A person is not guilty of an offence if
(a) they either believe on reasonable grounds that they are in peaceable possession of property or are acting under the authority of, or lawfully assisting, a person whom they believe on reasonable grounds is in peaceable possession of property;
(b) they believe on reasonable grounds that another person
(i) is about to enter, is entering or has entered the property without being entitled by law to do so,
(ii) is about to take the property, is doing so or has just done so, or
(iii) is about to damage or destroy the property, or make it inoperative, or is doing so;

(c) the act that constitutes the offence is committed for the purpose of

(i) preventing the other person from entering the property, or removing that person from the property, or

(ii) preventing the other person from taking, damaging or destroying the property or from making it inoperative, or retaking the property from that person; and

(d) the act committed is reasonable in the circumstances.

(2) Subsection (1) does not apply if the person who believes on reasonable grounds that they are, or who is believed on reasonable grounds to be, in peaceable possession of the property does not have a claim of right to it and the other person is entitled to its possession by law.

(3) Subsection (1) does not apply if the other person is doing something that they are required or authorized by law to do in the administration or enforcement of the law, unless the person who commits the act that constitutes the offence believes on reasonable grounds that the other person is acting unlawfully.

It is not necessary that a person actually own the personal property that is being protected, only that he or she is in peaceable possession of it or lawfully assisting someone else they reasonably believe is in peaceful possession of it. Therefore, someone renting a car would be able to rely on this section to use reasonable actions to stop someone from taking it.

In order to be able to raise the defence, a person must be in peaceable possession of the property. There is no definition of peaceable possession in the Code, but case law has defined it to mean two things:

- the person has actual possession of the property **and**
- the possession is not seriously challenged by others.

The phrase "not seriously challenged" in this context means that any challenge to the possession of the property that may arise would not likely lead to violence. In other words, if a person's possession of the property is likely to lead to a challenge that could result in a breach of the peace, the person is not in peaceable possession of that property and may not use the defence. For instance, a thief or a trespasser could not use the defence to try to stop the rightful owner of the property from reclaiming it, but likewise, the rightful owner could not use violence to take back his property because he is not in actual possession of it.

Once it has been established that the person is in peaceable possession of the property, whether it is real or personal property, s. 35 of the Code allows them to take reasonable action, including force, to protect that property if they have reasonable grounds to believe that it is about to be taken, damaged, or trespassed upon.

As with self-defence, it is not possible to take action to protect property from someone administering or enforcing the law unless there are reasonable grounds for believing that the law enforcement officials are acting unlawfully.

Consent

The defence of consent may be raised to some specific offences. In relying on this defence, the accused is claiming that the alleged victim consented to the accused's behaviour and therefore no criminal offence was committed.

One of the offences to which consent may apply is assault. While a person is not likely to agree to being hit, in some circumstances he is deemed to have consented to the physical contact. For instance, a person who voluntarily engages in a physical fight with the accused or who voluntarily plays a sport where physical contact is permitted by the rules of the game is deemed to have consented to the physical conduct. It is important to note that when playing a game the physical contact at issue must be permitted by the rules. A person playing hockey may be checked into the boards, and that type of contact is anticipated in a hockey game, but if a player starts hitting another player over the head with a hockey stick, that is not permitted as part of the rules of the game and would likely constitute an assault.

The consent also must be freely given. If it is obtained through fraud, threats, or trickery, it is not regarded as true consent and cannot be used as a defence.

Consent is not an allowable defence for some offences. For example, under s. 14 a person may not consent to having death inflicted upon him. This would prohibit someone who assisted in a suicide from using consent as a defence. There are also some sexual offences that do not allow the use of consent as a defence, particularly when the sexual offence involves a child.

Mistake of Fact

A mistake of fact involves an accused honestly believing in certain circumstances that do not exist but that would mean that he had not committed an offence if the circumstances did exist. If an accused believes that he is selling sugar instead of heroin, that would be a mistake of fact.[10] If the circumstances were as he believed, he would not be committing an offence.

Another example would be if a student picked up a copy of the *Criminal Code* after class and put it in her bag, believing the book was hers, but it instead belonged to another student. If the book actually belonged to the student who took it, there would be no offence committed.

The circumstance in which the accused believed must not involve the commission of an offence. For example, if the accused was selling a white powder that she believed was cocaine but which was actually heroin, mistake of fact could not be a defence because it is an offence to sell either cocaine or heroin.

There are some offences that specifically exclude mistake of fact as a defence. For the most part, these are sexual offences committed against young people. The accused may not simply claim as a defence that he was not aware of the age of the young person. He must show that he took reasonable steps to learn the actual age of the victim.

10. *Beaver v. R.* (1957), 118 C.C.C. 129 (S.C.C.).

Mistake of Law

It is a general presumption that people know the law. Ignorance of the law is not usually viewed as a defence. In fact, s. 19 of the Code specifically excludes it as a defence. Section 19 says:

> 19. Ignorance of the law by a person who commits an offence is not an excuse for committing that offence.

It is not always easy to tell the difference between a mistake of fact and a mistake of law, but generally speaking, not realizing that something is against the law amounts to a mistake of law and is not normally a defence. It is a mistake of fact to mistakenly think that the white powder one is selling is sugar and not heroin, but it is a mistake of law to mistakenly believe that selling heroin is not against the law.

CHAPTER SUMMARY

This chapter looks at the major defences available in Canadian criminal law. We learn that unlike criminal offences, which must be created by federal statute, s. 8(3) of the *Criminal Code* preserves all the common-law defences as long as they are not inconsistent with the Code or other federal statutes. Therefore, we have some defences that are statute-based, some that are created by the common law, and some that are combinations of both statute and common law.

Specifically, we look at the defences of mental disorder, intoxication, automatism, provocation, duress, necessity, self-defence, defence of property, consent, mistake of fact, and mistake of law. We note that the defences of mental disorder and provocation are both very limited defences. In the case of mental disorder, a successful raising of this defence results in a finding of not guilty by reason of mental disorder and confinement in a mental health facility until it is decided by a committee that the person is no longer a danger to society.

In the case of provocation, it may only be used as a defence in relation to murder, and it is not a complete defence in that, if proven, it does not lead to an acquittal, but only to a reduction of the offence from murder to manslaughter.

We also examine the more recent amendments to the *Criminal Code* regarding the defences of self-defence and defence of property, which have replaced much more complex and difficult provisions in the Code.

KEY TERMS

appreciate, 108
general intent, 109
intoxication, 109

know, 108
mental disorder, 108
specific intent, 109

REVIEW QUESTIONS

1. How is a mental disorder proved?
2. What is unusual about the defence of mental disorder?
3. What is a specific intent offence and what is the significance of this type of offence in relation to the defence of self-induced intoxication?
4. What's the difference between insane and non-insane automatism?
5. Can provocation be used as a defence to an assault?
6. Is duress a common-law defence or a statutory defence?
7. What is the test for successfully raising the defence of necessity?
8. When is it possible to raise the defence of self-defence?
9. What does the term "peaceable possession" mean?
10. When may a person defend their property?
11. Under what circumstances will a person be deemed to consent to physical contact that might otherwise be assault?

EXERCISES

1. The accused were charged with importing and possession of narcotics for the purpose of trafficking. They had been arrested in Canadian waters in possession of a large quantity of heroin. The accused claimed that the load of drugs was originally supposed to have been unloaded in international waters (where Canadian law does not apply). The drugs were never intended for delivery in Canada. However, they contended that their vessel encountered a number of serious mechanical problems as well as a major storm and that, for the safety of the crew, they were obliged to enter Canadian waters in order to seek refuge from the storm and make repairs.

   According to the accused, the vessel ran aground on the Canadian coast and started to list. At this point, it was decided to start unloading the heroin in order to prevent the vessel from capsizing. However, the police arrived, arrested the accused, and recovered almost 33 1/2 tons of heroin.

   Do you think the defence of necessity can be successfully raised in this case?

2. Bohdan was at a club in downtown Toronto with his friends. He had about 10 beers and was intoxicated. A group of men came into the pub and started pushing and shoving to get to the bar. Bohdan told one of them to stop pushing. An argument between the two men ensued. They were shouting and screaming at each other. The bouncers came and threw both Bohdan and the other man out of the club. Once outside, the two continued their argument and the other man started pushing Bohdan. Bohdan started pushing back. The other man had also been drinking and when Bohdan shoved him, he fell backward onto the curb.

   The police arrived and charged Bohdan with assault. He has retained you to represent him at his trial.

   a. Do you think that you could successfully raise an intoxication defence? Explain your answer fully.

   b. Do you think that you could successfully raise the defence of automatism? Explain your answer fully.

   c. Is there anything else that you could do for Bohdan in terms of defence?

3. Farah had been married to Sharif the sailor for 15 years. They had a good marriage, although Sharif had been away from home for long periods of time on voyages related to work. About 14 months ago, Sharif went away on a particularly dangerous voyage and did not return home. Farah believed he had perished at sea. She recently remarried and when she returned from her honeymoon she found Sharif in their bedroom. Sharif called the police, who charged Farah with bigamy under the *Criminal Code*.

   What defence(s) is/are available to Farah?

PART III

Criminal Procedure

Classification of Offences

11

LEARNING OUTCOMES

After completing this chapter, you should be able to:

- Explain the importance of the classification of offences in determining procedure.

- Describe the differences between the different types of offences.

- Demonstrate an ability to determine the classification of various offences.

- Explain the difference between a general summary conviction offence and a super summary conviction offence.

- Explain on what types of offences paralegals may represent an accused person in court.

Introduction

Nature of Criminal Procedure

Criminal procedure is the broad body of law that governs the legal route that must be taken as the accused makes his or her way through the criminal justice system. It includes the rules that surround the police investigation and the charging of the accused; it determines which court has **jurisdiction** to hear the case. The law of criminal procedure also decides the mode of prosecution, the trial process, and the process required for an appeal of the decision that determined the guilt or non-guilt of a person charged with a substantive criminal offence.

This area of law comprises a large collection of rules, many of which are very technical in nature, but it is important that these rules not be regarded as mere "technicalities." On the contrary, they are central to ensuring the application of the most essential principles of the criminal justice system. For instance, we cannot claim to have a system of criminal justice that recognizes the fundamental right under the Charter to be "presumed innocent until proven guilty according to law in a fair and public hearing by an independent and impartial tribunal" unless we have procedures that, in their operation, actually do reflect the presumption of innocence.

Sources of Criminal Procedure

The major source of criminal procedure is the *Criminal Code*; however, the procedural rules in the Code have been greatly affected by the *Canadian Charter of Rights and Freedoms*, often in dramatic ways, notably in the area of police investigatory powers. A procedural rule must be consistent with the Charter or it may be struck down unless it can be justified as a reasonable limitation under s. 1.

In addition to the procedural rules in the *Criminal Code*, each level of court in a province will have its own rules of practice that add administrative detail in relation to the administration of that court. An example of these rules in relation to the Ontario Court of Justice can be found in Chapter 18. These practice rules contain, for example, the document formats and contents for various kinds of motions, time requirements for filing material with the court, and steps for obtaining a motion date from the court office. Their primary purpose is to help provide a smooth and fair administration of the court. Unlike the procedural requirements of the *Criminal Code*, non-compliance with practice rules can be waived by the court as long as it would be just and fair to do so.

Classification of Offences in the Criminal Code

The nature of the procedure that will be followed in relation to an offence depends on how it is classified under the *Criminal Code*. All offences in the Code fall into one of three separate classifications. These are:

1. **summary conviction offences**,
2. **indictable offences**, and
3. **hybrid or Crown option offences**.

While there are three classifications for offences, there are only two procedures: summary conviction procedure and indictable procedure. The third classification, hybrid or Crown option offences, are offences that allow the Crown to choose or elect which of the two procedures the prosecution of the offence will follow.

We will now take a closer look at these three classifications.

Summary Conviction Offences

These offences are normally regarded as the least serious offences in the *Criminal Code*. Quasi-criminal offences created by the provincial legislature, such as traffic offences, are all classified as summary conviction offences, although in most provinces they are not prosecuted under the Code, but rather under a provincially enacted procedural code that will have different names in different provinces (e.g., Ontario's *Provincial Offences Act*; Nova Scotia's *Summary Proceedings Act*; and Alberta's *Provincial Offences Procedure Act*); however, our discussion will focus on summary conviction offences in the *Criminal Code*.

An example of a summary conviction offence in the Code is the offence of public nudity, s. 174:

174(1) Every one who, without lawful excuse,
(a) is nude in a public place, or
(b) is nude and exposed to public view while on private property, whether or not the property is his own,
is guilty of an offence punishable on summary conviction.

There is no specific penalty prescribed for this offence because summary conviction offences carry a general maximum sentence of six months' imprisonment, a maximum fine of $5,000, or both unless a higher sentence is specifically prescribed for a particular offence. Section 787 of the Code sets out the general penalty for these offences.

A number of offences in the Code do carry a higher maximum penalty than six months' imprisonment. For example, both assault with a weapon, s. 267, and sexual assault, s. 271, carry a maximum summary conviction sentence of eighteen months. These offences are sometimes referred to as "**super summary conviction offences**." At present, there is no sentence of imprisonment longer than eighteen months for any summary conviction offence.

summary conviction offences
offences that are the least serious offences in the *Criminal Code* and that follow the summary conviction procedure in the Code

indictable offences
offences that are the more serious offences in the *Criminal Code* and that follow the indictable procedure in the Code

hybrid or Crown option offences
offences that may be prosecuted as either summary conviction offences or indictable offences, at the choice or election of the Crown

super summary conviction offences
summary conviction offences that carry a higher maximum imprisonment penalty than the general penalty of six months

It is important to note that on super summary convictions an accused may not appear by or be represented by an agent. Section 802.1 of the Code prohibits representation by agent on summary conviction offences that carry potential maximum sentences longer than six months. Paralegals may therefore not appear on super summary conviction offences, even when they are regulated and licensed, as they are in Ontario.

limitation period
a period of time in which a legal action, including the laying of a summary conviction charge, must be taken or the power to take the action is lost forever

Another aspect of summary conviction offences relates to **limitation periods**. There is a legal requirement that a charge must be laid within a specific period of time after it is committed; if this requirement is not met, the person alleged to have committed the offence can never be charged with that offence. Limitation periods apply to summary conviction offences, but not to indictable offences. Generally, the charge on a summary conviction offence must be laid within six months of the offence being committed.

In addition to differences in penalties and the limitation period for laying the charge, the classification of an offence as summary conviction has other significant procedural implications. For instance, there are limitations on the police powers of arrest when charging an accused with a summary conviction offence: the accused will be tried before a provincially-appointed judge, and the appeal procedure is different from that for an indictable offence. Each of these aspects will be dealt with in detail in the chapters that deal with bringing the accused before the court and appeals (Chapter 14 and Chapter 21, respectively).

Indictable Offences

Indictable offences tend to be viewed as the most serious offences in the *Criminal Code* and include murder, kidnapping, and various types of arson. For instance, s. 434 deals with the indictable offence of arson causing damage to property:

> 434. Every person who intentionally or recklessly causes damage by fire or explosion to property that is not wholly owned by that person is guilty of an indictable offence and liable to imprisonment for a term not exceeding fourteen years.

However, there are some offences that are classified as indictable that most people would not regard as heinous offences. An example of such an indictable offence might be the offence of cheating at play, s. 209. While most would agree that a person cheating at a game of poker being played for money would be committing an illegal act, few would think that the offence would be classified in a group of offences that included the most serious criminal offences.

> 209. Every one who, with intent to defraud any person, cheats while playing a game or in holding the stakes for a game or in betting is guilty of an indictable offence and liable to imprisonment for a term not exceeding two years.

Potential sentences vary among the most serious indictable offences, for which the maximum term of imprisonment can be as much as life imprisonment, and indictable offences of a less serious nature. Unlike with summary conviction offences, there is no general sentence that applies to most offences in the indictable classification. Each offence carries its own specific penalty and penalties may vary greatly, as we can see from the two offences mentioned above.

As noted in the discussion of summary conviction offences, there is no limitation period for charging an accused with an indictable offence. A person can be charged at any time—years, even decades after the indictable offence was allegedly committed. There are some examples of charges being laid up to half a century after the offence was committed. In 2008, a 93-year-old man in Quebec was charged and convicted of sexually abusing his two young daughters some fifty years earlier.

Certainly, while there is no legal limitation period for indictable offences, there may be many practical, evidentiary reasons why a charge cannot be prosecuted many years later: witnesses may have died, memories may have faded, and physical evidence may have disappeared with the passage of time. But, as the sexual abuse case mentioned above illustrates, there is no time-limited legal impediment to charging, prosecuting, and convicting an accused if the evidence is there.

The classification of an offence as indictable determines which court has jurisdiction to hear the case, broadens the scope of police investigatory powers, and results in a different appeal process from the one used for summary conviction offences, all of which are discussed in the chapters on bringing the accused before the court and appeals (Chapter 14 and Chapter 21, respectively).

Agents and paralegals cannot represent an accused who has been charged with an indictable offence.

Hybrid or Crown Option Offences

Offences that fall within this classification may be prosecuted under either summary conviction procedure or indictable procedure, at the choice of the Crown. The large number of hybrid offences in the Code is regularly increasing. Assault causing bodily harm, s. 267, is an example of a hybrid offence:

> 267. Every one who, in committing an assault, …
>> (b) causes bodily harm to the complainant,
> is guilty of an indictable offence and liable to imprisonment for a term not exceeding ten years or an offence punishable on summary conviction and liable to imprisonment for a term not exceeding eighteen months.

A number of factors will determine the Crown's decision on the method of proceeding. Important issues to be taken into account will be the prior criminal record of the accused and the seriousness of the offence. For example, is the assault causing bodily harm charge based on the accused getting into a drunken punching match with a person of similar age, size, and physical condition outside the pub and breaking his nose? Or is it based on him pushing his elderly grandmother down the stairs in a fit of anger? In circumstances where the Crown might normally proceed by way of summary conviction, if the six-month limitation period for that type of offence has passed, then the Crown will have to proceed by indictment if it wishes to prosecute at all.

When all factors have been considered and weighed, if the Crown decides to proceed by way of summary conviction or, in courtroom lingo, proceed "summarily" against the accused, then all the aspects of that procedure apply, including the court jurisdiction and available sentencing provisions. Likewise, if the Crown elects to proceed by indictment, all of the elements of that procedure apply.

Prior to the Crown's election on the method of prosecution, all hybrid offences are considered to be indictable. They cannot be treated as summary conviction offences until after the Crown formally decides to proceed in that manner. Therefore, an agent or paralegal cannot appear on behalf of an accused on a hybrid offence until the Crown elects to proceed summarily.

CHAPTER SUMMARY

This chapter introduces the three classifications of offences under the *Criminal Code*: summary conviction, indictable, and hybrid or Crown option offences. Examples are given of each type of classification. We examine the features of each classification, including the seriousness, potential penalty, and whether or not a paralegal or agent may appear for a client.

Summary conviction offences comprise the least serious offences under the Code and carry the lowest penalties. Licensed paralegals may appear in court on these offences as long as they are punishable by the general sentence for summary conviction offences prescribed by s. 787 of the Code. The general penalty does not apply to all summary conviction offences. Some summary conviction offences carry higher potential jail terms of up to two years. These offences are sometimes referred to as "super summary

conviction offences," and paralegals may not appear for a client charged with this type of summary conviction offence.

Offences that fall into the indictable classification in the Code are more serious and, in fact, include the most serious offences in Canadian law, such as murder. Indictable offences carry different potential jail terms depending on the offence. Paralegals and agents may not appear on any indictable offence.

Hybrid offences or Crown option offences are offences that the Crown may choose, or elect, to prosecute as either a summary conviction offence or an indictable offence. All hybrid offences are regarded as indictable until the Crown informs the court how it wishes to proceed. A paralegal may not appear on a hybrid offence until or unless the Crown elects to prosecute it as a summary conviction offence.

KEY TERMS

criminal procedure, 126
hybrid or Crown option offences, 127
indictable offences, 127
jurisdiction, 126

limitation period, 128
summary conviction offences, 127
super summary conviction offences, 127

REVIEW QUESTIONS

1. What are the three classifications for offences and why is it important to be able to determine into which classification a particular offence falls?

2. What is a general summary conviction offence and how do we identify this type of offence?

3. What is a super summary conviction offence?

4. What is an indictable offence?

5. What factors will the Crown take into consideration when making an election on how to proceed with a hybrid or Crown option offence?

6. On what type of offences can a paralegal or agent represent a client?

7. What is the limitation period for laying a criminal charge?

EXERCISES

1. Paralegals and agents are very limited in the scope of their practice in criminal law. Discuss the limitations and what you think the policies behind the limitations are. Do you think the limitations are reasonable in terms of giving the public access to legal representation?

2. Examine each of the following sections of the *Criminal Code*. Determine what offence the section creates and whether it is a summary conviction offence, an indictable offence, or a hybrid offence. If the offence can be prosecuted by summary conviction, decide whether it is a general or super summary conviction offence.

   a. s. 145(5)   **e.** s. 137

   b. s. 335   **f.** s. 163.1(2)

   c. s. 120   **g.** s. 218

   d. s. 365   **h.** s. 264

Court Jurisdiction

12

LEARNING OUTCOMES

After completing this chapter, you should be able to:

- Explain various types of court jurisdiction in criminal matters.

- Discuss the importance of a court taking jurisdiction over an offence.

- Explain the basic structure of the courts in Canada.

- Explain the types of courts in the Canadian criminal justice system and the relationship of those courts to the basic Canadian court structure.

- Determine which court has jurisdiction over which classification of offence.

- Describe the various elections that can be made by the accused.

Introduction

jurisdiction
the power or authority of a
court to hear a case—
without jurisdiction,
the court cannot deal
with the matter

When we say that a court has **jurisdiction**, we mean that the court has the power or authority to hear a case. Not all courts have jurisdiction to hear all types of cases. A court that has jurisdiction over a criminal case is the court that has the authority to hear that case.

There are several different types of jurisdiction that relate to criminal matters and the court must have jurisdiction in each of them before it has the legal authority to hear the case. The three major types of criminal jurisdiction are:

1. geographical or territorial jurisdiction,
2. jurisdiction over the accused, and
3. jurisdiction over the offence.

Geographical or Territorial Jurisdiction

Section 6(2) of the *Criminal Code* provides that a court in Canada only has geographical jurisdiction to hear a case involving a criminal offence committed in Canada unless there is federal legislation that extends the jurisdiction for a particular offence that was committed outside the country. There are a number of offences for which the jurisdiction has been extended beyond Canadian territorial limits by specific legislation. For example, s. 7(4.1) of the Code extends the jurisdiction of Canadian courts to hear cases involving certain sexual offences against children that have allegedly been committed outside Canada by Canadian citizens or permanent residents.

In addition to federal legislation extending territorial jurisdiction outside Canada, the Supreme Court of Canada has ruled that criminal offences that have been partially committed inside Canada and partially committed elsewhere in the world may fall under the jurisdiction of Canadian courts if there is a **real and substantial connection** between the offence and Canada.

real and substantial connection
a legal test that is applied to determine whether a Canadian court may take geographical jurisdiction in a case

Even when an indictable offence has been committed within Canada, there are some jurisdictional rules that must be followed. Section 478(1) prohibits a court from trying an offence that occurred entirely in another province. If, for example, the accused is charged with arson in relation to a fire that occurred in Nova Scotia, he or she must be tried in Nova Scotia, normally in the specific Nova Scotia judicial division in which the fire occurred.[1]

But what happens if the accused leaves Nova Scotia and moves to British Columbia before an arrest takes place? The courts in British Columbia do not have jurisdiction to try the case because the alleged offence occurred entirely in Nova Scotia.

---

1. Although see *Criminal Code*, R.S.C. 1985, c. C-46, s. 599, which allows for a change of venue within the same province if doing so will expedite justice.

If the accused wants to plead not guilty, then the Code provides for the physical transfer of the accused back to the Nova Scotia judicial district for trial.[2]

However, if the accused wants to plead guilty to the offence, and it is not one of the offences listed in s. 469, the court in the province or territory where the arrest has occurred may, with the consent of that jurisdiction's Attorney General, take the guilty plea and sentence the offender. This makes sense, because on a guilty plea the Crown does not need to call evidence, but if the matter goes to trial, the evidence that will be required to prove the case will be in the province where the offence was committed.

Of course, in some instances, the offence may be a continuing offence that takes place in more than one province or territory. For example, a computer expert in Ontario hacks into the bank account of someone in Manitoba, electronically steals $10,000, and then transfers the money back into her own bank account in Ontario. The *actus reus* of this offence occurred in more than one place. In these circumstances, the courts of either province have jurisdiction to hear the case, although the accused can only be tried for the offence in one or the other province, not in both. This is called **concurrent jurisdiction**.

Jurisdiction Over the Accused

A court has the authority or jurisdiction to hear the case against the accused if he or she was found, arrested, or placed in custody in the territorial jurisdiction of that court or there is a lawful **order** that the accused appear before that court.[3] Most issues relating to jurisdiction over the accused are related to jurisdiction of the provincial or territorial courts, which are lower courts. These issues have largely been resolved by s. 485, which cures most procedural irregularities that arise in relation to an accused's appearance that if left unresolved might result in a loss of jurisdiction.

There are some persons who do not fall under the jurisdiction of a Canadian court. By virtue of s. 13, no person under the age of 12 can be tried and convicted of a criminal offence and therefore the courts hold no criminal jurisdiction over them. Foreign diplomats are also generally not subject to the laws of Canada while here and, in most instances, a Canadian court cannot take jurisdiction over them.

Jurisdiction Over the Offence

Overview of the Canadian Court System

The most complicated area of criminal jurisdiction in Canadian law relates to jurisdiction over the offence. In order to properly understand it, we must first know something about the general court system in Canada.

concurrent jurisdiction
the *actus reus* has taken place in more than one location, and courts in either location may have jurisdiction to hear the case; an accused may only be tried in one jurisdiction

order
a decision or direction made or given by the court

---

2. Sections 503(3) (arrest without a warrant) and 528 (arrest with a warrant that is not a Canada-wide warrant).

3. *Criminal Code* s. 470.

Although, as we know, criminal law constitutionally falls within the law-making power of the federal government, s. 92(14) of the *Constitution Act, 1867* gives the provinces the authority to set up and administer the court system within their geographical area. All provinces and territories in Canada basically have the same court structure, with the exception of Nunavut.

The courts of each province and territory, except Nunavut, can be divided into a higher and lower level.[4] The higher court judges are appointed at the federal level and the lower court judges by the province or territory.

The higher level of court can be further broken down into a court of appeal and a superior trial court. A province or territory's appeal court hears appeals from the superior trial court and the lower court of that province or territory.

The names of superior levels of trial court vary from province to province or territory to territory, but regardless of their different names they have the same role in the justice system. They are courts of "inherent jurisdiction," which means that they have the power to hear all cases except those specifically required by statute to be heard at another level.

The lower level of court in each province is a trial court and because these courts were created by statute they do not have the authority to hear the same broad span of cases as the superior courts. They have only the jurisdiction given to them by the statute that created them. Once again, the names of the courts vary from place to place, but they have the same function throughout the country.

Canadian Criminal Court System

Supreme Court of Canada

Provincial Courts of Appeal
Depending on the province, it may be called:
• Court of Appeal
• Supreme Court (Appeal Division)
• Supreme Court (Court of Appeal)

Provincial/Territorial Superior Courts
Depending on the province or territory, it may be called:
• Court of Justice
• Court of Queen's Bench
• Superior Court of Justice
• Supreme Court

Provincial Courts (lower courts)

---

4. Nunavut has only one level of court, the Nunavut Court of Justice, which is a superior court composed of federally appointed judges. It has the jurisdiction to hear all matters, including those that would be heard at a lower level court in the other provinces and territories.

Superior Level Trial Courts

- Court of Queen's Bench of Alberta
- Supreme Court of British Columbia
- Court of Queen's Bench of Manitoba
- Court of Queen's Bench of New Brunswick
- Supreme Court of Newfoundland and Labrador (Trial Division)
- Supreme Court of the Northwest Territories
- Supreme Court of Nova Scotia
- Nunavut Court of Justice
- Ontario Superior Court of Justice
- Quebec Superior Court
- Court of Queen's Bench for Saskatchewan
- Supreme Court of the Yukon Territory

Lower Level Trial Courts

- Provincial Court of Alberta
- Provincial Court of British Columbia
- Provincial Court of Manitoba
- Provincial Court of New Brunswick
- Provincial Court of Newfoundland and Labrador
- Provincial Court of Nova Scotia
- Ontario Court of Justice
- Provincial Court of Prince Edward Island
- Court of Quebec
- Provincial Court of Saskatchewan
- Territorial Court of the Northwest Territories
- Territorial Court of the Yukon

Types of Courts in the Criminal Justice System

The general court system in Canada is complex, and we must now look at how that court system functions in terms of jurisdiction to try criminal offences. It would be easy for students studying criminal court jurisdiction for the first time if court names in the *Criminal Code* exactly matched court names in the general justice system but, as with many aspects of the law, things are considerably more complicated than that. In order to determine which court has jurisdiction to try a particular criminal case it is necessary to examine the classification of the offence (e.g., is it summary conviction or indictable?); then, the types of court provided for in the *Criminal Code* must be matched with the general court system in Canada.

The *Criminal Code* talks about three types of court:

1. the summary conviction court,
2. the superior court of criminal jurisdiction, and
3. the court of criminal jurisdiction.

Summary Conviction Court

Not surprisingly, the court that is given jurisdiction under the Code to hear all summary conviction offences is the summary conviction court. Moreover, the summary conviction court can be very easily matched with the general court system.[5] This type of court is the lowest court in the criminal justice system and in the Canadian court system it is the provincial or territorial court for the province or territory where the offence was committed or partially committed. Trial in summary conviction court is always trial by judge alone, because the provincial and territorial courts do not have the authority to conduct jury trials.

Superior Court of Criminal Jurisdiction

The "superior court of criminal jurisdiction" referred to in the Code is the superior trial court division of the province or territory where the offence was committed, either wholly or in part.[6] As we know from the above discussion of the Canadian court system, although all these courts perform the same role, the actual name of the court will vary from province to province and territory to territory. These courts are given jurisdiction under s. 468 to hear any indictable offence but, as we will see, in practice they do not hear all of the offences that fall into that classification. The actual allocation of jurisdiction over indictable offences is considerably more complex.

Section 468 must be read in conjunction with s. 469, which provides that a court of criminal jurisdiction has jurisdiction to try an indictable offence except for the 14 specific offences listed in s. 469. The most commonly charged offence listed in s. 469 is murder. In other words, although the superior court of criminal jurisdiction has the authority to hear all indictable offences, the only offences that *must* be tried in this court are those listed in s. 469. When an offence must be tried in a specific type of court, we say that that court has exclusive or **absolute jurisdiction**.

When a superior court is trying an offence listed in s. 469, it sits with a jury unless both the accused and the Attorney General for the province or territory consent to dispense with the jury.

Let's now look at a court of criminal jurisdiction to clarify how it fits into the criminal justice system. Without a doubt, the Code has established a multi-faceted manner of allocating jurisdiction.

absolute jurisdiction
a court's exclusive authority to hear a case

---

5. *Criminal Code* s. 798.

6. See the definition of "superior court of criminal jurisdiction" in *Criminal Code* s. 2.

Court of Criminal Jurisdiction

We have learned to this point that summary conviction offences must be tried in summary conviction court, which is always a provincial or territorial court, and that offences listed in s. 469 of the *Criminal Code* must be tried in the superior court of criminal jurisdiction, which would be a province's or territory's superior trial court level. All other indictable offences must be tried in a "court of criminal jurisdiction." But what level of court is the court of criminal jurisdiction? This depends on a number of factors.

If the indictable offence is one listed in s. 553, then it must be tried in the provincial or territorial court of the jurisdiction where the offence took place. Section 553 provides that a provincial court judge has absolute jurisdiction over these offences.

If the offence is not listed in s. 553 or 469, then the level of court that hears the case depends on the choice of the accused. The process of the accused making a choice as to mode of trial is called the **election of the accused**. Section 536[7] states the procedure for the accused being put to an election.

The options are:

- trial by judge alone in the provincial or territorial court,
- trial by judge and jury in the superior trial court of the province or territory, or
- trial by judge alone in the superior trial court of the province or territory.

Failure of the accused to elect one of these options will result in him being deemed to have elected a trial in the superior court of the province or territory.

The court of criminal jurisdiction may be the provincial or territorial court, or the superior trial court composed of a judge sitting alone or a judge sitting with a jury.

election of the accused for indictable offences not listed in s. 469 or 553, the accused has a choice as to the level of court in which they want to be tried

Summary of Jurisdiction Over the Offence

The following is a simplified overview of the procedure relating to the court having trial jurisdiction over the offence:

1. All summary conviction offences are heard in the summary conviction court, which is the provincial or territorial court.

2. The indictable offences listed in s. 469, which include murder, treason, and piracy, are in the absolute jurisdiction of the superior court of criminal jurisdiction, which is the superior trial court of the province or territory.

3. The indictable offences that are listed in s. 553 are in the absolute jurisdiction of the provincial or territorial court.

4. Indictable offences that are not listed in s. 469 or 553 may be heard by either the provincial or territorial court or the superior trial court of a province or territory, depending on the election of the accused.

---

7. Or s. 536.1 if in Nunavut.

CHAPTER SUMMARY

In this chapter we examine the concept of jurisdiction and the three major types of jurisdiction that a court may take in the criminal justice system, geographical jurisdiction, jurisdiction over the accused, and jurisdiction over the offence. We then provide a general overview of the Canadian court system and look at how that system meshes with the level of courts described in the *Criminal Code*. We discuss in detail how the court takes jurisdiction over the various classifications of offences, previously examined in Chapter 11, and how the authority of a particular level of court to take jurisdiction over an offence is central to determining the procedure by which a charge moves through the court system.

KEY TERMS

absolute jurisdiction, 138
concurrent jurisdiction, 135
election of the accused, 139

jurisdiction, 134
order, 135
real and substantial connection, 134

REVIEW QUESTIONS

1. When we say a court has jurisdiction, what do we mean?

2. What types of jurisdiction apply in criminal matters?

3. Briefly explain the concept of geographical jurisdiction.

4. If an offence has been committed in a particular province in Canada, can it be tried in another province?

5. What determines whether a court may take jurisdiction over the accused?

6. What is meant by the term "absolute jurisdiction"?

7. What are the three types of courts mentioned in the *Criminal Code*?

8. What is a summary conviction court?

9. What is a superior court of criminal jurisdiction?

10. What do we mean when we say that the accused has an "election" for some offences?

11. What is a court of criminal jurisdiction?

EXERCISES

1. What level of court has the jurisdiction to hear the following offences?

   a. Public nudity

   b. Attempted murder

   c. Assault causing bodily harm

   d. Counselling a public bus driver how to accept lower bus fares than required and to keep the fares paid for himself. This is a fraud in relation to fares.

   e. Being found in a common gaming house

   f. Cheating at play

   g. Conspiracy to bribe a judge

2. When charged with an indictable offence not listed in s. 469 or s. 553, the accused has an election. She may choose to have a trial in the superior court of criminal jurisdiction or the summary conviction court. If she chooses trial in the superior court, she has a further choice to have a trial by judge alone or by judge and jury. Discuss what might influence her choices based on the legal advice she receives.

Investigatory Powers

13

LEARNING OUTCOMES

After completing this chapter, you should be able to:

- Explain the interaction between police powers to search and the *Charter of Rights and Freedoms*.

- Understand what actions constitute a police search, and explain the ramifications of an unauthorized or illegal search.

- Demonstrate an understanding of s. 8 of the Charter and what must be proved to establish a breach of that right.

- Describe the procedures required for the police to obtain a warrant to search a place and the necessary contents of such a warrant, as well as the procedure for obtaining a general search warrant.

- Demonstrate an understanding of the procedure for obtaining a warrant to search a person and the types of evidence police may be authorized to obtain under such a warrant.

- Explain under what circumstances the police may search without a warrant.

- Explain when the police may intercept private communications.

- Demonstrate an understanding of other investigative procedures, including line-ups, breath and sobriety tests, and polygraph tests.

Introduction

In the Canadian criminal justice system it is the function of the police to investigate and gather evidence in relation to offences and to charge, and possibly arrest, the people accused of committing them. Because police powers to search, arrest, and question an accused are some of the most intrusive powers in our legal system, they must be authorized by law and exercised in accordance with the *Charter of Rights and Freedoms*. Failure of the police to honour an individual's rights may result in evidence that is gathered in violation of the Charter being found to be inadmissible or, in some cases, a charge against an accused being dismissed or stayed.

The law in the area of investigatory powers has evolved, particularly since the advent of the Charter. Parliament and the courts are continually attempting to strike a balance between the duty of law enforcement to solve crimes and the protection of the rights of individuals in our society. It is not always an easy balance to create or maintain.

Search and Seizure

Section 8 of the Charter guarantees everyone the right to be "secure against unreasonable search or seizure." The section provides protection when an individual has a reasonable expectation of privacy from intrusion by the government and, in particular, law enforcement. Any evidence gathered as a result of an "unreasonable" search or seizure may be inadmissible in court, by virtue of s. 24 of the Charter. That section provides that evidence that brings the administration of justice into disrepute shall be excluded.

A person alleging a violation of his or her s. 8 Charter right bears the onus of proving the violation. To do that, it must first be established that he or she had a reasonable expectation of privacy in the circumstances. Once that has been proved, the question then becomes whether the search met the requirement of being "reasonable."

In *R. v. Collins*, the Supreme Court of Canada set out the test for determining whether or not a search is reasonable:

- the search must be authorized by law,
- the law itself authorizing the search must be reasonable, and
- the search must be conducted in a reasonable manner.

In addition, to be found reasonable, a search cannot be arbitrary and must be based on reasonable and probable grounds that an offence has been committed and that evidence relating to that offence is likely to be found at the place to be searched.

To be authorized by law, all searches conducted by law enforcement personnel must be permitted under a statute or by the common law. A lawful search may be conducted with a search warrant, or in much more limited circumstances, without a warrant. We will examine both searches carried out with and without warrants, but first let's look at what constitutes a search and what constitutes a **seizure**.

seizure
confiscation of
evidence by police

A "search" is all the things one automatically expects it to be—for example, pat-downs by police, a police hunt through a person's home, and so on. But telephone wiretapping and electronic surveillance also constitute searches. So does the collection of DNA samples from a suspect. If the police suspect that people inside a home are smoking marijuana, is it a search if they decide to knock on the door to see whether, when the door is opened, they can smell marijuana? Yes, says the Supreme Court of Canada, because the people in the house have a reasonable expectation of privacy.[1]

As we have already noted, "seizure" is distinct from a search, although the powers to seize are generally tied to the powers to search. A seizure is the confiscation of evidence by the police. The accused must prove that the seizure violated her reasonable expectation of privacy so that the gathering of evidence that was "found" by the police, such as a cigarette butt abandoned by the accused or blood drops or fingerprints taken at the scene of the crime, cannot be judged to have been "seized" by the police.

Search and Seizure with a Warrant

The *Criminal Code* provides procedures for law enforcement to obtain a search warrant prior to conducting a search or seizure. Although there is no definition of the term "search warrant" in the Code, the Supreme Court of Canada has defined it as "an order issued by a justice under statutory powers, authorizing a named person to enter a specified place to search for and seize specified property which will afford evidence of the actual or intended commission of a crime."[2]

A search conducted under the authority of a warrant is one in which the police have obtained an order from a justice of the peace or a judge prior to commencing the search. The Supreme Court of Canada has ruled that searches not conducted with a warrant are ***prima facie*** or presumed to be unreasonable, and therefore violations of s. 8 of the Charter.[3] However, like any legal presumption, it can be rebutted and in certain circumstances, which we will discuss below in our examination of warrantless searches, a warrantless search can be found to be reasonable.

Until relatively recently, warrants were available only to search places. However, over the last number of years, amendments have been made to the Code, adding provisions for obtaining warrants to conduct video and other forms of general investigation, and to search a person through the collection of their DNA, blood, fingerprints, and body impressions. The procedure for obtaining a warrant to search a place is slightly different from that for obtaining a warrant to search a person, so we will deal with them separately.

prima facie
Latin for "at first appearance" or "on the face of it": during the presentation of their evidence at trial, the Crown must prove enough facts beyond a reasonable doubt that the accused will be convicted unless he or she successfully raises a proper defence

Warrant to Search a Place

Section 487 provides a justice the authority for issuing a search warrant under the *Criminal Code* and any other federal statute that contains the power to search a building, receptacle, or place. A warrant issued under this section does not authorize

1. *R. v. Evans*, [1996] 1 S.C.R. 8, 104 C.C.C. (3d) 23.
2. *A.G. (Nova Scotia) v. MacIntyre*, [1982] 1 S.C.R. 175, 132 D.L.R. (3d) 385, 65 C.C.C. (2d) 129.
3. *Hunter et al. v. Southam Inc.*, [1984] 2 S.C.R 145, 14 C.C.C. (3d) 97.

the search of a person. The definition of "justice" in s. 2 includes both a justice of the peace and a provincial court judge. In practice, however, it is usually a justice of the peace who issues a warrant pursuant to s. 487.

To obtain a search warrant, law enforcement officials must make application under oath to a justice for prior approval for the search. This sworn application is called an Information and it is made in Form 1, an Information to Obtain a Search Warrant (see the Appendix where Form 1 is reproduced). An Information to Obtain a Search Warrant is a legal document that is similar to the Information that is used to lay a charge, which is discussed later in Chapter 16. The details on which the Information is based must have been legally obtained. For instance, for the search warrant to stand up to scrutiny, the police cannot use material in the Information that was gathered from an illegal wiretap. If it turns out that illegally obtained details were used to obtain a warrant, the warrant may later be **quashed** (overturned) by a judge, and the evidence gathered as a result of the search may be excluded.

quash
nullify or cancel

Other than in exceptional circumstances, such as in cases in which a warrant cannot be obtained because it would be impractical to obtain it by reason of urgent or **exigent circumstances**, the police, or other law enforcement officials, must obtain a warrant to conduct a search and seizure. A search with a properly obtained warrant is constitutional as long as there is nothing in the manner in which the search is conducted that is unreasonable.

exigent circumstances
an urgent situation

Before granting the request for a search warrant, the justice must be satisfied that there are reasonable and probable grounds to believe that there is physical evidence that is relevant to an offence that has been committed or is suspected of having been committed that can be found in the place that is to be searched. If so satisfied, the justice may issue a warrant authorizing a search. Peace officers who are searching under the authority of a warrant are said to be executing the warrant.

The warrant must contain:

- sufficient detail to identify the offence that was committed or is suspected of having been committed (i.e., the section number of the offence, the date and time of the offence, the name of the victim, and the manner in which the offence is alleged to have been committed);
- a list of the items to be seized, described sufficiently so that they can be identified; and
- a clear description of the place or receptacle to be searched (e.g., if it is a building, the address must be provided).

Sections 487(2.1) and (2.2) provide that the person authorized under a warrant to search for data may use a computer system in the place searched to locate or reproduce data stored on a computer at the premises.

Section 489 permits an officer executing a warrant or otherwise in the execution of his duties to seize things that are not mentioned in the warrant if there are *reasonable* grounds for believing that the things being seized

1. were obtained by the commission of any criminal offence,
2. were used in the commission of any criminal offence, or

3. will afford or provide evidence in respect of any criminal offence.

If the police obtain a warrant to search a place for stolen goods and the goods they are looking for comprise electronic equipment that is named in the warrant, but while in the building that they are authorized to search they discover drugs, despite the fact that the drugs are not specified in the search warrant, they may legally seize the drugs. The drugs may then be admitted into evidence in any charge related to the drugs.

Although the usual procedure for obtaining a warrant would require the person seeking the warrant to appear personally before a justice, the police may also obtain a warrant over the telephone.[4] However, this warrant, called a telewarrant, will be granted only in circumstances where the offence being investigated is an indictable offence and there is no time to obtain a warrant through the usual procedure. For instance, if the police had reasonable or probable grounds to believe that the time involved in obtaining a warrant through the regular procedure would result in the destruction of evidence, they could seek a telewarrant. In their request for the telewarrant, the police must clearly demonstrate that obtaining a warrant through a personal appearance is impracticable.

Remember, the Supreme Court of Canada has ruled that even if a search is authorized by law, it must be conducted reasonably.[5] The police officer must normally have the warrant in his or her possession and must present it if asked to do so by the occupants of the premises. Only reasonable force may be used in the execution of the warrant. Unless the police have reasonable grounds for believing that evidence will be destroyed unless they enter the premises without warning, they must make a "demand to open" before making a forcible entry. Finally, a warrant may only be executed during the day, unless the warrant specifically permits execution at night.

General Warrant

Section 487.01 authorizes the issuing of a warrant to a "peace officer"[6] to gather information through the use of "any device or investigative technique or procedure," including video surveillance. This type of warrant may only be issued by a judge of the provincial or superior court. In practice, a warrant of this type would usually be issued by a provincial court judge. A justice of the peace has no jurisdiction to issue a general warrant.

A search warrant of this nature is a powerful and potentially far-reaching investigative tool for law enforcement and, as such, it can only be issued in certain circumstances. It cannot be sought to permit bodily interference with any person. There must be reasonable grounds for believing that an offence has been or is about to be committed, and that information concerning that offence can be obtained through the use of the investigative technique, procedure, or device. The judge must be satisfied that it is in the best interests of the administration of justice to issue the

---

4. *Criminal Code*, R.S.C. 1985, c. C-46, s. 487.1.

5. *R. v. Collins* (1987), 33 C.C.C. (3d) 1 (S.C.C.).

6. See the definition in s. 2 of the *Criminal Code*.

warrant, and there is no other statutory provision that would authorize the use of the technique, procedure, or device. Section 487.01(3) requires the judge to impose any appropriate conditions on the warrant to ensure that the search or seizure is reasonable in the circumstances and s. 487.01(4) requires the judge to impose conditions to protect personal privacy where the warrant authorizes video surveillance in circumstances in which there is a reasonable expectation of privacy.

Furthermore, in relation to video surveillance, it is only available for the investigation of offences listed in s. 183 under the definition of "offence," and in the same circumstances under which the Code may authorize wiretaps or other electronic surveillance methods that intercept a private communication.[7] We will examine these circumstances below when we look at the topic of electronic surveillance.

While we are dealing primarily with search warrants under the *Criminal Code*, the *Controlled Drugs and Substances Act*[8] also authorizes searches or seizures in relation to drugs. Since s. 487 of the *Criminal Code* is the general power for issuing a search warrant, warrants to search for drugs under the *Controlled Drugs and Substances Act* are also issued under that section. However, s. 12 of the *Controlled Drugs and Substances Act* gives a peace officer executing a warrant for a drug search much broader powers than those permitted under an ordinary s. 487 search warrant. The peace officer may use necessary force, execute the warrant at night, search any person found in the place being searched, and enlist assistance from anyone even if the assister is not named in the warrant.

Miscellaneous Powers of Search or Seizure Under the Criminal Code Relating to Places

The Code also provides authorization for law enforcement in the issuing of search warrants for other purposes, including the following:

Criminal Code Section Number	Search Warrant Purpose
s. 117.04(1)	weapons, ammunition, and explosives[9]
s. 164	obscene publications, child pornography, or crime comics
s. 199(1)	common gaming and betting houses, bawdy houses, and places where book-making, betting, illegal lotteries, and games of chance are being conducted
s. 320	hate propaganda

7. See Part VI of the *Criminal Code*.

8. Supra footnote 1 and see s. 11 of the *Controlled Drugs and Substances Act*.

9. Note that s. 117.04(2) of the *Criminal Code* permits a search without a warrant where a peace officer has the basis for obtaining one but determines, on reasonable grounds, that it is not in the interests of public safety to take the time to obtain one.

s. 395	valuable minerals
s. 462.32	proceeds of crime
s. 492.1	to install, maintain, remove, and monitor a tracking device placed on a vehicle or some other thing
s. 492.2	to install a number recorder on a telephone

Warrant to Search a Person

Sections 487.04 to 487.09 provide authority to a provincial or superior court judge to issue a warrant to seize bodily substances for DNA analysis and provide the procedures for collection of the substances. Prior to the addition of these sections to the *Criminal Code*, there was no power to gather DNA or other biological specimens from a person without their consent. The provisions have withstood a challenge under the Charter and were held to be constitutional by the Supreme Court of Canada.[10]

As with a warrant to search a place, the peace officer seeking a warrant to collect bodily substances must swear an Information, but this type of warrant can only be issued by a judge of a provincial or superior court, not by a justice of the peace. In practice, it is usually a provincial court judge who hears the application. Form 5.01 (called Information to Obtain a Warrant to Take Bodily Substances for Forensic DNA Analysis) is the Information used in this situation (see the Appendix where Form 5.01 is reproduced).

Section 487.05(1) sets the conditions for the issuing of a warrant to collect DNA. The judge must be satisfied on reasonable grounds that:

- a designated offence as defined in s. 487.04[11] has been committed;
- a bodily substance has been found or obtained at the scene of the offence or within or on the body of or on anything carried by the victim or on a person or thing associated with the offence;
- the suspect is a party to the offence;
- forensic analysis of the DNA will provide evidence of whether the bodily substance is that of the suspect; and
- it is in the best interests of the administration of justice to issue the warrant.

DNA may be collected in only one of three ways: (1) by the plucking of an individual hair with its root, (2) by a buccal swab from the mouth, (3) or by taking a blood sample.[12]

Before an officer executes a warrant, the suspect must be informed of its contents, how the DNA samples will be collected, the purpose for taking them, the possibility

10. *R. v. S.A.B.*, 2003 SCC 60.
11. These are mostly murder, sexual offences, and other offences causing death or bodily harm, but hijacking, robbery, and arson are also included.
12. *Criminal Code* s. 487.06(1).

that the results of the analysis may be used in evidence, and that the officer is authorized to use necessary force in obtaining the samples.[13] During the taking of the samples, the privacy of the suspect must be protected, and if the suspect is a young person, that person must be informed of their right to a reasonable opportunity to consult with and have counsel, a parent, or, in the absence of a parent, an adult relative or another appropriate adult present while the samples are taken.

A collected sample may only be used in relation to the offence under the warrant[14] and must be destroyed: (1) if the sample is not from the suspect; (2) if the person is acquitted; or (3) one year after a discharge at a preliminary inquiry, a withdrawal of charges, or a stay of proceedings, although a judge does have the power to order the sample to be kept for an appropriate period of time if the result of the analysis is needed in the investigation of another designated offence.

An issue related to the collection of DNA samples under the authority of a search warrant is the provision in the *DNA Identification Act* for the establishment of a DNA data bank. As we have learned, a search warrant for DNA can only be issued when the offence is designated—that is, when it is an offence listed in s. 487.04. However, the offences listed in that section are broken down into two categories: primary designated offences and secondary designated offences. Upon conviction for an offence in the primary category, the court shall order the collection of a DNA sample from the offender to be added to the DNA data bank. If the offender has been convicted of a secondary designated offence, the court has discretion whether or not to order that a DNA sample be taken and added to the data bank.[15]

In addition, for DNA search warrants there is provision in the Code[16] for issuing a warrant to take an impression of a handprint, footprint, tooth impression, or impression of any other body part. These warrants may be issued by a justice for the investigation of any offence created by a federal statute, including all offences under the Code, as long as the justice is satisfied that there are reasonable grounds to believe that the impression will provide information concerning the offence. An additional condition is that the issuing of the warrant is in the best interests of the administration of justice.

Section 256 authorizes a justice to issue a warrant for the taking of a blood sample when there are reasonable grounds for believing that a person has committed the offence of impaired driving within the last four hours; has been in an accident causing bodily harm to himself or herself, or others; and a doctor is of the opinion that the suspect is, as a result of the accident, unable to consent to the taking of blood and that his or her health will not be compromised by the taking of the sample. This is the type of warrant that would be sought if a suspected impaired driver is unconscious as a result of a recent accident and is likely to sober up before they regain the capacity to consent to the blood sample.

---

13. *Criminal Code* s. 487.07(1).

14. *Criminal Code* s. 487.08(1); it is an offence under s. 487.08(3) for a person to fail to comply with this limitation.

15. *Criminal Code* s. 487.051.

16. *Criminal Code* s. 487.092.

Search and Seizure Without a Warrant

As we have already discussed, the Supreme Court of Canada has ruled that a search conducted without a warrant is *prima facie* unreasonable, which limits the circumstances in which a warrantless search will be permitted.

There are some statutory provisions that authorize warrantless searches. Section 487.11 of the *Criminal Code* allows law enforcement officials, acting in the course of their duties, to conduct a search without a warrant in exigent circumstances, as long as the actual basis for obtaining a warrant exists. Exigent circumstances are not specifically defined, but would include any emergency situation requiring immediate action to prevent imminent danger to life, to prevent the destruction of evidence, or when in hot pursuit of a suspect. An emergency situation makes it impractical for the police to obtain a warrant. An example of such a situation would be when the police arrive on the scene and hear someone screaming and crying for help inside a house.

In addition, ss. 117.02 and 117.04(2) of the Code permit an officer, in specific exigent circumstances, to conduct a search without a warrant for weapons, ammunition, and explosives; and the *Controlled Drugs and Substances Act* authorizes an officer executing a warrant to search a place to search a person found in the place if there are reasonable grounds for believing that the individual is in possession of drugs. Pursuant to s. 462(2), an officer is permitted to seize without a warrant counterfeit money or tokens, or equipment for making counterfeits, but this section has not been tested under the Charter.

The common law also permits searches without warrants in the following circumstances:

1. as incident to a lawful arrest;
2. during an investigative detention; and
3. upon informed consent.

Incident to a Lawful Arrest

When lawfully arresting a person, a peace officer may search him or her for anything that would be a threat to the safety of the officer, the public, or the accused, and anything that might constitute evidence or that might facilitate the escape of the accused. The search must be directly related to the purpose for which the accused was arrested and it must not be conducted in an abusive manner or in a way that would humiliate or degrade the accused. Because the Supreme Court of Canada has determined that strip searches are inherently humiliating and degrading, law enforcement is required to meet a higher standard and to justify that a strip search was incident to the arrest.[17]

---

17. *R. v. Golden*, [2001] 3 S.C.R. 679, 159 C.C.C (3d) 449.

During an Investigative Detention

Section 9 of the *Charter of Rights and Freedoms* affords individuals the right not to be arbitrarily detained or imprisoned and s. 10 sets out additional rights of a person that come into play once an arrest or detention has occurred. These latter rights include the right to be informed of the reason for the arrest or detention and the right to counsel. Evidence gathered by the police as a result of an arbitrary detention may be ruled inadmissible pursuant to s. 24(2) of the Charter.

However, the police and a citizen under investigation for a criminal offence do not always agree on what amounts to a detention. Officers may say that the person was free to go, but the person may believe that they had no choice but to remain and comply with the requests of the police. In situations where a person is actually physically confined by the police it may be easier for the court to determine whether there was a detention, but the law also recognizes the concept of psychological detention. Psychological detention occurs in one of two situations: (1) when the individual has a legal obligation to comply with a police demand or (2) when there is no legal obligation for compliance, but a reasonable person believes that there is.[18]

In the case of *R. v. Grant*[19] the Supreme Court of Canada attempted to clarify the law in relation to what constitutes a psychological detention. On that issue, the Court concluded:

1. Detention under ss. 9 and 10 of the *Charter* refers to a suspension of the individual's liberty interest by a significant physical or psychological restraint. Psychological detention is established either where the individual has a legal obligation to comply with the restrictive request or demand, or a reasonable person would conclude by reason of the state conduct that he or she had no choice but to comply.

2. In cases where there is no physical restraint or legal obligation, it may not be clear whether a person has been detained. To determine whether the reasonable person in the individual's circumstances would conclude that he or she had been deprived by the state of the liberty of choice, the court may consider, *inter alia*, the following factors:

    (a) The circumstances giving rise to the encounter as they would reasonably be perceived by the individual: whether the police were providing general assistance; maintaining general order; making general inquiries regarding a particular occurrence; or, singling out the individual for focussed investigation.

    (b) The nature of the police conduct, including the language used; the use of physical contact; the place where the interaction occurred; the presence of others; and the duration of the encounter.

    (c) The particular characteristics or circumstances of the individual where relevant, including age; physical stature; minority status; level of sophistication.

---

18. *R. v. Therens*, [1985] 1 S.C.R. 613, at 644.

19. [2009] 2 S.C.R. 353.

In the earlier 2004 case of *R. v. Mann*,[20] the Supreme Court of Canada had determined that police have a limited power to conduct an investigative detention, and during that detention they have the further limited common-law authority to search the detained person. An investigative detention is one, said the Court, where the police do not have reasonable and probable grounds to arrest an individual but do have, on the totality of the circumstances, a reasonable suspicion that the individual has a connection to the offence they are investigating. There must be considerably more than a hunch by the police to make the investigative detention lawful. Unlike in an arrest, during a lawful investigative detention there is no automatic right to search the individual, but if the police have reasonable grounds to believe that their own safety or that of the public is endangered, then they may conduct a pat-down search of the detainee for weapons.

Upon Informed Consent

Even though there may be no right to search as incident to an arrest or to an investigative detention, a person may be searched without a warrant if they consent to the search. However, to control situations where the police may be tempted to set up circumstances where a person believes that they have no right to refuse to be searched, the court requires the prosecution to establish that the individual has waived his or her constitutional rights in full knowledge of the consequences of the consent.[21] To do this, the Crown must demonstrate that the accused was not subjected to police oppression or coercion, and that he or she was informed of the right to refuse to be searched but consented anyway.

Electronic Surveillance

Part VI of the *Criminal Code* is entitled "Invasion of Privacy" and it deals primarily with the limitations on the power of law enforcement to secretly intercept telephone and other private communications while they are investigating criminal offences. These interceptions are often referred to informally as "wiretapping" or "bugging." It is often necessary to use such investigative tools in law enforcement, but due to their powerful nature, they are strictly controlled through application of the various sections in Part VI of the Code.

The term "private communication" is defined by s. 183[22] and it means, essentially, any oral communication or telecommunication made in circumstances where the originator of the communication reasonably expects that it will not be intercepted by anyone other than the person to whom the communication is directed. It must be made or intended to be received by a person who is in Canada. Interestingly, although the term applies to land-line telephones, it does not apply to a cellular telephone unless the phone has been specifically treated or scrambled to prevent

---

20. [2004] 3 S.C.R. 59, 185 C.C.C. (3d) 308.

21. *R. v. Wills* (1992), 70 C.C.C. (3d) 529 (Ont. C.A.).

22. Section 183 contains a number of definitions that are important in relation to this part of the *Criminal Code*.

interception. Unscrambled cellphone conversations can be picked up by anyone using fairly common equipment and therefore are not protected because there cannot be a reasonable expectation of privacy in the circumstances. However, if the interception of an unscrambled cellphone transmission is done maliciously or for gain, it is caught by the provisions in Part VI of the Code.

Section 184 makes it an offence to intercept a private communication by means of an "electro-magnetic, acoustic, mechanical or other device." There are two major exceptions to this rule. Interception of a private communication by these means is permitted where:

1. the originator or any person intended by the originator to receive the communication consented to the interception (s. 184(2)(a)), or
2. a judge has given prior authorization for the interception.

In the case of *R. v. Tse*,[23] the Supreme Court of Canada ruled that a further exception in s. 184.4 that permitted interception without a warrant of private communication in exigent circumstances was a violation of s. 8 of the Charter. This exception was struck down and is now of no force or effect, so only two exceptions now exist.

In addition to it being an offence, the unlawful interception of a private communication is regarded as a search and would therefore amount to a violation of the right to be protected against unreasonable search or seizure under s. 8 of the Charter. Any evidence gathered by the interception would likely be excluded under s. 24(2) of the Charter.

It is important to note that the consent exception in s.184(2)(a) applies only to private citizens. Any private party may legally tape a telephone conversation without the consent of anyone else in the conversation. However, law enforcement officials may not rely on the consent of one of the parties to the private communication to intercept it without court authorization unless the officer has reasonable grounds to believe that the person consenting to the interception is at risk of bodily harm and the purpose of the interception is to prevent bodily harm (s. 184.1). Any evidence gathered as a result of the interception may only be used in a trial of the offence related to the bodily harm. In any other circumstance, law enforcement officials must always obtain an authorization by a judge under s. 185, although s. 184.2 provides that authorization will be much easier to obtain from the court if one of the parties to the communication consents to the interception.

The major principle under this part of the Code is that law enforcement should obtain prior judicial authorization before attempting to intercept a private communication. Prior judicial authorization is generally only available for certain offences, which are listed in s. 183 of the *Criminal Code*. The listed offences are the most serious in the Code and include murder, sexual assault, *facilitating* terrorist activity, weapons trafficking, child pornography, child abductions, drug trafficking, and organized crime. However, if the originator or intended recipient consents to the interception, prior authorization may be given for any offence in the Code or any other federal statute.

The main procedure for obtaining prior authorization is contained in ss. 185 and 186 of the Code.

---

23. 2012 SCC 16, [2012] 1 S.C.R. 531.

Application for Authorization, s. 185

- Only specifically designated senior law enforcement officers may make an application for a prior authorization.

- An application must be made to a judge of the superior court.

- The application must be accompanied by an affidavit sworn by a proper law enforcement officer that sets out:

    1. the facts relied on to justify the issuing of an authorization;

    2. details about the offence;

    3. the names and addresses of the persons whose private communications would be intercepted;

    4. the number of prior applications made, if any;

    5. the length of time for which the application is being sought; and

    6. whether other investigative techniques have been tried and failed or why they would not succeed or cannot be attempted due to urgency.

Judge to Be Satisfied, s. 186

- Before issuing an authorization, the judge must be satisfied that it would be in the best interests of the administration of justice to authorize the interception.

- The judge must also be satisfied that, except in the case of an offence such as terrorism, other investigative techniques have been tried and failed, are unlikely to succeed, or there is an urgency that makes it impractical to use other investigative techniques. The judge may impose terms and conditions on the authorization, including conditions to ensure that the privacy of individuals is respected as much as possible during the surveillance.

Authorizations are issued for a period of not more than 60 days, but may be renewed by a judge who is satisfied that the same circumstances that applied to the original application for authorization still apply.

Under s. 188 of the Code, a specially designated peace officer may apply to a judge for an authorization in an urgent situation where there is not enough time to use the regular application procedure. An authorization issued in these circumstances may be issued for a period of up to 36 hours, and the judge may impose terms and conditions.

As noted above, s. 184.2 permits law enforcement to make an application for electronic surveillance when the originator of the private communication or the intended recipient of the communication consents. Because consent exists, the requirements for obtaining an authorization are less stringent than the regular authorization procedure under ss. 185 and 186. The application may be made to a provincial court judge; it can be made by any peace officer or public officer, not just those who are specially designated, and the judge need not be satisfied that other investigative measures have been tried or would succeed.

Finally, a peace officer may apply to a judge for a "general" warrant under s. 487.01 of the Code. This section provides for the issuing of a warrant for the use of surveillance by way of any device or investigative technique that is not contemplated elsewhere in the Code or in any other federal statute. The criteria for such a warrant were discussed above under General Warrants.

Other Investigative Procedures

The police may ask the accused to participate in other investigative procedures in addition to an interrogation.

Line-Ups

line-up
to establish the identity of a suspect, police gather a number of people with a similar appearance, line them up side-by-side, and then ask the victim of the crime to pick out the perpetrator of the offence

A suspect in a police investigation may be asked to participate in a **line-up**. There is no obligation on a person to do so and they may refuse. However, if the suspect refuses to participate in person, the police may still use a photo line-up in which the victim or other witnesses will be shown a set of photographs of different people and asked if they recognize anyone. To be admitted as evidence against the accused, the line-up must have included people of somewhat similar age and physical appearance to the suspect.

Breath and Sobriety Tests

If a police officer has reasonable grounds to believe that an individual has been driving while impaired by alcohol, s. 254 of the *Criminal Code* permits that officer to require the driver to take a breath test. The driver must comply with the request or she will be charged with the criminal offence of failing to comply with a breath demand. This offence carries penalties that are as serious as the charge of driving while impaired, so there is no advantage to the suspect in refusing to comply.

Polygraph Tests

Polygraph or lie detector tests are not admissible as evidence in any court of law in Canada. The technology is not regarded as reliable enough to meet evidentiary requirements. Nevertheless, the police use the test fairly regularly as an investigative tool. A suspect is never obligated to consent to take a test of this kind.

CHAPTER SUMMARY

In this chapter we examine the interaction between s. 8 of the *Charter of Rights and Freedoms,* the right to be secure against unreasonable search and seizure, and the duty placed on police to investigate and solve crimes. Parliament and the courts are continually attempting to strike a balance between these interests in this evolving area of the law.

We look at what must be proved by a person claiming a s. 8 Charter violation and what constitutes an unlawful search: there must be a reasonable expectation of privacy and it must be determined whether the search conducted by the police was reasonable. For a search to be reasonable, the Supreme Court of Canada has ruled that it must be authorized by law, the law itself must be reasonable, and the search must be conducted in a reasonable manner. We learn that evidence obtained through an illegal search may be inadmissible in court pursuant to s. 24 of the Charter.

We discuss the fact that, in most instances, a search will not be considered "authorized by law" unless a warrant is issued. *Criminal Code* sections that authorize searches are examined, as are the procedures for obtaining a warrant to search either a place or a person and the information each type of warrant must contain. We also look at how these warrants must be executed—that is, how they should be carried out.

We go on to discuss search and seizure without a warrant and the limited circumstances in which such a search may be carried out. First we look at what constitutes the exigent circumstances that permit a warrantless search under the Code, and then we examine the situations in which the common law may permit a search without a warrant.

Finally, we take a look at electronic surveillance and the interception of private communications and when such interception is allowed.

KEY TERMS

exigent circumstances, 144
line-up, 154
prima facie, 143

quash, 144
seizure, 142

REVIEW QUESTIONS

1. What must a person alleging a violation of his or her s. 8 Charter right first prove?

2. What is the *Collins* Test?

3. Besides meeting the *Collins* Test, what other factors are involved in determining whether a search was legal?

4. What is a search warrant?

5. Does a search warrant issued pursuant to s. 487 of the Code give the police the right to search a person?

6. When are law enforcement officials required to obtain a warrant in order to conduct a search?

7. Who is authorized to grant a search warrant?

8. Is a search conducted with a properly obtained search warrant always constitutional?

9. What information must a warrant to search a place contain?

10. When does the common law permit law enforcement officials to search without a warrant?

11. Under what circumstances is it not an offence to tape a private conversation?

EXERCISES

1. Sally asked her friend Nandani to pick her up in a parking lot down the street from the mall where she had been shopping. The two friends were planning to go to another friend's home to watch some television. When Nandani arrived in her car, she found Sally standing in the parking lot with a big green garbage bag, which Sally threw into the back seat. She told Nandani that the bag contained some clothes.

Nandani lost track of her driving speed and before she realized it, she was driving too fast. Just as she thought about slowing down, she noticed the blue flashing lights of a police car behind her and so she pulled over.

The officer came to the car window, told Nandani she had been going 25 km/h over the speed limit and that she was going to get a speeding ticket. While the officer was writing up the ticket, he noticed that the garbage bag in the back seat had partially spilled out, revealing a pile of clothes with price tags attached to them. The officer opened the back door of the car and began to go through the clothes. With further investigation, it was discovered that Sally had stolen all the clothes and she was charged with theft over $5,000.

Sally's lawyer wants to argue that the search was illegal because it was a violation of Sally's right to be protected from unreasonable search and seizure pursuant to s. 8 of the *Charter of Rights and Freedoms*. Do you think this argument will be successful?

2. The principal of the local high school was very concerned in general about the use of and possible sale of drugs by his students. In an attempt to deter students from being involved in drug-related activity, he made well known to students, teachers, and parents that he had given the police a permanent invitation to come to the school to conduct a drug sniffer-dog search whenever they had the time.

One day the police came to the school with the sniffer dogs to conduct a drug search. They had no reason to believe that there were any drugs in the school that day, but decided to come by because they had some extra time and wanted to take the principal up on his general invitation.

The students were required to put all their bags and backpacks on the gym floor and return to their classrooms while the dogs sniffed their belongings. The dogs' attention was drawn to one particular backpack. The police opened the pack and discovered a large quantity of drugs of various types inside. The owner of the backpack, Jerry, was charged with possession of drugs for the purpose of trafficking. He wants to argue that he was illegally searched and his s. 8 Charter right was violated. Do you think the argument will be successful?

3. Rhonda was receiving harassing phone calls and so she attached an electronic recording device to her telephone in an attempt to catch the caller. She recorded every call she received and then took the information to the police, who used the recorded material to charge her neighbour, Jorge.

Jorge wants to argue that Rhonda illegally intercepted his telephone calls and taped them without his consent. Is he correct?

4. Would your answer to the question about Rhonda and Jorge be different if, before putting the recording device on her phone, Rhonda had contacted the police, who asked her to come in to pick up such a device from them and instructed her on how to attach it to her phone and operate it?

5. Would your answer be different if instead of contacting the police, Rhonda called the telephone company, which put a recording device on her phone with the intention of catching Jorge and turning the information over to the police?

Bringing the Accused Before Court

14

LEARNING OUTCOMES

After completing this chapter, you should be able to:

- Demonstrate an understanding of the laying of a charge under the *Criminal Code*.

- Explain the process when the Information is laid first.

- Explain the process when the Information is laid second.

- Demonstrate an understanding of the powers of arrest of a police officer.

- Demonstrate an understanding of a private citizen's powers of arrest.

Introduction

Once the police have determined that a person is to be charged with an offence, a charge must be formally laid and the accused must be brought before the court to be dealt with according to law. The most surefire way to ensure that an accused is brought before the court would be for the police to arrest the person and detain him or her until the trial begins or the accused decides to plead guilty. In fact, many people who are untrained in the law believe that being charged with a criminal offence and being arrested are the same thing.

However, most people charged with a criminal offence are never arrested. If all accused persons were arrested and detained until trial, there would be a large number of people in detention who had been arrested for minor offences but who were not yet convicted. This would result in considerable public expense and, more important, it would be highly problematic in relation to the right to the presumption of innocence that is inherent in our system and enshrined in s. 11(d) of the *Charter of Rights and Freedoms*. Such a manner of proceeding would not stand constitutional challenge on a number of levels. Therefore, the *Criminal Code* establishes a number of different procedures for bringing the accused before the court, some of which involve the arrest of the person charged and some of which do not.

Process One: Laying the Information First and Obtaining a Summons or Arrest Warrant

A criminal prosecution formally begins with the laying of a document called an Information. This document and the procedure relating to it are discussed in detail in Chapter 16, Informations and Indictments. An Information is Form 2 of the *Criminal Code* forms. A reproduction of Form 2 can be seen in the Appendix to this text.

The process involves a person called an **informant**, who is most often either a police officer or, in some Canadian jurisdictions, a prosecutor, who appears before a justice and provides written, sworn allegations that there are reasonable grounds for believing that the accused has committed an offence.[1] The justice examines the Information in order to determine whether he or she is satisfied that there are indeed reasonable grounds to believe that an offence has been committed by the accused.[2]

If the justice is properly satisfied, he or she will **endorse** the Information and then do one of two things:

1. Issue a **summons**, in Form 6, Summons to a Person Charged with an Offence, commanding the accused to appear before the court on a specified day, at a specified time to answer the charge. Form 6 can be seen in the

informant
a person who swears an Information, usually a police officer

endorsement
a justice shows approval of a document by signing his or her name on it, indicating agreement

summons
a court order commanding a person to appear in court on a specific date and time to answer a criminal charge against him or her

---

1. *Criminal Code*, R.S.C. 1985, c. C-46, s. 504.

2. *Criminal Code* s. 507.

Appendix to this text. The summons must then be delivered personally to the accused. This personal delivery is called "**service**." Failure of the accused to appear as ordered will result in him or her being charged with the additional criminal offence of failing to appear. At that time, an **arrest warrant** will be issued for the accused's arrest and he or she will be arrested and brought before the court to answer both the original charge and the additional charges resulting from failure to obey the summons.

OR

2. Issue a warrant for the arrest of the accused directing the police in a particular location to take the accused into custody and deliver him to the court. Form 7 is the Warrant for Arrest. Form 7 can be seen in the Appendix to this text.

Normally, the warrant may only be executed in the province in which it was issued, but the Code also makes provision for a Canada-wide warrant. Such a warrant may only be issued by a judge of a superior court, not by a justice of the peace or a provincial court judge.

At the time of laying an Information the police will specify whether they are seeking a summons or an arrest warrant, but there is a positive duty on the justice[3] to issue a summons rather than an arrest warrant, unless the evidence of the informant establishes, on reasonable and probable grounds, that it is in the public interest to arrest the accused. This usually means that an arrest warrant will be issued for more serious offences, when there is concern that an accused might destroy evidence, or when it appears that the accused might try to escape justice by fleeing the jurisdiction.

An accused arrested with a warrant is normally held in custody by the police until he or she is brought before the court for a bail hearing. However, for offences not listed in s. 469 of the Code, the justice who issues the warrant may, at the time of issuing, authorize the police officer in charge[4] of the station or lock-up where the accused was taken following the arrest to release him or her. This authorization would be made in writing directly on the warrant and is called an endorsement. In this situation, the accused is permitted to wait for his or her first court appearance while living in the community,[5] but this type of release after an arrest is not the usual way of proceeding and, in most instances, once arrested, the accused would be held until brought into court for a bail hearing. The procedure for bail hearings is discussed in Chapter 15, Release of the Accused Prior to Trial under the heading Judicial Interim Release.

A summons must contain the accused's name, but a warrant may be issued based solely on a description of the accused, without a name. This type of warrant would be issued in circumstances in which the police have a good description of the accused but do not know his or her name.

service
legal delivery of a court document according to court rules

arrest warrant
a court order directed to the police in a certain geographical area to arrest an accused and bring him or her before the court to answer a criminal charge

---

3. *Criminal Code* s. 507(4).

4. See *Criminal Code* s. 493 for the definition of "officer in charge."

5. *Criminal Code* s. 507(6).

An arrest warrant does not expire, but instead remains in effect until it can be executed and the accused can be arrested. However, the justice has the discretion to hold back putting the warrant into effect for a specified period in order to allow the accused time to surrender to the police.

bench warrant
a type of arrest warrant issued by a justice when an accused person does not appear in criminal court as required

Even if a summons has been issued, the justice may ultimately issue a warrant for the accused's arrest if he or she does not appear in court at the time directed on the summons. This type of warrant is often referred to as a **bench warrant** because it is issued by the justice sitting on the bench in the courtroom in which the accused was directed to appear.

Process Two: Appearance Notice or Arrest Without a Warrant and Laying the Information Second

The above process is the one followed when police who have been investigating a crime believe that they have found the perpetrator and wish to now charge her with the offence. However, a great deal of crime comes to the attention of the police before they have an opportunity to lay an Information. For instance, while on patrol the police come across a crime in progress or they are directed to attend at a location as a result of a call to 911. When the police arrive, they conduct an investigation on the spot and as a result they may have reasonable grounds to charge a person who is present at the scene. Obviously, it is impractical for them to ask the accused to wait while they head off to find a justice and swear out an Information.

The *Criminal Code* therefore provides another procedure for dealing with this type of scenario. There are two options available to the officer at the scene, which are outlined below.

Arrest Without a Warrant

Section 495(1) permits an officer to conduct an arrest without a warrant in the following circumstances:

- when the officer has reasonable grounds to believe the person has committed or is about to commit an indictable offence;
- when the officer finds the person committing any offence, either indictable or summary conviction; or
- when the officer has reasonable grounds to believe that there is an executable warrant out for the arrest of the person.

However, s. 495(2) imposes a duty on an officer who has the power to arrest a person without a warrant not to do so for

- any of the less serious indictable offences listed in s. 553,
- a hybrid offence, or
- a summary conviction offence,

unless the officer has reasonable grounds to believe that it is in the public interest to do so or has reasonable grounds to believe that the person may not appear in court.

In determining whether it is in the public interest to conduct an arrest, the officer will consider all of the circumstances, including the need to

- establish the identity of the person,
- secure or preserve the evidence relating to the offence, and
- prevent the continuation or repetition of the offence or the commission of another offence.

The principle behind s. 495 is that although officers are granted a broad power of arrest they should not be exercising the power for less serious offences if it is not necessary to do so.

Issuing an Appearance Notice

Where a police officer has no reasonable grounds under s. 495 to arrest an accused without a warrant, the officer may issue an Appearance Notice to the accused under s. 496. The Appearance Notice is a document in Form 9 of the Code that requires the accused to attend in court on a specified day and time, to answer the criminal charge. If the accused fails to appear, he faces the same consequences as an accused who fails to obey a summons—that is, arrest and further criminal charges for failing to appear. The accused is required to sign the Appearance Notice, but failure to do so does not affect the validity of the notice. Form 9, called Appearance Notice Issued by a Peace Officer to a Person Not Yet Charged with an Offence, can be seen in the Appendix to this text.

In addition, if the charge involves an indictable offence, the accused may be required to attend at a time and place specified in the notice to have his fingerprints and photograph taken.

Once the officer has arrested the accused without a warrant or issued an Appearance Notice, she must attend before a justice as soon as practicable to swear an Information. The justice must be satisfied that there are reasonable grounds for believing an offence has been committed before he or she will endorse the Information and the laying of the charge. In the event that the justice is not satisfied that reasonable grounds exist, the Appearance Notice will be cancelled.

Other Aspects of the Power to Arrest

In the discussion above, we examined the power of a peace officer to arrest an individual. There is also a much more limited power for a private citizen to conduct an arrest. This is often referred to as a "citizen's arrest," and some people wrongly believe that it is a fairly broad power, but, in fact, s. 494(1) of the Code permits an ordinary person to arrest only in one of two circumstances:

1. the person arrested is found committing an indictable offence, or

2. the person conducting the arrest has reasonable grounds for believing that the person they intend to arrest has committed a criminal offence **and** is escaping from and is being freshly pursued by someone who has the lawful authority to conduct an arrest.

In the first instance, the private citizen must find a person who is apparently committing an indictable offence—having reasonable grounds for believing that an indictable offence has been committed is not enough. In addition, the commission of an indictable offence must actually be in progress or just completed. For instance, if you saw someone breaking into your neighbour's house, you would be able to arrest them, although it may be a bit foolhardy to do so. However, if you saw someone breaking into your neighbour's house two days before and then recognized that person later at the mall, you have no power of arrest because the offence was committed in the past.

Note that the citizen's power of arrest under s. 494(1) applies only to indictable offences or to the commission of any criminal offence, including a summary conviction offence. However, a citizen who merely finds a person in the act of committing a summary conviction offence has no power to arrest. A citizen only has the power to arrest for a summary conviction offence when they have reasonable grounds to believe that a criminal offence has been committed and the person who they believe committed the offence is escaping from and is being freshly pursued by persons who have the legal authority to arrest. In such circumstances, a citizen may arrest the fleeing person. Remember that a hybrid or dual procedure offence is regarded as an indictable offence until such time as the Crown elects to proceed summarily, so private citizen powers of arrest in this section do apply to this classification of offence.

Section 494(2) gives a specific power of arrest to property owners or their authorized agents to arrest someone they find committing any criminal offence, including a summary conviction offence, in relation to that property. This is the provision relied on by security guards in retail locations to arrest a person for shoplifting.

Section 494(2) has recently been amended[6] to permit a property owner or his agent to arrest a person without a warrant at the time they find that person committing a criminal offence on or in relation to the property or within a reasonable time thereafter, but they may only exercise the latter power when they have reasonable grounds to believe it is not feasible in the circumstances to have the arrest made by a police officer.

A private citizen who arrests someone is required by s. 494(3) to turn the accused over to a peace officer "forthwith." The courts have determined that "forthwith" does not mean immediately, but rather "as soon as is reasonably practicable."

Section 494(4) cross-references s. 25 of the Code, the section that deals with the use of reasonable force, and, as such, means that a private citizen may not use excessive force in conducting a citizen's arrest.

---

6. See s. 3(1) of the *Citizen's Arrest and Self-defence Act*, S.C. 2012, c. 9, which came into force on March 11, 2013 and amended s. 494(2) of the *Criminal Code*.

Since a person's Charter rights arise on their arrest or detention, there is an issue as to whether or not those rights arise in relation to an arrest conducted by a private person. The case law on this point is not settled. In the case of *R. v. Lerke*, the Alberta Court of Appeal determined that the arrest of one private individual by another is a "governmental function," and that the Charter therefore applies. However, in a later case of the British Columbia Court of Appeal, the court held that a private citizen is not required to read the accused his rights as the Charter requires a peace officer to do.[7] To date, the Supreme Court of Canada has not addressed the issue.

There is no specific process given in the Code for conducting an arrest, but the Supreme Court of Canada has held that merely telling a person that they are under arrest is only sufficient if the arrested person complies and voluntarily submits to the arrest. In the event that the person being arrested does not comply, to complete the arrest there must be the actual seizure or touching of the body.[8]

Section 25 of the Code permits anyone, including a private citizen, making a lawful arrest to use reasonable force to complete or effect an arrest, but if the line is crossed and the arresting person uses excessive force, they can be held criminally responsible. That means the arresting person could be charged with assault or another applicable criminal offence if the force used was not reasonable.

A peace officer and anyone lawfully assisting the officer may only use force that is likely to cause death or grievous bodily harm when the person being arrested is fleeing to avoid the arrest and the person using the force believes on reasonable grounds that the force is necessary to protect the officer or anyone else from imminent death or grievous bodily harm, and the flight cannot be prevented in a less violent manner. In addition, this level of force may only be used in situations where, even if there is a warrant, the offence for which the person is being arrested is one for which arrest without a warrant is permitted.[9]

---

7. *R. v. A.M.J.* (1999), 137 C.C.C. (3d) 213 (B.C.C.A.).

8. *R. v. Whitfield*, [1970] S.C.R. 46, [1970] 1 C.C.C. 129.

9. *Criminal Code* s. 25(4).

CHAPTER SUMMARY

In this chapter we examine the procedures for charging an accused and bringing him or her before the court. We learn that the presumption of innocence enshrined in s. 11(d) of the *Charter of Rights and Freedoms* shapes the procedure for laying a charge or charges. Although arresting the accused for any or all offences and keeping that person in custody while he or she is awaiting trial would be the most effective way to ensure that the accused would appear for trial and not endanger the public, this approach flies directly in the face of the Charter right to be presumed innocent until proven guilty beyond a reasonable doubt.

We then discuss the process for laying a charge, noting that it always begins with the swearing of an Information before a justice. We examine two different types of circumstances that can exist when laying an Information. In the first

process we look at for the laying of an Information, where it is laid before other steps are taken, the justice either issues a summons or issues an arrest warrant to bring the accused before the court. The second process studied begins when an officer finds the accused as he or she is committing an offence and the officer must deal with the situation before laying an Information. In the latter circumstance, the officer would either issue an Appearance Notice to the accused or arrest him or her without a warrant and the officer would later swear the Information before a justice.

The powers of a police officer to arrest without a warrant and the limitations on those powers are surveyed, and we also look at the much more limited powers of a private citizen to perform an arrest.

KEY TERMS

arrest warrant, 159
bench warrant, 160
endorsement, 158

informant, 158
service, 159
summons, 158

REVIEW QUESTIONS

1. Through what process is a charge laid under the Code?

2. Why aren't persons accused of crimes just all arrested and held in custody until trial?

3. Why is it necessary to have two different processes for the laying of an Information?

4. What is a summons?

5. What are the two options an officer can request when laying an Information before a justice before advising the accused that he or she is being charged?

6. What is the difference between a regular arrest warrant and a Canada-wide arrest warrant?

7. When may an officer arrest a person without a warrant?

8. Are there any limitations on an officer's power to arrest without a warrant?

9. What must an officer consider in relation to whether an arrest without a warrant is in the public interest?

10. What is an Appearance Notice?

11. What are the powers of arrest given to a private citizen?

EXERCISES

1. Officer Sharma is a police officer. What is the most appropriate manner in each of the following situations for Officer Sharma to bring the accused before the court?

   a. While in his police car on patrol, Officer Sharma came across George, who was scratching up someone's car in the Wal-Mart parking lot. He decided to charge George with mischief under s. 430(4) of the Code.

   b. After an investigation, there is sufficient evidence for Martin to be charged with 14 different violent sexual assaults.

   c. Officer Sharma received a call from 911 about an assault at a club and upon arriving there he found Desmond kicking a smaller man who was down on the ground. Officer Sharma is going to charge Desmond with assault under s. 265 of the *Criminal Code*.

d. Officer Sharma has been patrolling in his police car and has just encountered Mike, who is very drunk and is doing an Elvis impersonation, at the top of his lungs, out in front of his girlfriend's house. The neighbours say that Mike does this for hours when he's had too much to drink, but that when he's sober he's a great guy. Officer Sharma is going to charge Mike with causing a disturbance.

e. Betty wrote a bad cheque to The Bay. The police have investigated and are now ready to charge Betty with fraud. She has no criminal record, is a resident of Canada, and the bad cheque was in the amount of $75. Officer Sharma is going to go before a justice of the peace to lay an Information. He is also going to ask for a warrant for Betty's arrest. Is he likely to get a warrant? What other options are available to the justice of the peace?

Release of the Accused Prior to Trial

15

LEARNING OUTCOMES

After completing this chapter, you should be able to:

- Understand the powers and procedures of the arresting officer and the officer in charge in releasing the accused without a bail hearing.

- Describe the types of documentation required for the release of the accused by the police.

- Understand the types of conditions that may be placed on the accused when he or she is released by the police without a bail hearing.

- Understand the types of bail hearings and when they apply.

- Describe the grounds that must be established to hold an accused person without bail and the manner in which the grounds are applied.

- Identify the various types of documentation on which an accused person may be released on bail.

- Demonstrate an understanding of the types of conditions that may be placed on an accused when he or she is released on bail.

- Understand the role that a surety plays in the bail procedure.

Introduction

Remember that it is a right under s. 11(d) of the *Canadian Charter of Rights and Freedoms* that a person is presumed innocent until proven guilty beyond a reasonable doubt. Therefore, even if the accused has been arrested, either with or without a warrant, it does not automatically mean that she will remain in custody right up until trial. There are several processes in the *Criminal Code* that permit the accused to be released even after an arrest has been made. In fact, for most offences (other than those in s. 469), the processes in the Code *direct* that the accused be released while awaiting a court appearance or trial, if at all possible. In addition, only the most necessary restrictions should be placed on the accused's liberty as a condition of their release.

Release by the Arresting Officer

When an officer has arrested an accused person *without a warrant* for a summary conviction offence, a hybrid offence, or an offence listed in s. 553 of the Code, s. 497(1) requires the arresting officer to release the accused on a summons or an Appearance Notice that will compel them to attend court as specified. However, any release of the accused cannot be contrary to the public interest. In determining what is in the public interest, the officer must consider all the circumstances, including the need to:

- establish the identity of the accused;
- secure or preserve evidence of or relating to the offence;
- prevent the continuation or repetition of the offence or the commission of another offence; or
- ensure the safety and security of any victim of or witness to the offence.[1]

In addition, before releasing the accused, the officer must be satisfied that there are no reasonable grounds for believing that the accused will not attend court if released.

The authority for the arresting officer to release an accused does not extend to an arrest for an indictable offence allegedly committed in another province of Canada. A person arrested in those circumstances must be taken into custody.

Release by the Officer in Charge

If the arresting officer decides to not release the accused or is not authorized by the Code to do so, the accused who has been arrested *without a warrant* is to be brought before an officer in charge[2] at a police station or lock-up.

---

1. *Criminal Code*, R.S.C. 1985, c. C-46, s. 497(1.1).

2. See *Criminal Code* s. 493 for the definition of "officer in charge."

The first option available to the officer in charge is to release the person and not proceed with laying any charge against him or her. Remember, in these scenarios of release by the officer or officer in charge, we are dealing with arrests without a warrant, so no charge has yet been laid as there has not been enough time for an Information to have been laid before a justice.

If the officer in charge decides to proceed with laying a charge against the arrested person, he or she is still permitted, under s. 498, to release the accused if the alleged offence is a summary conviction offence, a hybrid offence, or an indictable offence listed in s. 553 of the Code, or any other offence that carries a maximum term of imprisonment of five years or less. The officer in charge should release an accused who has been brought in for one of these types of offences unless it is not in the public interest to do so or there are reasonable grounds for believing that, if released, the accused will not appear for his or her court date.

Release Procedure by the Arresting Officer or Officer in Charge

The accused may be released without any documentation, or the officer in charge may release the accused on a summons, an Appearance Notice, a Promise to Appear, or a recognizance.

A Promise to Appear is in Form 10 of the *Criminal Code* forms. It is a written promise, made by the accused, to appear in court on a specified date at a specified time. If the accused does not appear as promised, he or she will be charged with the additional offence of failure to appear, pursuant to s. 145 of the Code. Form 10, Promise to Appear, is reproduced in the Appendix to this text.

A recognizance is in Form 11, and it contains both a Promise to Appear and a requirement that if the accused does not appear as required, he or she will owe a debt, not to exceed $500, for that failure to appear. If the accused does not live in the province or lives more than 200 kilometres from the place where he or she was taken into custody, the officer in charge may require that the accused deposit money or other security, up to a value of $500, to ensure attendance. The money or security will be forfeited if the accused does not attend court as required. In addition, as with a Promise to Appear, failure to appear will result in a further criminal charge. Form 11, Recognizance Entered into Before an Officer in Charge or Other Peace Officer, can be seen in the Appendix to this text.

In circumstances where an accused is arrested without a warrant, release by the arresting officer or the officer in charge always takes place prior to the Information being laid before a justice. When the Information is laid, the justice is still required to decide if there are reasonable grounds for laying the charge. If the justice is not satisfied, then any documentation requiring the accused to appear will be cancelled and a notice will be sent to the accused advising him or her of the cancellation. If the justice is satisfied, the documentation issued by the police will be confirmed or, in some instances, a summons or arrest warrant will be issued.[3]

---

3. *Criminal Code* s. 508.

Finally, the *Identification of Criminals Act* authorizes the police to photograph and fingerprint an accused who is alleged to have committed an indictable offence. The photographing (often referred to as a "mug shot") and fingerprinting can be done immediately after the arrest; however, the accused may be required by the documentation relating to his release to appear at another date and time to have these steps completed. Failure of the accused to attend for this purpose is a criminal offence.[4]

The discussion so far relates to the police releasing the accused without a warrant. When the accused has been arrested *with a warrant*, the standard wording on the warrant commands the police to not only arrest the accused but also bring him or her before the court, judge, or justice to be dealt with according to law. This means that a person arrested with a warrant cannot be released by the police, but must be held in custody until a bail hearing is held before a justice. There is an exception to this in that as long as the offence being charged is not one listed in s. 469,[5] the justice issuing the arrest warrant may specifically authorize the officer in charge of the police station to release the accused and not hold the person for a bail hearing.[6] This authorization, which appears on the arrest warrant itself, is called an endorsement. We say that the warrant has been endorsed.

Section 499 outlines the process and documentation to be used when the police are releasing an accused after an arrest with a warrant that has been endorsed by the justice under s. 507(6). As with an accused arrested without a warrant, on an endorsed arrest warrant the officer in charge may release an accused on a Promise to Appear or on a recognizance; however, in these circumstances, the officer in charge has an additional option for release, an undertaking. This document is *Criminal Code* Form 11.1. Form 11.1, Undertaking Given to a Peace Officer or an Officer in Charge, appears in the Appendix to this text.

The undertaking requires that the accused, in order to be released, agree to do all or any of the following:

- remain within a specific territorial jurisdiction;
- notify the police of any change of address;
- abstain from communicating directly or indirectly with a victim, witness, or other named person, often a co-accused;
- deposit his or her passport with the police or other identified person as required;
- abstain from going to any specified places;
- abstain from possessing a firearm;
- report to the police or other identified person as required;
- abstain from alcohol or drugs;
- comply with any other specified condition that the officer in charge deems necessary to protect the victim or witnesses.

---

4. *Criminal Code* s. 502.

5. Murder is the most commonly charged offence listed in this section.

6. *Criminal Code* s. 507(6).

Judicial Interim Release

Judicial interim release, the formal name for bail, is determined at a bail hearing. A bail hearing is also referred to as a "**show cause hearing**" because, in regular situations, the Crown must show cause to a justice why the accused should not be released while he or she is awaiting trial.

show cause hearing
another term for bail hearing

If the police decide not to release the accused or do not have the authority to do so under the Code, the accused must be brought before a justice.[7] Section 503 of the Code requires that the police must bring an accused, arrested with or without a warrant, before a justice within 24 hours, or where a justice is not available within 24 hours, as soon as possible. The justice may adjourn the case for up to three days without the consent of the accused, or for a longer period with the consent of the accused, or the justice may hold a hearing.[8] The purpose of the bail hearing (or show cause hearing) is for a justice to determine whether the accused should be released while awaiting trial and, if so, what conditions should be placed on her. Both oral and documentary evidence may be called, although in most bail hearings, the Crown and defence simply make arguments to the court without witnesses or lengthy documents being introduced. In some instances, a bail hearing may take place by telephone or other telecommunication device rather than by a physical hearing.[9]

Section 518 of the Code permits a justice at a bail hearing to admit evidence that is viewed as credible and trustworthy in the circumstances even though it might not normally be admissible under the stricter rules of evidence. This section also ensures that the bail hearing cannot be used by the prosecution to examine the accused about the offence charged.

There are three types of bail situations that may arise under the *Criminal Code*:

1. regular bail situations,
2. reverse-onus situations, and
3. bail for offences listed in s. 469.

Regular Bail Situations

In regular bail situations, the Crown bears the onus of proving why the accused should not be released on bail while awaiting trial.[10] Generally speaking, the justice is required to release the accused on an undertaking or a recognizance without conditions, pending trial, unless the Crown is able to "show cause" or prove, on the balance of probabilities, one of the following:

1. that the accused is unlikely to appear for further court appearances and trial;

---

7. See *Criminal Code* s. 2 where "justice" is defined to mean "a justice of the peace or a provincial court judge."
8. *Criminal Code* s. 516.
9. *Criminal Code* s. 515(2.2).
10. *Criminal Code* s. 515.

2. that he or she poses a risk to public safety, including any victims or witnesses, if released; or

3. that confidence in the administration of justice will suffer if the accused is released.[11]

The likelihood of the accused to appear for further court appearances and trial is referred to as the primary ground. The risk the accused may present to the public is the secondary ground, and maintenance of confidence in the administration of justice is the tertiary ground.

In relation to the primary ground, the court will examine such factors as ties the accused has to the community, including family, friends, employment, and permanent place of residence. The court will also look at the accused's criminal record. Those accused who are closely tied to the community or have a criminal history where court appearances were made are viewed as more likely not to flee or fail to attend court. If the Crown is able to establish the primary ground, there is no need to move on to the secondary ground. However, if the Crown cannot prove the primary ground, he or she can then attempt to prove the secondary ground, that there is a risk to public safety if the accused is released.

In evaluating the risk to public safety, the court will consider such things as the seriousness of the alleged offence, the accused's criminal record, the strength of the case against him or her, and the danger he or she poses to any victims or witnesses or the integrity of the criminal justice system. An accused with a criminal record or who is involved in gangs or organized crime may be viewed as substantially more likely to commit further offences if released.

If the Crown cannot prove either the primary or the secondary ground, then the court will examine any proof provided in relation to the tertiary ground. This ground is somewhat of a catch-all, and as such has been both controversial and the subject of Supreme Court of Canada decisions that have led to Parliament amending the provisions so that they meet the requirements of the *Canadian Charter of Rights and Freedoms*. The factors to be considered by the court in determining whether this ground has been met are the strength of the Crown's case; the seriousness of the offence; the circumstances surrounding the commission of the offence, including whether a firearm was used; and the potential for a lengthy term of imprisonment upon conviction. The Supreme Court of Canada has also ruled that this ground should be used sparingly,[12] and it is therefore not commonly applied to hold the accused in custody.

In the event that the Crown cannot establish any of the grounds for holding the accused in custody, he or she must be released on an undertaking without conditions. However, the Crown may show cause why release should be given on certain restrictive conditions. Section 515(2) of the Code sets out an ascending order of restrictions that can be used to release an accused where the Crown shows cause why such restrictions should apply. These restrictions involve the release of the accused:

---

11. *Criminal Code* s. 515(10).

12. *R. v. Hall*, [2002] 3 S.C.R. 309, 167 C.C.C. (3d) 449.

515(2) …

(a) on his giving an undertaking with such conditions as the justice directs;

(b) on his entering into a recognizance before the justice, without sureties, in such amount and with such conditions, if any, as the justice directs but without deposit of money or other valuable security;

(c) on his entering into a recognizance before the justice with sureties in such amount and with such conditions, if any, as the justice directs but without deposit of money or other valuable security;

(d) with the consent of the prosecutor, on his entering into a recognizance before the justice, without sureties, in such amount and with such conditions, if any, as the justice directs and on his depositing with the justice such sum of money or other valuable security as the justice directs; or

(e) if the accused is not ordinarily resident in the province in which the accused is in custody or does not ordinarily reside within two hundred kilometres of the place in which he is in custody, on his entering into a recognizance before the justice with or without sureties in such amount and with such conditions, if any, as the justice directs, and on his depositing with the justice such sum of money or other valuable security as the justice directs.

When we say that the restrictions are ascending, we mean that the conditions go from the least restrictive to the most restrictive. This means that the justice may not make an order under ss. 515(2)(b) to (e) unless the Crown shows cause why an order under the preceding paragraph should not be made. In other words, the justice must first consider (a) an undertaking with conditions, then (b) a recognizance without sureties, then (c) a recognizance with sureties without a deposit of money, then (d) a recognizance with a deposit of money. Subsection (e) is a clause that applies to accused persons who are not ordinarily resident in the province, or if a resident of the province does not live within 200 kilometres of the place where he or she was arrested.

The forms for an undertaking and a recognizance are reproduced in the Appendix to this text. See Form 12, Undertaking Given to a Justice or a Judge and Form 32, Recognizance.

In a recognizance without sureties, the court will set a sum that the accused must pay if he or she does not appear or otherwise fails to comply with the conditions of the recognizance. A **surety** is a person who promises the court that he or she will take responsibility over the accused to ensure that the accused attends court as required and follows all conditions placed by the court on the accused's release. If the recognizance is with sureties, the surety signs the recognizance and agrees to pay a specified amount of money, set by the court, if the accused fails to attend at court or breaches a bail condition. This gives the surety an incentive to properly supervise the accused while he or she is out on bail. Since the surety takes a supervisory role in relation to the accused, it must be someone who is in a position to see the accused on a regular basis, preferably daily. The surety must also be able to show proof of sufficient income or assets to pay the amount of money set by the court if the accused fails to appear or does not comply with the conditions of the recognizance. A person willing to act as a surety must bring this proof to court with them.

surety
a person who agrees to supervise the accused while he or she is out on bail and ensure that the accused attends court and obeys any conditions placed on him or her; the promise to supervise is backed by a promise and an ability to pay the bail amount if the accused does not attend court or comply with conditions

In addition, the surety should be an adult who does not have a criminal record and should not be a victim or co-accused of the person seeking bail. A legal representative should never act as a surety because it would raise ethical concerns about the representative having a financial interest in the accused's case.

Normally a surety will continue to act until the case is completed, but a surety may apply to the court to be relieved of their duties and the court will relieve them of their responsibility without the surety being required to give a reason; however, once the surety is removed, the court will issue an arrest warrant for the accused unless the accused is already present in court at the time of the surety's removal.

If the accused does not comply with the conditions or fails to attend court and is charged and convicted with breaching the recognizance, the Crown may make an application to the court to require the surety to pay the money they promised to provide in the event of a breach. Both the accused and the surety will have notice of the hearing and the surety will have an opportunity to show why they should not be required to pay. The court may order that they pay the entire amount, part of the amount, or none of it.

Both an undertaking and a recognizance entered into under s. 515(2) of the Code will have conditions attached. Sections 515(4) to (4.3) set out both some general conditions that the court may apply and some conditions to be considered or applied to certain specific offences. Some commonly applied conditions are that the accused:

- report to the police or another person designated in the order on a regular basis;
- remain within a specified territorial jurisdiction;
- report any changes, such as in address or employment;
- deposit their passport with the court;
- abstain from contact with any named persons—this might include the victim, any witnesses, and any co-accused;
- abstain from going to specified locations;
- abstain from alcohol or other intoxicants, particularly if these substances were involved in the offence.

Even in a regular bail hearing where the onus is on the Crown to prove why the accused should not be released, a properly prepared defence will be ready to offer conditions that they have already cleared with the client so that the justice may be persuaded that the attendance of the accused in court is going to occur and that risk to the public can be minimized.

Reverse-Onus Situations

Although in most bail situations the onus is on the Crown to prove beyond a reasonable doubt that the accused should not be released on bail, s. 515(6) states that, in certain circumstances or for certain offences, the onus shifts from the Crown to the accused. This results in a reverse-onus bail hearing. The defence must prove, on the balance of probabilities, that the accused should not be detained while awaiting trial when:

1. the accused is charged with an indictable offence committed while she is out on bail awaiting trial for another indictable offence;

2. the offence charged is related to a criminal organization, terrorism, trafficking in or exporting or importing firearms or weapons, or one of certain listed offences involving a firearm;

3. the accused is charged with an indictable offence and is not a Canadian resident;

4. the accused is charged with the offence of failing to appear at a court hearing or with a breach of condition of a bail order; or

5. the accused is charged with committing an offence under the *Controlled Drugs and Substances Act*, which carries a potential sentence of life imprisonment.

If the accused is successful in showing cause why he or she should be released on bail, the judge or justice of the peace may order the accused to be released pursuant to an undertaking or recognizance under s. 515(2), as was discussed above in relation to regular bail hearings. The grounds for release are the primary, secondary, and tertiary grounds discussed above.

Bail for Offences Listed in Section 469

Section 469 contains some of the most serious offences in the *Criminal Code*, including murder and major offences against the state, such as treason. Unlike with all other offences, there is no automatic entitlement to a bail hearing for these offences. An accused must apply for release under s. 522 and if a bail hearing is granted, it must take place before a judge of a superior court. The onus is on the accused to show cause why they should not be detained in custody. If the accused is successful in showing cause, the court may release an accused on an undertaking or recognizance as described in s. 515(2) and attach any condition to the release as described in ss. 515(4), (4.1), and (4.2).

Publication Ban at Bail Hearings

A publication ban is a court order that prohibits the media from publishing or broadcasting information, for a specific period of time, about a case that is before the court. Section 517 of the Code requires that if the accused requests a publication ban on a bail hearing, the court must make an order that evidence taken, information given, representations made, and reasons given by the justice in a decision on a request for bail shall not be published or broadcast in any way. It is common for such publication bans to be requested.

Section 517 has been challenged under the *Charter of Rights and Freedoms*. The Supreme Court of Canada found that the section violated s. 2(b) of the Charter, freedom of the press and other media, but that it could be saved under s. 1 of the Charter.[13]

---

13. *Toronto Star Newspapers Ltd. v. Canada*, [2010] 1 S.C.R. 721.

Adjournments of a Bail Hearing

Although, as was noted above, s. 503 of the Code requires that the police must bring an accused, arrested with or without a warrant, before a justice within 24 hours or, where a justice is not available within 24 hours, as soon as possible, either the Crown or the defence may request an adjournment of the hearing. However, unless the accused consents, the adjournment cannot be for longer than three days.

The defence may require an adjournment of a hearing in order to investigate the possibility of a surety being available or for other information-gathering reasons. It is important that preparation for a bail hearing be properly carried out because if the accused is denied bail, he may lose his job or suffer other deleterious consequences as a result of incarceration. When bail is denied, there can be a delay in obtaining a date to have a superior court review the matter.

In addition, whether it is a regular bail hearing or a reverse-onus bail hearing, if there is any concern that the accused may not be released, the role of the defence legal representative would be to examine all the possibilities for restrictive conditions that can be suggested for consideration by the justice. A justice who is wavering on release may find it possible to order the release with assurances that the accused is more than willing to comply with the conditions that are suggested by his legal representative.

Bail Review

Any order made at a bail hearing remains in effect until the end of the trial unless it is amended by a further court order. Section 520 of the *Criminal Code* provides that the accused may challenge a denial of bail or the imposition of specific conditions that he believes are unfair or improper. Similarly, under s. 521, the prosecution may also request a review of the bail hearing if they wish to challenge an order made by a justice to release an accused pending trial or the adequacy of any bail conditions placed on the accused. This process, whether conducted under s. 520 or 521, is called a bail review.

An application for bail review must be made to a judge of a superior court and two days' notice of the request for a review must be given to the other side. At the hearing, the judge will hear any evidence, review the transcripts of the bail hearing, and either dismiss the application or vacate the original bail order and make a new order granting or denying bail, as the case may be, or altering the conditions of release. The onus at a bail review hearing brought by the accused is on the accused, not the Crown, even if the bail hearing was not reverse onus.

In cases in which the accused is not released at the bail hearing, and the offence is not one listed in s. 469, the accused is entitled to an automatic bail review under s. 525 if his or her trial has not started within 90 days of the first bail hearing for an indictable offence or within 30 days for a summary conviction offence.

CHAPTER SUMMARY

In this chapter, we review the procedures by which an accused who has been arrested either with or without a warrant may be released from custody while he or she is awaiting trial.

We first examine the responsibility of the arresting officer to review the continued detention of the accused arrested without a warrant for certain classifications of offences that are the more minor offences. Then we look at the role of the officer in charge in considering release if the arresting officer does not release the accused. We also survey the documents and conditions upon which the police may decide to release the accused.

A person arrested with a warrant or a person arrested without a warrant and not released by the police will be held for an automatic bail hearing for all offences not listed in s. 469. We examine in detail the types of bail hearings and the shifting of onus in different circumstances listed in s. 515(6).

We review the various types of release and the conditions that may be placed on the accused by the justice while the accused is in the community awaiting trial.

KEY TERMS

show cause hearing, 171
surety, 173

REVIEW QUESTIONS

1. Why is an accused, who has been arrested, not just automatically held in custody until trial?

2. Under what circumstances must an arresting officer release an accused without holding him or her for a bail hearing before a justice unless it is in the public interest not to do so?

3. What factors must be considered by the officer in determining whether or not it is in the public interest to release the accused?

4. Under what circumstances must an officer in charge release the accused without holding him or her for a bail hearing before a justice unless it is in the public interest not to do so?

5. What sort of documentation is required on the release of an accused by an officer?

6. What are the different types of bail hearings? Explain when each type applies.

7. In what circumstances is a reverse-onus bail hearing held?

8. When is a bail hearing held?

9. What are the grounds for the justice not granting bail to the accused?

10. What factors does the justice consider when examining whether the primary ground has been met?

11. What factors does the justice consider when examining whether the secondary ground has been met?

12. What types of restrictions may be placed on an accused released on bail by a justice?

13. What conditions can a justice place on an accused who is granted bail?

14. What is a surety?

15. What is a bail review?

EXERCISES

1. What type of bail hearing would the accused have in the following situations?

   a. George is arrested and charged with attempted murder.

   b. Ajit, a resident of New York, is arrested and charged with assault under s. 265. It is his first offence.

   c. Ajit is granted bail on the above assault offence and while out on bail he is arrested and charged with making harassing telephone calls.

2. Stephen is arrested and charged with robbery; he gets bail. Then two days after being released on bail, he is arrested and charged with aggravated assault. Both crimes took place in residential areas. Stephen had been drinking when he allegedly committed both offences. The public is frightened and outraged. Stephen is married and owns a house in the city where he lives.

   a. On whom will the onus rest should Stephen want to seek bail again? Explain why the onus rests where you believe it does. What will have to be proved in the bail hearing if Stephen is to be released?

   b. Identify four separate conditions you wish to suggest to the judge in the bail hearing in an effort to have Stephen released on bail.

   c. What would happen if Stephen, instead of being arrested on charges of aggravated assault while out on bail, was arrested for causing a disturbance by being drunk in a public place? Would the bail hearing be different?

Informations and Indictments

16

LEARNING OUTCOMES

After completing this chapter, you should be able to:

- Understand how criminal proceedings are commenced.

- Discuss the differences between an Information and an Indictment.

- Define the rules for the wording of Informations and Indictments.

- Understand the rule against duplicity.

- Understand when a defective Information or Indictment will be permitted to be amended.

- Discuss when separate trials may be ordered for two or more persons charged on a single Information or Indictment.

Introduction

Information
a sworn document that
commences the prosecu-
tion of a criminal offence

Indictment
a document signed by
a Crown attorney that
replaces an Information
when a criminal matter
is before the Superior
Court of Justice

Informations and **Indictments** are the documents that set out the charges against the accused. They are the legal documents that are prescribed by the *Criminal Code* and contain the written allegations that are made against the accused. They are analogous to the statement of claim in a civil action in that they set out the case against the accused. However, unlike with a civil matter, the accused is not required to prepare a written response to the allegations set out in an Information or an Indictment.

The Information

All criminal prosecutions begin with the laying of an Information, whether the accused is charged with a summary conviction offence, an indictable offence, or a hybrid offence.[1] An Information must be in writing and in Form 2 as set out in Part XXVIII of the *Criminal Code*. (See the Appendix to this text, where Form 2 has been reproduced.) The informant, who is usually a police officer, is identified in the Information. The Information will outline the allegations against the accused. In some cases the informant may have personal knowledge of the allegations made against the accused. If the informant has no personal knowledge of the matters, the Information may be based on the informant's belief on reasonable grounds that an offence has been committed. In other words, the informant will swear that the accused has committed a criminal offence or that the informant has reasonable grounds to believe that the accused has committed the specified offence.[2]

Swearing of the Information

An Information is laid when the informant appears before a justice and swears to the truth of the contents of the Information. Section 504 of the Code requires the justice to receive the Information if it is alleged that the offence was committed, or the accused resides, within the territorial jurisdiction of the justice. On its face, this appears to be a routine administrative function and the justice is compelled to receive the Information once territorial jurisdiction is established. In reality, however, the justice is obligated to perform a quasi-judicial function when receiving an Information. Section 507 requires the justice, if the accused has not been arrested, to conduct a hearing into the allegations of the informant and to consider the evidence of witnesses, if appropriate, before issuing a summons or warrant for the arrest of the accused. In other words, the justice is compelled to hold an inquiry into the sufficiency of the Information. This hearing is *ex parte*, which means that it is not held in open court and is not open to the public. However, the justice is obligated to act judicially and, after considering the allegations of the informant and any other

---

1. *Criminal Code*, R.S.C. 1985, c. C-46, s. 788 provides that all summary proceedings are commenced by the laying of an Information. Section 504 provides for the laying of an Information for indictable offences.

2. *Criminal Code* s. 504 provides that a person who has reasonable grounds to believe that an offence has been committed may appear before a justice to lay an Information.

evidence, must be satisfied that there are reasonable grounds to believe that the person named in the Information committed the specified offence. If the justice is satisfied, he or she will endorse the Information. It is at this moment that the person named in the Information is transformed from being a person suspected of committing a crime to a person accused of committing an offence.

What will happen if the justice endorses the Information without first conducting an inquiry into the sufficiency of the allegations contained in the Information? While there are some decisions to the contrary,[3] it appears that in Ontario the Information is a **nullity** and the court will be without jurisdiction to try the accused.[4]

nullity
a nullity is that which is legally void and has no legal validity

Private Informations

Sometimes an Information is not sworn by a police officer. In a private prosecution where the informant is not a police officer or other public official, the justice is required by s. 507.1 of the Code to refer it to a provincial court judge or designated justice. The judge or designated justice must provide the Attorney General with a copy of the Information and notice of the hearing into the allegations set out in the Information. This applies only to indictable and hybrid offences and there is no similar provision in the Code that requires a justice to inquire into the allegations of an Information that sets out a summary conviction charge.

Reading of the Information

The allegations in the Information will be read to the accused when the accused appears in court to answer the charges. This process is called the **arraignment** and is fully explained in Chapter 17, Pretrial Procedure. If the accused wishes to make a motion to quash the Information, it must be made before a plea is entered. If the trial will be held before a provincial court judge because the accused is charged with a summary conviction offence, an indictable offence that is within the absolute jurisdiction of a provincial court judge, or an indictable offence where the accused has elected to be tried by a provincial court judge, the Information is the document under which the accused will be prosecuted. For indictable offences where the accused has elected to be tried in the Superior Court of Justice, or for indictable offences listed in s. 469 of the Code, the Information will be replaced by an Indictment after the accused has been committed to stand trial.

arraignment
the formal reading of the charge in court; the arraignment signifies the start of a criminal trial

The Indictment

An accused who is tried in the Superior Court of Justice will be tried on an Indictment.[5] An Indictment usually replaces an Information after the preliminary inquiry.

---

3. See *R. v. Pottle* (1979), 49 C.C.C. (2d) 113 (Nfld. C.A.) and *R. v. Bachman*, [1979] 6 W.W.R. 468 (B.C.C.A.).

4. *R. v. Gougeon, R. v. Haesler, R. v. Gray* (1980), 55 C.C.C. (2d) 218 (Ont. C.A.), leave to appeal to the S.C.C. refused 35 N.R. 83n.

5. *Criminal Code* s. 566.

On those occasions where an accused agrees to waive the right to a preliminary inquiry, the Indictment will replace the Information after the accused is committed to trial in the Superior Court of Justice. On rare occasions the Attorney General may prefer a direct indictment, which has the effect of sending the accused directly to trial without a preliminary inquiry. Direct indictments are more fully explained later in this part.

Unlike an Information, an Indictment is not a sworn document. It is prepared and signed by the Crown attorney in Form 4 of the *Criminal Code*. (See the Appendix to this text, where Form 4 has been reproduced.) The Indictment will contain the charge for which the accused was committed to stand trial. It is often said that the Indictment must be drafted with sufficient particularity to permit the accused to make a full answer and defence to the allegations contained in it. The accused must know the exact charge against her, and the date and place that she is alleged to have committed the offence.

The Indictment will normally contain the charge or charges on which the accused was ordered to stand trial. However, in some cases the evidence on the preliminary inquiry may not support a committal for the charge that is contained in the Information. This might occur, for example, if the wrong charge was laid in the first place or if a witness on the preliminary inquiry gave unanticipated evidence. Section 574(1)(b) of the Code provides that an Indictment may also be preferred on "any charge founded on the facts disclosed by the evidence taken on the preliminary inquiry." This occurred following the preliminary inquiry of convicted serial murderer Robert Picton in 2005 when the Crown added seven new charges that arose from the evidence at the 2003 preliminary inquiry.

Preferred Indictment

As mentioned earlier, it is possible for an indictment to be preferred, which has the effect of sending the accused directly to trial without the benefit of having a preliminary inquiry. This form of indictment is called a **preferred indictment**. Section 577 of the Code permits a preferred indictment "even if the accused has not been given the opportunity to request a preliminary inquiry, a preliminary inquiry has been commenced but not concluded or a preliminary inquiry has been held and the accused has been discharged" with the consent of the Attorney General or Deputy Attorney General. The decision of the Attorney General to prefer a direct indictment is not reviewable by the court even if the accused was discharged at the preliminary inquiry.[6] Moreover, the power conferred by s. 577 does not infringe the *Charter of Rights and Freedoms* provided that the accused receives full and complete disclosure.[7]

The decision to prefer a direct indictment is rarely made but is almost always controversial since it deprives an accused of the right to have a preliminary inquiry to consider and determine the sufficiency of the charges facing the accused. While the power to send an accused directly to trial has been invoked after the discharge

preferred indictment
a special indictment (sometimes referred to as a direct indictment) that is signed by the Attorney General that sends an indictable offence directly to trial without a preliminary inquiry

---

6. *R. v. Balderstone* (1983), 8 C.C.C. (3d) 532 (Man. C.A.), leave to appeal to the S.C.C. refused.

7. *R. v. Ertel* (1987), 35 C.C.C. (3d) 398 (Ont. C.A.), leave to appeal to the S.C.C. refused.

of an accused following a preliminary inquiry, it has also been used to shorten an ongoing preliminary inquiry or to prevent a preliminary inquiry from occurring at all. In some instances, the decision to prefer a direct indictment is made when the preliminary inquiry is inordinately delayed. This happened some eighteen months into the 1996 preliminary inquiry of the four men charged in the shooting death of Georgina Leimonis at a popular Toronto restaurant. In 1997, a direct indictment was preferred against former Nova Scotia premier Gerald Regan after nearly one year of a preliminary inquiry into sex-related charges. A jury subsequently found Mr. Regan not guilty of the charges. More recently, in Brampton, Ontario, fourteen suspects facing terror-related charges were directly indicted during their preliminary inquiry in 2007. In that case, unreasonable delay and risk of jeopardy to witnesses and their families were cited as the reasons for sending the accused directly to trial.

Rules Respecting the Wording of Counts

Setting Out Charges

As already mentioned, the Information or Indictment will set out the charges against the accused. If the accused is facing more than one charge, the charges may be contained in one or more Informations or Indictments. Historically, a trial could only be held on a single indictment. This rule has been relaxed and it is now possible to hold a trial on two or more indictments with the consent of the accused or if the trial judge finds it in the interests of justice to hold a single trial, provided that the charges could have properly been contained in a single indictment. Normally, however, if the charges are in some way related, they will be contained in a single document.

Each charge will pertain to only one offence and will be set out in paragraphs that are called **counts**. There is no limit on the number of counts that a single Information or Indictment may contain.[8] Normally, the Information or Indictment will set out all of the offences that the accused has been charged with. It is, after all, much more efficient to hold a single trial for multiple offences than it is to hold multiple trials on single charges. Sometimes the accused may object to having a single trial when there are multiple charges. For example, the accused may wish to testify in relation to some of the charges, but not others. The accused would not be able to do this if all of the charges were tried together under a single indictment. In that case, the accused may apply to have the counts severed, which would result in separate trials for each charge. The power to sever counts is found in s. 591(3) of the *Criminal Code*, which provides the court with the power to sever counts "where it is satisfied that the interests of justice so require."

The *Criminal Code* does not set out the factors for determining whether it is in the interests of justice to sever counts in an Information or Indictment. The courts, however, recognize the value of avoiding a multiplicity of proceedings and have established that the onus is on the accused to demonstrate, on the balance of

counts
consecutively numbered paragraphs in an Information or Indictment that set out the charges against an accused person

---

8. *Criminal Code* s. 591.

probabilities, that the interests of justice require separate trials.[9] Some of the factors that the courts will look at when considering whether to sever counts include the accused's intention to testify in relation to some, but not all, of the counts, the complexity of the evidence, and whether similar fact evidence will be led on some counts. An application to sever counts will normally be made before the trial has started. However, if the accused has not asked for a severance until after the trial has commenced, it will only be allowed if there is prejudice that became apparent during the trial. For example, if the Crown's case turned out to be weak on some counts and strong on others, the accused might decide to testify on only those counts where the Crown had a strong case. If the counts were not severed, the accused might incriminate herself where the Crown had a weaker case while she was attempting to defend herself against the stronger case.

When There Are Several Accused

What happens where several accused are alleged to have committed a crime together? It is obviously much more practical to have a single trial under a single Information or Indictment naming all of the individuals who have been charged. It would be much more costly and time consuming to hold separate trials for each accused. One can hardly imagine the inconvenience of each witness offering the same testimony in multiple proceedings. Making things even worse would be the possibility of appeals based on the inconsistent verdicts that multiple trials might yield. It would be unfair to the others but of enormous benefit to an accused to have the last trial after having observed the testimony and demeanour of witnesses in prior proceedings. For these, as well as other, practical reasons, the general rule is that people who are alleged to have committed a crime together should be tried together.[10]

Ordering Separate Trials

The *Criminal Code* does permit the judge to order separate trials where there is more than one accused or defendant.[11] However, the courts are reluctant to order separate trials and the *prima facie* rule is that where accused are jointly indicted they should be jointly tried if it is alleged that they acted together.[12] It is only where an accused would be prejudiced in her defence or denied the opportunity of a fair trial that separate trials will be ordered.[13] Whether accused persons have antagonistic defences is one factor that may be considered by the court when considering whether to order separate trials. A separate trial may be ordered to make one co-accused a compellable witness for the second co-accused if the evidence could reasonably affect the verdict for the second co-accused by creating a reasonable

---

9. *R. v. McNamara (No. 1)* (1981), 56 C.C.C. (2d) 193 (Ont. C.A.).

10. *R. v. Chow*, [2005] 1 S.C.R. 384.

11. *Criminal Code* s. 591(3)(b).

12. *R. v. Agawa and Mallett* (1975), 28 C.C.C. (2d) 379 (Ont. C.A.).

13. *R. v. Quiring and Kuipers* (1974), 19 C.C.C. (2d) 337 (Sask. C.A.).

doubt.[14] The courts have also ordered separate trials for persons accused on a single indictment where the evidence is substantially stronger against one of two co-conspirators[15] and where one accused was prevented from cross-examining a co-accused after a series of rulings designed to protect the co-accused.[16]

Rules for the Wording of Counts

The *Criminal Code* has special technical rules that apply to the wording of counts.[17] The rules are generally the same for Informations, Indictments, and provincial offences. Each count can only contain a "single transaction." This means that each count can only contain one alleged offence. If the accused is charged with committing an offence against a number of victims, the allegations against the accused, in relation to each victim, must be contained in a separate count in the Information or Indictment. Further, if the accused is charged with more than one type of offence involving the same victim, for example, theft and fraud, each offence must be contained in a separate count.

There is no requirement that any special or "legal" words be used in the drafting of Informations or Indictments. Section 581(2) of the *Criminal Code* provides that the allegations may be in popular language or may set out the words of the section of the statute that created the offence. Informations and Indictments may, but are not required to, contain the section number of the specific offence in question. The basic requirement is that the wording is sufficient to provide notice to the accused of the specific offence she is charged with. Each count must be sufficiently detailed to enable the accused to identify the particular transaction. This means that the facts supporting each allegation against the accused must be set out in each count. Normally, the identity of the victim, the date when the offence was alleged to have been committed, and where the offence is alleged to have been committed will be set out in each count. This may, however, not always be possible. If the identity of a victim is not known, it is permissible to simply refer to the victim as "unknown" in the count. Further, a count may properly approximate a date or set out a range of dates where the exact date of the offence is not known. Similarly, if the authorities do not know exactly where the offence was allegedly committed, the count can set out a general location, such as "near or about the City of Toronto."

The **single transaction rule** does not necessarily mean that each count must refer to only a single incident or event. A transaction can occur over a period of time or involve a series of events. For instance, a fraud can be perpetrated over a period of time with a series of false statements made during the course of several days or weeks before the victim actually takes the bait. What is not permissible, however, is for a count to contain more than one charge or refer to more than one occasion on which an offence is alleged to have been committed. A count of fraud that sets out one transaction involving a series of false statements culminating in the commis-

single transaction rule
a rule requiring that each count in an Information or Indictment can only refer to a single transaction

14. *R. v. Torbiak and Gillis* (1978), 40 C.C.C. (2d) 193 (Ont. C.A.).

15. *R. v. Guimond*, [1979] 1 S.C.R. 960.

16. *R. v. Kendall and McKay* (1987), 35 C.C.C. (3d) 105 (Ont. C.A.).

17. *Criminal Code* s. 581.

sion of a single offence does not offend the single transaction rule. However, a single count setting out a series of falsehoods that results in multiple offences—for example, one where the victim was defrauded several times—would offend the rule. In the latter situation, each offence would constitute a single transaction and each would properly be the subject of a single count.

Duplicitous Counts

duplicitous count
a count that contains more than a single transaction

If a count contains more than a single transaction or offence, it is said to be "duplicitous." A **duplicitous count** is void and cannot be the basis for the prosecution of an accused person. The reason for the duplicity rule is that the accused is provided with too much information to enable her to have specific notice of the particular offence that she is facing. In other words, the count alleges two or more different offences and the accused is unable to know which case to meet. Interestingly, the rationale here is the same as in the sufficiency rule, which requires enough information to disclose the offence, except in this case the accused is provided with too much information as opposed to too little.

A count may appear to be duplicitous when in fact it is not. We have already seen that, without being duplicitous, a count may properly refer to a transaction that occurred over a period of time. A provision that creates an offence may provide for several ways of committing the offence. For example, s. 253 of the Code makes it an offence for a person to operate a motor vehicle while the person's ability to operate the vehicle is impaired by alcohol or a drug. The substance of the offence is operating a motor vehicle while impaired. The reference to alcohol or a drug sets out two ways in which the offence can be committed. Thus, an accused charged with operating a motor vehicle while impaired by alcohol or a drug is charged with committing a single offence. Similarly, it is also perfectly proper for a count to specify alternative modes of committing an offence without offending the duplicity rule. This is usually accomplished by using the word "alternatively" in one count to separate the two different ways in which the offence is alleged to have been committed.

The Supreme Court of Canada in *R. v. Sault Ste. Marie*[18] considered the test for a duplicitous count. In that case the defendant was charged with an offence under s. 32(1) of *The Ontario Water Resources Commission Act*. It was argued that s. 32(1) created three separate offences of discharging, causing to be discharged, and permitting to be discharged, deleterious materials. Speaking for the Court, the Honourable Mr. Justice Dickson framed the test for duplicity in the following manner:

> In my opinion, the primary test should be a practical one, based on the only valid justification for the rule against duplicity: does the accused know the case he has to meet, or is he prejudiced in the preparation of his defence by ambiguity in the charge?[19]

---

18. [1978] 2 S.C.R. 1299.

19. Ibid., at 1308.

Put another way, a count will be duplicitous only where the extent of any ambiguity prejudices the accused in preparing a defence to the charge.

In *R. v. Sault Ste. Marie*, the defendant knew the case it had to meet. Section 32(1) of the Act dealt with only one matter, pollution. Polluting waterways is the substance of the offence or as the Court stated, "That is the gist of the charge and the evil against which the offence is aimed."[20] Polluting was the only offence with which the defendant was charged. The fact that s. 32(1) specified three different ways that the offence could be committed did not establish three different offences. The defendant knew that it was charged with a pollution infraction and was not prejudiced in any way in preparing its defence.

History of the Rules for the Wording of Counts

The rules respecting the wording of counts are common-law principles that first developed in England in the 18th century during a time of extreme formality in the prosecution of crime. The rules evolved as a result of a lack of procedural and other safeguards for persons accused of crimes at a time when punishment was often swift and severe. Many crimes were categorized as felonies for which the penalty was death by hanging. The courts tried to balance the scales by applying an extremely formalistic approach to procedural issues that arose during the prosecution of persons charged with serious offences. Flawed Indictments were seen as a nullity incapable of supporting the trial of the accused on the specified charges. An Indictment would almost always be quashed if it was found to be defective and the accused would be freed.

There has been a shift in Canada over the past century from this formalistic approach to an approach favouring a trial on the merits of the case. The reasons behind this movement are twofold: first, the harshness of early penal statutes has been replaced by the proportionate and rational approach to crime and punishment contained in the *Criminal Code*; and second, the Code now allows for the amendment of Informations and Indictments, something that the common law did not permit. As Mr. Justice Dickson stated in *R. v. Sault Ste. Marie*:

> The slightest defect made an indictment a nullity. That age has passed. Parliament has made it abundantly clear in those sections of the *Criminal Code* having to do with the form of indictments and Informations that the punctilio of an earlier age is no longer to bind us. We must look for substance and not petty formalities.[21]

Mr. Justice Dickson is specifically referring to s. 601 of the *Criminal Code* that provides the court with broad powers to amend defective Indictments at any point in the proceedings. Amendments to an Indictment are permitted where there is a discrepancy between the Indictment and the evidence at trial to make the Indictment conform to the evidence.[22] Of even greater significance is that amendments

---

20. Ibid.
21. Ibid., at 1307.
22. *Criminal Code* s. 601(2).

can be made if the Indictment was preferred under the wrong statute, if it fails to state or states defectively anything required to make out the offence, or if it is in any way defective in form or substance.[23] In addition, the court has the power to amend or to divide duplicitous counts[24] and to order particulars, which are details of the allegations set out in a count, if it is necessary for a fair trial.[25] These curative provisions of the *Criminal Code* also apply to Informations in summary proceedings.[26]

Amendments and Motions to Quash

It does not necessarily follow that because an Indictment may be amended for virtually any reason, it will be amended in every case. The court will not permit an amendment and will quash the count if it does not disclose an offence known to law. This means the count is so flawed on its face that no offence has been disclosed. In other words, it is impossible to make out any offence from reading the count. In these instances, the court will quash the offending count. However, there would not be anything that would prevent the Crown from preferring a fresh Indictment properly setting out the offence since the accused was never in jeopardy of being convicted in the first place. Note, however, that for a summary conviction offence, a new Information cannot be laid if more than six months has elapsed from the time when the subject matter of the proceeding arose.[27]

An amendment may also be refused if the amendment would cause prejudice to the accused that could not be cured by an adjournment of the proceedings. For instance, an amendment during trial that fundamentally changes the Crown's case would not be permitted. Nor would an amendment that seeks to replace one charge with another of a totally different nature or seeks to substitute one victim for another. However, these situations do not arise frequently and, in most cases, the Crown would normally be permitted to amend a defective count.

Even if a motion will not result in the quashing of a charge, the accused may still wish to attack a defective Indictment if only to receive proper notice of the case against him or her. An objection to a count where the defect is on the face of the Information or Indictment must be made by way of a motion to quash before the accused has pleaded and only later with leave of the court.[28] In some cases the defect will not be known to the accused until after the trial has started. For example, the count may allege a particular charge, but the evidence later establishes the commission of an entirely different offence. In those cases, there is no requirement that a motion to quash be made by an accused prior to entering a plea.

---

23. *Criminal Code* s. 601(3).

24. *Criminal Code* s. 590(2).

25. *Criminal Code* s. 587.

26. *Criminal Code* s. 795.

27. *Criminal Code* s. 786.

28. *Criminal Code* s. 601(1).

CHAPTER SUMMARY

All criminal prosecutions are started by the laying of an Information. If the accused is charged with a summary conviction offence or a hybrid offence for which the Crown has elected to proceed summarily, the Information will be the document upon which the accused is tried. Where the accused is charged with an indictable offence or a hybrid offence where the Crown has elected to proceed by way of Indictment, the Information will be replaced by an Indictment after the accused has been committed for trial.

Although there is no formal requirement that Informations or Indictments contain any special words or language,

there are strict rules setting out how these documents are to be drafted. Essentially, each charge must be set out in a separate paragraph called a count. An Information or an Indictment may contain several counts, but each count can only refer to a single transaction. Historically, any defects in the way counts were worded usually resulted in the quashing of the count or charge against an accused. The *Criminal Code* now contains provisions that enable the court to amend most defects in the wording of counts. Accordingly, it is now only in rare instances where a defect in the wording of a count will result in the quashing of criminal charges.

KEY TERMS

arraignment, 181
counts, 183
duplicitous count, 186
Indictment, 180

Information, 180
nullity, 181
preferred indictment, 182
single transaction rule, 185

REVIEW QUESTIONS

1. How is a summary conviction offence charge laid?
2. What is an Indictment and what purpose does it serve?
3. What is the single transaction rule?
4. What is the difference between an Indictment and a preferred indictment?
5. In what circumstances would a court amend an Information?
6. What is the rule against duplicity?

EXERCISES

1. Rebecca and Stefan, a married couple, were arguing over the family budget. Unfortunately, the disagreement escalated into violence with Stefan striking Rebecca, and the police were called. The police arrived but did not charge Stefan. What, if anything, can Rebecca do to have Stefan charged with assaulting her?

2. Ali Sheik is charged with theft under $5,000. Ali's surname was misspelled as "Shiek" on the Information before the court. In addition, the Information mistakenly refers to the offence as having been committed in June, instead of in July. The Crown handling the matter noticed these errors on Ali's first appearance in court. What should the Crown do? How is the court likely to respond?

3. Jodi and Angela have been jointly charged with attempted robbery on a single Information. Jodi has a lengthy criminal record while Angela has never been in trouble with the police. Angela's defence is that she had no idea that Jodi was going to rob the bank. She will testify that she entered the bank believing that Jodi was simply paying some overdue bills. Angela also wishes to call Jodi as a witness to confirm her testimony. What problem does Angela face? Is there anything that she can do?

Pretrial Procedure

17

LEARNING OUTCOMES

After completing this chapter, you should be able to:

- Understand the Crown's obligation to provide disclosure to a person charged with a criminal offence.

- Discuss how disclosure is obtained by a person who has been charged with a criminal offence.

- Discuss the purpose of a preliminary inquiry.

- Discuss the purpose of a pretrial conference.

- Understand the concept of plea bargaining.

- Understand the impact of plea bargaining on the administration of justice.

- Understand situations where it may be appropriate for a person charged with a criminal offence to dispense with or waive formal proof of an element of the offence.

- Define the various pleas available to a person who has been charged with a criminal offence.

Introduction

A person does not go on trial immediately after being charged with a criminal offence. Most cases are tried several months after the accused has been charged with an offence. Sometimes it may take longer than a year for a complicated indictable case to go to trial. The process of bringing an accused to trial is complex and time consuming. The procedure will vary depending upon whether the accused is charged with a summary conviction offence, a hybrid offence, or an indictable offence. This chapter examines the major procedural steps in bringing a person who has been charged with a criminal offence to trial.

Disclosure

Disclosure refers to the Crown's obligation to provide the defence with all of the information relating to the prosecution of the accused that is in the possession of the Crown or the police. Prior to the entrenchment of the *Charter of Rights and Freedoms*, there was no formal obligation on the Crown to provide any material to the accused. The practice and procedure relating to disclosure varied from jurisdiction to jurisdiction. The obvious problem stemming from inadequate disclosure is the risk of wrongfully convicting an innocent person. A number of high-profile wrongful convictions can be attributed in part to deficient disclosure. As a result, the Law Reform Commission of Canada recommended the implementation of a comprehensive and consistent system of disclosure as early as 1973.[1] However, the right of an accused to obtain disclosure from the Crown did not exist until the 1991 decision of the Supreme Court of Canada in *R. v. Stinchcombe*.[2]

Purpose of Disclosure

In addition to permitting an accused person to make full answer and defence, full disclosure also facilitates a more efficient operation of the criminal justice system. When a person who is charged with an offence is provided with complete disclosure of the case against him, he can make informed decisions on how to best respond to the allegations. If it is disclosed that the prosecution has a very strong case, the accused may very well decide to plead guilty to the offence with which he is charged or try to plea bargain for a lesser offence. In other situations where the accused discovers a weakness in part of the Crown's case or where the accused may have a potential defence, the accused may decide to waive formal proof of part of the Crown's case and either target the weakness in the case against him or focus on asserting his defence. In both situations, where there is a guilty plea, or where parts of the Crown's case are admitted, the trial will be either shortened or eliminated altogether. This will obviously help reduce the strain on an already overburdened

---

1. Law Reform Commission of Canada, *Discovery in Criminal Cases* (Ottawa: The Commission, 1974).

2. [1991] 3 S.C.R. 326.

justice system. There is the added benefit to the accused that it is good advocacy to focus on the important areas of a case while admitting the parts that are not in dispute. From a practical standpoint, judges appreciate lawyers and paralegals who are well prepared and do not waste the court's time by futilely grasping at every last straw.

The Duty to Disclose: R. v. Stinchcombe

As mentioned earlier, the right of an accused to receive disclosure from the Crown was created by the Supreme Court of Canada in *R. v. Stinchcombe*. In that case the accused was a lawyer who was charged with breach of trust, fraud, and theft. A former employee of the accused made a statement to the police. The Crown disclosed the existence of the statement to the accused but did not provide the contents of the statement to the accused following a disclosure request. The Crown took the position that it was under no obligation to disclose the contents of the statement to the accused. Until *Stinchcombe*, the law regarding the obligation of the Crown to provide the accused with disclosure was not settled. The Supreme Court recognized that the element of surprise in litigation had historically been an acceptable tactic. The Court noted, however, that the tactic of surprising an adversary at trial had long since disappeared in civil cases and was replaced by rules setting out comprehensive schemes of disclosure. The Court concluded after reviewing the arguments both for and against a duty of disclosure "that there is no valid practical reason to support the position of the opponents of a broad duty of disclosure." Citing from earlier cases, the Court in *Stinchcombe* framed the duty of the Crown to provide disclosure in the following terms:

> [T]here is a general duty on the part of the Crown to disclose all materials it proposes to use at trial and especially all evidence which may assist the accused even if the Crown does not propose to adduce it.

In order for disclosure to be effective, it must be made in a timely manner. Disclosure will not serve any valid purpose if it is made too late in the game. The accused must have received disclosure well in advance of trial in order to properly assess the case and to prepare for trial. The Supreme Court of Canada has set down a rule that initial disclosure should be made before the accused is called on to either elect the mode of trial or enter a plea. The obligation to provide disclosure is triggered by a request for disclosure from the accused. The onus is on the person charged with a criminal offence to take the first step by making the appropriate request. It should be noted that the obligation to provide disclosure is a continuing one. If the Crown or police discover any further information that is relevant to a matter before the court, that information must also be disclosed to the accused.

Obtaining Disclosure

There is no central authority where requests for disclosure are made. Disclosure requests are normally directed to the Crown attorney's office that is responsible for prosecuting the charge. The procedure for obtaining disclosure varies depending upon the offence with which the accused is charged and the practice followed in the particular Crown's office. In many cases, some form of disclosure is provided to the accused when she first appears in court. For less serious infractions, such as provincial offences, disclosure may not be provided until the defendant has made a request for disclosure. In any event, where there is any uncertainty, it is good practice to contact the office of the Crown attorney responsible for the prosecution of the case to ascertain the process for obtaining disclosure.

Scope of Disclosure

inculpatory
evidence that is
incriminating

exculpatory
evidence that relieves
of blame or liability

In general, the Crown must disclose all relevant information to the accused. It does not matter whether the Crown intends to rely on the information at trial, or whether the information is **inculpatory** or **exculpatory**. All that matters is that the information is relevant. Of course it is not uncommon for the Crown and defence counsel to have a different view of what constitutes relevant information. A competent defence lawyer or paralegal will leave no stone unturned in satisfying her professional obligations to her client. On the other hand, the Crown will understandably be reluctant to disclose matters that are clearly not material or relevant in the proceedings. For example, the police may have embarked on investigations that have no bearing on the accused or the charges before the court. The discretion rests with the Crown to make an initial determination regarding the relevancy of information that will form the basis of disclosure. Or, as the Supreme Court of Canada put it in *Stinchcombe*, the "initial obligation to separate 'the wheat from the chaff' must therefore rest with Crown counsel."

The Crown is also permitted some latitude in terms of withholding privileged information and protecting the identity of informants. Generally, the identity of police informants is not disclosed to the accused for obvious reasons. If an informant's identity becomes known to the accused, the informant's life or safety may be endangered. The discretion of the Crown to withhold information is reviewable by the trial judge. Upon review, the Crown must justify the failure to disclose. The trial judge will be permitted to inspect any material that has not been disclosed before deciding the issue.

Inadequate Disclosure

In most cases, the Crown will provide full and timely disclosure to the accused. What happens in those infrequent situations where the Crown fails to live up to its obligations? The answer depends in part on when the issue of non-disclosure first arose. If it arose before or during the trial, the trial judge may rectify the non-disclosure by an order for disclosure and an adjournment to permit the accused the opportunity to properly assess the new material. If, however, the Crown continues to fail to meet its obligations in the face of the judge's order, it is possible that the proceedings against the accused may be stayed by the court. A stay of charges is available under s. 24(1) of the *Charter of Rights and Freedoms* in appropriate cases because it is now well established that s. 7 of the Charter includes a right to disclosure.

The situation is different when the non-disclosure is not discovered until after the trial. In that situation, an order for disclosure and an adjournment will not help the accused who has been convicted and is possibly serving a jail sentence. In *R. v. Taillefer; R. v. Duguay*[3] the non-disclosure was not discovered until several years later. In that case, one accused was convicted of first-degree murder after a trial and the second accused had pleaded guilty to the lesser charge of manslaughter. It was later discovered that the Crown and police had failed to disclose a considerable amount of evidence during the original trial. In this case, the Supreme Court of Canada made a distinction between an infringement of the right to disclosure and the right to make full answer and defence. In other words, the issue is whether the lack of disclosure had any impact on the trial. The fact is that a breach by the Crown of its disclosure obligations will not have an impact on the correctness of the decision in every instance. There is no injustice to the accused if the result would have been the same had disclosure been made. In these situations, there is no need for a remedy even though there has been an infringement of the accused's right to disclosure.

While the distinction between an infringement of the right to disclosure and the right to make full answer and defence is logical, it is not, practically speaking, always an easy distinction to make. There will be clear cases where it is obvious that the undisclosed material is trivial and the evidence against the accused is overwhelming. But in other cases there may be uncertainty about the impact that any undisclosed material may have had on the trial. In these less clear cases, how can a court determine, after the event, whether the undisclosed material would have resulted in a different outcome? The Supreme Court of Canada dealt with this problem in *Taillefer* and set the standard as follows:

> [71] … To determine whether there is an infringement of the right to make full answer and defence, the accused will have to show that there was a reasonable possibility that the failure to disclose affected the outcome at trial or the overall fairness of the trial process.

The Court in *Taillefer*, finding that the two accused persons had demonstrated that there was a reasonable possibility that the failure to disclose had affected the outcome or overall fairness of the trial, allowed the two appeals. The Court next turned to the question of remedies. The Court stated that ordering a new trial would normally be the appropriate remedy on successful lack of disclosure appeals. In paragraph 117, the Court, citing from an earlier case, recognized that a **stay of proceedings** would be ordered in exceptional circumstances

> where the prejudice to the accused's right to make full answer and defence cannot be remedied or where irreparable prejudice would be caused to the integrity of the judicial system if the prosecution were continued.

One accused was appealing his conviction for first-degree murder following a trial. In that case the Court granted a new trial. The other accused, however, had

stay of proceedings
a court ruling to stop or suspend legal proceedings

---

3. [2003] 3 S.C.R. 307.

pleaded guilty to manslaughter and had served eight years in jail. In staying the charges against the second accused the Court pointed out that the accused had already served enough time in jail to be eligible for parole even if he was ultimately convicted in this matter.

Pretrial Conferences

Pretrial conferences are informal meetings involving the Crown, the accused's representative, and a pretrial conference judge where various procedural and substantive issues relating to the case are discussed; this process leads to a more efficient use of court time. It should be noted that the judge hearing the pretrial will not be the same judge that hears the trial. This is to ensure that there is no risk that anything said during an informal pretrial conference will influence a trial where evidence is admitted only if it meets a much higher threshold.

Sometimes meetings between the Crown and the accused's representatives are also called pretrial conferences. These are technically not pretrial conferences according to the *Criminal Code*, but these conferences are commonly held and achieve many of the same goals as judicial pretrial conferences. There is often a combination of one or more so-called Crown pretrial conferences held along with a judicial pretrial conference. While the objectives of these two forms of pretrial conferences are similar, this part of the chapter will focus on judicial pretrial conferences that involve the participation of a judge.

The *Criminal Code* does not set out any procedural rules for pretrial conferences. In fact, the only part of the Code that expressly deals with pretrial conferences is s. 625.1, which provides that the court, upon application by the Crown or the accused, or upon its own application, may order a prehearing conference to consider matters that would promote a fair and expeditious hearing. In practice, a pretrial conference will almost always be ordered if requested by a party. In addition, most jurisdictions have adopted the convention of holding mandatory pretrial conferences for any trials that are expected to exceed one day in duration. Section 625.1(2) makes these pretrial conferences mandatory in cases that are to be tried with a jury.

There really is no end to the matters that can be discussed during a pretrial conference given that the purpose of a pretrial conference is to consider any issues that would promote a fair and expeditious trial. Sometimes it is even possible for the parties to resolve the case completely either through a plea bargain agreement or by the withdrawal of the charges against the accused. In some cases the defence may agree to waive formal proof of part of the Crown's case. Plea bargaining and the waiver of evidence are more fully explained later in this chapter.

The *Criminal Proceedings Rules for the Superior Court of Justice (Ontario)* contain provisions that govern the procedure for pretrial conferences in that court.[4] Rule 28.05(9) essentially mirrors the provisions of s. 625.1(2) of the *Criminal Code* by

---

4. S.I./2012-7. It should be noted that the provincial courts have various rules or directions regarding pretrial conference proceedings. For example, the *Criminal Rules of the Ontario Court of Justice* contain provisions that deal with pretrial conferences in that court. These provisions are dealt with in Chapter 18, Criminal Rules.

requiring the pretrial conference judge to "inquire about and discuss any matter that may promote a fair and expeditious hearing of the charges contained in the indictment." Rules 28.05(10), (11), (12), and (13) set out a plethora of matters that can be addressed at a pretrial conference. These include substantive inquiries into such things as the issues in dispute, the simplification of issues, the possibility of making admissions of fact, and the appropriate sentence upon a finding of guilt. The Rules also set out various procedural issues that can be addressed, including the scheduling of the trial, the nature of any pretrial applications or motions, the resolution of any outstanding disclosure issues, the need for interpreters, and the need for any technological equipment to facilitate the introduction of evidence at trial.

Rule 28.05(13) of the *Criminal Proceedings Rules for the Superior Court of Justice (Ontario)* permits the pretrial conference judge to make various recommendations to the parties, including recommendations about admissions of fact and any outstanding disclosure issues, as well as on various procedural issues. Further, the pretrial conference judge is permitted to express his or her opinion about the appropriateness of any proposed sentence. Obviously, the opinion of the pretrial conference judge will weigh heavily in influencing the decisions facing both the Crown and the accused, including the decision on how to plead. However, as mentioned earlier, pretrial conferences are informal meetings and the pretrial conference judge does not have the power to make orders that would affect the position of the parties; the pretrial conference judge is limited to making recommendations only. Similarly, there is normally no obligation on the part of the Crown or the defence to actually follow through on any representations made during a pretrial conference. This was illustrated in a Manitoba sexual assault case[5] where the defence indicated at a pretrial conference that the only issue at trial would be whether the victim had consented to have sexual relations with the accused. At trial, however, the accused was permitted to argue that no sexual relations had occurred between the victim and the accused notwithstanding the representations that had been made at the pretrial conference.

The only time where the Crown will be required to follow through on its promises is where the accused's right to a fair trial would be jeopardized. This would occur if the accused relied on the representations made by the Crown at the pretrial and undertook a course of action that later proved to be detrimental for the accused. For example, it would be unfair for the Crown to introduce a statement made by the accused, if the accused, in reliance on the Crown's promise to not use the statement, elected to be tried by a jury. There would, however, be no unfairness had the accused not relied on the Crown's statement in making her election.

Plea Bargaining

The reality is that most criminal cases do not require a trial and are resolved by a plea of guilty. In many cases, the guilty plea is pre-arranged through negotiations between the accused or her representative and the Crown. This process is commonly

---

5. *R. v. Christensen* (1995), 100 Man. R. (2d) 25 (C.A.).

referred to as "plea bargaining" or "plea negotiations." The fact that these negotiations occur in private sometimes results in the process being perceived negatively by the public. However, plea bargains are vital to the effective administration of justice and without them, the courts would likely soon be bogged down with delays attributable to an increase in trials or prolonged sentencing hearings.

Plea negotiations can occur at any time during the process, from before the first appearance by the accused in court, right up to and including trial. Generally, however, no meaningful discussions will occur before the accused has been provided with disclosure and is aware of the case against him. In addition to s. 625.1(2) of the Code that provides for mandatory pretrial conferences for any Superior Court trial with a judge and jury, most jurisdictions now have some form of pretrial for all criminal cases. As mentioned earlier, a pretrial is an informal meeting between the Crown and the accused, often with the assistance of a judge. One purpose of a pretrial is to canvass the possibility of resolving the case through a negotiated resolution. For example, if the accused is facing several charges, he may agree to enter a plea of guilty to the lesser charge and in return the Crown will withdraw the more serious charges. Even when the plea negotiations do not lead to a complete resolution of the case, they may lead to agreement on some of the issues or procedural matters and this may result in a more efficient trial.

Plea negotiations can have limitless possible outcomes. However, where an agreement is reached, there will usually be a plea of guilty to at least one charge. The Crown and defence may have agreed to a specific sentence, in which case there will be a **joint submission** as to the appropriate sentence for the accused. It is important to note that while many judges tend to accept a joint submission as the basis for sentencing the offender, no judge is bound by such a submission. It is up to the judge to impose an appropriate sentence and the parties' submissions are one of many factors that a judge will consider before sentencing a person who has been convicted of a criminal offence.

joint submission
a sentencing submission put forth to the court that has been agreed to by both the Crown and defence

Waiver of Evidence

Good advocacy does not necessarily mean relentlessly exploring every possible avenue. The simple reality is that a good advocate will zero in on the real issues in the case and admit without formal proof those elements that are not really in dispute. It may appear to the casual observer that this strategy of not pursuing every issue, however tenuous, could compromise an accused person's defence. In fact, the contrary is true. By focusing on the "real" issues there is less chance of confusing the trier of fact with irrelevant considerations that might result in the main argument being overlooked or missed. Further, judges (and Crown attorneys, for that matter) always appreciate a well-presented and well-considered case.

With the acknowledgment that waiving evidence might be helpful in the presentation of a case, the question arises: "Which evidence should be waived?" This question can only be answered on a case-by-case basis. What may be insignificant in one case may be an essential part of the defence in another case. For example, one element that the Crown must prove in every criminal case is identity. The Crown must prove beyond a reasonable doubt that the person sitting accused in court is the same person who committed the offence. In most cases identity is not really in issue. For instance, the accused may be well known by the victim or may have identified himself to the police. In other cases, however, identity may be a central issue in the case. Numerous appellate courts have commented on the frailties of identification evidence in cases where events occurred more than a year before trial and witnesses are attempting to identify the person sitting in the prisoner's box or next to the defence lawyer as the perpetrator. In these situations, the identity of the person who committed the crime would likely be a key issue as far as the defence is concerned and it would be perfectly proper, and perhaps expected, for a competent lawyer or paralegal to explore any weaknesses in the evidence.

Another situation where formal proof might be waived by the defence is when an accused makes a statement to the police. In order for the statement to be admitted into the trial, the Crown must prove beyond a reasonable doubt that it was made voluntarily by showing that the accused's will was not overborne by threats or promises of inducement, oppressive circumstances, or lack of an operating mind. In addition, for the statement to be admissible, the Crown must show beyond a reasonable doubt that there has not been any police trickery that has unfairly compromised the accused's right to remain silent. It might well be imagined that the Crown can face a lengthy and cumbersome process in having a confession admitted into evidence. The judge must hold a **voir dire**, which is a mini trial within the trial, to determine the admissibility of the evidence. During a *voir dire*, the Crown is expected to call on every police officer that had contact with the accused up to the point at which the statement was made. It is also open for the accused to testify during the *voir dire* as to the circumstances surrounding the making of his or her statement.

voir dire
a mini trial or trial within a trial that is designed to determine the admissibility of evidence

The defence may consider waiving formal proof of voluntariness if the statement is exculpatory or not harmful to the accused. There may be situations where the defence will consider waiving proof of voluntariness, even if the confession is inculpatory and hurts the accused. For example, if the Crown is capable of proving that a statement was made voluntarily, what is gained by putting the Crown to the test and needlessly prolonging the trial? This is especially true if there is a better defence available on a different point. The risk of putting the Crown to every test is that the real issues become clouded and the trial judge may have difficulty in distinguishing viable defences from courtesy defences.

Another area where the defence might consider waiving formal proof and making an admission is with regard to technical matters that are not in issue. These are matters where formal proof often requires the testimony of several witnesses to establish an element of the offence that is often not in serious dispute. These are situations where, if put to the test, the Crown will almost certainly call witnesses to make a point. In a drug prosecution, for example, the Crown must prove the chain of continuity to establish that the drugs tendered as evidence at trial are the actual drugs that were seized from the accused. As a result, every person who handled the drugs after they were seized must be called by the Crown to establish that the evidence was not tampered with or otherwise compromised. The Crown is fully able to prove the chain of continuity in most prosecutions, and experienced lawyers will consider admitting the chain of continuity in these cases to eliminate confusing issues and save court time.

Finally, while not really a waiver of evidence, a pretrial conference may be an opportune time to advise the Crown on whether the defence will be raising any Charter issues at trial.

The Arraignment and Plea

A person charged with an offence will usually make several appearances in court before the commencement of the trial. All of these initial appearances, including the arraignment and plea, will be before a provincial court judge regardless of whether the accused is charged with a summary conviction or an indictable offence.

The purpose of these initial appearances is to set a date for trial or the preliminary inquiry. In most cases the accused will not have obtained representation on the first appearance and will be provided with an adjournment to retain a lawyer or paralegal.

Before the commencement of the trial or preliminary hearing, the accused is read the charges by the clerk of the court and asked to enter a plea. This process is known as the arraignment and marks the formal commencement of the trial. The only pleas that are permitted by the *Criminal Code* are guilty, not guilty, or one of the special pleas of **autrefois acquit**, **autrefois convict**, or **pardon**. There is no special requirement to plead not guilty by reason of mental disorder.[6] The trial itself will begin after the accused has entered a plea.

The special pleas of *autrefois acquit* and *autrefois convict* are available if the accused has previously been tried on the charges to which he is now pleading. The pleas are only available if the charges have been finally disposed of. In the case of *autrefois acquit* the accused is pleading that he has been acquitted or found not guilty in respect of the charges. For *autrefois convict* the accused is stating that he has previously been convicted of the charges. Irrespective of whether the accused was acquitted or convicted, the fact that he was put in jeopardy on a previous occasion for the same charges prevents him from facing the same charges again.

The plea of pardon is similar to the pleas of *autrefois acquit* and *autrefois convict* except that instead of having been acquitted or convicted of the offence for which he is charged, the accused is pleading that he had been previously pardoned for the offence. These special pleas recognize the principle that a person cannot be tried twice on the same matter. They are popularly known as double jeopardy defences.

In most cases the accused will enter a plea of either guilty or not guilty. If the accused does not respond when asked to plea, the court will enter a not guilty plea on behalf of the accused and the trial process will move forward.

When a not guilty plea is entered the court will usually fix a date for the trial or the preliminary hearing, although it is possible for the trial to start right after the accused has entered a plea if the trial is to be before a judge of the provincial court. Normally, however, these dates are established on the **set-date** appearance with regard to the availability of court time, the witnesses in the case, the Crown, and the accused's representative. As a result, trials and preliminary hearings are usually set

autrefois acquit
a special plea that is made by a person charged with a criminal offence where the person has previously been acquitted or found not guilty in respect of the charge and thus cannot be tried again for the same offence

autrefois convict
a special plea that is made by a person charged with a criminal offence where the person has previously been convicted or found guilty in respect of the charge and thus cannot be tried again for the same offence

pardon
a special plea where the commission of a criminal offence and the relevant penalty are forgiven, usually by a head of state or by an act of Parliament

set-date
an early appearance in court to set a trial date in a case

---

6. The defence of mental disorder was formerly known as insanity.

several months into the future. If the accused is in custody, every effort is made to obtain an expedited trial date. Most jurisdictions keep some trial dates reserved for such in-custody matters.

If the accused pleads guilty, the court will inquire whether he admits to the essential allegations of fact. If the facts are admitted and they support a conviction by establishing all of the elements of the offence, the court will make a finding of guilt against the accused. After a finding of guilt has been made, the accused will be sentenced. Sentencing is discussed later in this text in Chapter 20.

The Election of the Accused on Indictable Offences

There are two forms of election under the *Criminal Code*. The reader will recall (with reference to Chapter 11) that the Crown will elect to proceed with the charge summarily or by way of indictment when the accused is charged with a hybrid offence. The Crown will make its election after the accused has been arraigned.

The second election is available to the accused. Generally, if the accused is charged with an indictable offence that is not listed in either s. 469 or s. 553 of the *Criminal Code*, the accused may elect the mode of trial. The accused will make this election prior to entering a plea during arraignment. The options that are available to the accused are trial by a judge of the Superior Court of Justice with a jury, trial by a judge of the Superior Court of Justice without a jury, and trial by a provincial court judge without a jury. The accused will be deemed to have elected to be tried by a judge of the Superior Court of Justice with a jury if the accused fails to make an election.

What happens next depends on the classification of the offence and how the accused has elected to be tried. The accused does not have the right to elect the mode of trial if charged with a summary conviction offence, a hybrid offence for which the Crown has elected to proceed by summary conviction, or an offence listed in s. 553 of the *Criminal Code*. In these instances, the accused will be tried by a judge of the provincial court without a jury and will enter a plea when asked by the clerk of the court. Sometimes the case is then adjourned and the accused will return at a later date for the trial or to be sentenced if a guilty plea has been entered. Normally, however, the process will continue before the provincial court judge following the election of the accused.

In all other instances (that is, cases that are to be tried in the Superior Court of Justice, either with a jury or without a jury), the accused is entitled to have a preliminary inquiry to determine whether there is sufficient evidence to warrant a trial. In those cases, a date will be set for the commencement of the preliminary inquiry and the accused will be expected to return to court on that date. It is possible for the accused to waive his right to a preliminary inquiry and be committed for trial immediately. If the accused is ordered to stand trial, the matter is then adjourned to the Superior Court of Justice for the purpose of setting a trial date in that court.

The Preliminary Inquiry

The function of the preliminary inquiry is to determine whether there is sufficient evidence to commit or send the accused to trial. An accused is entitled to a preliminary inquiry in the following situations:

1. The accused has been charged with an offence listed in s. 469 of the *Criminal Code*. These are the most serious offences in the Code—for example, murder and treason.

2. The accused has been charged with an offence that permits him to elect the mode of trial and he has elected to be tried by a judge of the Superior Court of Justice sitting alone or with a jury.

3. A provincial court judge has converted the trial of an indictable offence into a preliminary inquiry under s. 555 of the *Criminal Code*.

The last of these situations can occur if the accused was charged with an offence that is within the absolute jurisdiction of a provincial court judge or had elected to be tried by a provincial court judge. Under the wording of s. 555 of the Code, the presiding provincial court judge appears to have wide discretionary powers in deciding whether to convert a trial into a preliminary inquiry. However, case law has made it clear that the accused should be entitled to proceed in the manner of the election unless there is a judicial reason for overruling the accused's election.[7] Thus an accused will not normally have a preliminary inquiry if he is charged with an offence that is in the absolute jurisdiction of a provincial court judge or if he has elected to be tried by a provincial court judge. An accused charged with a summary conviction offence cannot have a preliminary inquiry under any circumstances.

Purpose of the Preliminary Inquiry

The preliminary inquiry is held before a judge of the provincial court. The object for the judge is to determine whether there is enough evidence to send the accused to trial. The test for determining this is whether there is any evidence upon which a reasonable jury, properly instructed, could convict the accused. The accused will be committed for trial if there is admissible evidence[8] that could, if believed, result in a finding of guilt. The judge on the preliminary inquiry does not assess or weigh the evidence. It does not matter whether the evidence is weak and not likely to convict the accused or if the Crown has not proven guilt beyond a reasonable doubt. The test for a committal is much lower than the test for a conviction and the accused will be committed for trial if the evidence is *capable* of resulting in a guilty verdict. It is only if the Crown fails to meet this test that the charges against the accused will be dismissed following a preliminary inquiry.

---

7. *R. v. Babcock* (1989), 31 O.A.C. 354 (C.A.).

8. While a preliminary inquiry judge generally has the power to exclude evidence, a preliminary inquiry is not a court of competent jurisdiction under the *Charter of Rights and Freedoms* and there is no power to exclude evidence that was obtained as a result of a Charter violation.

In the vast majority of cases the accused will be committed for trial. The matter is then sent to the Superior Court of Justice for trial. It is there that matters such as the strength, weight, and credibility of the Crown's evidence will be assessed in addition to any issues and defences that might be raised by the accused.

Before the advent of disclosure requirements by the Crown, defence counsel used the preliminary inquiry as a way to obtain disclosure and to test the strength of the Crown's case by cross-examining and assessing the credibility of the Crown's witnesses. After the Supreme Court of Canada set out disclosure rules in *R. v. Stinchcombe*, the need to use the preliminary inquiry for this purpose has virtually disappeared. As a result, there is currently some discussion on whether the preliminary inquiry continues to serve any useful purpose, especially when one considers the fact that the test for a committal to stand trial is not particularly onerous.

Procedure on the Preliminary Inquiry

Historically, the jurisdiction of the preliminary inquiry was limited to the charge or charges set out in the Information or any included offences that might be disclosed by the evidence. There was no jurisdiction to commit an accused for trial on other or more serious charges even if they were supported by evidence at the hearing. That changed in 1985 when the *Criminal Code* was amended to permit the accused to be committed for trial on any indictable charge disclosed by the evidence.[9] This means, for example, if the accused is charged with manslaughter, the preliminary inquiry judge has the power to commit the accused to stand trial for murder if the evidence is capable of supporting that charge.

The actual "inquiry" takes the form of a hearing that is very similar to a trial. However, instead of proving guilt beyond a reasonable doubt, the Crown has the burden to demonstrate that there is sufficient evidence to warrant a trial. This is normally accomplished by the calling of witnesses. The Crown will conduct a direct examination of each witness that it will call on the preliminary inquiry and the accused will have the opportunity to cross-examine each witness to test their evidence and credibility after the Crown has completed its questioning. The process of examining witnesses is fully explained later in Chapter 19, which deals with trials.

The evidence of each witness is recorded and forms part of the record of proceedings. This means that the evidence can be transcribed and may be used later at trial if the witness has died or is unavailable.[10] In addition, if the testimony of the witness is different at trial, pointing out the discrepancies to the witness can attack the witness's credibility.

In most cases, the accused will be ordered to stand trial after the preliminary inquiry because the threshold test for a committal is low. For this reason, the defence will often consider waiving the evidence of peripheral witnesses for the purpose of the preliminary inquiry. Instead, the defence will take the opportunity to test only the Crown's key witnesses, such as the complainant or eyewitnesses. Sometimes where complete disclosure has been made, the defence may consider waiving its

---

9. *Criminal Code* s. 535.

10. *Criminal Code* s. 715 permits the evidence to be used at trial if the witness is dead, has become insane, is too ill to testify, or is absent from Canada.

entitlement to a preliminary inquiry altogether and have the case sent directly to trial. In a situation where there are multiple persons accused in a single indictment, each is entitled to request a preliminary inquiry. In that event, a preliminary inquiry will be held for all of the accused and each will have the right to participate.

Although it is permitted, the defence will rarely present any evidence on the preliminary inquiry. There really is no reason for the defence to call witnesses after the Crown has met the test for committal. The preliminary inquiry judge will not assess the credibility of competing witnesses and accept the testimony of one witness while rejecting the evidence of another. Further, by calling evidence the defence may be inadvertently providing the Crown with disclosure, which may place the defence at a tactical disadvantage. One occasion where the defence may consider calling a witness might be if there is a risk that the witness might not be available for trial and the defence wishes to preserve the evidence for use later. Sometimes, if the prosecution fails to call a witness whose evidence is not vital in securing a committal for trial, the defence might call that witness to hear and see the witness in order to assess their credibility.

Publication Bans

A final note should be added about publication bans where the court prohibits the publication of any details of the evidence presented at a preliminary inquiry. Although publication bans are rarely imposed during trials, they are almost always made at a preliminary inquiry. This is to protect the accused, who is presumed innocent and is not at risk of conviction, from negative publicity prior to trial. A publication ban also shields witnesses in the same manner. The rationale for a publication ban is even stronger where there is a jury trial since there is a risk that potential jurors might be influenced by what is reported by the media. Section 539 of the *Criminal Code* provides that a preliminary inquiry judge may order a publication ban if one is requested by the Crown and must make one if requested by the defence.

The Preferred Indictment

Under the *Criminal Code*[11] the Attorney General of a province has the right to send an accused directly to trial without first holding a preliminary inquiry. This is an absolute right that exists before a preliminary inquiry has started, while a preliminary inquiry is in progress, and even after a preliminary inquiry has been completed with the accused being discharged. This power is rarely exercised because it deprives the accused of an important procedural safeguard in the preliminary inquiry. In addition, when the Attorney General decides to prefer an indictment the decision is often met with controversy and negative comments from civil liberty groups. Usually the Attorney General will only consider taking this step in extraordinary cases where there has been an inordinate delay in the preliminary inquiry or where the interests of justice may require it.

Preferred indictments are fully discussed in Chapter 16, Informations and Indictments.

---

11. *Criminal Code* s. 577.

CHAPTER SUMMARY

We often read and hear about delays in bringing accused persons to trial. There is sometimes an assumption that these delays are attributable to foot-dragging by the prosecution or the defence. The reality, however, is that much of this time is spent on pretrial procedural matters that are designed to facilitate a fair and efficient trial. While these pretrial procedures no doubt lengthen the time that it takes to bring the accused to trial, consider how inefficient and cumbersome trials would be without these steps.

KEY TERMS

autrefois acquit, 200
autrefois convict, 200
exculpatory, 194

inculpatory, 194
joint submission, 198
pardon, 200

set-date, 200
stay of proceedings, 195
voir dire, 199

REVIEW QUESTIONS

1. Why is the Crown required to provide disclosure to a person who is charged with a criminal offence?

2. Apart from satisfying a legal obligation, is there any other reason why it is desirable for the Crown to provide disclosure to a person who is charged with a criminal offence?

3. How is disclosure requested from the Crown by a person charged with a criminal offence?

4. What information is the Crown required to disclose to a person who is charged with a criminal offence?

5. What is the main purpose of a preliminary inquiry? Is there any other purpose served by a preliminary inquiry?

6. What purposes does a pretrial conference serve?

7. What pleas are available to a person charged with a criminal offence?

EXERCISES

1. Julia Wilkins was charged with impaired driving and "over 80" after being involved in a motor vehicle accident. Her lawyer, Ali Abdi, had made a request for disclosure and disclosure was provided by the Crown's office in a timely manner. However, at 9:30 a.m., just before the trial was to start, Ali was advised by the Crown attorney who was handling the matter that there was another civilian witness that the prosecution intended to call. The witness was expected to testify as to the manner in which Julia was driving her vehicle immediately before the accident. The police did not know about this evidence when disclosure was originally provided in this matter and the existence of this witness was not disclosed earlier. What should Ali do? How is the court likely to respond?

2. Murray Mitskovic is charged with theft of a motor vehicle under s. 333.1 of the *Criminal Code*. After negotiations between the Crown attorney and Murray's lawyer, Murray has agreed to plead guilty to the lesser charge of joyriding under s. 335. Both the Crown and Murray's lawyer have agreed to a joint submission for a suspended sentence with probation. The sentencing judge instead sentenced Murray to 60 days in jail after hearing that Murray has several prior convictions for theft of motor vehicles. Do you think that the sentencing judge was wrong in incarcerating Murray? Explain your answer.

3. Kathryn Kazeryk is charged with murder in the death of her husband. The Crown has called three eyewitnesses at Kathryn's preliminary inquiry. The witnesses gave contradictory evidence. One witness testified that she saw Kathryn stab her husband, while the other two testified that it was Kathryn's sister who in fact stabbed the deceased. What is the likely outcome of the preliminary inquiry?

4. Samantha Silvio was charged with possession of cocaine for the purpose of trafficking under the *Controlled Drugs and Substances Act* after a quantity of cocaine was found in her apartment following a search authorized by a search warrant. Following the discovery of the cocaine, Samantha was read her rights and she made a statement to the police readily admitting that the cocaine was hers and that she intended to use the cocaine in making a special tea that helped to ease her acute asthma. Samantha's defence to the trafficking charge is that the cocaine was for her own use and that while she can be convicted of the lesser charge of possessing cocaine, she has not committed the offence of possession of cocaine for the purpose of trafficking.

a. At Samantha's trial, the Crown attempted to enter as evidence the statement made by Samantha to the police following her arrest. Samantha's lawyer objected to this testimony on the basis that the Crown is obligated to first prove that the statement was made voluntarily. What do you think of the lawyer's objection?

b. Later, Samantha's lawyer objected to the introduction of the cocaine into evidence on the basis that the Crown had failed to establish a chain of continuity in the evidence. The objection was essentially based on the premise that it was not proven that the evidence that was seized from Samantha by the police is the evidence that is now before the court. What do you think of the lawyer's objection?

Criminal Rules

18

LEARNING OUTCOMES

After completing this chapter, you should be able to:

- Understand the function served by criminal rules.

- Define the authority for making criminal rules.

- Understand the *Criminal Rules of the Ontario Court of Justice*.

- Discuss the most common applications in criminal proceedings.

- Understand how to make an application in the Ontario Court of Justice.

- Understand how to respond to an application in the Ontario Court of Justice.

- Discuss the concept of case management in the Ontario Court of Justice.

Introduction

Canada's *Criminal Code* is a federal statute that sets out various offences and defences. It also includes the procedural steps involved in the prosecution of both indictable and summary conviction offences. However, the *Criminal Code* does not contain detailed step-by-step procedural rules for the prosecution of criminal offences across Canada. Using a painting analogy, the *Criminal Code* provides the broad brush strokes, but not the fine intricate details. These details are normally provided by rules established by the courts.

The Need for Rules

In a perfect world, the entire process for a legal proceeding would be contained in a single document. This, however, is simply not possible. One reason for this is that constitutional jurisdiction over criminal law in Canada is shared between the federal and provincial governments. Under s. 91.27 of the *Constitution Act, 1867*, the federal government has jurisdiction over

> [t]he Criminal Law, except the Constitution of Courts of Criminal Jurisdiction, but including the Procedure in Criminal Matters.

At the same time, s. 92.14 confers on the provincial legislatures jurisdiction over

> [t]he Administration of Justice in the Province, including the Constitution, Maintenance, and Organization of Provincial Courts, both of Civil and Criminal Jurisdiction, and including Procedure in Civil Matters in those Courts.

Since the two levels of government share the power to administer criminal law, it follows that both must have procedural rules specific to the needs of the particular jurisdiction.

Compounding the issue is that Canada is a vast territory with ten provinces and three territories comprising one level of government. This leads to a second reason for the lack of detailed rules in the *Criminal Code*. The simple reality is that no document or set of rules can be universally applied without regard to the nature and circumstances of the offence before the court and, more importantly, regional considerations. As a matter of practice, it is one thing to prosecute thousands of offences in a large metropolitan area such as the City of Toronto, and a very different thing altogether to prosecute a fraction of those offences in remote and widespread areas that might not even have a full-time judge. It will always be the case that different rules will be needed based on regional considerations and requirements.

Authority for Making Rules

The *Criminal Code* expressly provides rule-making authority to the various levels of courts in Canada. Section 482(1) confers power on every superior court of criminal jurisdiction and every court of appeal to "make rules of court not inconsistent with this or any other Act of Parliament." Section 482(2) extends the same rule-making power to every provincial and territorial court. All of the provinces and territories have various rules and practice directions that govern the procedure used in prosecuting criminal offences within their jurisdiction. It is far beyond the scope of this text to detail all of the provincial and federal criminal rules currently in force in every jurisdiction throughout Canada. The various rules are available online and can be accessed by visiting the website of the Department of Justice, the appropriate provincial attorney general, or a specific court. As a matter of convenience and to accommodate the needs of licensed paralegals in Ontario, this chapter will focus on the *Criminal Rules of the Ontario Court of Justice*.[1]

The Criminal Rules of the Ontario Court of Justice

The *Criminal Rules of the Ontario Court of Justice* came into force on July 1, 2012 and replaced the *Rules of the Ontario Court of Justice in Criminal Proceedings*. The *Rules of the Ontario Court of Justice in Criminal Proceedings* were composed of 32 different rules and 15 forms. These rules and forms were designed to be used by lawyers and contained complicated and technical legal language. They were not user-friendly. People charged with criminal offences who were self-represented had a difficult time navigating through the complex procedural requirements set out in the Rules. In addition, the *Rules of the Ontario Court of Justice in Criminal Proceedings* had been in force since 1997 and did not recognize that persons charged with minor summary conviction criminal offences now had the option to be represented by paralegals licensed by the Law Society of Upper Canada. The former rules spoke only of counsel and did not cover representation by licensed paralegals for persons charged with minor criminal offences. To remedy this, on July 1, 2012, the *Rules of the Ontario Court of Justice in Criminal Proceedings* were revoked and replaced with a completely different set of rules and court forms.

It is obvious that the new *Criminal Rules of the Ontario Court of Justice* were designed for ease of use and to accommodate the increasing number of people facing criminal prosecution who represent themselves or are represented by licensed paralegals. The number of rules has been reduced from 32 to just 5, and there are now only 3 different forms instead of the previous 15.

Fundamental Objective

Rule 1.1(1) provides that the fundamental objective of the Rules is to ensure that proceedings in the Ontario Court of Justice are dealt with justly and efficiently. Specific examples of how proceedings are dealt with justly and efficiently are set out in Rule 1.1(2) and include the following:

- dealing with the prosecution and defence fairly,

---

1. S.I./2012-30.

- recognizing the rights of the accused,
- recognizing the interests of witnesses, and
- scheduling court time and deciding other matters in ways that take into account:
  - the gravity of the alleged offence,
  - the complexity of what is in issue,
  - the severity of the consequences for the accused and for others affected, and
  - the requirements of other proceedings.

Rule 1.1(3) imposes an obligation on every counsel, paralegal, agent, and litigant to act in accordance with the fundamental objective of the Rules and to comply with the Rules and any practice directions and orders made by the court. Rule 1.1(4) requires the court to take the fundamental objective of the Rules into consideration when exercising any power under the Rules or when applying or interpreting any rule or practice direction.

Non-Compliance

The reason for having court rules in the first place is to facilitate the orderly administration of justice; sometimes the strict application of rules has the opposite effect and results in a miscarriage of justice. For instance, we would all agree that it would be unjust for an application under the *Canadian Charter of Rights and Freedoms* to be dismissed for a technical or trivial inadequacy where a person's rights have been violated by the police. The *Criminal Rules of the Ontario Court of Justice* expressly address this issue by providing for relief from non-compliance in Rule 5.3, which permits the court to excuse non-compliance with any rule to the extent necessary to ensure that the fundamental objective set out in Rule 1.1 is met.

Applications

application
similar to a motion, it is a hearing that usually concerns a procedural issue before a final decision is reached in the case

Rule 2 deals with all **applications** made to the court. Applications to the court are made in circumstances where the applicant is seeking an order or some form of relief. Applications can be made on the trial date or they can be made earlier. Rule 2.1 requires that an application is to be commenced by serving an application in Form 1 on the opposing party and every other party affected by the application and filing it, together with proof of service, with the court.

Form 1 is a two-page document that is completed by the applicant. The first page contains various fields and boxes that, when completed, provide basic background information about the application, such as the court file number; name of the case; date; application hearing date, time, and place; identity of the applicant; and whether the applicant is self-represented or has legal representation. The applicant is required to complete the second page of Form 1 by providing a concise statement of the subject of the application, a statement of the grounds to be argued, a detailed statement of the factual basis for the specific application, and a list of the material and evidence that will be relied on at the hearing of the application. Normally, evidence on an application is provided in the form of a sworn affidavit setting out the facts that are relied upon by the applicant. The applicant has the option to file an agreed statement of facts or rely on the oral evidence of witnesses on the application. Rule 2.1(3) states that the applicant is required to serve and file a transcript if one is required for the determination of the application. A transcript of previous proceedings would be needed, for example, to demonstrate the reason for a previous adjournment. The application must be signed and dated by the applicant. Form 1 is reproduced in the Appendix to this textbook.

While it is true that every criminal case is unique in terms of evidence and legal issues, the reality is that there are only a handful of different applications that are usually brought in criminal proceedings. Rules 2.4 and 2.5 require certain applications to be made before the trial begins and others to be made at the start of the trial or during trial. Rule 2.4(1) states that a pretrial application shall be heard at least 60 days before trial unless the court orders otherwise. A brief overview and some distinguishing features of some of the more common applications are provided below.

1. Applications for Removal as Legal Representative of Record

Once a legal representative has undertaken to represent a person charged with a criminal offence, he or she cannot withdraw from the case unless permitted by the court. An application to have a legal representative removed from the record can be made by either the prosecutor or the legal representative for the accused person. The affidavit in support of this application must contain sufficient information and facts to justify the removal of the legal representative. It is important to keep in mind that the legal representative must not disclose confidential and privileged information when making this application. Normally, the application will be served on the prosecutor and on the accused person. This application is a pretrial application that is expected to be made at least 60 days before trial.

2. Applications for Adjournment

It may sometimes become necessary to seek an adjournment of a trial after a date for the trial has been fixed. In that case, an application should be made for an adjournment before the trial. The affidavit in support of the application should contain information that is not privileged that pertains to the request as well as proposed trial dates in the event that the application is successful. The court may refuse to grant an adjournment in situations where an application has not been made in a timely manner. This is another example of a pretrial application that should be made at least 60 days before trial.

3. Applications to Exclude Evidence Under s. 24(2) of the Charter

Section 24(2) of the Charter provides for an exclusionary remedy in circumstances where evidence has been obtained in a manner that infringes or denies any rights or freedoms guaranteed by the Charter. Normally, this application is made to the judge who has been assigned to preside over the trial. Under the previous rules, a special form was used when the application raised any constitutional issues, but now

Form 1 is used for all applications, including those that deal with constitutional issues. However, it should be noted that when an application raises constitutional issues, it must be served on both the Attorney General of Ontario and the Attorney General of Canada. This application is usually heard at the start of or during a trial.

4. *Other Constitutional Applications*

Form 1 is also used for applications that raise constitutional and Charter issues other than applications seeking relief under s. 24(2) of the Charter. These would include an application to stay proceedings where there has been a violation of an accused person's Charter rights or freedoms, and an application for a law that is inconsistent with the provisions of Canada's Constitution to be declared of no force or effect to the extent of that inconsistency. This application is also required to be served on both the Attorney General of Ontario and the Attorney General of Canada. An application for a stay of proceedings for unreasonable delay under s. 11(b) of the Charter is a pretrial application that is to be heard at least 60 days before trial. However, unlike all other pretrial applications, an application for a stay of proceedings for unreasonable delay is to be brought before the assigned trial judge (see Rule 2.4(3)). All other applications involving constitutional matters are usually made at the start of or during a trial.

5. *Preparatory Applications*

It may be necessary to make an application for matters that must be determined before proceeding to trial. Such applications might include those relating to disclosure, the release of exhibits for testing, or for commission evidence that is intended for use at trial. A preparatory application is a pretrial application that is to be heard at least 60 days before trial.

6. *Evidentiary Applications*

An application can be made for complex evidentiary issues, such as applications for the admissibility of similar fact evidence, evidence of a complainant's prior sexual activity, and hearsay evidence. Further, an evidentiary application can also be made for access to records in the possession and control of non-parties—for example, doctors' notes. An evidentiary application will usually be heard at the start of or during a trial.

7. *Applications for Severance of Accused or Counts*

severance
separation of one matter or issue into two or more with each being decided on its own without regard for the other(s)

There are two situations where an application for **severance** can be made:

- where there are multiple counts in an Information, that the accused be tried separately on one or more of the counts, and
- where there is more than one accused on an Information, that one or more of them be tried separately.

This is another pretrial application that is to be made at least 60 days before trial.

8. Applications for Particulars

An application for **particulars** is made under the provisions of s. 587(1) of the *Criminal Code*, which permits the court to make an order that the prosecutor furnish particulars[2] in respect of an Information or a count where it is necessary in order for the accused to have a fair trial. An application for particulars is a pretrial application that is to be made at least 60 days before trial.

particulars
specific details supporting a more general statement or proposition; in criminal law, an application for particulars is normally a request for a detailed itemization of a count in an Information

Responding to an Application

A party who wishes to respond to an application is required by Rule 2.2 to serve a response in Form 2 on the applicant and any other affected party and file it with the court together with proof of service. A Form 2 response is similar to a Form 1 application and is to include a concise statement of the party's reasons for responding to the application, a response to the applicant's grounds, and a detailed statement of the factual basis for the party's position in the proceeding.

Rule 2.3 states that an application in Form 1 does not require any additional material. However, additional factual and legal material is permitted on an application at the option of a party or if ordered by the court, and such additional material may include a brief statement of the legal argument to be made, one or more affidavits, case law, and an agreed statement of facts. Note that Rule 2.3(2)(c) states that the parties are not required to file well-known case law. Under the previous rules the parties were expected to file factums on most applications containing a statement of each issue raised, immediately followed by a concise statement of the law and any authorities relating to that issue. The fact is that very few applications raise novel issues or rely on little-known case law. As a result, most factums were simply boilerplate-type reproductions that really served no useful purpose other than to make the practice of criminal law paper intensive.

Third-Party Applications

Not all applications are made by the accused person or by the Crown. Sometimes an application is made by a third party such as a witness in the proceeding or the media. These applications are required by Rule 2.6 to be heard at least 30 days before the trial, unless the court orders otherwise.

Consent Applications

Sometimes an application will not be opposed by the other side and will be made on consent. In instances where an application may have initially been opposed but is no longer opposed when heard, the parties may simply advise the court that the application is proceeding on consent and the court will normally make the order that has been agreed to by the parties. The court of course must still be satisfied that the order made is appropriate in the circumstances. However, it would be unusual for the court to not grant an order that the parties have consented to.

---

2. Particulars are a detailed itemization of a count. They will be ordered in situations where the accused needs these particulars to answer the charge against him or her.

In circumstances where the parties consent to an application before the hearing of the application, Rule 2.7(1) says that the application may be dealt with on consent and without a hearing if one of the parties files a consent in Form 3 with the court. This procedure is only available where all parties are represented by counsel or by licensed paralegals. However, according to Rule 2.7(2), the court may still order a hearing where the court is of the opinion that the application requires a hearing. Rule 2.7(3) states that an application made on consent where a party is not represented may also be dealt with by using a Form 3, but the self-represented party is required to appear in court and the court must first be satisfied that the party understands the nature of the consent and the consequences of giving it.

Times for Service and Filing

Rule 3 sets out the timing for service and filing of an application. Generally, an application in Form 1 is to be served on all other parties and filed in the court office with proof of service at least 30 days before the date of the hearing of the application, as stated specifically in Rule 3.1(1). Rule 3.1(2) tells us that a response in Form 2 is to be served and filed, with proof of service, at least 15 days before the date of hearing of the application, and Rule 3.1(3) says that these time periods can be lengthened or shortened by the court or with the consent of the parties. Rule 3.2 notes that on applications for adjournment and applications to be removed from the record, shortening these time periods requires both the approval of the court and the consent of the parties. For this reason it is vital that these applications be made in a timely manner. It would be grossly irresponsible for a legal representative to expect a matter to be adjourned without serving and filing the application in a timely manner. It is recognized that there may be occasions where unexpected developments occur, such as illness or a breakdown in the solicitor–client relationship that would make it impossible to give as much notice as required by the Rules. In those cases, the parties should not wait until the trial date and should bring the application as soon as possible on short notice.[3]

How Applications Are Served

The *Criminal Rules of the Ontario Court of Justice* have simplified the procedure for serving applications. Under the old *Rules of the Ontario Court of Justice in Criminal Proceedings* the mode of service varied depending on the nature of the document served, the identity of the party served, and whether the party served had legal representation. Now, according to Rule 3.3, service of any document can be made in person, by fax, or by email at the option of the party serving the document. While Rule 3.3 requires the filing of hard copies of documents with the court, Rule 3.3(2) permits the filing of documents electronically where the technology is available and the court has authorized electronic filing by a practice direction.

---

3. See commentary to Rule 3.2 of the *Criminal Rules of the Ontario Court of Justice*. Annotated *Criminal Rules of the Ontario Court of Justice* are available at http://www.ontariocourts.ca/ocj/files/rules/criminal-rules-EN.pdf.

Case Management

Compared to the former rules, which set out the procedure for pre-hearing conferences, the current rule on **case management** is broader in scope and deals with several other matters. From a reading of it, it is clear that Rule 4 has been designed to facilitate a just, efficient, and fair determination of criminal proceedings. The guiding principle is set out in Rule 4.1:

> 4.1 When conducting a hearing or trial, the Court has the power to make any order or direction in relation to the conduct of the proceeding that would assist in ensuring that it is conducted in accordance with the fundamental objective set out in rule 1.1.

Judicial pretrial conferences are dealt with in Rule 4.2. A judicial pretrial conference is an informal meeting involving the pretrial conference judge, the Crown, and legal representatives for all accused at which a full and free discussion of the issues raised may occur without prejudice to the rights of the parties in any subsequent proceedings. Normally the accused person will not be present at a pretrial conference unless the accused is not represented by counsel or a paralegal licensee.

Rule 4.2 requires that before attending a judicial pretrial conference it is desirable for the parties to review the file and meet in order to attempt to resolve issues. This initial pretrial conference held with the Crown should focus on agreements and admissions as well as matters in issue.[4]

It is expected that parties attending the judicial pretrial will have authority to make decisions on the following matters, as outlined in Rule 4.2(3):

- disclosure,
- applications, including Charter applications that will be made at trial,
- the number of witnesses each party intends to call,
- the admissions any party is willing to make,
- any legal issues that the parties anticipate may arise in the proceeding,
- an estimate of the time needed to complete the proceeding, and
- resolution of the matter if appropriate.

Rule 4.2(4) tells us that at least three days before the judicial pretrial, the Crown is required to provide the pretrial judge a copy of a synopsis of the allegations against the accused. If the defence is of the opinion that the Crown's synopsis is incomplete or inaccurate, the defence has the option to provide additional material to the pretrial judge. This material, according to Rule 4.2(5), should also be provided at least three days before the judicial pretrial, if possible. The pretrial itself is normally held in person, but Rule 4.2(6) states that if the pretrial judge agrees, it may be held by way of telephone or some other form of communications technology.

At the conclusion of the pretrial, the pretrial judge may, as outlined in Rule 4.2(7), take one or more of the following steps:

case management
supervision by the court of a legal case as it proceeds through the justice system; the concept of case management has existed for years in civil cases, but is a relatively recent phenomenon in criminal cases

---

4. See commentary to Rule 4.2 of the *Criminal Rules of the Ontario Court of Justice*.

- confirm or amend the estimates of the time required to hear the proceeding,
- set timetables for the exchange of materials on applications to be heard, or for the completion of disclosure on matters to be set for trial or preliminary hearing,
- set times for the hearing of applications, and
- set a date for a further pretrial, if required.

According to Rule 4.2(8), if there have been any admissions or agreements made at the pretrial, they may be signed or otherwise recorded, transcribed, and attached to the Information in the proceeding for the assistance of the trial judge.

Focus Hearing

focus hearing
an informal meeting between a judge, Crown, and defence to facilitate a more efficient preliminary inquiry; a new feature of the *Criminal Rules of the Ontario Court of Justice*

A **focus hearing** is held to facilitate the conduct of a preliminary inquiry. Rule 4.3 provides that a preliminary inquiry judge may order a hearing under s. 536.4 of the *Criminal Code*. The purpose of a focus hearing is to ensure that the process is streamlined and witnesses with non-contentious evidence are not inconvenienced or that non-contentious evidence is not necessarily called.[5]

Under Rule 4.3(3), the party who requested the preliminary inquiry shall serve the other parties and file a statement of issues and witnesses, and for each witness listed, a brief synopsis of the evidence, an explanation of why in-person testimony is necessary, and an estimate of the time required to examine or cross-examine the witness. In addition, the party shall provide a list of witnesses that the parties propose to examine through a discovery process, a brief statement as to whether committal for trial is at issue and on what basis, and a statement of admissions agreed on by the parties.

discovery
procedural devices that occur before trial where a party is able to obtain evidence from an adverse party: in civil law, any party can discover any adverse party; in criminal law, only the accused may have discovery rights

A **discovery** is an out-of-court examination of a witness that is recorded and transcribed; it is available in cases where the parties and preliminary inquiry judge agree to it (Rule 4.4). Evidence taken at a discovery forms part of the official record of the preliminary inquiry and can be used at trial in the same manner as evidence from a preliminary inquiry. The discovery process is intended to free up valuable court time by reducing the number of witnesses required on a preliminary inquiry.

The discovery process is most useful for expert or non-controversial witnesses and is not available in situations where a witness is under the age of 18 years or for a complainant in a proceeding involving sexual or physical violence (Rule 4.4).

Practice Directions

The purpose of the Rules is to fill in those procedural details that the *Criminal Code* lacks. Sometimes even the Rules themselves may not deal with specific local concerns. In those cases, the court may issue practice directions to complement the Rules. The chief justice, or his or her delegate, has the authority to issue practice directions that are consistent with the Rules. A practice direction may apply to the whole of Ontario or only to specified regions, and all practice directions are posted on the website of the Ontario Court of Justice (Rule 5.1).

---

5. See commentary to Rule 4.3 of the *Criminal Rules of the Ontario Court of Justice*.

CHAPTER SUMMARY

The procedure for criminal proceedings is found in several sources. The *Criminal Code* sets out the major procedural steps involved in the prosecution of a criminal offence. However, the actual details involved in these steps are usually found in court rules. The specific rules that apply in a given case depend on the province or territory involved and the level of court. In individual cases, the specific rules affecting the conduct of the proceeding should be carefully reviewed to ensure compliance. The appropriate rules are available at the website of the court having jurisdiction over the matter.

KEY TERMS

application, 210
case management, 215
discovery, 216

focus hearing, 216
particulars, 213
severance, 212

REVIEW QUESTIONS

1. What purpose do rules serve in criminal proceedings?
2. Where can Canadian criminal rules be found?
3. What is the difference between a preparatory application and an evidentiary application?
4. What form is used under the *Criminal Rules of the Ontario Court of Justice* to make an application? What form is used to respond to an application?
5. What is the difference between a rule and a practice direction?

EXERCISES

1. Seth Alkina represents Gwen Jenkinson, who has been charged with a criminal offence. Seth has issued an interim account to Gwen for legal services performed on the file. The account has not been paid and Gwen is no longer returning Seth's calls or emails. Gwen's trial is scheduled to start in three months. What should Seth do?

2. Assume in question 1 above that Seth's account has been paid and that Gwen telephoned Seth the night before the trial telling him that she has a new lawyer and does not want Seth to appear for her trial the next day. What should Seth do?

3. Which of the following are pretrial applications and which can be made at trial?

   a. Application for an adjournment
   b. Application to exclude evidence under the Charter
   c. Application for a stay under the Charter
   d. Application for a severance of counts
   e. Application for further disclosure

The Trial

LEARNING OUTCOMES

After completing this chapter, you should be able to:

- Discuss how a theory of the case is developed.

- Discuss how to collect and organize information for the trial.

- Understand the jury selection process.

- Understand the trial process.

- Discuss the difference between a direct examination and a cross-examination.

- Understand the purpose of the opening statement.

- Understand the purpose of a closing argument.

- Discuss how a jury reaches a verdict.

Introduction

The *Criminal Code* provides comprehensive rules that govern trial procedure. They are set out in Parts XIX, XX, and XXVII, which deal with indictable offence trials with a judge alone, indictable offence trials with a judge and jury, and summary conviction trials. The three different types of trials share many characteristics. Sections 572 and 795 make the procedures in Part XX governing jury trials apply, to the extent that they are not inconsistent, to non-jury and summary conviction trials.

Preparation for Trial

Trial preparation is a continuous process that starts the moment a file is opened or a case is assigned to a lawyer, paralegal, or other legal professional. It continues through the trial itself since no amount of preparation can anticipate the twists and turns that a trial might take. This part of the chapter will focus on several important aspects of trial preparation that should be considered in every case. These important aspects are the development of the theory of the case, the collection of evidence, the analysis of the case, and, finally, the organization of material for use at trial.

The Three Different Types of Trials

- Indictable offence trials with a judge alone
- Indictable offence trials with a judge and jury
- Summary conviction trials

The Theory of the Case

The theory of the case is the framework within which the facts and applicable law are presented. In some cases this might mean that there will be several different options available for the defence, while in other situations no viable defence will be disclosed. In the latter situation, plea negotiations (also called plea bargains) may be a viable option.

Preparing the theory of the case when defending criminal charges begins with the first interview with the client. This is where preliminary issues are raised and the initial theory of the defence is formulated. The file is usually not assigned to the Crown prosecutor until after the charges have been laid, and sometimes as late as the trial date for less serious offences. When this is the case, the officer in charge of the investigation will have prepared much of the case for trial. However, the Crown attorney prosecuting the charge must be completely familiar with the file because he is ultimately responsible for presenting the case to the trier of fact. With more serious charges, the Crown attorney will play a more active role in preparing the file for trial.

In most cases it is prudent to conduct research of the relevant law at an early stage. This may lead to the discovery of hidden issues that might affect the theory of the case and require further research. After all of the issues have been disclosed and researched, it becomes possible to begin the process of determining how the relevant facts will fit together and be presented to the trier of fact.

For the defence, the theory of the case cannot be fully formulated until after full disclosure of the Crown's case has been obtained and all issues have been thoroughly researched. There may be several viable options at this point, but through the process of fact-gathering and identifying and researching legal issues a dominant theory of the case should emerge. A helpful technique is to break down the offence into every element that the Crown must prove and to focus on any gaps or weaknesses in the Crown's case. In some cases there might be alternative theories that are available for presentation at trial, but care should always be taken to not overly confuse the trier of fact.

Collecting and Organizing Information for the Trial

After the theory of the case has been developed comes the collection stage. This is when all of the information that is required for trial is collected. While the specific information that will be used at trial will vary from case to case, the type of information that is necessary will be the same in every case. It starts with the marshalling of the evidence. This includes witnesses, real (or physical) evidence, and documentary evidence. Any potential exhibits should be identified and collected. Care should be taken to ensure that proper notice is given if any business records will be used at trial. Similarly, a report may need to be served if an expert will be testifying at trial. The lawyer or paralegal should take this opportunity to become completely familiar with all of the information that is available for use at trial.

Analyzing Information for Use at Trial

After the information has been collected it must be analyzed to determine how it can be best used or, if the information is detrimental to the case, how the negative impact can be lessened. A good way to start is by listing all of the information that is available for use by both the prosecution and the defence. Any gaps in the evidence should be noted and acted on. The lawyer or paralegal should interview each witness that they plan to call and prepare a series of questions for each witness. Although it is improper to "coach" a witness with regard to their evidence, it is useful to go through the questions when preparing a witness, and to ensure that the witness fully understands each question. There is nothing improper in knowing what a particular witness will say in court. In fact, most effective advocates will not only know what their own witnesses will state, but also have a good sense of the anticipated evidence that opposing witnesses will give. For this reason, each witness should also be prepared for **cross-examination** by the other side. It may seem trite, but witnesses should be advised on how to dress and act in court. They should also be told when and where to attend. In most cases, the attendance of the witness should be secured by issuing and serving a **subpoena**. Form 16: Subpoena to a Witness can be found in the Appendix.

In addition to preparing a series of questions that they will ask of each witness, most effective lawyers, paralegals, or other legal representatives will also prepare questions to ask of the other side's witnesses. It has often been said of cross-examination that no question should be asked unless the examiner is certain of what the witness will answer. The reality is that it is simply not possible to completely anticipate the evidence of adverse witnesses. However, by preparing properly, the examiner should be able to anticipate the general evidence that witnesses will give. The examiner should have some, and perhaps even a good, idea of how a question

cross-examination
principle of the adversarial system in which one side in a legal proceeding is given an opportunity to question the witnesses for the opposing party in order to challenge their evidence and the entire case

subpoena
a document that compels a witness to attend court; in civil proceedings the document is often called a summons (under the *Criminal Code*, however, a summons is a document that compels the accused to attend court)

will be answered. A careful review of the disclosure materials will go a long way in helping in this regard. Most experienced examiners will target areas that have potential for cross-examination as well as preparing specific questions. When testifying in **direct examination**, a witness might say something that is inconsistent or lacks credibility, in which case the examiner will have to adapt the cross-examination to take advantage of the opportunity that has presented itself.

In addition to preparing for the examination of each witness, the opening statements and closing arguments should be prepared before trial. Opening statements and closing arguments are discussed later in this chapter. Sometimes the case will not unfold exactly as expected and the closing argument may need to be modified in order to address the evidence that was presented to the trier of fact.

The Trial Book

Most lawyers and paralegals will organize materials for use at trial in a **trial book**. The trial book should contain in separate sections the opening statements and closing arguments, the questions that will be asked of the party's own witnesses, questions and areas for cross-examination, and copies of any exhibits and reports that will be used at trial. Copies of all exhibits and reports should be available to provide to the judge, the witnesses, and the other side. In addition, there should be an area where notes on the testimony of every witness can be made.

Research and Precedents

If the party intends to present the court with any research or precedents, copies of relevant cases and statutes should be provided to the judge and the other side. Normally, any case law or statutory authority that a party intends to rely on will be compiled into a **book of authorities** so that all of the research is in one place and is easily accessible. Most judges prefer specific passages and provisions that a party will rely on to be highlighted so that they are easier to locate.

Jury Selection

Not all cases require a trial with a jury. Jury trials are held in cases where the accused has a right to elect the mode of trial and has elected trial by judge and jury. Jury trials are also mandatory for the most serious criminal offences, which are listed in s. 469 of the *Criminal Code*, unless both the accused and the Attorney General consent to a trial without a jury. It should be noted that the *Canadian Charter of Rights and Freedoms* guarantees the right to a jury trial for any indictable offence that is punishable by five years' imprisonment or more. This does not mean that the accused must have a jury trial for those offences, but that the accused has the right to elect trial by jury if he or she so wishes. There are, of course, no jury trials in summary offence proceedings.

Juries are composed of 12 people who have been selected by the Crown and accused from a much larger pool called a **jury panel** or **jury array**. Summoning pro-

direct examination
initial questioning of a witness that is conducted by the party who called the witness to provide evidence in the proceeding; also called an examination-in-chief

trial book
a book for use at trial by a legal representative where all papers and documents relating to the proceeding are organized in an easy-to-use and easy-to-find way

book of authorities
a book for use at trial by the parties and the court containing all authorities, including cases and legislation that will be relied upon at trial

jury panel/jury array
these terms are used interchangeably and refer to the large pool from which a jury is selected

spective jurors is a provincial matter and each province has a jury act that sets out the procedure for selecting people for jury duty. While the rules of selecting a jury panel vary, the end objective is the same: to establish a body of jurors that will be large enough to meet the needs of justice in the province. Potential jurors are then summoned for jury duty when required. The number of prospective jurors on a jury panel depends on the number of cases expected in a session; in a large city, this number can exceed 1,000 people.

Not all people are qualified to sit on a jury. Again, this is a matter of provincial legislation so there is some variation across the provinces. Usually, jurors must be of the age of majority and be both a resident of the province and a Canadian citizen. All provinces exclude certain occupations, such as police officers, lawyers, judges, members of Parliament, members of the provincial legislature, senators, and, in some cases, certain health practitioners. Persons with serious criminal records are also normally excluded from serving on a jury. Most provinces also have rules for excluding people from jury duty who would suffer an undue hardship or who have a mental or physical disability that would impair their ability to sit on a jury. Some jurisdictions will excuse jurors on the basis of conscience or religion.

The Selection Process

The *Criminal Code* governs the process by which a jury is selected once the panel has assembled in the courthouse. The first point to note is that the Crown and the accused each have the right to challenge the entire jury panel, but "only on the ground of partiality, fraud or wilful misconduct on the part of the sheriff or other officer by whom the panel was returned."[1] However, this rarely occurs.

The actual jury selection process will begin after a jury panel has been accepted. Section 631 of the Code requires that the names of prospective jurors be placed in a box and then drawn randomly, one at a time, by the clerk of the court. This process continues until the number of persons called is, in the opinion of the judge, sufficient to provide for a full jury. Although juries in criminal trials are composed of 12 people, more names are called because some of those who have been called may be excused, challenged, or directed to stand by. If it turns out that there were too few names called to provide a full jury, the clerk will repeat the process of drawing names until such point that the jury has been filled.

Under s. 632 of the Code, the judge has the power to excuse any juror prior to the commencement of the trial if the juror has a personal interest in the matter to be tried, if the juror is related to certain people associated with the trial,[2] if the juror would suffer personal hardship by serving on the jury, or for any other reasonable cause. In addition, the judge has the power under s. 633 to direct a juror to "stand by" for reasons of personal hardship or for any other reasonable cause. If a juror is excused, the juror is free to leave. However, if a juror is directed to stand by, the

---

1. *Criminal Code*, R.S.C. 1985, c. C-46, s. 629.

2. A juror may be excused if related to the judge, prosecutor, accused person, counsel for the accused, or a prospective witness.

juror's name is returned to the bottom of the list of names that comprises the entire panel. What this means is that a juror who is directed to stand by will not be called again unless the entire panel has been exhausted without completing the jury and the juror will only be called on as a last resort.

Challenging a Prospective Juror

The next stage in the jury selection process permits the Crown or the accused to challenge any prospective juror. By challenging a juror, the Crown or accused is effectively questioning the appropriateness or fitness of the person to stand as a juror. There are two types of challenges available to the Crown and accused: the **peremptory challenge** and the **challenge for cause**. In a peremptory challenge, no cause need be shown. The challenging party is permitted to have a juror excused at the party's complete discretion. Challenges for cause can only be made on the grounds that are set out in s. 638 of the Code, and on no other ground. These grounds are summarized as follows:

peremptory challenge
the ability of the Crown and the accused to reject a potential juror without further explanation or reason

challenge for cause
the ability of the Crown and the accused to challenge a prospective juror's impartiality

1. the name of the juror does not appear on the panel;
2. the juror is not indifferent between the Crown and the accused;
3. the juror has been convicted of an offence for which he or she received a sentence of 12 months or more;
4. the juror is an alien;
5. the juror, even with aid, is physically unable to perform properly the duties of a juror; or
6. the juror does not speak the official language of Canada that is the language of the accused.

The grounds upon which a prospective juror can be challenged for cause are quite narrow and in most cases it will be a simple matter to determine whether sufficient grounds exist. The only difficult ground is the second, whether the juror is not indifferent between the Crown and the accused. It is important to understand that while the accused may want a sympathetic jury, he is entitled only to an unbiased one. As a starting point, all jurors are presumed to be indifferent or impartial. Counsel are not permitted to challenge jurors without first demonstrating that there is some reason to doubt the juror's impartiality. Only if the challenging party can satisfy the judge that there is a realistic possibility of partiality will a challenge for cause move to the next stage.

In the past, it was virtually unheard of for counsel to question every prospective juror regarding his or her partiality as between the Crown and the accused. Recently, however, the Supreme Court of Canada has relaxed this rule when it comes to the issue of attitudes about the race of the accused. In Ontario, challenges for cause on the basis of racial bias are permitted by any accused that belongs to a visible minority. This essentially means that in cases where a person accused of a crime is identified as a visible minority, every juror can face questioning on their attitude and views concerning the race of the accused.

A challenge for cause usually involves a hearing to determine whether the challenge is valid. Two jurors will be selected to make a decision regarding the validity of the challenge. If two jurors have not yet been selected, the judge will select any two people from those present in court. These two people are sworn to act as the trier of fact on the challenge. During the challenge, the Crown and the accused will question the prospective juror. The challenge can take the form of a hearing, with further evidence being called and both parties making **submissions**. If the two jurors cannot agree on a decision, two new jurors will be selected to decide on the validity of the challenge.

In addition to having an unlimited number of challenges for cause, the Crown and the accused are provided with a number of challenges that result in the automatic dismissal of a juror, irrespective of cause. These are peremptory challenges and they permit the Crown or accused to dismiss a potential juror without explanation or reason. The number of peremptory challenges that are available depends on the seriousness of the charge before the court. In cases of first-degree murder or high treason, the Crown and the accused are each entitled to 20 peremptory challenges. If the accused is charged with an offence that has a maximum penalty of five years' imprisonment or more, the number of peremptory challenges is 12. For all other offences, the number is 4. If the accused is facing trial for several offences, the number of peremptory challenges is determined by the most serious of the offences. If two or more accused are tried together, each accused receives their full entitlement of peremptory challenges. The Crown, however, is entitled to the same number of peremptory challenges that are available to all of the accused.

> **submission**
> in general, the act of making a presentation or an assertion; can also be used to mean "closing argument"

We have seen that peremptory challenges permit the Crown or the accused to excuse a juror without explanation. A separate issue is how peremptory challenges are used. Is it permissible to use peremptory challenges to select a sympathetic jury, or should prospective jurors be challenged only if there is a real issue concerning the suitability of a person to sit as a juror? The answer depends on whether we are talking about the Crown or the accused. It is clear that an accused may use peremptory challenges for any purpose, including the selection of a jury that is perceived as sympathetic to the accused. The same is not true when we are dealing with the Crown. The Crown is seen as having a greater duty to the administration of justice than the accused. It is not the function of the Crown to secure a conviction at any cost. The duties of the Crown are subject to the *Charter of Rights and Freedoms* and any discretion must be exercised in conformity with the principles and values that are enshrined in the Charter. As a result, the Crown should not use its peremptory challenges to produce a jury that does not appear to be impartial. The Crown should use peremptory challenges only where valid reasons exist. Peremptory challenges by the Crown should not be made on irrational or irrelevant considerations such as race or ethnicity. Similarly, it is not appropriate for the Crown to screen prospective jurors by performing background checks.

The order of challenging jurors is set out in the *Criminal Code*. Section 635 provides that the accused shall be called on to challenge, for cause or peremptorily, the first juror called. The Crown will have the opportunity to challenge the juror if the juror is acceptable to the accused. The parties then proceed in alternating fashion until 12 jurors are selected. If there is more than one accused, then all of the accused will challenge at the same time, one after another. For example, if there are two accused persons, the first accused may challenge the first juror, followed by the second accused, who is then followed by the Crown. The parties will alternate in challenging the next juror with the Crown challenging first, followed by the first accused, who is then followed by the second accused. This process will continue until 12 jurors have been selected. The *Criminal Code* permits the selection of alternate jurors to fill a vacancy in the jury prior to the start of the trial.

Reasons a Juror Might Be Discharged

Occasionally a juror may not be able to continue to act as a result of illness or for some other reason. Under s. 644 of the Code, the judge has the power to discharge a juror who can no longer continue by reason of illness or other reasonable cause. If the trial has not yet commenced, the judge may select another juror from the pool of alternate jurors or, if there are no alternate jurors, repeat the selection process by drawing names from the jury panel. If a juror dies or is discharged after the trial has commenced, the trial will continue with the remaining jurors, provided that a minimum of 10 jurors remain.

The Jury Process

Once a jury has been selected it will become the trier of fact. Its function is to weigh all of the admissible evidence, assess the credibility and reliability of the witnesses, and, finally, to render a verdict. As the trier of law, the judge is responsible for controlling the trial, determining the admissibility of the evidence put forth by the parties, and instructing the jury on the appropriate law.

Excluding the Jury—The Voir Dire

Not all evidence that is put forth at trial is admissible. Evidence may be excluded for any number of reasons. For example, a confession to the police may not be admissible if it was made under physical or emotional threat. However, a jury might have great difficulty in ignoring a confession by the accused that has been determined to be inadmissible. As a result, questions revolving around the admissibility of evidence are resolved in the absence of the jury. The judge will declare a *voir dire* and ask the jury to leave the courtroom when the admissibility of a piece of evidence is questioned. Counsel for each party will make submissions to the judge as to whether the disputed evidence is admissible. If the judge finds that the evidence is not admissible, the jury will return and not hear anything further about the evidence. If the evidence is ruled admissible, the jury will return from the *voir dire* and be presented with the evidence. A *voir dire* is often referred to as "a trial within a trial." Sometimes a *voir dire* is held at the start of a trial and before the taking of any evidence in order to not inconvenience the jury. This also results in a more orderly trial without the stoppages normally associated with a trial that involves a *voir dire*.

Indictable Trials

At trial, the onus or burden is on the Crown to prove each element of the offence beyond a reasonable doubt. The accused will be acquitted if the Crown is not able to discharge this onus. In most cases where an accused is found not guilty, the acquittal results from the inability of the Crown to prove the case, rather than from any affirmative defence put forth by the accused. The accused is under no obligation to testify or to offer any evidence.

The *Criminal Code* requires as a general rule that trials proceed continuously, subject to the court's discretion to adjourn the proceedings.[3] An accused person must be present for the trial unless the court orders and the parties agree to an appearance by closed-circuit television or other similar means.[4] The judge has discretion to excuse an accused for misconduct that interrupts the proceedings to the extent that it would make it unfeasible to continue the proceedings in the presence of the accused.[5] A similar power to exclude the accused exists during a hearing to determine whether the accused is fit to stand trial where the court is satisfied that the accused's continued presence might have an adverse effect on the mental condition of the accused.[6] If the accused absconds during the trial, the court has the choice to either issue an arrest warrant against the accused or continue the trial in the absence of the accused.

The trial judge has a broad discretion to control the trial process. This means that the judge will decide the hours that the court is in session and when the court will recess for breaks and lunch. Normally, trials will begin at 10:00 a.m. and end no later than 5:00 p.m., with two 15-minute recesses and a longer break for lunch. The judge's discretion also extends to such matters as where the Crown, defence counsel, and accused are seated. Counsel usually sits at a counsel desk located near the front of the court. An accused in custody will normally sit in the prisoner's dock. An accused that is not in custody may be permitted to sit beside or near his or her counsel.

The trial judge has the discretion to exclude the public from the court under s. 486 of the Code, although the presumption is that trials will be held in open court. This presumption does not, however, apply to witnesses. If either party requests an exclusionary order, witnesses will be excluded and directed to wait outside the courtroom until they are called to give their evidence. Witnesses are excluded in this manner so that their evidence is not tainted by anything that they may hear in court. The order excluding witnesses normally ends after they have given evidence and they will be allowed to remain in court for the rest of the trial, if they wish. The accused will not be subject to any exclusionary order since the accused has the right

---

3. *Criminal Code* s. 645.

4. *Criminal Code* ss. 650(1), (1.1), and (1.2).

5. *Criminal Code* s. 650(2).

6. Ibid.

to be present during the trial. Also, the accused is under no obligation to testify and is not required to advise the court of his or her decision in this respect in advance. There is normally an exception made to permit the police officer in charge of the investigation to remain in the courtroom and assist the Crown attorney presenting the case.

The Trial Process

The Opening Statement

The Crown presents its case first. Normally the Crown will be provided with the opportunity to make an opening statement to the jury. The opening statement involves explaining the theory of the case to the jury as well as highlighting the evidence that the Crown is expected to call. In most cases, the accused will make an opening statement at the conclusion of the Crown's case rather than immediately following the Crown's opening remarks. However, the trial judge has the discretion to allow the accused to make an opening statement at this time.

The Case for the Crown

The Crown is obliged to prove its case following the opening statement. This is normally accomplished by the calling of all of the Crown's witnesses to give evidence, one after the other, until the Crown has no further evidence to lead.

The Crown is free to call whichever witnesses it pleases. Naturally, the Crown will wish to lead sufficient evidence to secure a conviction. However, the Crown is under no obligation to call any particular witness in any particular order. Neither the judge nor the defence can require the Crown to call a specific witness. As each witness is called, they must take an oath or affirmation to tell the truth before testifying. The attendance of witnesses at trial is usually procured by serving a subpoena on each witness that requires them to attend at court to give evidence at a certain date and time. If a witness does not appear after having been properly served with a subpoena, the judge will normally grant an adjournment and may issue a warrant to apprehend the witness and have them brought to court.

EXAMINING WITNESSES

The process of examining witnesses is the same for all witnesses. First, the Crown will conduct a direct examination, also called an examination-in-chief, by asking the witness non-leading questions. A non-leading question is a question that does not suggest an answer. A question that suggests an answer is a leading question. For example, the question, "You were with the accused at 9:00 p.m., is that correct?" is a leading question. The question itself suggests or implies that the witness was with the accused at the material time. "At what time were you and the accused together?" is a non-leading question on the issue of time. In a non-leading question there is no answer suggested to the witness and the witness is unencumbered by suggestion in testifying before the court. As mentioned, normally it is not permissible for any party to ask its own witness leading questions.

While the onus is on the Crown to prove every element of an offence beyond a reasonable doubt, it is not uncommon for the accused to admit various parts of the Crown's case, thereby eliminating the need for examination of witnesses to establish those parts. This usually happens if a part of the Crown's case is not really in dispute. For example, in a drug case it is necessary for the Crown to prove continuity of possession as the seized substance is delivered to the police station, taken for testing and analysis, returned to the station, and then brought to court. This is clearly a cumbersome and time-consuming process that is often waived by experienced defence counsel if it is not really a live issue. A judge will always appreciate when a concession is made that does not impact on any live issues and has the effect of shortening the trial.

Most, but not all, evidence comes from witnesses. The *Criminal Code*, the *Canada Evidence Act*, and the common law all provide for alternative ways to prove various facts. For example, s. 657.1 of the Code provides that ownership and value of property may be proven by affidavit or solemn declaration of the lawful owner. Another example is found in s. 657.3, which permits the evidence of an expert to be provided by means of a report from the expert.

When the Crown has completed examining each of its witnesses, the accused will have the opportunity to ask questions of each witness. This is referred to as "cross-examination." During cross-examination a witness may be asked leading questions. This is a powerful tool that is used to test and probe the evidence of the witness or to attempt to demonstrate that the witness is not credible. A skillful advocate may be able to elicit concessions from the witness, point out weaknesses in the witness's evidence, and highlight the parts of the evidence that are consistent with or support the position of the defence. If any new matters have been raised during cross-examination, the Crown will be provided with the opportunity to re-examine the witness to clarify those points after the defence has finished. As with direct examination, only non-leading questions are permitted during **re-examination**.

re-examination
a second questioning of a witness that is conducted by the party who called the witness to provide evidence in the proceeding; a re-examination will follow a cross-examination

Normally, the judge will not assume an active role in the trial itself, leaving the questioning of witnesses to the Crown and the accused. On occasion, however, the judge may have some questions for a witness. These questions are usually intended to clarify a witness's evidence rather than to elicit further evidence from the witness. If the judge does have questions, each party will normally be provided with the opportunity to ask follow-up questions to clarify anything that the witness may have said in response to the judge's questions.

directed verdict of acquittal
a motion to the court by the accused for an acquittal immediately following the completion of the Crown's case when there has not been any evidence upon which a reasonable jury, properly instructed, could convict the accused; sometimes referred to as a non-suit

The Case for the Accused

The Crown will close its case after having called all of its witnesses and tendering all of the evidence that it will be relying on. At this point, an accused will have several options. If the accused believes that the Crown has failed to provide any evidence on an essential fact or element of the case, the accused may make a motion to the judge for a **directed verdict of acquittal**. A directed verdict of acquittal, or a non-suit, is a common-law right of the accused to ask that the judge direct the jury to make a finding of not guilty. The test is the same as for a preliminary inquiry: whether there is any evidence upon which a reasonable jury, properly instructed, could convict the accused. The judge is required to deny a request for a directed verdict in which there is admissible evidence that could, if believed, result in a finding of guilt. A directed verdict is therefore not available if the Crown's case is weak, or is not proven beyond a reasonable doubt. It is only available where no evidence was adduced on an essential fact that must be proven in order to secure a conviction. If a motion for a directed verdict is successful, the case will end there with an acquittal and the accused will be free to leave. There is no penalty if the motion is not successful.

If the accused has not made a motion for a directed verdict, or if the motion did not succeed, the accused will have the opportunity to call witnesses and present evidence. However, the accused may elect to call no evidence at all if the accused believes that, although some evidence establishing guilt was put forth by the Crown, there was not enough evidence presented to the court to prove guilt beyond a reasonable doubt. In other words, if the accused believes that the Crown has failed to prove all elements of the charge beyond a reasonable doubt, the accused may call no evidence because he or she anticipates a finding of not guilty based on the perceived weakness of the Crown's case. The risk of calling no evidence is obvious; it is possible that the accused will be found guilty without taking advantage of the opportunity to respond to the Crown's case by putting forth a different version of events or an affirmative defence if the trier of fact disagrees with the accused's assessment of the evidence.

Why then would the accused essentially gamble on the outcome by not calling evidence? There are several reasons. The accused may not have any witnesses to call and the defence strategy is to put the Crown to the burden of proving every element of the offence beyond a reasonable doubt. Sometimes the only witness that is available for the defence is the accused person. If this is the case, the accused might not testify in order to avoid being subjected to cross-examination. This is especially true if the accused has a criminal record, which can be brought to the attention of the court if the accused testifies. Finally, the order of closing arguments is determined by whether the accused has testified or not. If the defence has not called any evidence, the Crown would go first. The opposite is true when the accused leads evidence.

EXAMINING WITNESSES

competent witness
a witness who is lawfully capable of giving evidence; a competent witness may give evidence

compellable witness
a witness who can be lawfully required to give evidence; a compellable witness can be forced to give evidence

The same rules that applied to the Crown also apply to the accused if the accused elects to call evidence. It is entirely within the discretion of the accused as to how the defence will be presented. Every witness will be directly examined by the accused. The Crown will have the opportunity to cross-examine the witnesses in an attempt to discredit their testimony. In some instances there may be a re-examination and the judge may have some additional questions for the witness.

The accused is a **competent witness**, but is not **compellable** by the Crown. This means that the accused may testify if he or she wishes, but cannot be forced by the Crown to testify. The failure of the accused to testify cannot be commented on by the Crown or the judge and no adverse inference can be drawn from the fact that the accused did not testify. The defence will close its case after having completed calling all of the evidence that it relies upon.

Reopening the Case for the Crown

In the usual course of events, the trial will move to the closing argument stage after the defence has completed its case. There is, however, a very limited right for the Crown to reopen its case at this point. It is well established that the Crown is not permitted to "split its case" by leading evidence after the defence has completed its case. Thus, it is only in rare and exceptional circumstances that the Crown will be permitted to reopen its case and lead new evidence. These situations are generally limited to instances where the Crown has discovered new evidence and where the defence contributed to the Crown's failure to lead the evidence earlier, or where the Crown has made a purely technical mistake on a non-controversial matter that really has no bearing on the substantive matters in the case.

The Crown does, however, have a wider right to lead **rebuttal evidence** after the defence has closed its case. Rebuttal evidence is generally permitted in situations where the defence has raised a new issue during the presentation of its case that the Crown could not have reasonably anticipated. If this is the case, the Crown can lead evidence on the new issue but cannot lead any other evidence that could have been tendered earlier that would bolster the Crown's case. Rebuttal evidence is permitted because it does not prejudice the accused in the sense that the accused has had the opportunity to make a full answer and defence to the case presented by the Crown. The issue was raised by the defence and therefore it cannot be seen as surprising the defence after the completion of its case. For example, rebuttal evidence of the accused's whereabouts may be permitted if the accused raised the defence of **alibi** for the first time at trial. In that event, it would not have been possible for the Crown to anticipate the evidence and it would be contrary to the interests of justice to deny the Crown the opportunity to lead evidence that places the accused elsewhere. If the Crown has presented rebuttal evidence, the accused will normally be permitted to lead **surrebuttal evidence**, which essentially gives the accused the opportunity to rebut the rebuttal evidence.

rebuttal evidence
evidence that contradicts or refutes earlier evidence

alibi
generally, evidence of innocence—usually that the accused was somewhere else when the crime was committed; the word "alibi" derives from the Latin term for "elsewhere"

surrebuttal evidence
evidence that contradicts or refutes rebuttal evidence; it is essentially a rebuttal to a rebuttal

Closing Arguments[7]

After the Crown and the accused have completed presenting their cases, the parties are permitted to sum up their cases by making submissions to the judge. For a jury trial, closing arguments are made to the jury. The order of making submissions has already been discussed and is determined by whether or not the accused led any evidence. If not, the Crown goes first. The order of closing arguments is set out in s. 651 of the *Criminal Code*. It is generally considered an advantage to have the last word, especially in a jury trial. The Supreme Court of Canada has held that the order of closing arguments does not offend the rights to fundamental justice and a fair trial as guaranteed by ss. 7 and 11(d) of the *Charter of Rights and Freedoms*.[8] Although the trial judge does not have the power to change the order of closing arguments, there is discretion to permit the accused a limited right of reply following the Crown's closing argument where there has been an irregularity in the closing

---

7. Note that closing arguments are variously referred to as "submissions to the judge," "closing statements," "closing addresses," "closing remarks," and "summing up."

8. *R. v. Rose*, [1998] 3 S.C.R. 262.

argument that jeopardizes the fairness of the trial. This would occur only if the theory of the Crown's case had so dramatically changed that the accused could not be expected to answer the new argument, or where the accused was actually misled as to the theory of the Crown's case.[9]

The purpose of a closing argument is to persuade the trier of fact to find in the party's favour. While a party will obviously try to cast its case in the best possible light, it does not mean that a party can say anything it wishes to say in closing. Primarily, final arguments must be based on the evidence that was presented at trial. A party may emphasize the evidence that supports its position and can attempt to diminish the effects of any negative evidence by drawing other inferences from the evidence or by bringing facts to the attention of the trier of fact that challenge the credibility or trustworthiness of the evidence. For non-jury trials, a party will usually advise the judge on the appropriate law and how it should be applied to the facts of the present case. Inflammatory remarks should be avoided, as should making reference to extraneous matters, which may be prejudicial to a fair trial. Counsel is not permitted to offer their own opinion on the evidence or state their personal views of the case. When making closing remarks, the onus to be impartial and fair is heavier on the Crown than it is on the accused.

The Verdict

Non-Jury Trials

In a non-jury trial the judge will render the verdict after the parties have completed their submissions. The judge might require additional time to consider the evidence and determine the appropriate law. If this is the case, the decision of the judge will be reserved and the case will be adjourned to a later date for the judge's decision.

Jury Trials

If there is a jury, it will receive instructions from the judge on how to perform its duty in reaching a verdict. The process of instructing a jury is commonly referred to as "charging the jury." In charging the jury, the judge will summarize the evidence for the jury. The judge will also go over the closing arguments of the parties and explain the theory of each party's case. Finally, the judge will instruct the jury on the law that applies to the case. The charge to the jury should be fair, even-handed, and dispassionate. Although it is permissible for a judge to offer opinions on questions of fact when charging a jury, it would be an error for the judge to be seen as preferring one party over the other. It might be necessary for the judge to charge the jury on any number of particular issues in the trial that require special instruction, such as the frailties of eyewitness evidence, the law relating to alibi, or how the jury is to deal with the accused's criminal record. The charge should also include procedural instructions on how the jury is expected to proceed through the process of reaching a verdict. Section 650.1 of the Code permits a judge to confer with the Crown and

---

9. Ibid.

the accused regarding what should be explained to the jury and how the jury should be charged in general. The judge will usually canvass the parties for their views on the adequacy of the charge after the jury has been instructed. The jury may be re-charged on any aspect of the original charge that was unclear or confusing.

After the jury has been charged it will be excused to begin deliberations. The jury is sequestered or isolated from any external contact until it has either reached a verdict or is unable to proceed further. The jury may sometimes have questions, and these are sent to the judge. The judge will consider submissions from the parties before answering any questions. If it is determined that the jury requires clarification or further information, it will be brought back into the courtroom to be re-charged.

A jury must be unanimous in reaching a verdict. If a jury is not able to agree on a verdict, the judge will usually call the jury back into court and encourage them to reach a verdict. This is referred to as "exhorting the jury." When exhorting a jury the judge should focus on the process of coming to a verdict rather than offering any suggestion of an appropriate verdict. If a jury is deadlocked and cannot come to a unanimous decision, the judge will have to discharge the jury and order a new trial with a new jury.

Once a verdict has been reached, the jury will send a note telling the judge that the deliberations have been successfully concluded. The foreman of the jury will announce the verdict in open court. If requested, the jury will be polled and each member will announce in court whether they agree with the verdict that was rendered. In most cases, the jury is discharged and the verdict is final, subject only to review by an appellate court. In one unusual case,[10] the verdict of the jury was improperly recorded when the judge misheard the foreman state "not guilty" when the foreman actually stated "guilty." Even though the error was noticed in a matter of minutes, the jury had already been excused. In the end, it was determined that it was not within the power of the judge to change the verdict nor could the jury be recalled without there being a reasonable apprehension of bias. The only options available were to permit the verdict to stand or to declare a **mistrial**. The Supreme Court of Canada did not permit the not guilty verdict to stand because it would have resulted in a miscarriage of justice, and so a mistrial was declared.

mistrial
a trial that has been terminated before reaching its conclusion because of an irregularity

Disclosure of Jury Deliberations

In Canada, unlike in the United States, jurors are required by law to keep the details of their deliberations secret. Section 649 of the Code makes it an offence for any juror, or person providing support to a disabled juror, to disclose any information relating to the proceedings of the jury when it was absent from the courtroom. In other words, it is a crime to disclose any information involving the deliberations of a jury that was not made public in court. An exception is made if there is an investigation or charge of obstructing justice. The purpose of the rule is to protect jurors from fear of recrimination for unpopular verdicts and to create a climate where jurors can conduct their deliberations candidly, knowing that nothing that was said in the jury room will ever be publicly revealed. The secrecy rule only applies to

---

10. *R. v. Burke*, [2002] 2 S.C.R. 857.

matters that are intrinsic to the deliberation process and not to external factors that may have affected the jury.

Irregularities

Sometimes a serious irregularity or problem arises during a trial. Examples include an improper or inflammatory opening statement or closing argument, inadmissible evidence that was improperly put before a jury, widespread bad publicity, or inappropriate contact between a juror and the accused. In some cases, the judge may be able to remedy the problem by granting an adjournment or by instructing the jury to ignore the offending information. Sometimes, however, it may not be possible to undo the damage, and the accused's right to a fair trial will be compromised. If this is the case, the judge has the discretion to end the trial by declaring a mistrial. A mistrial is a remedy of last resort and is normally only declared if there is no other available remedy that would cure the defect. It is possible for a mistrial to be declared at any point in a trial, from the jury selection process right through to sentencing. Usually it is the accused that would seek a mistrial but it is open for the Crown to ask for one. A mistrial can be declared in both jury and non-jury trials, although it is extremely rare for there to be a defect that cannot be rectified where there is no jury. Normally, after a mistrial has been declared, a new trial will be held unless the Crown decides not to proceed with the prosecution.

Summary Conviction Trials

Summary conviction trials are governed by Part XXVII of the *Criminal Code*. As mentioned at the beginning of this chapter, summary conviction trials share many similarities with indictable trials. The most obvious difference is that there is no possibility of a jury trial in a summary conviction matter. As a result, the procedures for jury selection set out in Part XX have no application to summary conviction trials. Otherwise, the trial is conducted very much like an indictable offence trial, with a few notable differences.

A person charged with a summary offence is referred to as a "defendant" in the Code rather than as an "accused." The defendant has no right to elect a mode of trial and will be tried by a "summary conviction court," which in most cases is a provincially appointed judge. Section 800 permits the defendant to appear personally or by counsel or agent. This means that, unlike an accused in an indictable matter, the defendant does not have to be actually present in court for every step in the trial process as long as an agent is appearing on behalf of the defendant. However, the judge can require that the defendant appear personally. In Ontario, it is no longer permissible for a person to represent a defendant in summary conviction matters unless the person is licensed by the Law Society of Upper Canada as either a lawyer or a paralegal.

A person can be charged, tried, and convicted of an indictable offence at any time after the offence was committed. There is no limitation period within which an indictable charge or a hybrid charge must be laid when the Crown elects to proceed by indictment. A summary conviction charge, however, must be laid within six months from when the offence was alleged to have been committed unless the Crown and the defendant both agree to extend the time period. There may be times when the Crown and defendant will agree to an extension of time. For example, if a hybrid charge has been laid outside of the six-month limitation period, it would be in the best interests of the accused to agree to extend the limitation period to permit the Crown to proceed summarily rather than face trial by indictment.

The trial itself will be virtually identical to a trial of an indictable offence without a jury. The prosecution is required to prove the guilt of the defendant beyond a reasonable doubt and the defendant will have the opportunity to make full answer and defence. The process of calling and examining witnesses is the same for the two modes of trial. Each party will be provided with an opportunity to make closing submissions at the end of their case. The summary conviction court has the power to convict the defendant or to dismiss the information, which is the same as an acquittal or a finding of not guilty. The range of sentencing options available to the court is limited by the provisions of s. 787, which sets out a maximum fine of $5,000 or a maximum term of imprisonment of six months' imprisonment, or both, unless otherwise provided by law.

Not all matters that are before a summary conviction court involve the prosecution of a criminal offence. Section 810 of the *Criminal Code* permits a summary conviction court to require a person to enter into a recognizance to be of good behaviour and keep the peace where reasonable grounds exist to believe that the person will cause injury to another person, their family, or their property. This is commonly referred to as a **peace bond**. The process is started by the laying of an Information before a justice. A hearing will be held that is very similar to a trial, with the taking of evidence and the making of submissions. A recognizance may be made for a period of up to 12 months and may contain other conditions that the court considers appropriate. A person who refuses to sign a recognizance order faces 12 months' imprisonment. There are similar provisions[11] that permit the court to require a person to enter into a recognizance if there are reasonable grounds to believe that the person will commit any one of a number of other specified offences.

peace bond
a court order that requires a person to keep the peace and be of good behaviour for a specified period of time; it is not a conviction or a finding of guilt

---

11. *Criminal Code* ss. 810.01, 810.1, and 810.2.

Indictable and Summary Conviction Trials: Differences		
	Indictable Trials	**Summary Trials**
Jury possible	yes	no
Trier of fact	judge or jury	judge
Trier of law	judge	judge
Person charged with an offence	accused	defendant
Accused/defendant permitted to appear by agent	no	yes
Limitation period	none	6 months
Maximum penalty	as specified	generally $5,000 fine or 6 months
Recognizance provisions	none	yes

CHAPTER SUMMARY

A criminal trial is conducted generally in the same manner irrespective of whether the trial is for an indictable or summary offence. In all trials the burden is on the Crown to prove beyond a reasonable doubt that the accused or defendant committed a criminal offence. The Crown will present evidence that it hopes will establish guilt, normally through the sworn testimony of witnesses. The accused or the defendant will be provided with the opportunity to cross-examine each witness to test their evidence. After the Crown has completed its case, the accused will have the opportunity to also present evidence to the court. The accused is under no obligation to testify or to tender any evidence at all. If there is no jury present, the judge is both the trier of law and the trier of fact. The jury, if there is one, will be the trier of fact and has the task of determining guilt or innocence.

KEY TERMS

alibi, 231
book of authorities, 222
challenge for cause, 224
compellable witness, 230
competent witness, 230
cross-examination, 221

directed verdict of acquittal, 229
direct examination, 222
jury panel/jury array, 222
mistrial, 233
peace bond, 235
peremptory challenge, 224

rebuttal evidence, 231
re-examination, 229
submission, 225
subpoena, 221
surrebuttal evidence, 231
trial book, 222

REVIEW QUESTIONS

1. What are the major steps in the jury selection process?

2. What are the differences between a direct examination and a cross-examination?

3. What is a trial book? What purpose does it serve?

4. What is the difference between a competent witness and a compellable witness?

5. What is a mistrial? In what type of trial are mistrials most likely to occur?

EXERCISES

1. Yulia Nemovskaya is representing Devin Holden who is charged with theft and possession under $5,000. The Crown has alleged that Devin stole a laptop computer from a local office supply store. Devin has denied taking the computer and told Yulia he got it from a friend. Yulia asked Devin to tell his friend to attend court on the trial date to be a defence witness. Devin's friend did not show up for the trial as he had promised.

   What should Yulia do? Is there anything that she should have done differently in this case? Explain your answers.

2. Dwayne is charged under s. 362 of the *Criminal Code* with false pretence under $5,000 in relation to a cheque that he used to purchase clothing from an upscale clothing store that was subsequently dishonoured by Dwayne's bank. The Crown called two witnesses, the clerk that served Dwayne and the cashier that accepted Dwayne's cheque. The defence called only one witness. Dwayne testified in his defence that he did not in fact pay for the clothing by cheque but instead had used his debit card. After Dwayne completed giving evidence, the Crown sought to lead rebuttal evidence by attempting to enter the dishonoured cheque into evidence.

   Do you think that the Crown will be successful in having this evidence entered? Why or why not? Would you have handled this matter differently if you were acting for Dwayne in these circumstances?

3. Raj is charged with a hybrid offence and has asked his lawyer to explain the trial process to him. What would you tell Raj?

Sentencing

LEARNING OUTCOMES

After completing this chapter, you should be able to:

- Understand the principles of sentencing and discuss the sentencing guidelines set out in the *Criminal Code*.

- Discuss the differences between aggravating and mitigating circumstances and how these will impact on the sentencing process.

- Define the circumstances where a sentencing court will consider the recommendations set out in a pre-sentence report.

- Define the circumstances where a sentencing court will consider a victim impact statement.

- Discuss the sentencing process and how a sentencing court determines an appropriate sentence.

- Define the various sentencing options that are available under the *Criminal Code*.

- Understand the rules relating to parole and the different types of parole that are available to offenders who are sentenced to a period of incarceration.

- Discuss the process of obtaining a record suspension for persons who have been convicted of a criminal offence.

Introduction

Up to this point we have focused mainly on the determination of guilt or innocence. If the accused is found not guilty by a judge or jury, she is free to go as she pleases (unless of course she is facing other charges or is under the supervision of the court for a prior conviction). In the event that the accused is convicted of an offence, the trial will shift to the next phase, which is to determine the appropriate sentence to impose on the convicted person. It should be noted from the outset that not all criminal charges require a complete trial to determine whether the accused is guilty or not guilty of the charged offence or offences. The vast majority of charges are resolved through plea negotiations and/or a plea of guilty by the accused. Sentencing is dealt with in Part XXIII of the *Criminal Code*.

Principles of Sentencing

There has been much discussion and debate about the purpose and principles of sentencing. Understanding why people are punished for committing crimes is vital to being an effective advocate during the sentencing phase of a trial. As a starting point, the stated purpose and principles of sentencing are set out in s. 718 of the *Criminal Code*, which provides as follows:

> 718. The fundamental purpose of sentencing is to contribute, along with crime prevention initiatives, to respect for the law and the maintenance of a just, peaceful and safe society by imposing sanctions that have one or more of the following objectives:
>   (a) to denounce unlawful conduct;
>   (b) to deter the offender and other persons from committing offences;
>   (c) to separate offenders from society, where necessary;
>   (d) to assist in rehabilitating offenders;
>   (e) to provide reparations for harm done to victims or to the community; and
>   (f) to promote a sense of responsibility in offenders, and acknowledgment of the harm done to victims and to the community.

In most cases, the court has a number of options when sentencing the offender. The court will look to the basic principles for guidance in determining the appropriate sentence. These basic principles are briefly discussed below and reference will be made to the appropriate principle when discussing the various sentencing options open to the court.

Denunciation

denunciation
a principle of sentencing that focuses on denouncing or condemning criminal behaviour

The root word of **denunciation** is denounce. This underscores the purpose of denunciation, which is to denounce or condemn the offender's behaviour. Under this view, any sentence imposed must be sufficient to demonstrate society's condemnation of those who commit criminal acts. The idea is that people must be punished because there is a need to denounce bad behaviour.

Many critics of the justice system have argued that denunciation has no place in a modern society and that the only valid rationale for punishment is deterrence or rehabilitation.

Deterrence

The purpose of **deterrence** is to deter or prevent certain types of conduct. There are two types of deterrence: specific and general.

deterrence
a principle of sentencing that focuses on deterring or discouraging criminal behaviour

Specific deterrence focuses on the offender, and its object is to impose a sentence that is sufficient to discourage the offender from reoffending. This is why first offenders often receive lighter sentences than repeat offenders. Repeat offenders have not yet learned to not reoffend, and a harsher sentence is justified to discourage further transgressions.

General deterrence is about the message the sentence sends out to other members of society. The focus here is on preventing others from engaging in wrongful conduct by demonstrating that such behaviour will be punished. The rationale behind this principle is that people will not engage in wrongful conduct if they are aware that they will be punished if apprehended.

There may exist, in some cases, a conflict between general and specific deterrence when sentencing an offender. For example, by simply going through the entire criminal process, from apprehension and arrest to trial, a first offender may be deterred from committing further crimes, yet the gravity of the offence may require additional punishment in order to send a message to other members of society.

Social Protection

Section 718(c) recognizes that there may be a need in some instances to separate offenders from society. The purpose of this provision is to protect society from offenders who pose a danger to others or where there is a risk that they will reoffend. This principle applies to the most serious offences or worst offenders where incarceration is seen as a last, but necessary option.

Rehabilitation

The focus of the principle of rehabilitation is to treat, rather than to punish, the offender. The courts are much more likely to rely on this principle when sentencing a youthful offender or when addressing any underlying issues that may have contributed to the commission of the offence, such as a lack of education, mental disorder, drug addiction, alcoholism, or adverse socio-economic conditions. The theory is that by addressing and remedying the underlying causes of deviant conduct, offenders will be far less likely to reoffend.

Reparations

The 1988 Daubney Report has had a significant effect on sentencing in criminal law. The Report recommended an evaluation and expansion of programs that focus on both the offender and the victim at all stages, including sentencing, of the criminal

reparations
a principle of sentencing that focuses on repairing the harm done by the offender to the victim or to society as a whole

process. With respect to sentencing, the Report recommended **reparation** of harm to both the victim and community. The Report resulted in an amendment to the *Criminal Code* that incorporates the objectives in s. 718.

Reparations are more commonly referred to as restitution, and the focus is on the victim of the crime rather than on the offender. The purpose is to compensate the victim or the greater community for any harm that was suffered in the commission of an offence.

Self-Responsibility

Another recommendation of the Daubney Report is that sentencing should promote a sense of responsibility in offenders for their actions and an acknowledgment of the harm done to victims and their community. This reflects the fact that the first step in rehabilitation is often the offender's self-awareness of the harm that he or she caused to others.

Other Considerations

The *Criminal Code* contains other provisions that expressly deal with the principles of sentencing. Section 718.1 sets out the following as a fundamental principle of sentencing:

> 718.1 A sentence must be proportionate to the gravity of the offence and the degree of responsibility of the offender.

What this means is that a sentence must reflect the seriousness of the offence and the moral blameworthiness of the offender. It has been often said that the most severe sentences are reserved for the worst offence and worst offender. The focus should be on the behaviour of the accused rather than the consequences of his or her actions. A sentence should not be unduly harsh because of the tragic consequences of the event. For example, a person who has a momentary lapse of judgment while operating a motor vehicle may be guilty of an offence, but the offender should not be overly penalized if their brief inattention results in the death of an innocent pedestrian.

In addition, ss. 718.2(b) to (e) of the Code provide a series of principles that serve as sentencing guidelines:

> 718.2 …
> (b) a sentence should be similar to sentences imposed on similar offenders for similar offences committed in similar circumstances;
> (c) where consecutive sentences are imposed, the combined sentence should not be unduly long or harsh;
> (d) an offender should not be deprived of liberty, if less restrictive sanctions may be appropriate in the circumstances; and
> (e) all available sanctions other than imprisonment that are reasonable in the circumstances should be considered for all offenders, with particular attention to the circumstances of aboriginal offenders.

Aggravating and Mitigating Factors in Sentencing

Aggravating and **mitigating factors** play important roles in the sentencing of an offender. Aggravating factors are circumstances that increase the seriousness of the offender's actions and tend to result in a harsher sentence than when such circumstances are not present. Mitigating factors have the opposite effect. They are factors that tend to lessen the seriousness of the offender's actions and may favourably affect the offender during sentencing.

The *Criminal Code* expressly requires that both aggravating and mitigating factors be taken into account by the court when considering an appropriate sentence. Section 718.2 provides:

aggravating factors
circumstances surrounding the commission of an offence that increase the penalty associated with the offence

mitigating factors
circumstances surrounding the commission of an offence that reduce the penalty associated with the offence

718.2 A court that imposes a sentence shall also take into consideration the following principles:

(a) a sentence should be increased or reduced to account for any relevant aggravating or mitigating circumstances relating to the offence or offender, and, without limiting the generality of the foregoing,

(i) evidence that the offence was motivated by bias, prejudice or hate based on race, national or ethnic origin, language, colour, religion, sex, age, mental or physical disability, sexual orientation or any other similar factor,

(ii) evidence that the offender, in committing the offence, abused the offender's spouse or common-law partner,

(ii.1) evidence that the offender, in committing the offence, abused a person under the age of eighteen years,

(iii) evidence that the offender, in committing the offence, abused a position of trust or authority in relation to the victim,

(iii.1) evidence that the offence had a significant impact on the victim, considering their age and other personal circumstances, including their health and financial situation,

(iv) evidence that the offence was committed for the benefit of, at the direction of or in association with a criminal organization, or

(v) evidence that the offence was a terrorism offence

shall be deemed to be aggravating circumstances.

The *Criminal Code* does not set out a corresponding list of mitigating factors for consideration by a sentencing court. However, the following are generally viewed as mitigating factors that tend to reduce the severity of a sentence:

- the age of the offender, especially a youthful first offender;
- any mental or physical disability of the offender;
- cooperation with the police;
- remorse, especially as evidenced by an early plea of guilty;
- whether the offender had been provoked; and
- any particular hardship that may have caused or contributed to the reason that the offender committed the crime.

The Sentencing Process

The sentencing process begins after an accused is found guilty of an offence either by a plea of guilty or after a trial when the offender is convicted. Section 726.1 of the *Criminal Code* provides that in determining the appropriate sentence, the court shall consider any relevant information. This part of the chapter looks at the information that the court will consider when sentencing the accused. It is important to stress that while the court may access information from many sources, it is ultimately the function of the sentencing judge to impose the appropriate sentence.

As discussed previously in this text, a great number of criminal cases are resolved after the Crown and the defence agree on an appropriate sentence. This process is called plea bargaining. Although the sentencing judge normally accepts the joint recommendations of the parties in passing sentence, the judge is free to impose whatever sentence is deemed appropriate. Of course, the Crown and the defence do not always reach an agreement on an appropriate sentence. In those instances, the accused may still plead guilty in the hope that the guilty plea will result in a lesser sentence. If the accused does plead guilty, s. 606(1.1) of the Code sets out that the plea will only be accepted if the court is satisfied that the accused is making the plea voluntarily and understands that the plea is an admission of the essential elements of the offence, the nature and consequences of the plea, and that the court is not bound by any agreement made between the accused and the prosecutor. After the accused has pleaded, the Crown will read into the record a summary of the essential facts of the case. If the accused admits the essential facts and they are capable in law of supporting a conviction, the judge will enter a finding of guilt if the requirements of s. 606(1.1) have been met. After the finding of guilt, the sentencing process is the same regardless of whether the accused was convicted following a trial or the accused pleaded guilty.

Pre-Sentence Report

The offender may be sentenced immediately by the court or may have sentencing adjourned for a number of reasons. Sentencing is commonly adjourned if the judge requires a pre-sentence report. The power to request a pre-sentence report is found in s. 721 of the Code. A pre-sentence report is prepared by a probation officer and will usually contain information on the offender's age, maturity, character, behaviour, attitude, willingness to make amends, previous findings of guilt, and previous sentences. The report can also contain any other information that was requested by the sentencing judge. The probation officer will often make a recommendation as to an appropriate sentence or types of sentences for the offender. The sentencing judge will receive a copy of the report before sentencing the offender and use it to help determine the appropriate sentence for the offender.

Victim Impact Statement

Another type of report that may be used at the sentencing hearing is a victim impact statement. The victim of a crime or, if that person is not available to provide a statement, a relative of the victim may provide a written statement that outlines the effect the offence has had on them. Section 722.2 requires the court as soon as practical after a finding of guilt to inquire of the Crown or victim of the offence or their representative as to whether the victim has been advised of the opportunity to provide a victim impact statement. The provisions dealing with the procedure and presentation of victim impact statements are set out in s. 722 of the *Criminal Code*. The court is obligated to consider any victim impact statement that has been filed that is in writing and was prepared in accordance with procedures established by a designated victim impact program. In addition, s. 722(3) permits a court to "consider any other evidence concerning any victim of the offence for the purpose of determining the sentence to be imposed on the offender," whether or not a victim impact statement was prepared and filed.

Sentencing Submissions

Once the sentencing process has commenced, the Crown and the offender are provided with the right to make submissions with respect to any facts relevant to the appropriateness of the sentence. As discussed earlier, there may be a joint submission made as to sentence. If the Crown and offender are not joining in the making of submissions, each will make submissions to the sentencing judge. The process is more or less adversarial, with each party putting their best case forward. The offender will point out all of the factors supporting a lesser sentence, including any mitigating circumstances. On the other hand, the Crown will offer submissions that support a harsher sentence and make note of any aggravating circumstances that were present in the commission of the offence. The Crown and offender may, if they wish, call evidence at the sentencing hearing if they feel that it will help their cause. The normal rules of evidence are relaxed for sentencing and the court will generally accept hearsay evidence. The court also has the power to require the production of evidence if it will assist the judge in determining the appropriate sentence.

One of the factors that will influence a court in imposing a sentence is whether the offender has any previous convictions. In some cases, the Crown may be entitled to seek a higher range of sentence if the accused has been convicted of a similar offence in the past. This is true, for example, where the Crown seeks a longer driving prohibition for alcohol-related motor vehicle offences under s. 259 of the *Criminal Code*. If this is the case, s. 727 requires that the Crown notify the accused of its intention to seek an increased sentence before the accused enters a plea. In other cases, the Crown may wish to bring the offender's prior convictions to the attention of the court as a matter that is relevant to the determination of an appropriate sentence. Repeat offenders are generally dealt with more harshly by the courts because they have demonstrated that the previous sentence had little effect in rehabilitating or deterring them. Where the Crown is alleging a record of previous offences, the offender will normally be asked to admit her record for the purpose of sentencing. The offender will admit the previous convictions unless there has been some mistake. If this is the case, the Crown will be required to prove the particulars of the previous convictions if it intends to rely on them. Section 667 of the Code provides that a certificate signed by the person who made the conviction, the clerk of the court in which the conviction was made, or a fingerprint examiner is proof that the offender is the person referred to in the certificate and that the person was convicted and sentenced as stated.

Types of Sentences

In this part we will examine the various sentencing options that can be imposed on an offender. The sentencing options can all be found in the *Criminal Code*. They may be imposed individually or some of them may be combined. The various options will be dealt with in order of severity, from least to most severe.

Absolute or Conditional Discharge

The major feature of either type of discharge is that there is no conviction registered against the offender. There is a finding of guilt made, but if the offender is granted a discharge when sentenced, they will not have a criminal record. The purpose of this sentencing option is to provide certain offenders with a "second chance" for a single mistake or transgression that would normally result in a criminal record. However, this is not entirely a free pass and the fact that the offender has been granted a discharge will be recorded.

The authority to impose either an absolute or conditional discharge is found in s. 730(1) of the *Criminal Code*. These sentences are not available where an offender is a corporation or has been convicted of an offence for which a minimum penalty is prescribed by the Code or where a maximum penalty of 14 years or life is prescribed. Before deciding to grant a discharge, a court must be satisfied that it would be in the best interests of the offender and not contrary to the public interest. A discharge is in the best interests of an offender where the offender does not require specific deterrence or rehabilitation, except to the extent that may be required in a probation order. In most instances, the offender who is granted a discharge will be a person of good character without previous convictions.

Depending on the circumstances of the offence, there may be several considerations to the second part of the test, which is whether it is contrary to the public interest to grant a discharge. One element that the courts will invariably look at is the need for general deterrence. The imposition of a discharge on an offender will not deter others as much as other types of sentences. Accordingly, a court will generally consider granting an absolute or conditional discharge to a first time offender where the offence is relatively minor.

An **absolute discharge** is effective immediately and the offender will have no further obligation to deal with the criminal justice system in relation to the discharged offence. Courts will use this sentence only in cases where there is no need for any specific deterrence or rehabilitation.

A **conditional discharge** requires the offender to abide by certain conditions made in a probation order under s. 731(2) of the Code for a specified period of time. For instance, he may be required to keep the peace and be of good behaviour, or

absolute discharge
a sentence where there has been a finding of guilt made against the offender, but where no conviction is registered

conditional discharge
a sentence similar to an absolute discharge except that it takes effect only after the offender has satisfied specified court-imposed conditions

may be required to abstain from alcohol. The purpose of imposing conditions is to keep the offender under the supervision of the court. In this way, the offender is more apt to learn his lesson, and any specific concerns relating to the rehabilitation of the offender can be addressed through the use of appropriate conditions. If the offender abides by the conditions for the probationary period, the discharge will come into effect and he will have no conviction registered. If the offender fails to obey the conditions, he may be sentenced for the original offence and, in addition, be charged with the further offence of failure to comply.

Fines, Restitution, and Victim Surcharge

Fines

Section 734 of the Code provides that the court can sentence an offender, other than a corporation, to pay a fine. This sentencing option may be imposed with any other sentence that the court has the power to make. A fine is only available where there is no minimum sentence of imprisonment prescribed for the offence for which the offender was convicted. In addition, unless there is a minimum fine, the court may only impose a fine after it is satisfied that the offender has the ability to pay or that he or she is eligible for the fine option program established under s. 736. The fine option program permits the offender to discharge a fine by performing certain work over a period of two years. These programs have not been established in every jurisdiction. Section 735 permits a court to fine a corporation.

Under s. 734.1, any order for a fine must specify the amount of the fine, the manner in which it is to be paid, the time within which it must be made, and any other order respecting the payment of the fine that the court deems appropriate. Section 734(4) has a formula for determining the term of imprisonment that is imposed in default of payment of a fine. In most cases, however, at the time the fine is imposed, the court will provide an alternate jail sentence in the event that the fine is not paid. For example, the court may order a fine of $500 to be paid within 90 days and, in the alternative, 30 days in jail. If the offender requires more time to pay the fine, the court may grant an extension of the time period for making payment. In addition to incarceration, both the federal and provincial levels of government may enforce a fine in the same manner as a civil judgment. Both levels can also refuse to issue or renew, or may suspend, any defaulting offender's driver's licence or permit until the fine has been paid.

Section 787 states that unless otherwise provided by law, everyone who is convicted of a summary conviction offence is liable to a maximum fine of $5,000. In the case of a corporation, s. 735 permits a maximum fine of $100,000. There is no maximum fine for an indictable offence for either a natural person or a corporation. Fines are typically imposed on natural persons only for fairly minor criminal offences and for provincial offences. Fines are used more often as a sentencing option in the case of corporations.

Restitution

The *Criminal Code* provisions that deal with **restitution** are set out in ss. 738 to 741.2. The concept of restitution essentially requires an offender to pay money directly to a victim or to help cover the victim's losses and damage to property caused by the crime. The purpose of restitution is to provide the victim with some financial compensation for the crime committed against him or his property and to promote a sense of responsibility in the offender and an acknowledgment of the harm she has caused. Restitution is also available to members of the victim's family to compensate them for certain expenses in cases of bodily harm or threat of bodily harm.

Restitution is available in addition to any other sentence that has been imposed on an offender, including a discharge. A restitution order is enforceable against the person ordered to make the payment in the same manner as a civil judgment. It does not, however, take the place of a civil order and no civil remedy is affected by an order of restitution.

It should be noted that making restitution voluntarily to a victim of a crime might be considered to be a mitigating factor by the sentencing court. In property offence cases, many experienced lawyers advise their clients to make restitution in the hope that they will get a less severe sentence than would otherwise be given in the circumstances.

Victim Surcharge

Section 737 of the *Criminal Code* requires that everyone who has been convicted of a criminal offence or received a discharge shall pay, in addition to any other punishment imposed on the offender, a victim surcharge. The money is paid to the provincial and territorial governments to help develop and provide programs, services, and assistance to victims of crime. The amount of the victim surcharge is 15 percent of any fine that is imposed on an offender or, if no fine is imposed, $50 for a summary conviction offence or $100 for an indictable offence. The amount of the victim surcharge can be increased if the court considers it appropriate in the circumstances and is satisfied that the offender can pay the higher amount. Conversely, the victim surcharge may be waived if the offender can establish that undue hardship would result to the offender or the offender's family from payment of the victim surcharge.

A victim surcharge may also be payable for infractions of various provincial offences. For instance, in Ontario, the provincial government adds a victim fine surcharge to every non-parking fine imposed under the *Provincial Offences Act*. The amount is usually 20 percent of the imposed fine, but fines over $1,000 carry a surcharge of 25 percent.

Suspended Sentence and Probation

Section 731(1)(a) of the *Criminal Code* permits the court to suspend the passing of a sentence and release the offender on conditions contained in a probation order. This sentencing option is only available for offences that do not carry a minimum sentence. (Form 46, Probation Order is reproduced in the Appendix to this text.)

An offender who is placed on **probation** with a **suspended sentence** will remain out of custody but is released under the supervision of a probation officer. The probation order will set out a number of conditions that the offender must follow. These conditions will require the offender to do certain things or to refrain from certain behaviour. Section 732.1(2) sets out three compulsory conditions of any probation order: the offender must keep the peace and be of good behaviour; appear before the court as required by the court; and notify the court or probation officer of any change in name, address, or employment. Section 732.1(3) lists additional conditions that may be included in a probation order. These include reporting to a probation officer at a particular time and place, remaining within the jurisdiction of the court, abstaining from the consumption of alcohol and non-prescription drugs, abstaining from owning or possessing a firearm or weapon, providing for the support or care of dependants, and performing up to 240 hours of community service over a period not exceeding 18 months. In addition, if the offender consents, the court may order that the offender participate actively in a treatment program approved by the province or use an alcohol ignition interlock device when operating a motor vehicle.

The court also has a broad discretion to impose any "such other reasonable conditions … for protecting society and for facilitating the offender's successful reintegration into the community." These might include conditions that require the offender to reside at a specific place, reside with a specific person, maintain a curfew, refrain from contacting specified individuals, and/or to seek and maintain employment.

It is not the sentence itself that is suspended, but the passing of the sentence. This means that if the offender breaches any of the conditions of the probation order, she can be brought back to court and sentenced for the offence for which she was originally convicted. Further, if the offender does breach any of the terms of the order, she can be charged with the further criminal offence of breach of probation. A suspended sentence, unlike a discharge, will result in a criminal record even if the offender has met all of the probation terms.

Conditional Sentence of Imprisonment

For most offences where the court imposes a sentence of less than two years' imprisonment, s. 742.1 of the *Criminal Code* provides that the court may order, subject to certain conditions, that the sentence may be served in the community instead of in jail. Unlike a suspended sentence, where the court suspends the passing of a sentence, a conditional sentence of imprisonment actually imposes a sentence of imprisonment. The offender, if granted a conditional sentence of imprisonment, is permitted to serve the sentence out of custody. Before imposing this sentence, the court must be satisfied that serving the sentence in the community will not endanger the safety of the community and would be consistent with the fundamental purpose and principles of sentencing as set out in ss. 718 to 718.2 of the Code. This sentencing option is not available if the offender has been convicted of certain serious criminal offences, regardless of the length of time that the offender is jailed. These offences include any terrorism offence, any criminal organization offence that

probation
a sentence that permits an offender to live in the community but under supervision and subject to various conditions

suspended sentence
a sentence where the sentencing court suspends or holds in abeyance the passing of a sentence on an offender

carries a maximum sentence of 10 years or more, any offence punishable by a minimum term of imprisonment, or a serious personal injury offence as defined by s. 752 of the Code.

Section 742.3 sets out the compulsory and additional conditions of conditional sentences of imprisonment. These conditions are similar to those in s. 732.1 that apply to orders of probation. Of note is the power of the court to impose other reasonable conditions for securing the good conduct of the offender and for preventing the offender from committing further offences. The Supreme Court of Canada has dealt with conditional sentences of imprisonment in several cases, and in *R. v. Proulx* the Supreme Court made it clear that a conditional sentence of imprisonment is intended to address both punitive and rehabilitative objectives. Accordingly, the Supreme Court said that these sentences should normally contain punitive conditions that curtail an offender's liberty. In most cases, the offender will be placed on house arrest or on a strict curfew. This means that a conditional sentence of imprisonment can still provide a significant degree of denunciation and act as a deterrent while meeting the goals of rehabilitation, reparation, and promotion of a sense of responsibility. If the offender breaches any of the conditions, the court has the power to change any conditions, if appropriate, or require the offender to serve part or all of the remaining sentence in jail.

Imprisonment

Imprisonment is the most serious sentence available in Canada and it is used for the more serious offences or for repeat offenders. The *Criminal Code* provides that an offender should not be imprisoned if less restrictive sanctions may be appropriate and, further, that all other sanctions that are reasonable in the circumstances should be considered by the court before sentencing the offender.[1] Unless otherwise provided, the maximum period of imprisonment for a summary conviction offence is six months. For indictable offences, reference must be made to the provisions that create the offence because the maximum period of imprisonment varies according to the offence. For the most serious offences, such as murder, the sentence can be as high as imprisonment for life. While all offences set out a maximum penalty, some offences prescribe a mandatory minimum period of incarceration.

Where Will a Sentence Be Served?

Sentences of less than two years' imprisonment are served in a provincial correctional facility, while longer sentences are served in a federal penitentiary. In Ontario, provincial correctional facilities are the responsibility of the provincial government through the Ministry of Community Safety and Correctional Services. Federal penitentiaries are the responsibility of the federal government through the Correctional Service of Canada. The Correctional Service of Canada is headquartered in Ottawa, but its administration is coordinated regionally through five regional headquarters. In some cases, inmates are held in a remand or detention centre. These institutions

---

1. *Criminal Code*, R.S.C. 1985, c. C-46, s. 718.2.

are the responsibility of the provincial governments and primarily house persons awaiting trial or those who have recently been convicted and are awaiting sentencing or transfer to a longer-term facility. If an offender has been given a very short sentence, it may sometimes be served in this type of facility. Usually, however, after a person has been convicted, he or she will be transferred to a federal penitentiary or to a provincial correctional facility depending upon the length of the sentence.

All offenders who have been sentenced to imprisonment are assessed to determine where they will serve their sentence. In general, there are three levels of security: minimum, medium, and maximum. A minimum-security facility may bear very little resemblance to higher security institutions. There may be no walls or fences surrounding the institution and inmates will generally have more freedom and privileges within the facility. At the other end of the spectrum, in a maximum-security institution, inmates are allowed very limited movement within the institution, and are basically kept under lock and key for most of the day.

An offender who is serving a sentence in a provincial correctional institution is generally better off than an inmate of a federal penitentiary. Generally, the conditions in a provincial institution are better than the conditions in a federal penitentiary. In addition, those serving time in provincial institutions are likely to be closer to home, and in most instances this means that the offender is also closer to his or her family and support network while serving his or her sentence. Maintaining these connections can be very important for the offender's rehabilitation and reintegration back into the community at the end of the period of incarceration.

Credit for Time Served

A person who has served time in a detention centre while waiting for trial is usually provided with credit for time served when sentencing takes place. The period of pretrial custody is commonly referred to as "**dead time**." The normal practice of the court is to provide a "two-for-one credit" for time spent in pretrial custody, which means that the sentence that would ordinarily be imposed would be reduced by twice the amount of time that the offender spent in custody awaiting trial. For example, an offender who has spent a year in pretrial custody will have a 24-month credit applied to his or her sentence. In that case, a five-year sentence would be reduced to a sentence of three years.

dead time
credit for the period of time that an offender spends in pretrial custody

Serving a Sentence Intermittently

If the offender is sentenced to 90 days or less, the court may permit him or her to serve an **intermittent sentence** under s. 732 of the *Criminal Code*. This means that offenders are permitted to leave the institution at various times for specific purposes, such as attending school or work. In most cases, they will be released during the week so that they can work or attend school, but must report back to the institution on weekends. They will be given credit toward their sentence for each day spent in custody. No credit is given for time spent out of custody. This type of sentence must be accompanied by an order of probation that the offender must comply with when not confined. As with any order of probation, if the offender breaches any of the conditions he may be charged with the offence of breach of probation.

intermittent sentence
a jail sentence that is served in small blocks of time instead of all at once

How Multiple Sentences Are Served

It is not uncommon for offenders to be convicted of more than one offence and be sentenced to a period of incarceration for multiple offences. The sentencing court must decide between imposing a **consecutive** or a **concurrent sentence**. Consecutive sentences are separate sentences. The total length of the time that will be served in custody is the sum of the sentences. For example, if an offender has received consecutive sentences of three and six months, the total period of incarceration will be nine months. Concurrent sentences are two or more sentences that run concurrently, or at the same time. The period of time that will be spent in custody is the length of the longest sentence. If the three- and six-month sentences were to be served concurrently, the total time served would be six months.

consecutive sentence
a sentence in which the time that is actually spent in custody is the sum of all sentences, and the sentences are served one after another

concurrent sentence
a sentence in which the time that is actually spent in custody is determined by the longest sentence, and the sentences are served at the same time

Long-Term Offender Designation

A person who has been convicted of a serious personal injury offence or of a specified serious sexual offence may be designated as a long-term offender (LTO) and, in addition to any original sentence, may be subject to long-term supervision for up to 10 years. The period of long-term supervision begins after all original sentences have been served.

Under s. 753.1(1) of the Code, the court will find an offender to be an LTO where it is satisfied that:

a. it would be appropriate to impose a sentence of imprisonment of two years or more for the offence for which the offender was convicted;

b. there is a substantial risk that the offender will reoffend; and

c. there is a reasonable possibility that the risk the offender presents in the community can eventually be controlled.

An LTO will be placed in the community after having served all sentences under the supervision of the Correctional Service of Canada. An offender who does not abide by the conditions of a long-term supervision order is guilty of an indictable offence under s. 753.3 of the Code and may be imprisoned for a term of up to 10 years.

Indeterminate Sentence for Dangerous Offenders

A sentence of imprisonment will set out the specific amount of time that the offender must serve. The offender will be released at some point, usually before the expiry of the sentence on conditional release or after having completed the entire sentence. It is possible, however, for the Crown to seek a dangerous offender designation for offenders who have been convicted of violent offences. A person who is declared a dangerous offender will be incarcerated with no fixed date for release. This means that the offender may very well spend the rest of his or her life in jail.

The dangerous offender provision is contained in s. 753 of the *Criminal Code*. The Crown may make an application under this provision when the offender is convicted of a serious personal injury offence as defined in s. 752. These offences are essentially violent or potentially violent indictable offences that carry a maximum sentence of at least 10 years and various specified sexual assault offences. The application is started by applying for a 60-day psychiatric assessment. The Crown will rely on the psychiatric assessment in determining whether to proceed with the application. The application requires the written approval of the Attorney General. Before making a dangerous offender designation, the court must be satisfied that a person constitutes a threat to the life, safety, or physical or mental well-being of other persons or, in the case of the specified sexual assault offences, has shown a failure to control his or her sexual impulses with the resulting likelihood of causing injury to other persons.

A person who has been declared a dangerous offender will receive a sentence of detention in a penitentiary for an indeterminate period with no fixed day for release. The Parole Board of Canada will review the case after the dangerous offender has served seven years, and every two years after that. Most dangerous offenders are never released from prison. As of April 2011 there were 458 individuals who were living with the dangerous offender designation. Of these, only 17 were paroled and 441 remained incarcerated.[2]

Parole

At some point, most offenders will be released from prison. For some, their sentence will have expired, but most will be released on **parole** prior to completing their sentence. The *Corrections and Conditional Release Act* (CCRA) authorizes early release. The purpose of releasing inmates early is set out in s. 100 of the CCRA:

parole
the release of an offender from custody before the sentence has been fully completed, subject to various conditions

> 100. The purpose of conditional release is to contribute to the maintenance of a just, peaceful and safe society by means of decisions on the timing and conditions of release that will best facilitate the rehabilitation of offenders and their reintegration into the community as law-abiding citizens.

The CCRA requires that offenders be considered for some form of conditional release prior to completion of their sentence. This means that offenders are eligible for parole, but not that parole will necessarily be granted. Even if parole is granted, the remainder of the sentence is served in the community, subject to specified conditions and under the supervision of the Parole Board of Canada. The function of the Parole Board of Canada is to assess the risk that an offender poses when he or she becomes eligible for parole. The paramount consideration is the protection of society. The criteria for granting parole are set out in s. 102:

> 102. The Board or a provincial parole board may grant parole to an offender if, in its opinion,
> (a) the offender will not, by reoffending, present an undue risk to society before the expiration according to law of the sentence the offender is serving; and

2. See Public Safety Canada, "Frequently Asked Questions About the Release of Offenders" at http://www.publicsafety.gc.ca/prg/cor/tls/faq-eng.aspx.

(b) the release of the offender will contribute to the protection of society by facilitating the reintegration of the offender into society as a law-abiding citizen.

The various types of parole are outlined below.

Temporary Absence

The CCRA provides for various types of conditional release. The first is temporary absence. Temporary absence is granted for a specific purpose, such as attending a specified function, receiving medical attention or therapy, spending time with family, performing community service, and so forth. Temporary absence may be escorted or unescorted. Generally, offenders may apply for escorted temporary absence at any time while serving their sentence. Eligibility for unescorted temporary absence is more restrictive. Maximum-security offenders are not eligible for unescorted temporary absence. The eligibility of other offenders varies depending on the length of the original sentence.

Day Parole

The second form of conditional release under the CCRA is day parole. This form of release permits the offender to leave the institution for a specified period of time each day. Normally, the offender is required to return to prison or to a halfway house for the night. Offenders serving sentences of three years to life are eligible for day parole six months before becoming eligible for full parole. Those serving life sentences can apply for day parole three years before becoming eligible for full parole. Offenders serving from two to three years are eligible after completing six months of their sentence. Any offenders serving less than two years become eligible after serving one-sixth of their sentence.

Full Parole

The next form of conditional release is full parole, where the offender is permitted to spend the remainder of his or her sentence in the community under the supervision of a parole officer. Most offenders are eligible for full parole after having served one-third of their sentence or 7 years, whichever occurs first. Eligibility for full parole for offenders serving sentences for second-degree murder will be set by the sentencing court at between 10 and 25 years. Offenders convicted of first-degree murder are not eligible for full parole until they have served 25 years of their sentence.

Statutory Release

Finally, the CCRA provides that most penitentiary inmates will be released after having served two-thirds of their sentences if they have not yet been granted full parole. This form of release is called statutory release and does not require a decision from the parole board. An offender may be denied statutory release if the Correctional Service of Canada has recommended that an offender, while on statutory release, is likely to commit an offence causing death or serious bodily harm, a sexual offence involving a child, or a serious drug-related offence. As with other forms of conditional release, offenders on statutory release are subject to various conditions and supervision by a probation officer. The offender may be required to complete the balance of the original sentence if any conditions are breached or the offender poses an undue risk to the public. Any offender serving a life sentence or an indeterminate sentence is not eligible for statutory release.

Record Suspensions

A **record suspension**, formerly known as a pardon, is not a sentence but serves to separate from other criminal records the criminal record of offenders who have completed their sentence without having committed any further offences. In this respect, the purpose of a record suspension is similar to that of a discharge—to provide an offender with a "second chance" by removing convictions from the database of the Canadian Police Information Centre (CPIC). The CPIC, which is administered by the RCMP, is responsible for the delivery and sharing of national police, law enforcement, criminal justice, and public safety information. After a person has obtained a record suspension, the *Criminal Records Act* (CRA) removes information about convictions from the CPIC and prohibits the disclosure of this information without the consent of the Minister of Public Safety Canada.

The main benefit of a record suspension is that federal and provincial human rights legislation prevents discrimination in employment based on a conviction where a record suspension has been ordered.[3]

The *Canadian Human Rights Act*, which applies to federal agencies, Crown corporations, the Canadian Forces, and any business under federal authority, makes discrimination on the basis of a conviction for which a record suspension has been ordered a prohibited ground of discrimination. Section 3(1) provides as follows:

> 3(1) For all purposes of this Act, the prohibited grounds of discrimination are race, national or ethnic origin, colour, religion, age, sex, sexual orientation, marital status, family status, disability and conviction for an offence for which a pardon has been granted or in respect of which a record suspension has been ordered.

Provincial legislation serves a similar purpose and applies to both public and private employers within the province. For example, s. 5(1) of the Ontario *Human Rights Code* provides:

> 5(1) Every person has a right to equal treatment with respect to employment without discrimination because of race, ancestry, place of origin, colour, ethnic

record suspension
an order granted by the Parole Board of Canada that permits a qualifying offender to have a criminal record separated and kept apart from other criminal records; formerly called a pardon

---

3. It should be noted that discrimination for an offence for which a record suspension has been ordered is permissible in very limited circumstances. Generally, this occurs where the offence for which the record suspension was ordered is relevant to the job requirements. For example, a bank may be permitted to refuse to hire a person who has obtained a record suspension for theft or fraud.

origin, citizenship, creed, sex, sexual orientation, gender identity, gender expression, age, record of offences,[4] marital status, family status or disability.

A record suspension does not restore the status of an offender to that of a person who has never been convicted of a criminal offence. The following are the specific limitations of a record suspension:

- A record suspension does not change the fact that a person has been convicted of an offence. A criminal record is not erased; it is kept separate and apart from other criminal records.
- A record suspension may not guarantee entry to other countries.
- The CRA does not apply to provincial authorities. This means that provincial court and police services are not required to keep records of convictions separate and apart from other criminal records.
- A person who has obtained a record suspension for certain sexual offences will be identified in the CPIC computer system and will be required to release his or her record to an employer if the person wants to work with children or other vulnerable groups.
- Prohibition orders, such as a driving or firearm prohibition order, imposed under the *Criminal Code* will survive a record suspension.

A record suspension is not available for certain offences. A person is not eligible to apply for a record suspension if the person has been convicted of an offence referred to in Schedule 1 of the CRA or of three or more indictable offences each with a prison sentence of two years or more.[5] Schedule 1 of the CRA contains various sexual offences involving a child. Under s. 4(3) of the CRA a person who has been convicted of an offence referred to in Schedule 1 may apply for a record suspension if the person satisfies the Parole Board of Canada that:

(a) the person was not in a position of trust or authority towards the victim of the offence and the victim was not in a relationship of dependency with him or her;

(b) the person did not use, threaten to use or attempt to use violence, intimidation or coercion in relation to the victim; and

(c) the person was less than five years older than the victim.

A person who has been convicted as an adult of an offence under a federal statute such as the *Criminal Code* can apply to the Parole Board of Canada for a record suspension after they have completed their sentence(s) and a prescribed period of time has elapsed. Persons convicted under the *Young Offenders Act* or the *Youth Criminal Justice Act* generally do not need to apply for a record suspension because

---

4. "Record of offences" is defined in s. 10(1) in part as "a conviction for … an offence in respect of which a pardon has been granted."

5. *Criminal Records Act*, R.S.C. 1985, c. C-47, s. 4(2).

those records will be destroyed or archived after the expiry of prescribed time periods. Similarly, a person convicted of a criminal offence who received a discharge need not apply for a record suspension. An absolute discharge is removed from the CPIC after one year, and in the case of a conditional discharge, after three years.

The waiting period for a record suspension starts only after a sentence has been completed. A sentence is completed when:

- all fines, surcharges, costs, restitution, and compensation orders have been paid;
- a person has served all sentences of imprisonment, including parole and statutory release; and
- a person has satisfied all probation orders.

The waiting period depends on the offence for which a record suspension is sought. The waiting period is:

- 5 years for a summary conviction offence, and
- 10 years for an indictable offence.

Under the *National Defence Act*, the waiting period is 10 years for a service offence where a fine of more than $5,000 was imposed or where a person was detained or imprisoned for more than six months. For all other service offences under the *National Defence Act*, the waiting period is 5 years.

The Parole Board of Canada may order a record suspension if the Board is satisfied that the applicant has been of good character and was not convicted of a criminal or other federal offence during the prescribed waiting period. In addition, the applicant has the onus to demonstrate that a record suspension would provide a measurable benefit to the applicant and sustain his or her rehabilitation in society as a law-abiding citizen and would not bring the administration of justice into disrepute.[6] In cases where the Board refuses to order a record suspension, the applicant may reapply after one year.

The Parole Board of Canada has the authority to revoke a record suspension if the person is later convicted of a summary conviction offence, is found to be no longer of good character, or if a false/deceptive statement was made or relevant information was withheld in the application for the record suspension.[7] A record suspension that has been ordered to a person will cease to have effect if the person is subsequently convicted of an indictable offence or a hybrid offence, or in circumstances where the Board is convinced by new information that the person was not eligible for a record suspension at the time it was ordered.[8]

---

6. *Criminal Records Act* s. 4(1).

7. *Criminal Records Act* s. 7.

8. *Criminal Records Act* s. 7.2.

The process for applying for a record suspension is relatively straightforward and involves the following nine steps:

Step 1	Obtain applicant's criminal record from the RCMP in Ottawa
Step 2	Obtain Court Information Form from every convicting court
Step 3	Obtain Military Conduct Sheet (for members of Canadian Forces only)
Step 4	Obtain local police records check
Step 5	Obtain proof of citizenship or immigration documents
Step 6	Obtain copy of proof of identity
Step 7	Complete Record Suspension Application Form
Step 8	Complete Measurable Benefits/Sustained Rehabilitation Form
Step 9	Complete Record Suspension Application Checklist

The Parole Board of Canada's website provides complete instructions on the process of applying for a record suspension and details each of the nine steps. In addition, the website contains the various forms used to apply for a record suspension and sets out the current prescribed fees. Particularly helpful is the downloadable *Record Suspension Guide*, which contains step-by-step instructions on applying for a record suspension and all application forms. In all cases, reference should be made to the Parole Board of Canada's website for current instructions, forms, and fees.

CHAPTER SUMMARY

Sentencing is part art and part science. The *Criminal Code* sets out a number of sentencing options in varying degrees of severity. The art in sentencing is in matching the appropriate sentence to the offender. When sentencing an offender, the court will focus on the principles of deterrence and denunciation, assess the need to protect the public from the offender, and consider the impact that the offence had on the victim. In addition, the court will assess and consider opportunities to rehabilitate the offender, promote a sense of responsibility in the offender, and encourage the offender to acknowledge the harm caused.

KEY TERMS

absolute discharge, 246
aggravating factors, 243
concurrent sentence, 252
conditional discharge, 246
consecutive sentence, 252
dead time, 251

denunciation, 240
deterrence, 241
intermittent sentence, 251
mitigating factors, 243
parole, 253
probation, 249

record suspension, 255
reparations, 242
restitution, 248
suspended sentence, 249

REVIEW QUESTIONS

1. What is the difference between general deterrence and specific deterrence?

2. What is meant by the principle that a sentence must be proportionate to the gravity of the offence and the degree of responsibility of the offender?

3. What are the similarities and differences between a pre-sentence report and a victim impact statement?

4. What is the difference between a discharge and a record suspension?

5. What are the differences between probation and a conditional sentence of imprisonment?

6. What role does the sentencing judge perform in determining the location of incarceration?

7. What is the test for obtaining a record suspension?

EXERCISES

1. Tasha Spinks, a 19-year-old single mother, was charged with selling marijuana to high school students near a local school that she attended before dropping out three years ago. When she was arrested, Tasha readily admitted selling the drugs and even provided the name of her supplier when asked by the police. Tasha told police that she sold the drugs so that she could flee an abusive relationship and provide care for her young child. She has no prior criminal record. Tasha pleaded guilty on her second court appearance before a trial date had been set. What are the circumstances in Tasha's case that require a harsh sentence? Are there any circumstances that might result in a reduced sentence?

2. Neil Jermaine is a lawyer who has acted on behalf of Brandon King on several criminal matters in the past. Brandon has been arrested for assaulting his common-law spouse. Brandon was not released on bail because of his criminal record and history of abuse against the complainant. Brandon spent two weeks in pretrial detention. On Brandon's set date, Neil was instructed by Brandon that Brandon wanted to plead guilty to the assault charge. Although Brandon denied the allegations, he told Neil, "I want to plead guilty so that I can get out of jail now."

   What do you think of Brandon's strategy?

3. Ashraf Natawami was convicted of three counts of assault causing bodily harm. He was sentenced to 12 months concurrent on each of the counts. Ashraf spent a total of 6 months in pretrial detention. Assuming a "two-for-one" credit for dead time, how long would you expect Ashraf to be incarcerated? What would your answer be if the sentences were to run consecutively?

4. Parole is a "get-out-of-jail-free card" for criminals. Do you agree or disagree with this statement? Why?

5. Sami Sharif has been charged with three counts of break and enter. While on bail for those charges, Sami was charged with attempted robbery, breach of bail conditions, resisting arrest, and assaulting a police officer. Sami has admitted to his lawyer, Gwen Moodie, that he committed the offences and wants to make a deal. What should Gwen do in this situation?

Appeals

21

LEARNING OUTCOMES

After completing this chapter, you should be able to:

- Understand the rights of appeal for indictable offences and summary conviction offences.

- Understand the grounds of appeal for indictable offences and summary conviction offences.

- Discuss the differences between appeals by the accused and appeals by the Crown.

- Understand the limitations on appeals by the accused.

- Discuss the differences between appeals from conviction and appeals from sentence.

- Define the procedure for indictable offence appeals.

- Define the procedure for summary offence appeals.

Introduction

Criminal case appeals are entirely creatures of statute. What this means is that neither the Crown nor the accused person has a right to launch an appeal whenever they are unhappy with the determination of guilt, innocence, or the sentence imposed by the trial judge. Rather, the aggrieved party must look to see whether the *Criminal Code* provides for a right to appeal to a higher court in their particular situation.

In some situations there may be an absolute right to launch an appeal, while in other cases the appellant may be required to obtain "leave" or permission from the appeal court to bring the appeal. At some point, all cases reach a point where no further appeal is possible. For example, there is no possibility of appealing a decision of the Supreme Court of Canada because there is no higher level of court.

We have already discussed the distinction that the *Criminal Code* makes between summary conviction offences and indictable offences. This distinction continues when dealing with the question of appeals. We will examine rights of appeal for the Crown and the accused and outline the procedure for making an appeal for both indictable offences and summary conviction offences.

Indictable Offences

Appeals by the Accused Person

Part XXI of the *Criminal Code* governs appeals for indictable offences. At the outset, it should be noted that appeals follow the procedure of trial, not the offence appealed from. What this means is that if a trial proceeded by way of indictment but the accused was convicted of a lesser and included summary conviction offence, the appeal would be treated as an appeal from an indictable offence.

Rights of Appeal

The *Criminal Code* makes a distinction between the right to appeal and the basis or **grounds for appeal** on which an appeal will succeed. The rights of appeal provided to the accused are quite broad. Section 675(1)(a) of the *Criminal Code* sets out that appeals from conviction can be made on the basis of a question of law, a question of fact, a question of mixed law and fact, or on any other ground that "appears to the court of appeal to be a sufficient ground of appeal." However, the test for determining whether an appeal will be successful is far more stringent. This makes sense since it would not be apparent from the outset to the appellate court whether the appeal has any merit. The court of appeal would need to hear the appeal first in order to determine whether or not it had merit.

> **grounds for appeal**
> basis upon which an appeal can be commenced and be successful

Grounds of Appeal

Section 686(1)(a) sets out the circumstance when an appeal may succeed. The court of appeal may allow an appeal against conviction or a finding of not criminally responsible on account of mental disorder where it is of the opinion that

(i) the verdict should be set aside on the ground that it is unreasonable or cannot be supported by the evidence,

(ii) the judgment of the trial court should be set aside on the ground of a wrong decision on a question of law, or

(iii) on any ground there was a miscarriage of justice;

UNREASONABLE VERDICT

The first ground upon which an appeal can be granted is if the appellant demonstrates a verdict that is unreasonable or cannot be supported by the evidence. The test for determining whether a verdict is unreasonable or cannot be supported by the evidence is set out by the Supreme Court of Canada in the case of *R. v. Yebes*:[1]

> [T]he test is "whether the verdict is one that a properly instructed jury acting judicially, could reasonably have rendered."[2]

Although the use of such phrases as "a properly instructed jury acting judicially" and "could reasonably have rendered" suggests a test of an objective nature, the Supreme Court has made it clear that the test has both a **subjective** and an **objective** component. The objective part of the test requires the appeal court to look at what verdict a *properly instructed* and *reasonable* jury could judicially arrive at. The focus is on a fictitious reasonable jury, not the actual trial jury. In fact, it would be difficult in most cases to conduct a subjective review of a jury's decision in Canada because jurors are not permitted to speak or communicate about their deliberations. In most cases, the appeal court would not have any information concerning the deliberations of a jury and whether it in fact had acted reasonably in the circumstances of any particular case.

The test is not, however, entirely objective. The Supreme Court has made it clear that in assessing the **reasonableness** of a jury's verdict it is necessary for the appeal court to weigh the evidence that was before the jury. In *R. v. Yebes* the Supreme Court stated:

> While the Court of Appeal must not merely substitute its view for that of the jury, in order to apply the test the Court must re-examine and to some extent reweigh and consider the effect of the evidence.[3]

This is the subjective part of the test.

While the appeal court must consider the evidence that was presented to the jury, it is not enough for the appeal court to conclude that it would have come to a different verdict from the jury and to substitute its view for that of the jury. This is the case because the appeal court is at a disadvantage when it comes to assessing the evidence that was presented at trial. The jury has had the advantage of observing the demeanour and manner of the witnesses at trial. The appeal court mostly relies upon a transcript of the evidence that was presented at trial and normally does not hear any evidence at all. Many cases are decided on the basis of credibility. It is not

objective test
a legal test that focuses on the actions and beliefs of a hypothetical reasonable person; includes a consideration of reasonableness

subjective test
a legal test that focuses on the actions and beliefs of the person in issue; does not include a consideration of reasonableness

reasonableness
a standard of review that permits an appellate court to substitute its decision for the decision of a lower court only when the decision of the lower court is unreasonable

---

1. [1987] 2 S.C.R. 168.

2. Quoting from a previous decision of the Supreme Court of Canada in *Corbett v. The Queen*, [1975] 2 S.C.R. 275.

3. *Supra* footnote 1, at para. 25.

unusual to have one witness testify as to a certain version of the facts, while another offers a completely different story. Witnesses are not always truthful and their ability to observe or to recall events might be impaired. Two people who saw the same event from different vantage points can offer contrasting evidence. Trials occur months or even years after the events in question took place. Clearly the passage of time and a witness's propensity to fixate on a particular version of events will affect testimony in many cases. Without question, a judge or a jury observing evidence during a trial is in a much better position to make sense of it than an appeal court reviewing a transcript of the trial.

standard of review
the manner in which an appellate court will evaluate the decision of a lower court

What then is the **standard of review** when the appeal court is dealing with the question of the sufficiency of evidence? The answer to this question depends largely upon whether the appeal court is reviewing the decision of a jury or the decision of a judge. While the *Yebes* case deals with a jury verdict, the reality is that most indictable offences are tried by a judge sitting alone without a jury. Appeal courts are much more reluctant to disturb the findings of a jury than those made by a judge sitting alone. Judges will usually provide reasons for their judgment, while jurors are prohibited by law from offering any information on the process or rationale that led to their decision. Accordingly, it is much easier for an appeal court to determine whether a judge had acted unreasonably in coming to a conclusion. The appeal court has no such benefit when it comes to jury verdicts and the threshold for intervention by an appellate court is set higher. The simple fact of the matter is that it is not possible for an appeal court to determine how any properly charged jury reached a verdict.

In *R. v. Biniaris*,[4] the Supreme Court of Canada dealt with the standards for reviewing the reasonableness of decisions of both judges and juries. This case illustrates how appellate courts have traditionally struggled when reviewing the reasonableness of jury verdicts. There are many instances where the reviewing court may have come to a different conclusion from the jury, but cannot conclude that the verdict was unreasonable. However, where appeal courts are left with a "lurking doubt" or "feeling of unease" with the correctness of a jury verdict, that doubt may call for deeper or special scrutiny of the verdict. In those cases, the appeal court will examine whether the jury had acted in a non-judicial manner in coming to a decision. Acting judicially has been traditionally defined as meaning "acting dispassionately, applying the law and adjudicating on the basis of the record and nothing else." The Supreme Court, however, has extended the meaning of "acting judicially" in this context to include "arriving at a conclusion that does not conflict with the bulk of judicial experience." In other words, the expertise and experience of the court of appeal provides a type of filter that helps to identify unreasonable jury verdicts.

This does not mean that an appellate judge is free to substitute her view for that of the jury. Rather, it calls on the appeal court to draw on a collection of judicial experiences. In doing this, the appeal court must identify as specifically as possible what features of the case support the conclusion that a verdict is unreasonable. A good way to come to terms with this approach is to understand and appreciate that

4. 2000 SCC 15, [2000] 1 S.C.R. 381.

judges are very good at their jobs: appeal courts do nothing but hear appeals and appeal court judges have had the benefit of reviewing thousands of cases. Over time, a number of areas of concern have emerged for judges when performing reviews of the reasonableness of jury verdicts. For example, appellate courts have historically taken a hard look at appeals where identification of the accused is at issue. Judges understand the frailties of identification evidence, especially when an accused is being identified in court months or sometimes years after the event took place. Accordingly, a court of appeal would be justified in interfering with a jury's finding of guilt based on obviously flawed identification evidence.

It is easier for an appeal court to review a judge's decision than a jury's verdict, especially where reasons have been provided. In reviewing a judge's decision, the reviewing court

> may be able to identify a flaw in the evaluation of the evidence, or in the analysis, that will serve to explain the unreasonable conclusion reached, and justify the reversal.[5]

In other words, the appeal court can properly review how the trial judge evaluated or analyzed the evidence in determining the reasonableness of a decision. The significance of this is that it appears that it is now open for a court of appeal to conclude that a verdict is unreasonable if there is an error in the reasons provided by the trial judge. The Honourable Mr. Justice Fish for the majority of the Supreme Court of Canada in *R. v. Beaudry*[6] wrote:

> No one should stand convicted on the strength of manifestly bad reasons—reasons that are illogical on their face, or contrary to the evidence—on the ground that another judge ... could *but might not necessarily* have reached the same conclusion for *other reasons*.[7]

Therefore, even a decision of a judge that is supportable for other reasons may be set aside if it is based on either illogical reasons or reasons that are contrary to the evidence at trial.

ERROR OF LAW

The second ground contained in s. 686(1)(a) on which the judgment of a trial court can be set aside is on a wrong decision on a question of law. An **error of law** is any decision made by the trier of law that is based on either an erroneous interpretation of law or an erroneous application of law. For example, an error of law would occur if the trial judge provided flawed instructions to a jury. The standard of review is **correctness**. This means that the court of appeal is free to substitute its opinion for that of the trial judge. After all, the court of appeal is in as good a position as—and often a better position than—the trial judge to determine questions of law.

error of law
an error in the interpretation or application of law; an error of law is understood by contrasting it with an error of fact, which is an error in the resolution of the facts in issue

correctness
a standard of review that permits an appellate court to substitute its decision for the decision of a lower court when, in its opinion, the decision of the lower court is incorrect or wrong

---

5. Ibid., at para. 37.

6. 2007 SCC 5, [2007] 1 S.C.R. 190.

7. Ibid., at para. 97.

MISCARRIAGE OF JUSTICE

Finally, the court of appeal has the power to allow an appeal on any ground where there was a miscarriage of justice. This provision applies to those situations where there has been no error of law or unreasonable verdict yet it is necessary to allow an appeal in the interests of justice. The line between an error of law and a miscarriage of justice is not always clear. For example, if a trial judge improperly instructs a jury, there has been an error of law. However, if the trial judge is unaware of a problem and does not address it in her instructions to the jury, she has probably not committed an error, but a miscarriage of justice may have nonetheless occurred. This was the case in *R. v. Cameron*[8] where there was improper contact with a juror during deliberations that was discovered after the verdict. There was no way for this to be categorized as an error of law because the situation became known only after the trial. On the facts of the case it was also not possible for the accused to meet the stricter test for an unreasonable verdict. However, the Ontario Court of Appeal allowed the appeal on the basis that a miscarriage of justice had occurred.

Remedies

If an appeal by the accused is successful, the court of appeal may either enter a verdict of not guilty or order a new trial. In most cases, a new trial will be ordered. Only if there is no evidence on which a reasonably instructed jury could convict will the court of appeal enter an acquittal. This is consistent with the purpose of appellate courts, which is to review for errors and not be the trier of fact.

Appeal to the Supreme Court of Canada

It is possible to appeal indictable offences from a court of appeal to the Supreme Court of Canada. The grounds on which appeals to the Supreme Court of Canada are made are narrower than the grounds for appealing to the court of appeal. Even narrower are the circumstances under which the Supreme Court of Canada will permit appeals. These grounds are set out in ss. 691 to 695 of the Code. Basically, appeals are permitted only on a question of law. Further, appeals are generally only allowed when there is a dissenting opinion in the provincial court of appeal on a question of law or when the Court grants **leave to appeal** on a question of law. There is also an appeal available to accused persons that arises when the accused was acquitted at trial but had the acquittal replaced with a conviction by the court of appeal.

leave to appeal
where permission to appeal is a prerequisite to hearing the appeal; the purpose is to establish a threshold that must be met before an appeal can be heard by an appellate court

Limitations on Appeals by Accused Persons

We have already seen that in order for an appeal to succeed, an accused person must be able to meet the stringent requirements of s. 686(1)(a). This is only the first hurdle facing the accused. There are several additional provisions in s. 686(1) that the Crown can rely on when responding to an appeal.

---

8. (1991), 2 O.R. (3d) 633, 64 C.C.C. (3d) 96 (C.A.).

CURATIVE PROVISIONS

First, on the basis of the wording of s. 686(1)(ii), it appears that all an appellant must do to succeed is demonstrate to the court of appeal that the trial court committed an error in law. However, this is not necessarily the case, because the court of appeal has an overriding power to refuse an appeal in some situations where there has been a wrong decision on a question of law. The so-called curative provision of s. 686(1)(b)(iii) provides the court of appeal with the power to dismiss an appeal where there has been a wrong decision that is based on law if the court "is of the opinion that no substantial wrong or miscarriage of justice has occurred." In other words, even if the accused is able to demonstrate that there has been an error of law, an appeal may still be refused if the court of appeal is of the view that there has been no substantial wrong or miscarriage of justice. The reason behind this provision is simple: not all errors of law are the same. Some errors are serious and may substantially contribute to the making of a wrong decision, while others might be of a minor nature and have no effect on the outcome of a case. The curative provision requires that for an appeal based on a question of law to succeed, it must first be established that there is a reasonable possibility that the verdict would have been different had the error not been made.[9] In other words, the appeal will only succeed if the accused can demonstrate a causal connection between the error of law and the decision appealed from.

There are two situations in which the Crown can establish that there was no substantial wrong or miscarriage of justice:

1. Where the error is harmless. In this case the error would not have had any impact on the trial or caused prejudice to the accused.

2. Where the evidence against the accused is so overwhelming that even if an appeal succeeded and a new trial was ordered, the result would be the same. In other words, even though the error itself may not have been minor, it did not affect the result because of the overwhelming evidence against the accused.

OTHER PROVISIONS

The other provisions that permit the court of appeal to refuse otherwise meritorious appeals are set out elsewhere in s. 686(1)(b). Section 686(1)(b)(ii) confirms the power of the court to dismiss an appeal where the accused has failed to meet one of the required grounds. However, an otherwise valid appeal may also be dismissed if the appellant, while improperly convicted on one count in an Indictment, was properly convicted on another count.[10] Further, where the appeal is based on a procedural irregularity, the court of appeal may dismiss the appeal if the appellant suffered no prejudice.[11] This is similar to the curative provision that applies to errors of law, except that it extends to procedural irregularities. A procedural irregularity

---

9. *R. v. Khan*, 2001 SCC 86, [2001] 3 S.C.R. 823.

10. *Criminal Code*, R.S.C. 1985, c. C-46, s. 686(1)(b)(i).

11. *Criminal Code* s. 686(1)(b)(iv).

is a technical defect in the trial process, such as an improperly worded Indictment. Basically, this provision permits the court of appeal to dismiss those appeals that are based on technicalities if there is no prejudice suffered by the accused.

Sentence Appeals

There may be cases where an accused person wishes to appeal the sentence that was imposed by the trial court. The accused can choose to appeal the sentence alone or appeal both the conviction and sentence. Section 675(1)(b) permits the accused to appeal against the sentence passed by the trial court. However, this provision requires that leave must be obtained from the court of appeal or a judge of the court of appeal for all sentence appeals unless the sentence is one that is fixed by law. Under s. 687 a court of appeal may either vary the sentence within the limits prescribed by law or dismiss the appeal.

Appeals by the Crown

Grounds of Appeal

Crown appeals are dealt with under s. 676 of the Code. The Crown has a much more limited right of appeal than does the accused. Under s. 676(1)(a) the Crown can only appeal a verdict of acquittal or a verdict of not criminally responsible on account of mental disorder on any ground that involves a question of law alone. Unlike the accused, the Crown does not have the right to appeal from an unreasonable verdict or one that cannot be supported by the evidence. In other words, the Crown cannot appeal unreasonable acquittals. Section 676(1)(a) provides as follows:

> 676(1) The Attorney General or counsel instructed by him for the purpose may appeal to the court of appeal
> (a) against a judgment or verdict of acquittal or a verdict of not criminally responsible on account of mental disorder of a trial court in proceedings by indictment on any ground of appeal that involves a question of law alone;

Error of Law

The phrase "question of law alone" is different from the wording used in s. 686(1)(a) that refers to a "question of law." The Supreme Court of Canada has indicated that the two phrases have the same meaning and that the word "alone" is used to emphasize that there is no other basis for Crown appeals from acquittals. It is therefore important to understand the meaning of "a question of law" in order to appreciate the limited extent of the Crown's right of appeal. There are some things that are obviously questions of law. These include the interpretation or application of statutes, case law, and legal standards. Further, Charter and evidentiary issues are also easily categorized as questions of law. However, the Supreme Court of Canada in *R. v. Morin*[12] found that it is possible for an error of law to occur in assessing facts as they apply to the law. This can occur in three situations:

---

12. [1992] 3 S.C.R. 286.

1. where the trial judge has erred as to the legal effect of undisputed or found facts rather than the inferences to be drawn from such facts;

2. where the trial judge misdirects himself or herself with respect to the relevant evidence, provided that such misdirection is based on a misapprehension of some legal principle; or

3. where the reasons of the trial judge demonstrate a failure to consider all of the evidence in its totality.

Remedies

After the appeal has been heard, the court of appeal may either dismiss or allow the appeal. Section 686(4) provides that if a Crown appeal under s. 676(1)(a) is successful the court of appeal shall set aside the verdict. One option for the court is to order a new trial for the accused. In addition, the court of appeal has the power to enter a verdict of guilty with respect to the offence of which the accused should have been found guilty but for the error of law. In that event, the court of appeal may either pass an appropriate sentence on the accused or remit the matter back to the trial court for sentencing. It is important to note, however, that the power to enter a verdict of guilty as opposed to ordering a new trial is not available if the trial court was composed of a judge and jury. In other words, the court of appeal cannot substitute a finding of guilt in cases where an accused person was acquitted by a jury. In those cases, the only remedy that is available is to remit the matter back for a new trial.

Not all Crown appeals will be from an acquittal. For example, there will be situations where a trial judge quashes a defective Indictment or stays the proceedings. Sections 676(1)(b) and (c) permit Crown appeals in those situations.

Sentence Appeals

The Crown may be content with the decision or verdict of the court below, but may be unhappy with the sentence that was imposed. Section 676(1)(d) allows the Crown to appeal against the sentence that was passed by a trial court. However, as with sentence appeals by an accused, leave must be obtained from the court of appeal or a judge of the court of appeal for all sentence appeals unless the sentence is one that is fixed by law. Section 687 permits the court of appeal to either vary the sentence within the limits prescribed by law or dismiss the appeal.

Procedure

Section 482 of the *Criminal Code* provides the court of appeal in every province and territory with the power to make rules setting out the procedure for appeals from indictable offences. The rules vary accordingly for each jurisdiction, but are readily available on the Internet. The rules share many similarities and this section will focus on the Ontario Court of Appeal *Criminal Appeal Rules*.[13]

---

13. S.I./93-169.

Notice of Appeal

A person who wishes to launch an appeal must first complete a notice of appeal in either Form A or Form B. Form A: Notice of Appeal for Inmate Appeal and Form B: Notice of Appeal or Application for Leave to Appeal can be found in the Appendix. Form A is used if an inmate is representing themselves and Form B is used for all other appeals. The various forms used for appeals are part of the Ontario Court of Appeal *Criminal Appeal Rules* and so are available on the Internet along with the Rules. The notice of appeal has space for background information, such as the place of conviction, name of the judge, details of the conviction, and sentence imposed. The appellant is required to list the grounds for appeal in the appropriate place on the form. The notice of appeal must be served within 30 days of sentencing or, in the case of a Crown appeal, 30 days from acquittal. The Rules provide that service is effected "by delivering to the office of the Registrar or by mailing to the Registrar by registered mail three copies of the notice of appeal, and, in addition, in an appeal by the Attorney General, by personal service on the person in respect of whose acquittal or sentence the appeal is brought, or as may be directed by a judge."

Release from Custody Pending Appeal

In the event that the accused is serving a jail sentence, it is possible to apply for a release from custody pending appeal. The appellant is required to file an affidavit in support of the application. Rule 32 sets out the required contents of the appellant's affidavit. The Crown has the opportunity to file a responding affidavit if necessary. Each party has the right to conduct cross-examinations upon the affidavits filed by the opposing party. In the event that the appellant is released from custody, an order must be formally entered at the court and taken to a justice of the peace at the place of detention to secure the release of the appellant. Any proposed sureties must also attend at the place of custody before the appellant is released.

If bail pending appeal is granted, the appellant is usually released on a number of strict conditions. These conditions are imposed to ensure that the appellant does not pose a risk to others and that the appellant will return to custody if the appeal is not successful. One usual condition is that the appellant surrender into custody at the institution from which he or she was released, or such other institution as may be specified in the order, by 6:00 p.m. on the day prior to the hearing of the appeal or such other day as is specified in the order. If the appellant fails to surrender in this manner, the appeal is deemed to have been abandoned and will not be heard.

Transcript

After the notice of appeal has been filed, a transcript must be ordered by the appellant from the court reporter who recorded the proceedings in the trial court. In order to ensure that an order for the transcript has been placed in a timely manner, the Rules require that a copy of the court reporter's certificate confirming that an order for the transcript has been placed is to be filed with the notice of appeal. A court reporter's certificate is not required if the appeal is funded by Legal Aid Ontario. In those cases, the appellant is provided with additional time to permit Legal Aid Ontario to assess the merits of the appeal and to authorize the appeal. Rules 8(8) to 8(11) set out the required contents of the transcript. The court reporter shall notify the parties and the registrar when the transcript has been prepared. Upon payment from the appellant, the court reporter will forward the transcript to the registrar.

The appellant has 14 days following the filing of the notice of appeal to requisition the delivery of various documents from the trial court to the registrar of the court of appeal. These documents from the trial court include copies of the conviction, order, Indictment or Information, pre-sentence report, criminal record, and other documents relating to the appeal. The requisition must be filed with the registrar within 15 days from the date that the notice of appeal was filed.

Appeal Book

After the transcript has been prepared, the appellant generally has 90 days to perfect the appeal. To accomplish this, the appellant must serve on the opposing party one copy of the **appeal book**, one copy of the transcript, and one copy of the appellant's factum, and immediately thereafter must file proof of service of these together with copies of the appeal book and factum. The number of appeal books and factums that are to be filed depends on the number of judges that comprise the panel that is hearing the appeal.

appeal book
a book that contains all of the documents that are necessary for the hearing of an appeal by an appellate court

Rule 14(1) sets out the contents of the appeal book:

14(1) Except in an inmate appeal, the appeal book shall contain, in consecutively numbered pages arranged in the following order, a copy of,

(a) a table of contents describing each document, including each exhibit, by its nature and date, and, in the case of an exhibit, identified by exhibit number or letter;

(b) the notice of appeal and any supplementary notice of appeal;

(c) the order granting the leave to appeal, if any, and any order or direction made with reference to the appeal;

(d) the information or indictment, including all endorsements;

(e) the formal order or decision appealed from, if any, as signed and entered;

(f) the reasons for judgment, if not included in the transcript of the trial or hearing, together with a further typed or printed copy if the reasons are handwritten;

(g) any order for release from custody pending appeal and any other order suspending the operation of the sentence;

(h) all documentary exhibits filed at the trial arranged in order by date or, where there are documents having common characteristics, arranged in separate groups in order by date;

(i) all maps, plans, photographs, drawings and charts that were before the trial judge and are capable of reproduction;

(j) the agreed statement of facts, if any;

(k) where there is an appeal as to sentence, the pre-sentence report, the criminal record of the convicted person and any exhibits filed on the sentencing proceedings;

(l) any notice of constitutional question served in accordance with section 109 of the *Courts of Justice Act*, and proof of service of the notice upon the Attorney General of Ontario and the Attorney General of Canada;

(m) any agreement made by the parties under subrule 8(18);

(n) the certificate referred to in subrule 18(2); and

(o) a certificate in Form 61H of the *Rules of Civil Procedure* signed by the appellant's solicitor, or on the solicitor's behalf by someone specifically authorized to do so, stating that the contents of the appeal book are complete and legible.

Factum

A factum is a concise statement of a party's version of the facts, the issues, the law, and the order requested. It also includes a list of authorities that a party will rely on when the appeal is heard, and the text of all relevant statutes except any provisions contained in the *Criminal Code* or *Youth Criminal Justice Act*. The respondent may prepare his or her own factum for use at the hearing. The respondent's factum must be served and filed no later than 10 days before the week in which the appeal is to be heard.

Certificate of Perfecting and Scheduling

After the appeal has been perfected, the appellant must file a certificate of perfection with the registrar stating that the appeal book, transcript, and appellant's factum have all been served and filed and that the transcript is complete. Additionally, the appellant must provide an estimate of the total length of time that it will take for the parties to argue the appeal in order to permit for proper scheduling of the appeal. If an appeal is not perfected within the time limits set out in the Rules, it may be summarily dismissed as abandoned.

Final Preparation

The parties will receive notice from the court setting out the date that the appeal will be heard. If the parties are relying on any authorities, they must file books of authorities with the court no later than the Thursday of the week before the week the appeal is to be heard. To prevent unnecessary waste, parties are encouraged not to file duplicate authorities already filed by another party.

It should be noted that the Ontario Court of Appeal *Criminal Appeal Rules* contain special provisions for appeals by inmates or others who are not represented by a lawyer. In those cases, there is far less paperwork involved for the unrepresented appellant. The Crown will be required to prepare more of the documentation required for the hearing of the appeal, including the appeal book.

Appeals in Writing

It should finally be noted that the Rules also contemplate for a written appeal without an oral hearing under s. 688(3) of the *Criminal Code*. If an appeal is in writing, the appellant will perfect the appeal by filing all of the material required for an oral appeal with the exception of a factum. The court may dismiss the appeal after reviewing the material if the court is of the view that the appeal has no merit. If the appeal is not dismissed in this manner, the parties will be asked to provide written submissions for the court to consider. The court may decide the appeal on the basis of the material that was filed or may require further oral submissions from the parties.

Summary Conviction Offences

Part XXVII of the *Criminal Code* governs appeals from summary conviction offences. As a starting point, it should be noted that summary offence appeals are similar to appeals from indictable offences. Rather than repeat the contents of the section on indictable offence appeals, this section will focus on the major differences between the two forms of appeal.

Appeals by the Defendant

A person who is charged with a summary conviction offence is called a defendant instead of an accused. A defendant's rights of appeal are much broader than those of a person who was tried by indictment. Section 813(a) provides:

> 813. Except where otherwise provided by law,
>   (a) the defendant in proceedings under this Part may appeal to the appeal court
>   (i) from a conviction or order made against him,
>   (ii) against a sentence passed on him, or
>   (iii) against a verdict of unfit to stand trial or not criminally responsible on account of mental disorder;

As with indictable offences, however, the grounds on which an appeal may succeed are narrower. This is a reflection of the fact that s. 822(1) incorporates most of the provisions of ss. 683 to 689, which apply to indictable offence appeals and also to summary offence appeals. As a result, the grounds on which an appeal may be granted and the powers of the appellate court to dismiss otherwise meritorious appeals are the same as they are for indictable offences.

There are various other differences between summary offence and indictable offence appeals. The biggest difference is that s. 822(4) permits the possibility of appeals being heard by way of **trial *de novo*** in appropriate cases. A trial *de novo* is essentially a complete rehearing of the case, including the taking of evidence. This can occur if the record of the original trial was in some way defective or "for any other reason" where the interests of justice would be served by holding a trial *de novo*.

Another difference is that appeals from summary conviction offences are made to provincial superior courts of criminal jurisdiction. A further appeal lies to the court of appeal with leave of the court and only on a question of law.[14] Sections 673

trial *de novo*
a form of appeal where the appellate court holds a new trial without any regard to the first trial; the appeal essentially takes the form of a completely new trial, as if the previous trial had not occurred

---

14. *Criminal Code* s. 839.

to 689, which govern indictable appeals, also apply to summary offence appeals to the court of appeal.

Finally, there is an alternative method of appeal available for summary conviction offences. Sections 829 to 838 provide for appeals based on a transcript of the proceeding in the lower court or on an agreed statement of facts that the Crown and the defendant have agreed to that set out the facts of the case. However, the grounds for appeal are more limited, and this method is rarely used.

Appeals by the Crown

The only difference of note between appeals by the Crown and appeals by the defendant is the verdict that is appealed from. Both the Crown and the defendant may appeal from the sentence that was imposed at trial, but the Crown would only be interested in appealing acquittals or other similar dispositions. Section 813(b) sets out the Crown's rights of appeal:

> 813. Except where otherwise provided by law, ...
>   (b) the informant, the Attorney General or his agent in proceedings under this Part may appeal to the appeal court
>   (i) from an order that stays proceedings on an information or dismisses an information,
>   (ii) against a sentence passed on a defendant, or
>   (iii) against a verdict of not criminally responsible on account of mental disorder or unfit to stand trial,

Otherwise, the provisions that apply to appeals by the defendant also apply to Crown appeals.

Procedure

As is the case with appeals for indictable offences, the procedure for summary offence appeals varies from jurisdiction to jurisdiction. However, as with indictable offence appeals, the rules share many of the same features. The reader will recall that the first level of appellate court for summary offence appeals is the superior court of criminal jurisdiction. Accordingly, reference must be made to the general rules of the provincial superior courts of criminal jurisdiction in order to access the rules for first-level summary appeals. The specific rules for each jurisdiction can be found online. A review of the *Criminal Proceedings Rules for the Superior Court of Justice (Ontario)* reveals that the rules for summary offence appeals are substantially the same as those for indictable offence appeals in the Ontario Court of Appeal *Criminal Appeal Rules*, with one significant difference: summary offence appeal rules provide for the possibility of an appeal by way of trial *de novo*. Otherwise, both levels of court have essentially the same process for perfecting appeals. This is true for most other provinces, which either parallel the rules for indictable offence appeals or incorporate them by analogy. Appeals are generally commenced by serving a notice of appeal; transcripts must be ordered and appeal books and factums must be served and filed to perfect appeals. It serves no point to repeat the detailed information that is provided in the section on the procedure for indictable offence appeals. As always, the reader should refer to the specific rules applicable to their jurisdiction.

Appeal Routes in Ontario

The following chart outlines appeal routes for both summary offence and indictable offence appeals in Ontario.

Indictable offences	Summary offences
Trial court ⬇	Trial court ⬇
Court of Appeal ⬇	Superior Court of Justice* ⬇
Supreme Court of Canada	Court of Appeal ⬇
	Supreme Court of Canada
* In the other provinces and territories, the appeal court for summary offence appeals is defined in s. 812 of the *Criminal Code*.	

CHAPTER SUMMARY

Appeals are entirely a creation of statute. Generally, the provisions of the *Criminal Code* that deal with appeals reflect the view that trial courts are in a far better position to make findings of fact than are appeal courts. Accordingly, appellate courts are unlikely to intervene when an appeal is based on a question of fact, especially in cases where the Crown is appealing a verdict of acquittal. Conversely, an appeal court has no inherent weakness in reviewing questions of law. In fact, a court of appeal may be in a better position than a trial court to make decisions on questions of law because it is removed from the immediacy and emotion of a trial. When acting on any appeal of a criminal charge, indictable or summary conviction, it is important to review the specific *Criminal Code* provisions that provide for both the right of appeal and grounds on which an appeal may succeed. It is equally important to make reference to the specific rules that govern the procedure for perfecting the appeal. The rules are technical and impose strict requirements and deadlines that must be followed before an appeal can be heard.

KEY TERMS

appeal book, 271
correctness, 265
error of law, 265
grounds for appeal, 262

leave to appeal, 266
objective test, 263
reasonableness, 263
standard of review, 264

subjective test, 263
trial *de novo*, 273

REVIEW QUESTIONS

1. What is the difference between the standard of reasonableness and the standard of correctness?

2. Which standard is more difficult to meet: the standard of reasonableness or the standard of correctness? Why?

3. What are the available grounds for appeal for a person who has been convicted of an indictable offence?

4. What are the circumstances under which a meritorious appeal by an accused person can still be denied?

5. Briefly describe the procedure for an indictable offence appeal.

6. What is contained in an appeal book?

EXERCISES

1. Jeremy Laroche was convicted of assault under s. 266 of the *Criminal Code*. Jeremy wishes to appeal both his conviction and sentence. Which court will hear Jeremy's appeal?

2. In question 1 above, will Jeremy need to obtain leave before his appeal will be heard?

3. Shauna O'Leary was charged with first-degree murder and convicted of second-degree murder after a trial by judge and jury. Shauna's lawyer believes that the jury came to the wrong verdict based on the evidence. Do you think that an appeal will have a good chance to succeed? Explain your answer.

4. Do you think the Crown can successfully appeal from Shauna's acquittal on the first-degree murder charge in question 3 above?

Alternative Measures

22

LEARNING OUTCOMES

After completing this chapter, you should be able to:

- Define the concept of alternative measures.

- Define the conditions under which alternative measures are considered as a viable option.

- Discuss the various forms of alternative measures.

- Discuss Ontario's specialized courts.

- Understand the roles that lawyers and paralegals play when representing offenders with special needs.

Introduction

Most criminal charges do not result in a trial. A large proportion of persons who have been charged with a criminal offence will plead guilty to the offence or to a lesser offence. Still, criminal courts continue to overflow with relatively minor cases and in many jurisdictions it may take months or even years for a criminal charge to be tried. One way to deal with the backlog of criminal cases is to divert minor transgressions away from the criminal justice system. The simple fact is that it may not always be appropriate to prosecute certain minor offences with the full force of the law. What purpose is really served by convicting a young single parent for stealing food for his or her family? Clearly the needs of the young parent will not be addressed by the criminal justice system. Similarly, the goals of deterrence and rehabilitation may not be met, for example, by incarcerating offenders who suffer from an addiction or from mental illness.

General Programs

Crown attorneys have always had the discretion to divert minor charges from the criminal justice system. This discretion is formalized for young offenders under the extrajudicial provisions of the *Youth Criminal Justice Act*. While not as extensive as the provisions in the *Youth Criminal Justice Act*, s. 717 of the *Criminal Code* provides for the establishment of **alternative measures** programs that serve to divert appropriate cases from the criminal justice system.

alternative measures
various options outside the traditional criminal justice system that are available for dealing with offenders

Section 717(1) states:

> 717(1) Alternative measures may be used to deal with a person alleged to have committed an offence only if it is not inconsistent with the protection of society and the following conditions are met:
>
> (a) the measures are part of a program of alternative measures authorized by the Attorney General or the Attorney General's delegate or authorized by a person, or a person within a class of persons, designated by the lieutenant governor in council of a province;
>
> (b) the person who is considering whether to use the measures is satisfied that they would be appropriate, having regard to the needs of the person alleged to have committed the offence and the interests of society and of the victim;
>
> (c) the person, having been informed of the alternative measures, fully and freely consents to participate therein;
>
> (d) the person has, before consenting to participate in the alternative measures, been advised of the right to be represented by counsel;
>
> (e) the person accepts responsibility for the act or omission that forms the basis of the offence that the person is alleged to have committed;
>
> (f) there is, in the opinion of the Attorney General or the Attorney General's agent, sufficient evidence to proceed with the prosecution of the offence; and
>
> (g) the prosecution of the offence is not in any way barred at law.

According to *Criminal Code* s. 717(2), alternative measures are not available to deal with a person charged with an offence who denies participation or involvement in the commission of the offence or who expresses the wish to have the charge dealt with by the court.

Ontario has formally established alternative measures programs for young offenders and offenders with special needs. However, there is no coordinated, generally available program that has been designated for all adult offenders. Instead, programs vary from jurisdiction to jurisdiction and from courthouse to courthouse. Normally, **diversion** is offered as an option only to first time offenders who have been charged with a relatively minor offence such as property offences under $5,000, causing a disturbance, or possession of a small quantity of marijuana for personal use. Charges are initially screened by a Crown attorney who will determine whether diversion is appropriate in the circumstances of the case. Where a person who has been charged with an offence has not been screened as eligible for diversion, defence counsel or a paralegal may be able to convince a Crown attorney to reconsider their decision. However, the final decision is made by the Crown attorney and there is no further recourse.

diversion
redirection of a criminal charge from prosecution to an alternative program that often focuses on rehabilitation

Not all minor infractions are diverted into an alternative measures program. For example, the existence of an **aggravating circumstance** will normally prevent a person who has been charged with a minor offence from participating in the program. Aggravating circumstances include crimes involving hate, vulnerable victims, breach of trust, employee theft, and possession of even a small amount of marijuana near a school or while operating a motor vehicle.

aggravating circumstances
circumstances surrounding the commission of an offence that increase the culpability associated with the offence

Alternative measures can take many forms. These include:

- Attending a specified rehabilitation or educational program.
- Performing some form of community service.
- Performing some form of personal service.
- Making restitution to the victim.
- Making a payment or donation to a charity or specified program.

Normally, the offence with which the person has been charged will be withdrawn by the Crown attorney upon successful completion of the alternative measure. While this will not result in a formal conviction for the person, a record is kept and if the person is later charged with another offence, alternative measures will not normally be offered.

Specialized Courts

Four areas have emerged where the needs of special offenders would be better served outside the traditional court system. Specialized courts have been established in the City of Toronto and, in some instances, elsewhere in Ontario and Canada, to deal with the individual and special needs of certain offenders. These are: the Gladue courts, the Domestic Violence Court Program, the Toronto Drug Treatment Court, and the Toronto Mental Health Court.

The Gladue Courts

This type of court was established in response to the Supreme Court of Canada's decision in *R. v. Gladue*. In that case, the Court looked at s. 718.2(e) of the *Criminal Code*, which essentially directs a sentencing judge to look at alternatives to jail for all offenders that are reasonable in the circumstances of the offender as well as the circumstances surrounding the commission of the offence. The section also expressly directs the sentencing court to pay particular attention to the circumstances of Aboriginal offenders. As a result, Gladue courts have been established to serve the particular needs of Aboriginal offenders.

Gladue courts accept guilty pleas, sentence offenders, and conduct bail hearings. The court employs caseworkers who prepare reports on the life circumstances of an Aboriginal offender. The reports are provided to the court, defence counsel, and Crown counsel. The Gladue reports permit the sentencing court to consider an appropriate disposition other than incarceration for individual offenders.

The Domestic Violence Court Program

The traditional court system has historically been poorly equipped to handle cases involving domestic violence. Domestic violence is a serious and widespread social problem with complex issues. However, at the same time, there is often a goal of reconciliation and reunification of families where there has been domestic violence. In order to deal with the complex and often conflicting needs of offenders, victims, and their families, the Domestic Violence Court Program was created in Ontario in 1997.

The objectives of the Domestic Violence Court Program are to:

- prosecute cases involving domestic violence efficiently,
- intervene earlier in cases involving domestic violence,
- provide better support to victims of domestic violence, and
- increase the accountability of offenders.

The objectives of the Domestic Violence Court Program are achieved through a combination of the Early Intervention Program and a coordinated prosecution involving specialized Crown attorneys, police, and staff from the Victim/Witness Assistance Program. First-time offenders may be offered an opportunity to learn non-violent conflict resolution skills in cases where no weapon was used during the assault and where the victim has not suffered significant harm.

The Domestic Violence Court Program has two streams for eligible offenders: a sentencing stream and a diversion stream. In the sentencing stream, offenders are offered an opportunity to plead guilty and enroll in the Partner Assault Response (PAR) Program. Upon successful completion of the PAR Program, the Crown will recommend that a conditional discharge and probation for a period of 12 months be imposed on the offender. The Crown also has the option of diverting the case by agreeing to a peace bond under s. 810 of the *Criminal Code* and withdrawing the underlying charges for those who entered the program before a finding of guilt.

Toronto Drug Treatment Court

Substance abuse can lead to a cycle of repeat offending. Traditional sentencing options, including incarceration, do not necessarily provide the best options for treating the addicted offender. The Toronto Drug Treatment Court was established to meet the needs of non-violent offenders who are clinically assessed cocaine or heroin addicts.

The Toronto Drug Treatment Court operates through the partnership of three stakeholders: the court system, clinical treatment providers, and community stakeholders. The function of the court is to screen for potential applicants, manage the legal process, monitor the progress of the offender, and ensure compliance with the program. There is an initial 30-day screening period before a participant is accepted into the program. All treatment programs are administered by the Centre for Addiction and Mental Health. Therapists and case managers are assigned to each participant. Community/Court Liaison Workers coordinate between treatment providers, the courts, and community stakeholders. The Community Advisory Committee was formed to address the needs of community stakeholders and to provide support and advice to the Toronto Drug Treatment Court. This program has been very successful, with only 3 percent of graduates reoffending. The entire program lasts about 12 months. To graduate, participants must:

- demonstrate control over their addiction and attain a minimum of three months of substance abstinence;
- provide evidence of stable housing;
- be employed or registered in a job training program, school, or volunteer work program; and
- have had no new convictions during the past three months.

Toronto Mental Health Court

The Toronto Mental Health Court was established in 1998 to deal with pretrial issues of fitness to stand trial expeditiously, to house the Diversion of Mentally Disordered Accused program, and to otherwise accommodate the needs of the mentally disordered accused.

The Toronto Mental Health Court holds bail hearings, accepts guilty pleas, and holds "consent not criminally responsible trials" (where the accused and Crown consent to the defence). The court also holds disposition hearings after findings of "unfitness to stand trial" and "not criminally responsible by reason of mental disorder."

The Toronto Mental Health Court is staffed by Crown attorneys who have expertise in dealing with offenders who suffer from mental disorders. Many of these accused individuals with mental disorders may still be fit to stand trial or may not be exempt from criminal responsibility. In the past, such individuals were tried and sentenced in the same manner as any other offender. However, as the number of these offenders continued to increase, it became apparent that the criminal courts were not meeting the needs of these individuals. Now, the Crown attorney will screen any accused coming before this specialized court for mental health diversion.

In order to qualify for mental health diversion, the accused must meet the requirements of the Crown Policy on Diversion of Mentally Disordered/Developmentally Disabled Offenders. Essentially, an accused will be diverted from the normal criminal stream where the Crown is satisfied that the accused suffers from a mental disorder or from a developmental delay that contributed to the commission of an offence. Certain serious charges are excluded from diversion, and diversion is only available where it is not inconsistent with public safety.

In cases where diversion is appropriate, the accused is referred to the court's mental health worker who will coordinate treatment plans and canvass housing and community support options. The Crown will stay the charges once the accused has been successfully integrated into the community.

Lawyer and Paralegal Roles

While it is the Crown attorney's decision as to whether a particular charge is suitable for diversion from criminal prosecution, in appropriate cases it is important that a lawyer or paralegal raise the issue with the Crown in the first instance. Sometimes the Crown will not have reviewed the file completely or will have overlooked some detail, and matters that would justify diversion can be brought up by the lawyer or paralegal. If these issues are raised, the Crown attorney may very well agree to divert a case from criminal prosecution.

It is equally important for a lawyer or paralegal to recognize the existence and mandate of the various specialized courts. In nearly all instances it is advantageous for the accused to be streamed into the appropriate court at an early stage. In some cases the accused may already be aware of the available options. However, in many cases the accused is either unaware of or unable to consider the options and there is an obligation on the lawyer or paralegal to identify whether a client would qualify for inclusion in one of these programs. In order to identify potential applicants, particular attention should be paid to the behaviour and circumstances of a client. A thorough interview that includes a detailed background of the accused is essential. It may be necessary for the lawyer or paralegal to speak to family and friends of the client or to contact health-care professionals to gather further relevant information. However, care should be taken to maintain client confidentiality. Once an accused has been identified as a candidate for one of the specialized courts, the matter should be brought to the attention of the Crown attorney's office or to the court at the earliest opportunity.

CHAPTER SUMMARY

An effective criminal justice system will not prosecute all persons who have been charged with a criminal offence. It is clear that a variety of situations exist where the circumstances surrounding the commission of an offence or the circumstances of the offender call out for different treatment. The *Criminal Code* reflects this by providing a mechanism in s. 717 for the establishment of alternative measures programs to divert those cases from the criminal justice system.

This chapter outlined the general provisions of the *Criminal Code* that authorize the establishment of alternative measures programs to divert appropriate cases from regular criminal prosecution. The Ontario government has identified four categories of offenders whose specific needs are not well served by the criminal justice system—Aboriginal offenders, domestic violence offenders, offenders with mental illness, and addicted offenders—and has incorporated alternative measures programs for each. As a result, specialized courts have been established that are designed to meet the needs of offenders that the criminal justice system does not address particularly well.

KEY TERMS

aggravating circumstances, 279
alternative measures, 278
diversion, 279

REVIEW QUESTIONS

1. Under what circumstances are alternative measures appropriate for a person who has been charged with a criminal offence?

2. What are some specific examples of alternative measures?

3. What are the four specialized courts in Ontario?

4. Is it possible to appeal a Crown attorney's decision to refuse to divert a case from criminal prosecution?

EXERCISES

1. "The problem with the criminal justice system is that it is too easy on criminals. There should be meaningful consequences for breaking the law."

   What do you think of the above statement in relation to alternative measures programs?

2. Lawyer Michael Gulliver is representing 53-year-old Gary Wilkinson, who has been charged with "theft under $5,000" after taking a bottle of mouthwash from a local drugstore without paying for it. Gary has no prior criminal record. During the initial client interview, Gary advised Michael that his permanent address was a local men's shelter. When Michael attended court on Gary's first appearance he noticed that Gary looked haggard and unwashed, was wearing old and dirty clothing, and smelled of alcohol. During a court recess, Gary lit a cigarette in the courtroom and was immediately told by the Crown attorney to put it out, which Gary did by dropping the cigarette on the carpet and stepping on it.

   If you were Michael, how would you handle this case?

PART IV

Young Persons and Criminal Law

CHAPTER 23 The Youth Criminal Justice Act

The Youth Criminal Justice Act

23

LEARNING OUTCOMES

After completing this chapter, you should be able to:

- Understand how the courts have historically dealt with youth crime.

- Discuss why the *Young Offenders Act* was replaced by the *Youth Criminal Justice Act*.

- Define the principles of the *Youth Criminal Justice Act*.

- Understand the various parts of the *Youth Criminal Justice Act*.

- Discuss extrajudicial measures under the *Youth Criminal Justice Act*.

- Understand how youth crime is prosecuted under the *Youth Criminal Justice Act*.

- Define the various sentencing options that are available under the *Youth Criminal Justice Act*.

Introduction

The criminal justice system treats young offenders differently from adult offenders. Common sense dictates that children may not have the ability to fully appreciate their actions in the same manner that adults do. A very young child may not have the capacity to form the *mens rea* that is required to establish many crimes. Reflecting this is that children 11 years of age and younger cannot be convicted of a criminal offence in Canada. Section 13 of the *Criminal Code* provides that no person can be convicted of a criminal offence that was committed when they were under the age of 12 years. Older offenders who have not reached adult status can be found criminally responsible for their actions, although our justice system treats these offenders differently from adult offenders. Young persons who are 12 years of age and older but under the age of 18 are prosecuted for their offences under the provisions of the *Youth Criminal Justice Act* (YCJA).

History and Purpose

Children who committed criminal acts were not always treated differently from adult offenders. The age of criminal responsibility was 7 under the British common law, and in Canada, historically, children aged 14 and over were tried in adult courts. Children aged 7 and over were also tried in adult court if it could be shown that they had the ability to form criminal intent. This all changed in 1908 when the federal government enacted the *Juvenile Delinquents Act*.

The Juvenile Delinquents Act

welfare model of criminal justice
a model of criminal justice that focuses on the welfare and well-being of the offender

The *Juvenile Delinquents Act* (JDA) applied to children aged 7 to 16. It recognized that children had special needs and should be tried separately from adult offenders. The JDA provided a **welfare model** of dealing with young offenders that focused on treating young offenders as children in need of aid, encouragement, help, and assistance rather than as criminals. The JDA was intended to provide informal and flexible mechanisms for dealing with wayward children who ran afoul of any municipal, truancy, provincial, or federal law. Such children were found to be in a state of delinquency that required help and guidance. However, the informality and flexibility of the JDA proved to be a two-edged sword. The determination of whether or not a delinquency had been committed was made informally and without due process. Juvenile delinquents were often denied a right to counsel, rights of appeal, and were given open-ended (as opposed to definite) sentences. Sentencing options included suspension of disposition, adjournment *sine die* (no penalty), fines, probation, placement with the Children's Aid Society, and indeterminate committal to training school. The sentences did not always fit the crimes. A delinquent who breached a minor municipal standard might be "reformed" by an indeterminate length of stay at a training school.

The Young Offenders Act

The JDA with its social welfare approach to child crime remained as law for 76 years until 1984 when the *Young Offenders Act* (YOA) was proclaimed into force. The YOA was radically different from the JDA in that instead of focusing on social welfare, it provided for a **justice model** of criminal justice for young offenders. While the YOA continued to recognize the special needs and vulnerability of youths, it also valued both protection of the public and the rights of young people. The YOA was a much more detailed statute than the JDA, setting out a complete code that governed the prosecution of young offenders. It was less about social welfare and more about rights and obligations.

The YOA raised the age for criminal responsibility to 12 years old and extended the definition of a youth up to the age of 18. Young offenders would face the same charges as adult offenders. The difference was that the YOA established a youth court with special procedures and different sentencing options for young offenders. Young offenders faced a maximum sentence of two years in custody except in cases where an adult could face life imprisonment. In those cases, the maximum sentence was three years. The YOA also protected the identity of young offenders. It was possible for the Crown to apply to have youths over the age of 14 tried as adults.

Increased public pressure in response to a dramatic rise in the number of violent juvenile crimes resulted in several amendments to the YOA. In 1986 the maximum sentence was increased for offences committed while under sentence for a prior offence. In 1992 the maximum sentence for murder was raised from three to five years, and the rules for transferring offenders to adult court were relaxed. In 1995 the maximum sentence for murder was raised again to 10 years and the rules for transferring violent offenders to adult court were relaxed further. Victims of crime were also permitted to participate in the sentencing process through the use of victim impact statements. Notwithstanding these tough new measures, in the late 1990s an overwhelming majority of 77 percent of Canadians believed that the YOA was too lenient on offenders and only 26 percent were somewhat or very confident in the effectiveness of the YOA.[1] In reality, however, the rate of incarceration for young offenders was higher than the rate of incarceration for adult offenders, and young offenders usually served their entire sentences, unlike most adult offenders.[2]

There were a number of other problems associated with the YOA. For example, there was no mechanism available to ensure the proper reintegration back into society of those offenders who had served their sentences. Another major problem was that the YOA failed to distinguish between violent offenders and those convicted of less serious or minor offences. Compounding this problem was that unlike in adult court, there was a lack of consistency in sentencing young offenders. Finally, there was very little opportunity for the victims of youth crime to be heard during the sentencing process.

justice model of criminal justice
a model of criminal justice that focuses on the protection of the public and the rights of the person charged with an offence

1. Canadian Centre for Justice Statistics, *A Profile of Youth Justice in Canada* (Ottawa: Statistics Canada, 1998), at 11.
2. *Youth Crime in Canada: Public Perception vs. Statistical Information* (Edmonton: John Howard Society of Alberta, 1998).

As a result of mounting public pressure, the government instituted a program called the Youth Justice Renewal Initiative in 1998, which culminated in an overhaul of the entire youth criminal justice system. The Youth Justice Renewal Initiative attempted to balance the competing interests of law and order versus social justice. The objectives of the Youth Justice Renewal Initiative were to:

1. instigate greater citizen and community participation in the youth justice system;
2. increase public confidence in the youth justice system;
3. improve public protection through reduced youth crime;
4. make increased use of measures outside the formal court process;
5. reduce overreliance on custody;
6. increase emphasis on rehabilitation and reintegration of young offenders; and
7. target measures for violent offenders.

The most significant outcome of the Youth Justice Renewal Initiative was the adoption of the YCJA in 2003. The principles of the YCJA are expressed in the Declaration of Principle set out in s. 3 of the Act:

> 3(1) The following principles apply in this Act:
> (a) the youth criminal justice system is intended to protect the public by
> (i) holding young persons accountable through measures that are proportionate to the seriousness of the offence and the degree of responsibility of the young person,
> (ii) promoting the rehabilitation and reintegration of young persons who have committed offences, and
> (iii) supporting the prevention of crime by referring young persons to programs or agencies in the community to address the circumstances underlying their offending behaviour;
> (b) the criminal justice system for young persons must be separate from that of adults, must be based on the principle of diminished moral blameworthiness or culpability and must emphasize the following:
> (i) rehabilitation and reintegration,
> (ii) fair and proportionate accountability that is consistent with the greater dependency of young persons and their reduced level of maturity,
> (iii) enhanced procedural protection to ensure that young persons are treated fairly and that their rights, including their right to privacy, are protected,
> (iv) timely intervention that reinforces the link between the offending behaviour and its consequences, and
> (v) the promptness and speed with which persons responsible for enforcing this Act must act, given young persons' perception of time;
> (c) within the limits of fair and proportionate accountability, the measures taken against young persons who commit offences should
> (i) reinforce respect for societal values,
> (ii) encourage the repair of harm done to victims and the community,

(iii) be meaningful for the individual young person given his or her needs and level of development and, where appropriate, involve the parents, the extended family, the community and social or other agencies in the young person's rehabilitation and reintegration, and

(iv) respect gender, ethnic, cultural and linguistic differences and respond to the needs of aboriginal young persons and of young persons with special requirements; and

(d) special considerations apply in respect of proceedings against young persons and, in particular,

(i) young persons have rights and freedoms in their own right, such as a right to be heard in the course of and to participate in the processes, other than the decision to prosecute, that lead to decisions that affect them, and young persons have special guarantees of their rights and freedoms,

(ii) victims should be treated with courtesy, compassion and respect for their dignity and privacy and should suffer the minimum degree of inconvenience as a result of their involvement with the youth criminal justice system,

(iii) victims should be provided with information about the proceedings and given an opportunity to participate and be heard, and

(iv) parents should be informed of measures or proceedings involving their children and encouraged to support them in addressing their offending behaviour.

Jurisdiction

The YCJA applies to young people (persons who are 12 years of age and older but under the age of 18) who are charged with a federal offence. Section 13(1) establishes a **youth justice court** to administer the Act. A youth justice court judge is usually a provincial court judge appointed for this purpose, but can be a superior court justice because the YCJA permits a young person to be sentenced as an adult in certain circumstances.

Section 14(1) of the YCJA confers exclusive jurisdiction on the youth justice court to deal with any federal offences committed by a young person. The YCJA, like the legislation preceding it, does not create offences. It is a procedural statute setting out the process for young persons to be tried for criminal offences. In order to determine the substantive law—that is, the elements of offences and the various defences available—reference must be made to the federal statute that created the offence, which is usually the *Criminal Code*. What this means is that any young person age 12 or over and under the age of 18 who has been charged with a federal offence that is criminal in nature will have the matter proceed under the provisions of the YCJA and have it ultimately dealt with by a judge of the youth justice court.

The youth justice court has no jurisdiction for offences committed by persons 18 years of age and older. The court similarly has no jurisdiction in respect of offences committed by children under the age of 12, regardless of the nature of the offence or the present age of the offender. Offenders in this age group are dealt with by the appropriate provincial child welfare agency and not by the criminal justice system.

youth justice court
the court that has exclusive jurisdiction over persons under the age of 18 who have been charged with a criminal or other federal offence

Jurisdiction over the young person is determined by the young person's age at the time of the offence. Often, a young person will have turned 18 by the time his or her charges are finally dealt with by the youth justice court. Sometimes charges are laid several years after the commission of an offence. This occurs most frequently when a victim has been so traumatized by a crime that he or she suffers from repressed memory syndrome and is unable to recall the circumstances until a triggering event occurs much later. While certainly rare, it is possible for someone in their 20s or 30s to be tried by a youth justice court for an offence that was committed when they were a young person. As a result, there are some provisions of the YCJA that do not apply once a young person reaches a certain age; for example, notice to a parent is not required if the young person is 20 years old on the date of their first appearance in court, and the special rules relating to statements made to police do not apply to persons 18 years of age and over.

Since the YCJA applies only to offences created by an act of Parliament, persons under the age of 18 who are charged with a provincial offence will be dealt with in accordance with the provisions and procedures set out in the applicable provincial legislation. This means, for example, that in Ontario the 16-year-old driver of a speeding motor vehicle would be charged and tried under the provincial *Highway Traffic Act*.

Overview

The YCJA provides a complete code for dealing with youth crime. It is organized into eight parts, with each part setting out its own particular subject matter. The eight parts are summarized below.

Part 1: Extrajudicial Measures

extrajudicial measures
various options outside the traditional criminal justice system that are available for dealing with offenders

These are measures such as warnings, cautions, and referrals to community youth assistance programs that are available to the police and Crown before they initiate or continue a prosecution under the YCJA. **Extrajudicial measures** are dealt with in greater detail later in this chapter.

Part 2: Organization of Youth Criminal Justice System

This part sets out the jurisdiction and power of youth justice courts. These courts are set up to deal only with young persons who have been charged with offences and are separate from the regular courts that deal with adult offenders. The provinces can designate either provincially or federally appointed judges to deal with matters under the YCJA. In Ontario, provincially appointed judges of the Ontario Court of Justice are designated under the YCJA. These are the same judges that deal with adult offenders, but separate courts have been established that deal exclusively with youth crime.

Part 3: Judicial Measures

judicial measures
the manner in which offenders are tradition-ally dealt with by the criminal justice system

The part of the YCJA dealing with **judicial measures** provides a complete code governing the prosecution of young persons. There are a number of important features in this part. First, it establishes an absolute right to counsel for young people. If legal aid is not available to a young person, a youth justice court will appoint counsel at the request of the young person. In addition, the parents of a young person who has been charged with an offence must be provided with written notice that contains complete details of the proceedings. This requirement does not apply if the young person has attained the age of 20 years on the date of his or her first appearance.

Part 3 also sets out the procedures for detaining young persons prior to trial or sentencing and for the release of any young persons so detained. Under this part, youth justice courts have the power to order medical or psychological assessments of young persons. Finally, Part 3 makes the appeal provisions of the *Criminal Code* in respect of indictable and summary conviction offences apply to the YCJA.

Part 4:   Sentencing

This part sets out the principles of the YCJA and the types of sentences available for young persons. The YCJA has expanded the sentencing options that were available under the YOA. The current options are set out in s. 42 and range from a reprimand, discharge, fine, or restitution to community service, prohibition, probation, and custodial sentence. The various sentencing options under the YCJA are discussed in detail later in this chapter.

Part 5:   Custody and Supervision

Under the graduated sentencing principles set out in the YCJA, a custodial sentence is to be imposed only as a last resort and is generally reserved for violent offenders and serious repeat offenders. Part 5 of the Act sets out the various levels of custody and provides procedural safeguards and an annual review of the sentence with the possibility of early supervised release from custody.

Part 6:   Publication, Records and Information

Under the YCJA, criminal youth records can be disclosed only to authorized individuals or organizations for specified purposes. It is also permissible to use prior findings of guilt under the YCJA against adults at bail hearings and sentencing. Section 110 prohibits the publication of a name or other information that would identify a young person who is dealt with under the Act. Publication is permitted, however, if the young person has received an **adult sentence** for a violent offence[3] and the youth court has ordered a lifting of the publication ban. Finally, publication may be permitted by order of a judge if a young person is at large and is a danger to others and publication is necessary to assist in apprehending the young person. Any such order will expire five days after it is made.

Criminal records of young persons are not automatically destroyed at age 18. A youth record is retained for a period of time in all proceedings under the YCJA, including acquittals and withdrawals, and where extrajudicial sanctions are imposed. The record is retained for longer periods following a conviction, but will be de-

adult sentences
sentences that are available for offenders over the age of 18 under the *Criminal Code* and other federal statutes

---

3. "Violent offence" is defined in YCJA s. 2(1) as an offence or an attempted offence that includes the element of causing bodily harm or an offence that endangers the life or safety of a person by creating a substantial likelihood of causing bodily harm.

stroyed after a period of time if no further offences have been committed. In the case of conviction in a summary matter, the record will be retained for three years following the completion of the sentence. The time period is five years for most indictable offences, and a record for more serious offences is retained for ten years. Youth records may be retained indefinitely for a serious violent offence[4] for which an adult sentence is sought. Finally, if an adult commits an offence before the mandatory crime-free period for a youth record has expired, the record will automatically become part of that person's adult record.

Part 7: General Provisions

Part 7 deals with assorted procedural matters and sets out special rules regarding the **admissibility** of statements made by young offenders. The conditions for admitting statements under the YCJA are dealt with later in this chapter.

Part 8: Transitional Provisions

This part contains provisions that aid in the transition from the YOA to the YCJA.

admissibility
refers to whether or not a particular piece of evidence is capable of being used at trial

Extrajudicial Measures

Many matters that end up in the criminal justice system involve relatively minor crimes such as shoplifting and theft. In fact, nearly three out of four matters that appear in youth justice court can be categorized as minor offences.[5] Often, these offences are committed by first-time offenders who learn their lesson and will have no further involvement with the criminal justice system. The police and Crown attorneys have always had the discretion to divert offenders from the criminal justice system. This discretion was authorized by statute for the first time under the *Young Offenders Act*, which provided for the use of alternative measures instead of formal prosecution in appropriate cases. The YCJA has retained this feature and one of the objects of the Act is to effectively intervene and deal with young persons who are charged with minor offences. Many of these cases simply do not justify using the full force of the criminal justice system to deal with minor transgressions. Early intervention and diversion from traditional prosecution may provide more meaningful consequences that address the specific circumstances of the young person and/or the victim. It is also worth mentioning that by diverting appropriate cases, the more expensive and formal court process can be used to deal with serious crime.

Section 4 of the YCJA expressly sets out four principles that apply to extrajudicial measures. These are:

1. Extrajudicial measures are often the most appropriate and effective way to address youth crime.

---

4. "Serious violent offence" is defined in YCJA s. 2(1) as murder, attempted murder, manslaughter, or aggravated assault.

5. According to Statistics Canada, theft, possession of stolen property, fail to appear, fail to comply, mischief, break and enter, and minor assaults account for 74 percent of the matters dealt with by the youth justice court.

2. Extrajudicial measures allow for effective and timely interventions focused on correcting offending behaviour.

3. Extrajudicial measures are presumed to be appropriate for a first-time offender who has been convicted of a non-violent offence.

4. Extrajudicial measures should be used if they are adequate to hold an offender accountable for his or her behaviour, and the use of extrajudicial measures is not precluded if an offender has previously been dealt with by extrajudicial measures or has been convicted of an offence in the past.

The YCJA incorporates a graduated scale of extrajudicial measures for police and Crown attorneys to consider when dealing with youth offenders. In particular, the police and Crown are required to consider the following options:

1. No further action to be taken by the officer.

2. A warning (an informal warning by a police officer(s)).

3. A police caution (a formal warning by the police). The caution may be in the form of a letter to the young person and his or her parents or may require the attendance of the young person and his or her parents at a police station.

4. A Crown caution. A Crown caution is similar to a police caution, but is given by the Crown. The caution may take the form of a letter to the young person and his or her parents.

5. A referral. The police can refer the young person to community agencies to help keep the offender from reoffending. There are a number of programs available that offer services ranging from recreation to counselling.

6. Extrajudicial sanction. An extrajudicial sanction may only be used if the young person cannot be adequately dealt with by a warning, caution, or referral. This is the most formal extrajudicial measure available under the YCJA, and it is only available if the young person admits responsibility for the offence and has consented to the extrajudicial sanction. The sanction must be authorized by the Attorney General and be part of a designated program. Typical sanctions include providing compensation or personal services to a victim, community service, educational programs, an apology to a victim, attending a workshop or mediation, writing an essay that is relevant to the offence, or making a presentation.

    Extrajudicial sanctions cannot be used where the evidence does not support a prosecution. They are only authorized in cases where there is sufficient evidence to proceed with the prosecution of the young person. The charges may proceed in regular fashion through the court system if the young person fails to comply with the sanctions.

Pretrial Detention

It is a fundamental principle of criminal law that a person is presumed innocent until proven guilty. It follows that persons who are charged with an offence should not be incarcerated until they have been tried and convicted of the offence. However,

pretrial detention
the period of time that
a person who has been
charged with an offence
spends in custody
without being released
while awaiting trial

it is necessary in certain instances to detain an individual before trial, and this is known as **pretrial detention**. Under the YCJA, this is generally permitted on one of two grounds: (1) to ensure that the young person will appear in court or (2) where detention is necessary for the protection or safety of the public.

Section 28 of the YCJA provides that the provisions of Part XVI of the *Criminal Code* that deal with compelling the appearance of an accused and interim release also apply to the release of young persons. This means that when dealing with young offenders, police have the same powers of detention and arrest that they have in situations that involve adults. One significant difference is that police must give written notice to a young person's parent (or other suitable adult if a parent is not available) after a young person has been arrested or charged with an offence.

Except in cases that involve the serious charges set out in s. 469 of the *Criminal Code*, the police have broad powers to release young persons who have been arrested. Where the arrest is made without a warrant, a young person must be released unless the police officer believes on reasonable grounds that detention is necessary in the public interest or there are reasonable grounds to believe that the young person will fail to appear in court. In cases where an arrest is made with a warrant, the police officer will first appear before a justice to swear an Information. The justice may issue a summons requiring the young person to attend court at a specified date and time instead of issuing a warrant for arrest. There is a positive duty on the justice to issue a summons unless there are reasonable and probable grounds that it is in the public interest to arrest the young person. This means that arrest warrants are usually reserved for more serious offences for which there is a risk that the accused might destroy evidence or where there is a risk of flight. If an arrest warrant is issued, the justice may authorize the officer in charge to release the young person upon arrest. Further, s. 503 of the *Criminal Code* authorizes the release of a young person who has been charged with an offence other than a s. 469 offence if the police are satisfied that the person should be released from custody. The release may be subject to conditions that the young person must comply with.

A young person who has been detained by the police is entitled to have a bail hearing under the provisions of the *Criminal Code*. The same rules that govern bail hearings for adults also apply to young persons. In most cases the Crown will have the onus to justify the detention of the accused on one of three grounds: (1) that the young person will not appear for trial, (2) that the young person is a risk to public safety, or (3) that the detention of the young person is necessary to maintain confidence in the administration of justice. In certain circumstances, the young person may have a reverse-onus bail hearing where the onus will be on the young person to justify his or her release with regard to the three grounds.[6]

In cases where the youth justice court is considering whether the detention of a young person is necessary for the protection or safety of the public, s. 29(2) of the YCJA presumes that detention is not necessary if the young person would not be facing a custodial sentence if found guilty.

---

6. Section 515(6) of the *Criminal Code*, R.S.C. 1985, c. C-46, sets out the circumstances when the onus in a bail hearing will shift from the Crown to the young person.

Every province must establish facilities for the detention of young persons. Any young person who has been detained must be kept separate and apart from any adult who is detained or held in custody unless a youth court orders otherwise or the young person is 20 years of age or older.

Admissibility of Statements

The common-law confession rule applies to prosecutions under the YCJA and any statement that has been made by a young person to a police officer or other person in authority is not admissible unless the Crown can prove beyond a reasonable doubt that it has been made **voluntarily**. However, the YCJA recognizes that young persons may be particularly vulnerable when dealing with police officers and persons in authority. As a result, young persons are afforded enhanced procedural protection before a statement can be admitted into evidence.

Before a statement made to a police officer or person in authority can be admitted into evidence against a young person, the following additional conditions must be met:[7]

1. Before the statement is made, the person in authority must have explained in language appropriate to the young person's age and understanding that:

    a. the young person is under no obligation to make a statement;

    b. the statement may be used as evidence against the young person;

    c. the young person has the right to consult with counsel and a parent or other appropriate adult; and

    d. the statement must be made in the presence of counsel or a parent if either is consulted by the young person.

2. Before the statement is made, the young person must have been provided with a reasonable opportunity to consult with counsel, a parent, or any other appropriate adult.

3. If counsel, a parent, or another appropriate adult is consulted, the young person is to be provided with an opportunity to make the statement in that person's presence.

These additional conditions are not absolute and are subject to certain exceptions. They do not apply to any oral statements that are made spontaneously before the police officer or person in authority had the opportunity to comply with the requirements of the Act. A young person may also waive conditions 2 and 3 above, provided that the waiver is recorded or contained in a written and signed statement. If a technical irregularity in obtaining the waiver of rights arises, the court has the discretion to find the waiver valid on determining that the young person was informed of his or her rights and voluntarily waived them.

voluntariness in all criminal and quasi-criminal prosecutions, a statement made by a person charged with an offence is not admissible as evidence against that person unless the Crown proves beyond a reasonable doubt that it was made voluntarily

---

7. *Youth Criminal Justice Act*, S.C. 2002, c. 1, s. 146.

When there has been a technical irregularity in complying with any of the additional conditions under the YCJA, the court has the discretion to admit the statement "if satisfied that the admission of the statement would not bring into disrepute the principle that young persons are entitled to enhanced procedural protection to ensure that they are treated fairly and their rights are protected."[8] Further, a statement may be admitted if the young person represented himself or herself as being 18 years of age or older at the time the statement was made.

The YCJA offers procedural protection in two other ways with respect to statements made by young persons. First, a statement may be inadmissible if a young person can convince the court that the statement was made under duress imposed by any person who is not, in law, a person in authority. The effect of this is that no statements obtained under duress are admissible regardless to whom they are made. Second, a statement made by a young person during a medical or psychological assessment can only be used for limited purposes unless the young person consents to the admission of the statement.

Pleas and Trial

Section 140 of the YCJA makes the provisions of the *Criminal Code* applicable to any offences committed by young persons unless there is an inconsistency between the two statutes. Further, s. 142 sets out that trials in the youth justice court are governed by Part XXVII (summary conviction offences) and any other provisions of the *Criminal Code* that apply in trials of summary conviction offences unless there is an inconsistency between the two statutes. This essentially means that subject to a few important differences, the trial process in the youth justice court is virtually the same as it is for adult trials in cases involving summary conviction offences.

The biggest difference is that all trials of young persons are held in a special court called the youth criminal justice court irrespective of whether an adult sentence is sought. Each province is provided with the authority to establish a youth justice court within the province. The judges that preside over matters in the youth justice court come from the bench of the provincial or superior court of the province, depending on the classification of the offence.

When a young person first appears in the youth criminal justice court, the judge or justice is required to do the following:

1. read the Information or Indictment to the young person;
2. if the young person is not represented by counsel, inform the young person of the right to retain and instruct counsel; and
3. advise the young person if the Crown is seeking an adult sentence.[9]

In addition, before taking a plea from a young person who is not represented by counsel, the youth justice court must ensure that the young person understands the

---

8. *Youth Criminal Justice Act* s. 146(6).
9. *Youth Criminal Justice Act* s. 32(1).

charge; explain the consequences of being sentenced as an adult if an adult sentence could be imposed; explain that the young person can plead guilty or not guilty; and, where applicable, explain that the young person may elect the mode of trial. The youth justice court shall direct that the young person be represented by counsel if it is not satisfied that the young person understands these matters.[10]

The YCJA ensures that young persons charged with serious offences have the same procedural protection as adults. A young person facing a potential sentence of five years or longer has the right to elect his or her mode of trial. The right to elect the mode of trial will arise only in those situations where the young person is charged with either first- or second-degree murder or is facing the possibility of an adult sentence of at least five years. In all other cases an election is not available because the longest available sentence under the YCJA is three years.

Where an election is available, the young person may elect trial by youth justice court judge without a jury, trial by judge without a jury following a preliminary inquiry, or trial by judge and jury following a preliminary inquiry. Any preliminary inquiry will be conducted under the procedure set out in Part XVIII of the *Criminal Code*. Following a preliminary inquiry, trial procedure is governed by Parts XIX and XX of the *Criminal Code*, which set out the rules for jury and non-jury indictable offence trials. Regardless of the mode of trial that has been elected, all trials take place in youth court.

Sentencing

As previously mentioned in this chapter, there are a number of sentences that are available under the YCJA. Some of these sentences closely mirror sentences that are contained in the *Criminal Code*, while others are available only for young persons.

Types of Sentences

Reprimand

A reprimand is a severe warning or scolding of an offender by a judge in open court. It is used in minor cases, usually for first offenders, where it appears that warning the offender will provide sufficient deterrence.

Discharge

This is essentially the same option that is available under the *Criminal Code* for adult offenders. A discharge can be granted absolutely or with any conditions that the court considers to be appropriate.

Fine

Young persons can also be subjected to a fine. The fine cannot exceed $1,000 and the court may provide that the fine be paid over time.

---

10. *Youth Criminal Justice Act* s. 32(3).

Restitution

The YCJA provides for three forms of restitution: (1) restitution for personal injuries caused by an offender, (2) restitution for loss or damage to property, and (3) restitution through an order for compensation by way of personal services for loss or damage to property or for an injury caused by the offender.

Community Service

The court may order community service and require the young person to report to a probation officer on dates and times fixed by the court. An offender under a community service order will perform a specified number of hours of unpaid work, up to a maximum of 240 hours, in a community service organization. The community service order cannot extend for more than 12 months from the date that it is made.

Prohibition Order

A youth justice court has the power to make any prohibition, seizure, or forfeiture order that can be imposed under any federal statute, including the *Criminal Code*. The court therefore has the power to order an offender to refrain from owning or possessing firearms or other weapons, and can also order the seizure or forfeiture of any weapons in the custody of the offender.

Probation

In addition to ordering community service, the court may place an offender on probation for up to two years.

Intensive Support and Supervision

This option is essentially an intensive probation order that results in greater contact between the young offender and his or her probation officer. The expectation is that a more active role by the probation officer will have a positive influence and guide the young person in the right direction.

Attendance Order

A young person can be ordered to attend a specified program for up to 240 hours for a period not exceeding six months. The purpose of this option is to treat and rehabilitate the young person.

Deferred Custody and Supervision

This is similar to the conditional sentence of imprisonment sentencing option contained in the *Criminal Code*. In appropriate cases that do not involve a serious violent offence, a young person may be permitted, under conditions, to serve his or her sentence in the community. As with a conditional sentence of imprisonment, if the conditions are breached, the young person may have to serve the balance of the sentence in custody.

Custody and Supervision

A major criticism of the YOA was that there were no provisions for reintegrating an offender back into society after he or she had served a custodial sentence. The YCJA addresses this problem by splitting custodial sentences into two periods. An offender must serve the first period in normal custody and the second under supervision in the community, subject to conditions imposed by the court. The time spent under supervision would be one half of the time that was served in custody. Together the two periods constitute the entire sentence. For example, an offender who was sentenced to serve three months would serve two months in custody and one month in the community.

Particulars of Custody and Supervision

All young persons in custody must be held at a youth facility that is separate from adult offenders. If a young person will be held past the age of 18, the youth justice court may direct that the balance of the sentence be served in an adult facility if it is in the best interests of the young person or in the public interest.

There must be at least two levels of custody in the youth custody system in each province distinguished by the degree of restraint imposed on the young persons in them. Young persons will be placed in a level of custody that relates to the seriousness and circumstances of the offence, the needs and circumstances of the young person, the safety of other young persons in custody, the interests of society, the findings of any assessment, and the likelihood of escape.

After release from custody and while on supervision, a young person will be monitored and controlled to ensure that he or she receives the necessary treatment and programs to be successfully reintegrated into the community. Conditions such as keeping the peace and reporting to authorities are mandatory during all periods of supervision. In addition, specific conditions particular to a young person's needs may be applied, such as attending school or an educational program and attending counselling or treatment programs. A young person may be returned to custody if he or she fails to abide by these conditions, although existing conditions may be varied or further conditions may be imposed to address minor transgressions.

Length of Sentences

For most offences, the total maximum sentence is two years. For offences other than murder (for which an adult may face life imprisonment), the maximum sentence under the YCJA is three years. The YCJA provides for longer periods of incarceration for murder. In the case of second-degree murder the maximum sentence is seven years, with no more than four years served in custody, with the balance under conditional supervision. For first-degree murder the maximum sentence is ten years, composed of no more than six years in custody, followed by a maximum of four years of supervision in the community.

Intensive Rehabilitative Custody and Supervision

Many young offenders suffer from various mental health issues. In fact, it is estimated that 20 to 25 percent of the most serious violent youth offenders have various mental health issues. These young persons have special requirements that must be addressed before they can be successfully reintegrated into the community. The major feature that distinguishes this sentence from an ordinary sentence of custody and supervision is that the custodial portion of the sentence is served in intensive rehabilitative custody. Intensive rehabilitative custody and supervision is a sentencing option if:

1. the offender has been found guilty of a serious violent offence or the offender has been found guilty of an offence where the offender caused or attempted to cause serious bodily harm for which an adult is liable to imprisonment for more than two years and the offender has been convicted on at least two previous occasions of such an offence;

2. the offender suffers from a mental illness or disorder, a psychological disorder, or an emotional disturbance;

3. a treatment plan has been developed for the offender; and

4. there is an appropriate program available for the offender.

Adult Sentences

The YCJA continues to provide for the imposition of adult sentences in certain circumstances. In the past, it was necessary for the Crown to first make an application to transfer the case to adult court before trial. This is no longer the case under the YCJA. Now once a young person aged 14 and over has been found guilty of an offence, the youth justice court, in certain circumstances, may apply an adult sentence. The Crown can make an application for an adult sentence if the young person has been convicted of an offence that would attract a sentence of more than two years if committed by an adult. The Crown is obligated to consider whether it would be appropriate to seek an adult sentence in all situations where a young person is charged with a serious violent offence.

The young person will receive notice where there is a risk of receiving an adult sentence. The notice must be provided by the Crown before the young person enters a plea, or before the commencement of the trial with leave of the youth justice court.

An adult sentence will be imposed if the Crown is able to rebut the presumption of diminished moral blameworthiness or culpability of the young person and can satisfy the youth justice court that a youth sentence would not be of sufficient length to hold the young person accountable for their offending behaviour.

Where an adult sentence is applied to a young person under the age of 18, it will be served in a youth facility rather than an adult prison unless it would not be in the best interests of the young person or would jeopardize the safety of others.

Appeals

Section 37 of the YCJA contains the provisions that deal with appeals. As with much of the YCJA, appeals under the statute are conducted in accordance with the applicable provisions of the *Criminal Code*, subject to any modifications that the circumstances may require. Appeals for indictable offences are subject to Part XXI of the *Criminal Code*, and Part XXVII governs appeals for summary conviction matters. Reference can be made to Chapter 21 of this text for more information on appeal procedures and rights of appeal under the *Criminal Code*.

As might be expected, given that the YCJA is designed to deal with young persons, there are some unique features respecting appeals under the Act. These include the following matters, which are treated as indictable offence sentence appeals:

1. a judicial determination that the crime was a serious violent offence;
2. the imposition of an adult sentence;
3. a ban on publication; and
4. an order that a sentence be served in an adult facility.

In addition, all appeals that take place in a youth justice court that is a superior court are made directly to the court of appeal. All appeals to the Supreme Court of Canada require leave. See Chapter 21 for more on leave.

CHAPTER SUMMARY

How we view and treat youth crime in Canada has changed profoundly over the years. The *Juvenile Delinquents Act* used a social welfare approach to youth crime, seeing offenders as wayward children requiring guidance and compassion. There was, however, a cost associated with this approach. In addressing the special needs of children in an informal manner, the *Juvenile Delinquents Act* failed to provide adequate procedural protection to the children that it was designed to help and protect. At the same time, the incidence of violent youth crime increased and it became apparent that more emphasis was required on protecting society against youth crime, particularly violent youth crime. As a result, the focus in dealing with youth crime shifted from a social welfare model to a justice model while at the same time recognizing the special needs of youth offenders. This shift in focus resulted first in the enactment of the *Young Offenders Act* in 1984 and, later, in the passage of the *Youth Criminal Justice Act*. The basic theme of the *Youth Criminal Justice Act* is to balance the competing interests of law and order versus social justice.

KEY TERMS

admissibility, 294
adult sentences, 293
extrajudicial measures, 292
judicial measures, 292
justice model of criminal justice, 289

pretrial detention, 296
voluntariness, 297
welfare model of criminal justice, 288
youth justice court, 291

REVIEW QUESTIONS

1. How did the *Juvenile Delinquents Act* deal with youth crime? What were the advantages and disadvantages of this approach?

2. What are the major differences between the *Young Offenders Act* and the *Youth Criminal Justice Act*?

3. What are the various extrajudicial measures available under the *Youth Criminal Justice Act*?

4. What special considerations apply before a statement made by a young person to a police officer can be admitted as evidence against the young person?

5. Under what circumstances can a young person who has been charged with a criminal offence elect the mode of trial?

6. Describe the various sentencing options that are available under the *Youth Criminal Justice Act*.

EXERCISES

1. Fourteen-year-old Liliana Rajovic was shopping with her friends at the mall. Her friends were teasing Liliana about her shoes — she was wearing cheap knock-offs of a popular and more expensive brand. Liliana was tired of the teasing and decided to shoplift a pair of the more expensive shoes. Liliana was apprehended outside the store by store security and the police were called. It is Liliana's first offence. What options are open to the police? What do you think that the police should do? Why?

2. Seventeen-year-old Brian Jenkins was driving his parents' car when he was involved in a car accident. Brian was charged with careless driving under the Ontario *Highway Traffic Act*. Describe how Brian will be prosecuted.

3. Natalie Caruso was convicted of assault when she was 17 years old and received a discharge. She is now 18 years old and has been charged as an adult with assaulting the same victim. For what purposes can Natalie's youth conviction be used by the Crown in the present case?

4. Fifteen-year-old Hoang Tran is a student at a local high school where a number of lockers had been broken into. The principal of the school believes that Hoang belongs to a gang that is responsible for the thefts and speaks to him about the incidents. During the conversation the principal tells Hoang that she knows that Hoang is involved with the thefts and that, in addition to criminal prosecution, he will be expelled from school unless he tells the principal everything he knows about the thefts. Hoang confesses and implicates a number of his friends. Police are called and Hoang repeats what he told the principal to the police and he and his friends are ultimately charged with a number of criminal offences. Can the Crown use the information Hoang provided to the principal and the police against Hoang at his trial?

PART V

Office Procedures for Criminal Law

CHAPTER 24 Common Office Procedures

Common Office Procedures

LEARNING OUTCOMES

After completing this chapter, you should be able to:

- Understand how to draft legal correspondence.

- Discuss the concepts and sources of privilege and confidentiality.

- Understand how to bill a file.

- Define the various meanings of the term "retainer."

- Discuss the various legal aid plans in Canada.

- Understand how to bill Legal Aid Ontario for criminal matters.

- Define the purpose of the most commonly used forms in the practice of criminal law.

Introduction

Criminal law offices tend to be smaller than most other law offices. In fact, many criminal lawyers are sole law practitioners. This means that anyone working in a criminal law office is likely to have considerable contact and interaction with the firm's lawyers, as well as with the firm's clients. A result of this is that the work generated in a criminal law office can provide an exciting and challenging career. All law office staff must possess various technical skills, such as computer and keyboarding abilities, as well as have some substantive knowledge of law. In a criminal law office, however, there are various office procedures that are of special importance. There are many excellent texts that review and outline general law office procedures; one, for example, is *Working in a Legal Environment*, 2nd ed. by Diana Collis and Cynthia Forget (Toronto: Emond Montgomery, 2011). The purpose of this chapter is not to provide a complete review of all law office procedures; rather, this chapter focuses on office procedures that are particularly relevant to the criminal law office.

Correspondence

legalese
language that uses obscure legal terms and that is difficult to understand without legal training

The popular perception is that lawyers and legal professionals use obscure legal terminology, commonly referred to as "**legalese**," when speaking or writing. The idea is that specialized knowledge and expertise are required to compose or decipher the meaning of legal correspondence. The reality is quite the opposite. The most effective letters and documents are written clearly and concisely and use plain language. All correspondence that leaves a law office should be easy to read and understand.

Plain Language

The first rule of effective legal writing is to use plain language. Plain language is language that is clear and understandable. If a choice must be made between two words, one that is short, clear, and universally understood and another that is technical, specialized, or ambiguous, the correct choice is the former. The purpose of writing a letter is not for the writer to impress the reader with his or her knowledge, but to convey a message. It is much easier to write effectively if this goal is kept in mind.

There are three main benefits in using plain language in legal correspondence.

1. The use of ordinary words helps the writer to organize his or her thoughts better. A clearly written letter reflects clear thinking, whereas a poorly written letter may be the result of a confused mind. There is no doubt that not everyone who uses legalese fully appreciates what they have written.

2. A clearly written letter that employs ordinary language makes it much easier for the reader to understand the message that the writer is attempting to convey. Remember that many letters are directed toward lay people who

have no specialized legal knowledge or training. These letters should "speak the reader's language" and must not be used to demonstrate the writer's skill with legalese.

3. A commonly heard complaint is that legal professionals frequently use indecipherable language. By using everyday, plain language in a straightforward manner, legal professionals can reduce readers' frustration and enhance the reputation of the profession.

In a legal context plain-language writing should be clear, well-organized, and understandable. Clear and familiar language that most people can understand should be used. Plain-language writing is generally less formal and more relaxed than what is normally associated with the legal profession. Plain-language writing is characterized by concise word use—that is, using only the words that are necessary. If legal concepts and technical terms must be used, they should be clearly defined by the writer. In short, plain-language writing is the opposite of legalese.

Standard Format

Most law offices have a standard format that is used to prepare correspondence. All letters must have the date on them and be clearly addressed to the recipient. There is a movement in modern business correspondence toward removing the salutation and directing the correspondence by title or to the appropriate department. Where a salutation is used, it should be in neutral form. Gone are the days when there was a distinction made in salutations between married and unmarried women. The problem now is that it may sometimes be difficult to identify gender when all that is known about the recipient is their name. Androgynous names are not uncommon and it can also be difficult to identify gender where the writer and recipient have different cultural backgrounds.

Elements of Correspondence

Reference Line

All correspondence should include a reference line that contains the subject matter, client's name, and both the law firm's and the recipient's reference numbers. This makes the correspondence relevant to both the recipient and the writer, and permits them to locate their respective files.

Opening Paragraph

The opening paragraph should introduce you and your topic, and establish the entire theme of the letter. Sometimes it is useful to refer to a particular piece of previous correspondence or a previous conversation in the opening paragraph. When doing this, summarize any letter or conversation referred to by its date and contents. For example: "I confirm our conversation of this morning ..." or "My client disputes the contents of your letter dated ... ."

Content

The content and message will be set out in the body of the letter. This is the most creative and difficult part of legal letter writing. The most important thing to keep in mind is that the letter should fully set out all of the essential and relevant facts necessary to convey your message. Think about the "Five Ws": *who, what, when, where,* and *why*—your letter should address all that are relevant to the message you want to convey. If you are requesting that something be done, you should explain how that can be accomplished.

The following five steps will help you in conveying your message to the reader when writing the body of a letter:

1. *Know your reader.* Write to the level of the reader and write with a purpose. The reader should know the purpose of the letter and what action, if any, to take.

2. *Plan the correspondence.* Do not write without a plan. Think about what message you wish to convey and how best to convey it. It is helpful to make a list for any letter that will contain more than one piece of information. Use as few words as possible for each idea. After you have listed all of the information that is to be contained in the letter, sequence the list so that the letter will flow logically. Generally, it is good to start with the most important matters first.

3. *Write the letter.* Expand each listed item into a simple sentence and link the sentences together. Use short sentences whenever possible and confine each paragraph to one thought or point. It is acceptable, and in many cases preferable, to use headings and bullets. Try to be as concise as possible and stay on topic. You are not writing a novel.

4. *Review and edit.* Look for errors and edit for content and style. This tests how well your letter was written.

5. *Consider asking for feedback.* Show your letter to someone else in the office if you are unsure of its content or effectiveness. In some offices it may be standard practice for more experienced staff to review all correspondence.

Closing

You should always close a letter with care and purpose. Instead of reciting stock phrases in your closing paragraph, select words that will create a positive impression and invite a constructive response or action from the recipient. Take the opportunity to summarize what you want from the recipient or what your next course of action will be. This may take the form of a direct request: "Please send me all of your receipts"; a specific statement: "I will be sending you details of the meeting as soon as they are available"; or a question: "When would you like to come in for a meeting?"

Complimentary closings (e.g., "Yours truly") should be consistent in tone and style with opening salutations. Letters that contain formal salutations such as "Sir" or "Madam" should end with a formal closing salutation such as "Yours respectfully."

The slightly less formal "Dear Ms./Mr." should be followed by "Yours truly" or "Yours sincerely." Letters that start with the familiar salutation "Dear Ivan" or "Dear Ivan Hersch" can be closed with "Regards" or "Best regards." Particular care should be taken when addressing a member of the judiciary. The proper title in the inside address for a judge is "The Honourable Mr./Madam Justice Singh" followed by "Dear Justice Singh" as the salutation. A chief justice or associate chief justice should also be referred to by title in a salutation. Letters to judges should close with the most formal ending: "Respectfully" or "Respectfully yours."

Revisions

Other than for straightforward form letters, changes will usually be made at some point when writing a letter. It may be necessary for the writer to loop back to an earlier stage in the writing and work forward again; this process may have to be repeated several times before the letter is completed and the desired result achieved.

Electronic Correspondence

It should be noted that legal correspondence includes electronic communication and email. Many people wrongfully assume that it is permissible to be less formal when using electronic forms of communication. This is probably because it is usually instantaneous, and taking informal shortcuts makes communicating even faster. After all, the faster a letter is drafted, the sooner it can be sent. The reality is, however, that when working in a law office there should be no distinction made between electronic communication and hard copy mail. The same rules apply to both with regard to the salutation, reference line, content, and complimentary closing. Note that it is not appropriate to use short forms for words; for example, do not use "u r" for "you are" or "c" for "see."

Take the time to carefully review all electronic correspondence. Because of the ease and speed with which electronic communication is sent, it is imperative that the correspondence be reviewed. It is a good idea to print an email for review before it is sent so that you can check for formatting and other errors that are difficult to spot on a display screen. One common mistake that can be embarrassing and may compromise a client's position is to mistakenly choose "reply to all" instead of "reply to sender." Once "send" has been selected, it is too late to take back the message.

Privileged Communications

Solicitor–Client Privilege

The concept of **solicitor–client privilege** means that certain communications are to be treated as confidential and kept private from the rest of the world. It is essential to the solicitor–client relationship that communications between a solicitor and client remain privileged. Imagine for a moment what the relationship would be like if a lawyer went to the police with information that was obtained from a client. What do you think would happen if a client admitted to a lawyer that he had

solicitor–client privilege
a form of privilege that applies to communications between a lawyer and his or her client

committed a crime and the lawyer made the details public? There really would be no relationship at all. No client would ever again speak candidly with their lawyer and provide information that might prove harmful if something like this took place. It is essential to the operation of our criminal justice system that a client be able to speak freely with his or her lawyer without fear of repercussions. In order to properly advise and act in the best interests of a client, a lawyer must be armed with all available information, including the client's candid story. Employees and agents of lawyers are subject to the same privilege rules that apply to lawyers. It is important that those who work in a law office fully understand how the concept of **privilege** applies to them. A paralegal, law clerk, or anyone else in the employ of a lawyer is bound by the same rules regarding privilege that apply to their employer.

privilege
a rule that requires certain communications to be kept confidential and private

When Is a Communication Privileged?

There are several rules that must be canvassed in order to fully understand what privilege is, how it arises, and when it can be waived. The starting point for any discussion on privilege is the common-law evidentiary rule that requires lawyers to keep confidential any information that has been provided by a client. Solicitor–client privilege is the oldest and most recognized form of privilege. In order for a communication to be privileged, it must be in relation to the *seeking, forming, or giving of legal advice*, so not all communications are privileged. A conversation or written communication is only privileged when a client is communicating with a lawyer to obtain legal advice. A casual conversation on non-legal matters with a lawyer is not privileged. This means that a conversation may not be privileged in one context, while the same conversation may very well be privileged in another context. For example, privilege may not apply in a situation where a person playing golf with a lawyer casually discloses that he or she is contemplating purchasing stocks in a certain company; however, the same discussion would be considered privileged if the disclosure was made within the context of obtaining legal advice about the proposed purchase.

In addition, for a communication to be privileged, it must also be made in confidence. This means that the person making the communication has an obligation to protect the information. For example, a client speaking to a lawyer in a crowded elevator has opened the privilege door and released the information to the world. In a situation like this, the communication is not privileged because it was not made in confidence. It was, instead, released to the public.

When Is a Communication Not Privileged?

Even if a communication concerns legal advice and is confidential in nature, it will not be privileged if the communication itself is criminal or made for the purpose of facilitating a crime. Privilege would not attach to any communication where a lawyer, for example, was involved in a criminal conspiracy with a client, aided a client in committing real estate fraud, or laundered drug money on behalf of a client. It would be absurd for these and other similar situations to be privileged just because they involved a lawyer and a client. A lawyer's function is to help clients who have been charged with committing an offence, not to help them commit offences.

When Is Disclosure Permitted Under the Common Law?

Even if a communication is privileged, its disclosure would be permitted in two situations:

1. Where a threat of imminent harm has been made to an identifiable person or group, a lawyer must take all necessary steps to protect the person or group, even if it means that confidential information must be revealed. However, the lawyer can only reveal as much information as is necessary to protect the person or group in question.

2. Disclosure may also be permitted if the lawyer has confidential information that would serve to establish the innocence of an accused who had been wrongfully charged with a crime. In that case, there is available a narrowly applied exception to privilege called "innocence at stake." This exception applies only in very unusual cases.

> In summary, communications between a solicitor and client are privileged where they
>
> - are of a confidential nature,
> - relate to the seeking, forming, or giving of legal advice, and
> - are not criminal in nature or do not facilitate criminal activity.
>
> Communications between a solicitor and client are not privileged where they
>
> - are necessary to establish the innocence of an accused person, or
> - put public safety at risk.

Whose Privilege Is It? or Alternatively, Who Owns the Privilege?

It is important to realize that the privilege "belongs" to the client and not to the lawyer or others in the law office. Solicitor and client privilege continues even after the client is no longer a client of the lawyer or the client has died. The lawyer, as well as the lawyer's employees and agents, continues to be obligated to respect the privilege.

Litigation Privilege

Another common-law form of privilege that is similar to solicitor–client privilege is **litigation privilege**. The purpose of litigation privilege is to facilitate a smoothly functioning litigation system. Unlike solicitor–client privilege, which applies to communications between a lawyer and client, this form of privilege protects communications between a lawyer and third parties, if the dominant purpose of the

litigation privilege
a form of privilege that applies to communications between a lawyer and third parties where the dominant purpose of the communication is pending or actual litigation

communication is to obtain information for either existing or contemplated litigation. For example, letters from a lawyer to an expert seeking the expert's opinion about a technical aspect of a case or a client's medical condition would be privileged, as would be the expert's response.

With this privilege in place, a lawyer is able to freely seek the opinion of an expert without fear of having to disclose a harmful opinion or report to the other side in the litigation. While it may at first seem unfair to allow lawyers to keep unhelpful reports hidden from the other side in litigation, the fact is that no lawyer could properly assess and prepare for a case involving complex technological or medical issues without the help of an expert. If this information were not privileged, lawyers would be much more reluctant to obtain opinions and reports from experts and could not effectively represent their clients' interests, and it would be much more difficult for cases to be resolved prior to trial or to prove at trial. This rule permits a lawyer to fully assess, without fear of reprisal, the strengths and weaknesses of his or her client's case, prepare for trial, and put forth the best evidence at trial in support of the client's case.

Waiving Litigation Privilege

As with all forms of privilege, litigation privilege may be waived. This means, for example, that the report of an expert may be used in the litigation that supports the client's case if privilege has been waived for the report. In that event, a copy of the report would be provided to the other side. It must be noted that all provinces and territories have special rules in both criminal and civil matters that set out minimum notice periods for providing to the other side copies of any reports that will be used at trial.

Without Prejudice Communications

Sometimes communications with the other side in litigation are privileged. Settlement discussions, including any plea negotiations, enjoy a form of privilege and cannot be disclosed to the court during a trial. The reason is evident: by their nature, settlement discussions provide a forum during which sensitive information will be revealed. Further, the fact that a party may be discussing a negotiated resolution to the case may raise an inference of guilt or liability. After all, some might think, why would a person talk about settlement if they were completely blameless? Because of this risk, it is always prudent to expressly note that settlement negotiations are to be treated confidentially. The best way to ensure this is to preface any written offers or compromises with the words "**without prejudice**." This is clear evidence that the parties intend the discussion to remain privileged and off-limits to the court.

without prejudice communications
a form of privilege that extends to communications concerning settlement discussions

Rules and Codes of Conduct

The common-law privilege rules that arise in a solicitor–client relationship have been modified and extended by the rules that regulate and govern the way lawyers conduct themselves. The 14 provincial and territorial law societies have ethical codes of professional conduct that regulate the behaviour of their members. As part of belonging to a law society, these codes of conduct obligate lawyers to keep confidential all information that is acquired in the course of providing legal services to clients. The ethical rules are wider than the common-law evidentiary rules of privilege and apply irrespective of the nature and source of the information possessed by the lawyer and whether or not the information is shared by others. While the evidentiary rules are all about excluding evidence from the litigation process, the ethical rules provide a blanket obligation of confidentiality over all information that has been acquired by a lawyer during a professional relationship. By way of example, Rule 2.03(1) of the *Rules of Professional Conduct* of Ontario's Law Society of Upper Canada is quite typical and provides as follows:

> 2.03(1) A lawyer at all times shall hold in strict confidence all information concerning the business and affairs of the client acquired in the course of the professional relationship and shall not divulge any such information unless expressly or impliedly authorized by the client or required by law to do so.

Disclosure of Confidential Information

Generally, confidential information can only be disclosed if disclosure is authorized by the client, by law, by order of a court or tribunal, or when there is an imminent risk of death or serious harm to an identifiable person or group. Disclosure may also be permitted where it is necessary for the lawyer to respond to allegations of wrongdoing or to collect fees. Even where disclosure is permitted, the lawyer is not permitted to disclose any more information than is necessary in the circumstances.

Respect for the Client Is Paramount

Everyone who works for a lawyer is obliged to treat information concerning the affairs of a client confidentially. Even the identity of a client or the fact that a certain individual may have consulted with a lawyer must be treated confidentially and cannot be disclosed to others. Those who receive confidential information are obliged to protect it from careless disclosure. Confidential communications must not be discussed in public places such as elevators or restaurants. Similarly, gossiping may result in confidential matters being disclosed and should be avoided, as should careless disclosure to friends and family members.

Billing

In addition to providing clients with legal services, a private law office is also a business. Salaries, rent, office and equipment expenses, expenses incurred on behalf of clients, law society levies, and other costs associated with running a law office must all be accounted for and paid. The money to cover these expenses comes from fees that are charged to clients. In most cases, a law firm will be paid only after issuing a bill or invoice to the client.

Accounting

It is first necessary to understand some basic accounting principles as they relate to lawyers before discussing how invoices are issued. Most lawyers will have at least two bank accounts: (1) a general account from which general expenses and salaries are paid and (2) a trust account, which is the account where a client's money is kept before it is disbursed. Lawyers will usually require that a **retainer** be paid to the firm before they undertake any work on behalf of a client. A retainer, in this sense, is a deposit of money from the client. All retainers are initially deposited into a lawyer's trust account because a lawyer is entitled to be paid only after having earned his or her fees through having provided legal services to a client and, generally, a bill can only be issued after legal services have been provided to a client. Any funds held on behalf of a client in the trust account can be transferred to the general account after the client's file has been billed and a copy of the invoice has been provided to the client. If there are no funds held in trust on behalf of a client, bills will remain outstanding until they have been paid by a client. A client can be billed in full after completion of the case, or at intervals as legal services are provided. It is permissible to use money that is held in a trust account to pay for out-of-pocket disbursements incurred on behalf of a client.

Provincial law societies have rules that require lawyers to maintain various detailed accounting journals and records. Some of the records that must be maintained include the following:

- a trust record detailing all moneys that are received in trust for a client,
- a trust record detailing all moneys that have been disbursed from funds held in trust for a client,
- a client's trust ledger showing all trust transactions for that client,
- a record showing all transfers of money between clients' trust ledger accounts,
- a record detailing all receipts other than trust receipts,
- a record detailing all disbursements other than trust disbursements,
- a billings journal,
- a record detailing all property other than money held in trust for a client, and
- a record detailing all moneys that have been received in the form of cash.

Lawyers are also required to keep the usual records and ledgers that are kept by any other business. These include ledgers for payroll, employment insurance, Canada Pension Plan benefits, harmonized sales tax (HST), and so forth.

Accounting Software

In the past, keeping such a variety of records was a time-consuming and expensive task that was often left to an accountant or bookkeeper. Most firms now use specialized legal accounting software such as PCLaw, which was designed for ease of use and maintains all of the journals required in a law office. PCLaw is a "one-write"

retainer (deposit)
a deposit paid by a client before legal services have been provided by a lawyer

system that automatically institutes all of the necessary entries in the appropriate journals by entering the data in one place. For example, the appropriate journals and records are updated when a trust or general cheque is prepared using the software. Similarly, general and trust receipts are only recorded once. The software will also track expenses incurred on behalf of a client, as well as keep track of **dockets** (time spent working on a file). All of this information will appear on an invoice when the software is used to prepare bills. PCLaw will also track items that are not specific to law offices, such as the HST, and will create records and ledgers for those entries. Finally, PCLaw can generate productivity reports and financial statements for the law firm.

docket
a record of time spent working on a client matter

Billing Methods

Criminal lawyers will issue bills to clients based on either the amount of time that has been spent working on a file, or on a **block fee** arrangement. **Contingency fees** (i.e., fees contingent upon success) are generally not permissible in criminal matters.

block fee
a pre-arranged amount that will be paid to the lawyer for providing specified legal services to the client

Dockets

Most law firms will have a system to track the time that is spent working on files. Lawyers keep track of their time using dockets. Dockets are simply records of time spent and are used to prepare bills that are based on time. Most lawyers keep track of their own dockets using either a manual system or software such as PCLaw. Dockets are recorded in increments of six minutes or tenths of an hour, as the following table indicates:

contingency fee
an agreement between a lawyer and client that legal fees will be payable and based on a future event occurring; normally, a contingency fee is payable upon successful completion of a matter and is calculated as a percentage of any moneys recovered by the lawyer

Docket Time Increments		
Tenths of an Hour	**Time in Minutes**	**Docket Time**
1	Up to 6	0.1
2	Up to 12	0.2
3	Up to 18	0.3
4	Up to 24	0.4
5	Up to 30	0.5
6	Up to 36	0.6
7	Up to 42	0.7
8	Up to 48	0.8
9	Up to 54	0.9
10	Up to 60	1.0

So, for example, a lawyer who worked on a file for 45 minutes would docket 0.8. If, later in the day, the lawyer worked another 90 minutes on the same file, he or she would then docket a further 1.5. The total time docketed in the day for the file would be 2.3 (0.8 plus 1.5).

When a file is ready to be billed out, the dockets are itemized on the bill. The bill will show the total of all dockets and the fee will be determined by multiplying the total docketed time by the lawyer's hourly rate. Therefore, if a lawyer with an hourly rate of $400 has docketed a total of 12.3 hours, the client would be billed a total fee of $4,920. Added to this amount would be any expenses (also called disbursements) incurred on behalf of a client, plus the applicable HST.

Block Fees

A block fee is pre-arranged and does not depend on time spent working on a file. As an example, a lawyer may agree to defend a client for a fee of $5,000 without regard to the amount of time that will be spent working on the file. Block fees can also be modified to account for variables such as whether there will be a plea of guilty or a trial. So, using this method, a matter would be billed a certain amount for a guilty plea and a higher amount if there were a trial. Block fees may be inclusive of disbursements or there may be an additional charge for any disbursements. HST would be charged as applicable.

Most criminal lawyers charge block fees for their work.

Retainer Agreements

The word "retainer" has several different meanings in the legal profession. It can be used to describe the existence of a relationship between a lawyer and client. More specifically, a lawyer is said to be retained by a client when the lawyer undertakes to provide specified legal services to the client. A **retainer** can also mean moneys paid to a lawyer by a client to secure the lawyer's services. In this sense, a retainer is a deposit on account from which the lawyer can pay expenses incurred on behalf of a client and to satisfy any outstanding accounts for providing legal services. This is the meaning discussed above under the heading "Billing."

retainer (engagement)
the engagement by a client of a lawyer to provide specified legal services

In this section, **retainer** refers to a written agreement between a lawyer and his or her client that specifies the rights and obligations of both parties. Most law offices will have a standard form of a retainer agreement that can be modified to meet the particular needs of individual clients. A typical retainer agreement will cover some or all of the following points.

retainer (agreement)
a written agreement or contract that sets out the rights and obligations of the lawyer and client

Scope of Engagement

In a criminal matter the client will usually retain the lawyer for a specific charge or for several charges. The retainer may simply set out that the lawyer will represent the client in a specified matter and take all actions and proceedings necessary to defend the client. Sometimes the retainer will be restricted to certain procedures such as attending at a preliminary inquiry or appearing at a sentencing hearing. Most retainer agreements will include clauses that permit a lawyer to use his or her discretion in incurring **disbursements** on behalf of a client—for example, the retaining of medical or technical experts. Sometimes a retainer will include a clause that permits the lawyer to employ other lawyers as agents in performing work for the client.

disbursements
out-of-pocket expenses incurred by a lawyer on behalf of a client

Fees

A necessary component of every retainer agreement is a provision that details how and when fees will be charged to the client. As previously outlined in this chapter, criminal lawyers use an hourly rate or block fee in calculating a client's bill. The retainer agreement should specify which method will be used. In the case of an hourly rate, the retainer agreement will normally specify that all time spent working on a file will be recorded, and will set out the applicable rate for each person in the firm who will work on the client's file. The billing period will vary depending on the practice of the lawyer and the nature of the matter. Some matters may be billed periodically, usually quarterly, while other matters may be billed by progress on the file or upon completion of stages. Many retainer agreements also set out that the specified hourly rates are subject to periodic revision upon notice to the client.

Where billing is on a block fee basis, the amount of the fee and the billing date should be set out in the retainer agreement. In addition, a clause may be inserted that will cause the fee to be adjusted in the event that extra or unanticipated matters arise in the course of completing the matter.

Disbursements

Lawyers usually incur expenses on behalf of clients when working on their cases. In the case of block fees, these disbursements may be included in the fee that is charged to the client. However, the retainer agreement should specify whether disbursements will be billed in addition to fees. In that case, a comprehensive retainer agreement may list typical disbursements, such as long distance telephone calls, photocopies, courier charges, travel expenses, and any government filing or search charges, as well as fees charged by agents who may undertake various tasks on behalf of a lawyer.

Interest

Most lawyers charge interest for accounts that are not paid within 30 days. The retainer agreement should specify when interest is charged, the date from which interest is charged. and the interest rate.

Retainer (Deposit)

Many lawyers have experienced the harsh reality of having completed legal work on behalf of a client that goes unpaid. This is why most lawyers prefer to keep a sum of money on deposit in a trust account on behalf of a client from which they draw funds to cover billed fees and disbursements. This ensures that legal accounts are paid and are paid in a timely manner. Accordingly, a typical retainer agreement will require that the client provide the lawyer with a deposit before any legal services are undertaken by the lawyer. The amount of the deposit will vary and will depend on a number of factors, such as the lawyer's hourly rate, any block fee, the complexity of the work, the anticipated time that will be devoted to the client's file, and any expected disbursements that will be incurred on behalf of a client. If the retainer agreement requires that a deposit be made, there will also usually be a provision that requires the client to replenish the deposit from time to time as it is drawn upon to satisfy the lawyer's fees and disbursements. In that case, the deposit acts essentially as an account that the client must keep in good standing.

Termination of Retainer

Sometimes a solicitor–client relationship is terminated before the completion of the client's matter. The relationship may be terminated either by the client or by the lawyer. This can happen for many reasons. The client may have lost confidence in the lawyer, retained a new lawyer, or may no longer require the lawyer's services. Some of the common reasons for lawyers to terminate the relationship include:

- the client fails to either accept or give instructions,
- the client fails to disclose important facts,
- the client fails to cooperate with reasonable requests,
- continuing to act for the client would be illegal or unethical,
- the retainer has not been paid, or
- accounts have not been paid.

The retainer agreement will outline situations in which the solicitor–client relationship can be terminated. There is a complicating factor in criminal cases in that the retainer agreement cannot derogate from the lawyer's obligation as an officer of the court. Once a lawyer has represented to the court that he or she is acting on a matter, the lawyer is duty-bound to complete the matter unless permission is received from the court to withdraw from the case. Permission to withdraw requires that the lawyer make an appearance before the court that has jurisdiction over the matter to ask to be removed as solicitor of record. A court may not grant the request if the matter is close to trial or if the client's case would be prejudiced by the lawyer's withdrawal. Normally, however, the request will be granted.

Legal Aid

The Development of Legal Aid

Legal aid is administered and provided at the provincial level in Canada. Prior to 1967, legal aid did not formally exist in any province in Canada. Instead, senior criminal lawyers would often agree to provide pro bono legal services for people who were charged with criminal offences and could not afford to retain a lawyer. In other words, legal aid was provided by volunteer lawyers who would agree to take on criminal cases free of charge. This changed in 1967 when Ontario became the first province to adopt a legal aid plan that funded the provision of legal services to qualified applicants based on need. In 1972 the federal government agreed to contribute about half the cost of providing legal aid for criminal matters in each province. Today, all of the provinces provide one form or another of legal aid to those in need of legal representation and who cannot afford to privately retain a lawyer.

Licensing and Regulation

It is noteworthy that while the Law Society of Upper Canada currently licenses and regulates paralegals, only lawyers and those working under the supervision of a lawyer are permitted to provide legal aid services in Ontario. Paralegals are not licensed in any other Canadian province and are unable to provide legal aid services directly to the public.

The Provision of Legal Aid

Most provinces provide legal aid by using one or a combination of different service delivery models—salaried legal aid staff or lawyers in private practice are paid a prescribed fee or tariff. Currently, Prince Edward Island is the only province that does not have a legal aid act. Instead, Prince Edward Island offers legal aid through a salaried staff **judicare** model.

judicare
a government-funded program that provides free legal services to those who meet financial eligibility requirements

The salaried legal aid staff model provides legal aid by offering summary or basic legal advice by telephone or over the Internet, by providing salaried duty counsel to courthouses, or by operating legal aid clinics staffed by salaried lawyers. Duty counsel are normally assigned to work in courthouses and they provide basic legal advice to those facing criminal charges. In addition, duty counsel may appear at bail hearings and guilty pleas on minor matters, or speak to the court on procedural issues such as adjournment requests. Accused persons seeking full representation attend a legal aid clinic and receive legal services from clinic lawyers and staff. Under this model, clients are assigned lawyers to handle their cases. The disadvantage of this system from a client's perspective is that the client cannot be represented by a lawyer of his or her choosing.

Under the private practice model, clients meeting eligibility requirements[1] are typically issued a voucher or certificate that they are free to take to any lawyer in private practice who agrees to represent them. Under this model, the client chooses their own lawyer. The lawyer will be paid by the legal aid plan for providing the services that are specified in the legal aid certificate. The lawyer may be paid either a block fee or an hourly rate, depending on the criminal charge.

---

1. Eligibility for legal aid is usually determined by a combination of financial need and the seriousness of the charges the client is facing.

Fees

Block Fees

Block fees are fixed fees that are usually paid on common criminal charges where specified services are provided to the client. In Ontario, block fees are payable in summary conviction matters and for less serious indictable charges. Block fees are paid for specified services and the amount of the fee varies with the nature of the service provided to the client. For example, Legal Aid Ontario provides block fees for the following services: guilty pleas, withdrawal/stay of charges, bail hearings, pretrial hearings, Charter motions, and bail review, as well as for attendance in specialized courts. The amount of the block fee varies with the service provided, with less paid for procedural matters such as bail hearings and pretrial hearings and more paid for complex resolution matters such as guilty pleas and withdrawal of charges.

Block fees are usually calculated to include payment for the types of disbursements most commonly incurred in completing client matters. These include facsimile and photocopying charges. Other disbursements, such as experts' or private investigators' fees, are payable in accordance with a prescribed tariff.

Block fees are calculated to provide a reasonable level of remuneration to a lawyer for providing specified legal services. There is a risk to lawyers that hourly earnings will be lower on matters that require more of a lawyer's time to resolve than on matters that can be completed quickly. In other words, the disadvantage of block fees from a lawyer's point of view is that longer, more complex matters will result in an effectively reduced hourly rate being paid to complete the client's file. However, on the whole, the goal of providing fair compensation to the lawyer and cost certainty to the legal aid plan is best achieved through the use of block fees.

In addition to providing a fair level of remuneration, block fees provide the following benefits to lawyers:

- They eliminate the need for lawyers to keep dockets or track time.
- They reduce billing administration.
- They provide financial certainty to a lawyer.
- They reward efficient and effective lawyers.

Billing by Time

Billings based on time spent working on a file is the other method commonly used to determine the amount a lawyer will be paid for his or her work. When billing by time, a lawyer (and in some instances, office staff) is required to keep dockets that are submitted to the legal aid plan on an interim or final basis. This method is intended to compensate a lawyer for the actual time it takes to complete a matter instead of compensating a lawyer on completion of a matter.

Legal Aid Ontario

Legal Aid Ontario does not offer lawyers the option to select a preferred billing method. As discussed earlier, block fees are paid for the most common criminal offences. All other criminal matters are billed by time. The amount of time that can be billed to any one matter is usually subject to a maximum limit. In Ontario, the legal aid certificate authorizes the particular services that a lawyer will be paid to provide to a client. Billings are subject to a tariff that sets out a prescribed hourly rate that is based on experience and expertise as well as the maximum hours that can be billed for the matter.[2] Lawyers are entitled to be paid one of four prescribed hourly rates. The first three rates increase with the billing lawyer's certified years of experience. The fourth and highest rate is reserved for lawyers who have been approved to take on complex cases. The tariff maximum limit of hours that can be billed on a matter depends on the charges authorized, the progress of the case, and how the charges are disposed of. The first step in calculating the tariff maximum is to determine the legal aid tariff category of the most serious charge authorized by the legal aid certificate. All offences fall into one of four legal aid categories: (1) summary conviction offences, (2) indictable Type I offences, (3) indictable Type II offences, and (4) provincial offences and other federal summary conviction offences. Next, there are tables for each of the categories that set out the maximum time that can be billed for providing various services. This means that there is a tariff maximum for each type of service provided. For example, offences within the same category that are resolved by a guilty plea are subject to a lower tariff maximum than matters that are concluded with a trial. Additional services such as bail hearings or judicial pretrial conferences generate additional tariff maximums. In short, the effective hourly rate increases with the seriousness of the offence, and the tariff maximum is determined by what services were provided to the client.[3]

Disbursements

Most disbursements that have been incurred while working on a file will be reimbursed. Some common disbursements, such as those for photocopying and postage, do not require prior authorization. Many larger disbursements, however, require authorization for payment before they are incurred. Most of the disbursements that require authorization are subject to a tariff maximum.[4]

---

2. The current tariff for Ontario is available on the website of Legal Aid Ontario. Other provincial legal aid plans have made similar resources available online.

3. For complete details on the Ontario tariff, see the Legal Aid Ontario website (http://www .legalaid.on.ca), where you can find in downloadable form the *Tariff and Billing Handbook*, which contains detailed billing instructions for all legal aid matters in Ontario. Similar resources are available for other provinces; for example, the Legal Services Society of British Columbia, in addition to making its forms, tariffs, and instructions available online, also publishes a handy electronic newsletter entitled the *Legal Aid Brief* several times a year.

4. For complete instructions, see the *Disbursements Handbook*, which is available as a download on the Legal Aid Ontario website.

Submitting Bills

Legal Aid Ontario accounts are billed online using the Legal Aid Online billing system (http://www.legalaid.on.ca/en/info). The system was designed for ease of use, especially for block fee billings. After signing in, lawyers are able to create on-line accounts with an easy-to-use form. A legal aid certificate number is either entered or selected from a list of all outstanding certificates. The account page for each certificate is pre-populated with basic background information about the file. The lawyer is prompted to complete certain required fields by using a drop-down menu, answering yes and no questions, and filling in blanks. For matters to be billed and paid by time rather than by block fee, the lawyer must enter the time that was spent on the file by each person in the office and the amounts of individual disbursements. The account itself is generated by the online system. The final step is to submit the account electronically. The system then provides a confirmation number and produces a printable account.[5]

It is expected that all accounts submitted to Legal Aid Ontario will fall within the allotted time limits. Where exceptional circumstances can be demonstrated, a discretionary increase in payment may be permitted where the tariff maximum has been exceeded. Requests for a discretionary increase should be made only after the tariff maximum has been exceeded, and not in advance. Discretionary increase requests must be made in writing either by using Legal Aid Ontario's Request for Discretion—Criminal Law form or by writing a letter. The request should be attached to the account for which the discretionary increase is sought and should include detailed reasons that justify the request. Some of the factors that may justify a discretionary increase include the following:

- where an exceptional result was obtained;
- where the matter was more complex than anticipated;
- when extra preparation time was spent on a lengthy trial; and
- any other relevant factors that would warrant an increased fee, such as use of exceptional Crown resources, disclosure problems, or a high-profile case.

The Request for Discretion—Criminal Law form lists several other reasons that would justify a discretionary increase.[6]

---

5. Complete instructions are available in the *Legal Aid Online User Guide* available on the Legal Aid Ontario website (http://www.legalaid.on.ca/en/info/legalaidonline_billingtutorials.asp); the website also features a step-by-step short video on how to submit electronic accounts.

6. The Legal Aid Ontario website provides several examples of other factors that would justify a discretionary increase. These include, among others, the seriousness and number of charges, the length of trial, the number of parties, the volume of disclosure, the complexity of evidence, the amount of court time saved, and the amount of money saved by Legal Aid Ontario.

Legal Forms and Documents

Unlike in civil proceedings, there are very few forms used in criminal law. There are two reasons for this. First, the practice of criminal law is not paper intensive. There are no pleadings and discovery rules in criminal law and the process is not driven by motions and applications. Further, many criminal charges are resolved by a plea of guilty at a relatively early stage of the proceeding. Even when cases are resolved later or proceed to trial, the process normally flows disruption-free and there is usually very little reason to use the few forms that do exist.

The second reason that criminal practice is less paper intensive than civil litigation lies in the nature of criminal law itself. Criminal law is a form of public law that pits the Crown against a single offender. Not only is the burden of proof on the Crown, but so is the onus to take the case to trial. As a result, a person who has been charged with an offence does not have to do anything other than to appear as required in court for a case to be brought to trial. It is the Crown and police who are responsible for completing whatever little paperwork is required to initiate and maintain the prosecution of a person who has been charged with committing a criminal offence.

Criminal Code Forms

The following is a brief summary of the most commonly used forms in the *Criminal Code*. The actual forms are reproduced in the Appendix to this book.

Form 1: Information to Obtain a Search Warrant

This is the form that is used by the police when appearing before a justice to obtain a search warrant. The process for obtaining a search warrant is described in Chapter 13, Investigatory Powers.

Form 2: Information

This document initiates the prosecution of all criminal offences. Informations are dealt with in Chapter 16, Informations and Indictments.

Form 4: Indictment

An Indictment replaces an Information where the accused is charged with an indictable offence and the matter is before the Superior Court of Justice. Indictments are dealt with in Chapter 16, Informations and Indictments.

Form 5: Warrant to Search

This form is commonly referred to as a search warrant and provides the police with authority to search a building, receptacle, or place. There are also a number of forms following Form 5 that sequentially relate to warrants for the taking of bodily substances for DNA testing. The process for obtaining and executing search warrants is dealt with in Chapter 13, Investigatory Powers.

Form 5.1: Warrant to Search

Where a peace officer believes that an indictable offence has been committed and it is impractical to appear before a justice, an Information in Form 1 may be submitted by telephone or other means of electronic communication for a search warrant in Form 5.1.

Form 6: Summons to a Person Charged with an Offence

A summons in Form 6 is issued by a justice in circumstances where it is not appropriate for the justice to issue a warrant for the arrest of a person who is charged with an offence. The procedure for obtaining a summons is set out in Chapter 14, Bringing the Accused Before Court.

Form 7: Warrant for Arrest

A justice has the power to issue a warrant for the arrest of a person who has been charged with a criminal offence. This topic is covered in Chapter 14, Bringing the Accused Before Court.

Form 7.1: Warrant to Enter Dwelling-House

This warrant permits the police to enter a dwelling house to arrest a person who has been charged with a criminal offence.

Form 9: Appearance Notice Issued by a Peace Officer to a Person Not Yet Charged with an Offence

This form is issued by a peace officer to a person who has not yet been charged with an offence. Appearance notices are fully dealt with in Chapter 14, Bringing the Accused Before Court.

Form 10: Promise to Appear

A peace officer may release a person who has been arrested upon the person giving their promise to appear in court. This topic is covered in Chapter 15, Release of the Accused Prior to Trial.

Form 11: Recognizance Entered into Before an Officer in Charge or Other Peace Officer

A peace officer may release a person who has been arrested upon the person entering into a recognizance before a peace officer. This topic is covered in Chapter 15, Release of the Accused Prior to Trial.

Form 11.1: Undertaking Given to a Peace Officer or an Officer in Charge

A person released from custody by way of a Promise to Appear or recognizance may be required to enter into an undertaking to abide by specified conditions. This topic is covered in Chapter 15, Release of the Accused Prior to Trial.

Form 12: Undertaking Given to a Justice or a Judge

This form is used when a person who has been arrested is released by a justice on the person's undertaking to appear in court and abide by specified conditions. This topic is covered in Chapter 15, Release of the Accused Prior to Trial.

Form 16: Subpoena to a Witness

A subpoena is used by the Crown or defence to compel the attendance of a witness to give evidence in court. Subpoenas are issued by a judge, justice, or clerk of the court. The defence normally obtains a subpoena from the clerk of the court. A subpoena must be served personally on the witnesses. The preparation of witnesses is canvassed in Chapter 19, The Trial.

Form 32: Recognizance

A person who has been arrested may be released by the court upon entering into a recognizance. This topic is covered in Chapter 15, Release of the Accused Prior to Trial.

Form 46: Probation Order

A person who has been convicted of a criminal offence may be sentenced to a period of probation. Probation is fully discussed in Chapter 20, Sentencing.

Superior and Provincial Court Forms

The superior and provincial courts also have forms for procedures that are not covered by the forms contained in the *Criminal Code*. All of these forms are available online at the websites of the appropriate provincial Attorney General or the Department of Justice Canada. While it is simply not possible to reference and reproduce all of the forms, the following are the forms used under the *Criminal Rules of the Ontario Court of Justice*. These three forms are reproduced in the Appendix to this book.

Form 1: Application

An application is used when the applicant is seeking an order or some form of relief, usually prior to trial. Non-constitutional applications are typically made for procedural matters such as a request for an adjournment, an order to sever counts or accused, an order for particulars, or an order to remove counsel of record.

Form 2: Response

A party responding to an application will use Form 2.

Form 3: Consent

Where the parties agree to the disposition on an application, the parties can file a consent using Form 3.

CHAPTER SUMMARY

Working in a law office is a rewarding yet demanding career. In addition to general office procedures, law office staff need to possess specialized skills and knowledge that can be gained through experience and/or education. Given the nature of the work and the pressures associated with representing persons who have been charged with criminal offences, working in a criminal law office can be even more challenging than working in a general law practice. However, the rewards associated with guiding and helping clients through potentially life-altering events easily outweigh the special challenges of working in a criminal law office.

Today's law offices are very different from those of as recently as 20 years ago. The biggest changes are based on emerging technology, and there is no doubt that technology will continue to evolve and that new advances will be made. However, there are things that have remained the same over the past 20 years, and will continue to remain the same. Lawyers operate a business that provides legal services, and those services are subject to regulation and special rules—this is something that will not change, and everyone working in a law office must be familiar with and keep up-to-date on criminal law regulations and rules.

KEY TERMS

block fee, 319
contingency fee, 319
disbursements, 321
docket, 319
judicare, 323

legalese, 310
litigation privilege, 315
privilege, 314
retainer (agreement), 320
retainer (deposit), 318

retainer (engagement), 320
solicitor–client privilege, 313
without prejudice
   communications, 316

REVIEW QUESTIONS

1. What are the advantages of using plain language instead of legalese when corresponding with clients and other law offices?

2. What are the five steps to follow when writing the body of a letter?

3. What are the various types of privilege and confidentiality obligations that you should be familiar with when working in any law office?

4. What are the three methods used by lawyers to bill their work? Which of these methods are used by criminal lawyers?

5. The word "retainer" has several meanings in the legal profession. Identify and define three different meanings for "retainer."

6. What specific provisions does a typical retainer agreement contain?

7. What are the two different ways that legal aid services can be provided to the public? How is legal aid provided in your province?

EXERCISES

1. Assume that you work for criminal lawyer Natalie Persaud, who represented Ellen Habbid. Ellen was charged with theft under $5,000 and possession under $5,000. Ellen was acquitted of both charges following a half-day trial. Write a reporting letter to the client. You can provide any missing details such as dates and addresses.

2. Ryan Jyles was charged with assault causing bodily harm. He met with his lawyer, Francis Capote, at a downtown bar to discuss the case. Ryan told Francis that he did in fact commit the assault but was confident that the Crown would withdraw the charge because Ryan was certain that the victim of the assault would not testify against him. This conversation was overheard by an off-duty police officer sitting at the next table. Is this conversation privileged? Why or why not?

3. What are the advantages and disadvantages associated with the block fee billing method?

4. Kelly Wrock works in a criminal law office and is responsible for issuing bills to clients. Kelly is preparing a bill and has been provided with the following dockets by the lawyer who is responsible for the file:

Date	Service	Time
Jan. 17	meet with client	2.5
Jan. 27	arrange disclosure	0.2
Feb. 3	obtain and review disclosure	1.7
Feb. 5	conduct research re: possession	0.8
Feb. 7	telephone call to Crown	0.2
Feb. 8	attend set date — negotiate withdrawal of charge	3.5

The lawyer charges $300 per hour for her time. Calculate the total docketed time and the amount that will be billed to the client as fees from the information above.

Checklists and Forms

CLIENT GENERAL INFORMATION

[*This form should be completed at the first interview with the client. The information gathered will be of assistance in preparing for a bail hearing and speaking to sentencing.*]

Date

Date of next hearing   Type of hearing

Client Information

Name   Date of birth   Age

Place of birth   Citizenship

Current address   How long?

Phone   Alternate phone

Previous addresses   How long?

Aboriginal?

First Nation affiliation

Work or School History

Occupation

Employed?   Employer   How long?

                             Address

Salary or wage?

Position held?

Supervisor   Phone

Past employers   How long?

Future employment/advancement plans?

Unemployed?   How long?

Receiving gov't benefits?   Type   Amount   How long?

Education   Currently attending?

Grades

Level or qualification attained

School(s)

Plans for further education

Family Information

Marital status   Single [ ]   Married [ ]   Divorced [ ]   Widow(er) [ ]   Common Law [ ]

How long?

Spouse
Name   Age

Years together

Employer   Occupation

Phone

Supporting spouse?   Amount

Children
Name   Age   Sex

Supporting child?   Amount

Other Dependants
Name   Relationship   Age

Any issues with dependants (*e.g., health-care requirements*)

Immediate family circumstances

Any particular family difficulties (*finances, relationships, health, etc.*)

Other Relatives

Who else lives in the client's residence?

Name   Age   Relationship   Occupation

Community Ties

Any church, temple or other religious affiliations?

Length of affiliation

Close Friends

Name   Length of relationship   Contact Information

Any other close community ties?

Surety Information   *[Once a possible surety has been identified, complete a Bail Hearing Surety Checklist.]*

Are any family members or friends willing to act as a surety?

Contact information

Medical Issues

Does the client have any current major medical issues (including psychiatric or psychological)?

What are they?

Treatment

Doctors

Name   Contact information

Financial Information

Source(s) of income (*employment, gov't benefits, other income, support payments*)

Annual amount

Any recent changes?

Own or rent residence?

Own [ ]   Value?   Mortgage?

Rent [ ]   Monthly amount

Other assets (*name, type, and value for each*)

Criminal Charge Information

Present charges

Any outstanding charges

Co-accused
Name   Name of legal representative

Has the client been held in custody awaiting trial?

If so, how long has he or she been incarcerated?
(*This time counts as part of any jail sentence and may even count as more than day for day.*)

Criminal record

Offence(s)	Place	Date	Penalty	Circumstances

Notes:

Currently on probation?   Details

Currently on parole?   Details

BAIL PROCEDURAL CHECKLIST

[*This checklist should be used with the Client General Information form and the Bail Hearing Surety Checklist.*]

	N/A	Date Completed
1. Meet with the client and gather information for the Client General Information form.		
2. Advise the client on the nature of the bail hearing and the likelihood of release pending trial.		
• Make a preliminary determination of appropriate conditions (no alcohol or drugs; surrender of passport; no contact order; curfew, etc.)		
• Discuss the client's willingness to comply with conditions		
• Determine whether there is someone who may act as a surety		
3. Determine the type of bail hearing: regular or reverse onus. Is it a s. 469 offence?		
4. Should the bail hearing be held at first opportunity? Or is a defence-requested adjournment required to arrange for a surety, appropriate conditions, etc., thereby increasing chances for the client's release?		
5. Contact the Crown to determine whether:		
• they will seek any delay under s. 516(1)		
• they will proceed by summary conviction or indictment if the offence is hybrid		

• they will seek the detention of the accused and, if so, what their principal concern is:		
i. possible failure to attend court (s. 515(10)(a))		
ii. protection of the public (s. 515(10)(b))		
iii. maintaining public confidence (s. 515(10)(c))		
• Determine whether the Crown will consent to release if your suggested conditions are put in place.		
• Can mutually agreeable bail terms be reached?		
• What evidence is the Crown intending to present in relation to the offence charged?		
• Will the hearing take place in court or by video link?		
6. Is the client a young person? If so, review ss. 28 to 33 of the *Youth Criminal Justice Act*, particularly s. 29, with regard to the limitations on a young person being detained.		
7. Contact all potential sureties and determine whether they are prepared to act. Determine the type of security and maximum amount that they would be willing to provide. Complete the information on the Bail Hearing Surety Checklist.		
8. Determine whether the client lives more than 200km from court. If so, a cash bail will likely be imposed (s. 515(2)(e)).		
9. With the client's consent in writing, contact those who may assist in setting up the client's release plan: employer, treatment facility, First Nation community if the client is Aboriginal and has a connection to the community, doctors, psychiatrist, etc.		
10. Determine whether the client has accommodation if released, and if not, try to arrange this through family, friends, or community and social agencies.		

11. Arrange for a translator through the court if one is required.		
12. Prepare defence submissions (to do so, you must consider what the Crown is likely to argue in opposition) and review s. 515 for factors that the justice will consider in determining whether the client will be released.		
• If addressing a concern that the client may not attend court (s. 515(10)(a)), consider all of the following:		
i. Does the client have strong ties to the community? For example, a good job, strong family connections, ownership of property in the jurisdiction.		
ii. Is the client a Canadian citizen? Does he or she have dual citizenship in another country? Does he or she have a passport? Will a surrender of all passports address this concern?		
iii. What is the seriousness of the offence charged? The more minor the offence, the less likelihood the client will flee.		
iv. If there were prior "fail to appears," what was the reason? Was he or she impaired due to an addiction that is now treated? Was he or she young and not prone to paying attention to dates and times, etc.?		
v. If the Crown raises any prior criminal history, it can be submitted that the client attended court for all of those hearings, if that is the case. (If the Crown does not raise any prior criminal history, this is not something that would likely be in the client's interests to raise.)		
• If addressing a concern that the client may pose a danger to the public (s. 515(10)(b)), consider all of the following:		
i. Is it likely that the client will re-offend while out on bail?		

ii. If the answer is yes, is it possible to put strong conditions in place to satisfy the court that he or she is unlikely to re-offend? For example, curfew, house arrest, no alcohol or drugs, no firearms.		
iii. Nature of the alleged offence. If violence was involved, how can the public be protected with the type of conditions listed in ii. above?		
iv. If a child was involved in the offence as a victim or witness, that is a specific issue that the justice must address when considering release and conditions for release. Will a no-contact condition address this issue?		
v. If the client is Aboriginal, are there services in the Aboriginal community that may be able to assist him or her with any problems that he or she may be suffering that led to the charge or charges?		
vi. Has the client been cooperative with police?		
vii. Is this a gang- or organized crime-related offence and, if so, is it possible to fashion conditions that would stop or strongly deter the client's contacts with gang members or organized crime?		
viii. Is the client a leader or a follower?		
• If addressing a concern that the client's detention is necessary to maintaining confidence in the administration of justice (s. 515(10)(c)), consider all of the following:		
i. How serious is the alleged offence? Only the most heinous or horrific offences are likely to raise this concern.		
ii. How strong is the Crown's case?		
iii. Is there a minimum sentence for this offence?		

13. Other considerations for submissions:		
• Is an early trial date available?		
• The availability of sureties and any financial limitations		
• Aboriginal identity of the client (see the Gladue considerations in Chapter 22 of the text)		
• Charter arguments, ss. 9 and 11(c)		
• What is the defence proposal on bail conditions and the possible forms of release (for example, undertaking, recognizance, etc.)?		
14. Speak with the client before the bail hearing and advise him or her on how the hearing will proceed.		
15. If bail is set, obtain a copy of the related documents (undertaking, recognizance, etc.) from the court clerk or monitor and check the documents to ensure that they properly reflect the court order.		
16. Meet with the client in lock-up to advise him or her of the legal ramifications of the bail order and ensure that he or she understands the conditions imposed. Follow up with a letter. Include the next court date in the letter.		

BAIL HEARING SURETY CHECKLIST

Name:

Address: How long?

Prior address: How long?

Occupation: Employer: How long?

Surety's relationship to accused:

How long has the surety known the accused?

Does the surety know details of present charges?

Does the surety know client's criminal history, if any?

Does the surety know of client's outstanding charges, if any?

Does the surety know the duties and responsibilities of acting as such?

Does the surety have a criminal record?

If yes, what is the surety's criminal record?

Has the person previously acted as surety?

If so, was it for the accused?

Did the previously supervised person stay out of trouble?

How often does the surety see the accused?

How close does the surety live to the accused?

How close does the surety live to the accused's workplace?

What plans does the surety have to supervise the accused while the surety is working?

Surety's financial information:

Does the surety own his or her home?   If so, is there another owner on title?

> Name

> Relationship

Is the home a matrimonial home?

> Value of home

> Mortgages outstanding on home

What is the maximum the surety would be prepared to pledge?

Does the surety understand that the Crown may place a lien on the property?

Surety's understanding of obligations:

If the accused was breaking bail conditions, what would the surety do?

Does the surety realize that bail lasts until trial?

Are there any bail conditions the surety would suggest be placed on the accused?

Would the surety be willing to have the accused reside with him or her if the Court found this necessary?

TRIAL PROCEDURAL CHECKLIST

[*This checklist should be used with the Client General Information form. (This checklist relates to summary conviction trials.)*]

	N/A	Date Completed
1. In the initial interview, complete a Client General Information form.		
• Prior to trial, review the form and gather additional information required.		
2. Determine whether the offence is summary conviction, hybrid, or indictable.		
• If hybrid, is it likely that the Crown will proceed summarily?		
3. Decide whether or not to accept the case based on		
• Nature of charge		
• Conflicts of interest		
• Complexity of case and skill level required		
4. If you decide to act, obtain the client's instructions, complete a retainer with client, and ensure that a letter confirming the retainer and instructions from the client has been sent.		
5. If the client is in custody, prepare for a bail hearing (see Bail Procedural Checklist).		
6. If there is a co-accused, contact his or her representative.		
7. Open a file and diarize all dates.		
• Confirm all dates in writing with client		
• Diarize date for commencement of trial preparation one month in advance of trial		

Preparation Prior to Trial		
8. Confirm trial date and any other dates in writing with the client.		
9. Contact the Crown to arrange for disclosure, which will include		
• A copy of the Information		
• Crown allegations of circumstances of the offence		
• A copy of the officer's notes—get notes from all officers involved		
• A list of all Crown witnesses (including police) and their full contact information (ensure that you ask for and obtain a full list of witnesses, including those the Crown does not intend to call at trial)		
• A copy of any statement made by the client		
• A copy of the client's criminal record, if any		
• A copy of any statements made by witnesses		
Determine the Crown's position on sentencing, including its position on an early guilty plea.		
10. Determine the *actus reus* and *mens rea* of the offence and make a preliminary determination about the likelihood that the Crown will be able to meet the standard of proof on the *actus reus* and *mens rea*.		
11. Determine whether there are any Charter issues that might apply.		
12. Do preliminary research on the likelihood of the Crown's success at trial.		
13. Review disclosure material and discuss the Crown's position with the client.		

14. How does the client wish to plead? Obtain written instructions in this regard.		
• If the client wishes to plead guilty, discuss with the client the possibility of acquittal if the matter goes to trial; advise the client on the likely sentence if he or she pleads guilty or is found guilty after trial.		
• If the client wishes to plead guilty, fix a date and prepare for a sentencing hearing (refer to the Client General Information form to determine factors that may influence sentencing. Gather any further information as needed).		
• If the client does not wish to plead guilty, proceed with preparations for trial.		
Trial Preparation		
15. Consider whether a pretrial is necessary to narrow the issues or prepare an agreed statement of facts. Discuss with the Crown. (Pretrials are not usually required for simple summary conviction matters.)		
16. Research:		
• Conduct legal research on all applicable issues.		
• Conduct factual research—visit the scene of the alleged offence; are expert witnesses required on any issue?		
17. Witnesses:		
• Interview potential witnesses and obtain any statements in in writing.		
• Determine whether a witness should be referred for independent legal advice on the potential consequences of their evidence.		
• Consider whether the Crown should be given notice of any alibi witnesses. Where the accused fails to give notice of an alibi to the Crown in advance of the trial, the trier of fact may draw an adverse inference.		

• Decide which witnesses to call and draft subpoenas to be taken to the court and signed. Always subpoena witnesses even though they promise to come to trial because if they do not and they were not subpoenaed, the justice may not be disposed to grant an adjournment to get the witness to trial.		
• Determine the order of calling witnesses.		
• Prepare witnesses for examination-in-chief and cross-examination.		
• Prepare and deliver to the Crown a notice of intention to call any expert witnesses at trial. (See s. 657.3 of *Criminal Code*: notice must be delivered to the Crown at least 30 days before trial.)		
• Determine whether an application for production of third-party records is required. If so, the application must be made well in advance of trial, and will require notice to all third-party record-holders and persons whose privacy may be affected; see the provisions in ss. 278.1 to 278.7 of the *Criminal Code*, as well as *R. v. O'Connor*, [1995] 4 S.C.R. 411.		
18. Decide whether the client should testify, considering any past criminal record and any ethical duties you may have.		
19. If the client is going to testify, prepare the client for examination-in-chief and cross-examination.		
20. Prepare any opening comments to the court.		
21. Prepare questions for examination-in-chief.		
22. Prepare cross-examination of Crown's witnesses based on what they are anticipated to say after a review of the disclosure material.		
23. Prepare any evidentiary arguments such as admissibility of documents or real evidence, admissibility of statements, etc., for *voir dires*.		

24. Obtain and review copies of any defence expert reports and give notice of expert and summary of report to the Crown pursuant to s. 657.3(3)(c) of the *Criminal Code* (notice must be given of intention to call an expert and the report or a summary must be given to the Crown at least 30 days in advance).		
25. Prepare any Charter argument and give notice to the Attorneys General and the Crown within the required time limits.		
26. Prepare for closing.		
27. Prepare the client on how to dress and behave in the courtroom and how to answer when the charge is read in courtroom.		
Trial		
28. When the case is called, introduce yourself for the record, say that your client is present, and announce that you are ready to proceed.		
29. Deal with any preliminary motions—for example, to exclude evidence, for a stay of proceedings under ss. 11(a) or (b) of the Charter, for severance, etc.		
30. If the Crown seeks an adjournment, decide, based on the client's instructions, whether you will consent or oppose. Keep in mind that any Crown adjournments will add to a Charter argument about delay and a possible stay of proceedings under s. 11(b) of the Charter.		
31. If the trial proceeds:		
• Take notes while Crown witnesses are being examined.		
• Be prepared to object to any evidence that may be inadmissible—for example, hearsay.		
• Decide whether to cross-examine. Sometimes it is best to not examine a Crown witness; if you do, it may give them an opportunity to strengthen their testimony—instead, call a witness in rebuttal in the defence part of the case.		

• When the Crown concludes its case, determine whether they have met the required burden of proof on all of the elements of the case or whether you should bring a motion for dismissal on the basis that they have not.		
32. Call your witnesses.		
33. Make your closing argument.		
34. If the client is convicted, be prepared to speak to sentencing.		
35. If the client is convicted, discuss with the client the advisability of an appeal.		
36. Send the client a reporting letter.		

FORM 1

(Section 487)

INFORMATION TO OBTAIN A SEARCH WARRANT

Canada,

Province of ....,

(*territorial division*).

This is the information of A.B., of .... in the said (*territorial division*), (*occupation*), hereinafter called the informant, taken before me.

The informant says that (*describe things to be searched for and offence in respect of which search is to be made*), and that he believes on reasonable grounds that the said things, or some part of them, are in the (*dwelling-house, etc.*) of C.D., of ...., in the said (*territorial division*). (*Here add the grounds of belief, whatever they may be.*)

Wherefore the informant prays that a search warrant may be granted to search the said (*dwelling-house, etc.*) for the said things.

Sworn before me this .... day of ...., A.D. ....,

at ....

_____

(*Signature of Informant*)

_____

A Justice of the Peace in and for

_____

FORM 2

(Sections 506 and 788)

INFORMATION

Canada,

Province of ....,

(*territorial division*).

This is the information of C.D., of ...., (*occupation*), hereinafter called the informant.

The informant says that (*if the informant has no personal knowledge state that he believes on reasonable grounds and state the offence*).

Sworn before me this .... day of ...., A.D. ....,

at ....

_____
(*Signature of Informant*)

_____
A Justice of the Peace in and for

_____

Note: The date of birth of the accused may be mentioned on the information or indictment.

FORM 4

(Sections 566, 566.1, 580 and 591)

HEADING OF INDICTMENT

Canada,

Province of ....,

(territorial division).

In the *(set out name of the court)*

Her Majesty the Queen

against

(name of accused)

(Name of accused) stands charged

1. That he *(state offence).*

2. That he *(state offence).*

Dated this .... day of .... A.D. ...., at ....

_____

(Signature of signing officer, Agent of Attorney General, etc.,
as the case may be)

Note: The date of birth of the accused may be mentioned on the information or indictment.

FORM 5

(Section 487)

WARRANT TO SEARCH

Canada,

Province of ....,

(territorial division).

To the peace officers in the said *(territorial division)* or to the *(named public officers)*:

Whereas it appears on the oath of A.B., of .... that there are reasonable grounds for believing that *(describe things to be searched for and offence in respect of which search is to be made)* are in .... at ...., hereinafter called the premises;

This is, therefore, to authorize and require you between the hours of *(as the justice may direct)* to enter into the said premises and to search for the said things and to bring them before me or some other justice.

Dated this .... day of ...., A.D. ...., at ....

_____

A Justice of the Peace in and for

_____

FORM 5.01

(Subsection 487.05(1))

INFORMATION TO OBTAIN A WARRANT TO TAKE BODILY SUBSTANCES
FOR FORENSIC DNA ANALYSIS

Canada,

Province of ....

(*territorial division*)

This is the information of (*name of peace officer*), (*occupation*), of .... in the said (*territorial division*), hereinafter called the informant, taken before me.

The informant says that he or she has reasonable grounds to believe

(*a*) that (*offence*), a designated offence within the meaning of section 487.04 of the *Criminal Code*, has been committed;

(*b*) that a bodily substance has been found

(i) at the place where the offence was committed,

(ii) on or within the body of the victim of the offence,

(iii) on anything worn or carried by the victim at the time when the offence was committed, or

(iv) on or within the body of any person or thing or at any place associated with the commission of the offence;

(*c*) that (*name of person*) was a party to the offence; and

(*d*) that forensic DNA analysis of a bodily substance from (*name of person*) will provide evidence about whether the bodily substance referred to in paragraph (*b*) was from that person.

The reasonable grounds are:

The informant therefore requests that a warrant be issued authorizing the taking from (*name of person*) of the number of samples of bodily substances that are reasonably required for forensic DNA analysis, provided that the person taking the samples is able by virtue of training or experience to take them by means of the investigative procedures described in subsection 487.06(1) of the *Criminal Code* and provided that, if the person taking the samples is not a peace officer, he or she take the samples under the direction of a peace officer.

Sworn to before me this .... day of ...., A.D. ...., at ....

_____

(*Signature of informant*)

_____

(*Signature of provincial court judge*)

FORM 5.1

(Section 487.1)

WARRANT TO SEARCH

Canada,

Province of [*specify province*].

To A.B. and other peace officers in the [*territorial division in which the warrant is intended for execution*]:

Whereas it appears on the oath of A.B., a peace officer in the [*territorial division in which the warrant is intended for execution*], that there are reasonable grounds for dispensing with an information presented personally and in writing; and that there are reasonable grounds for believing that the following things

[*describe things to be searched for*]

relevant to the investigation of the following indictable offence

[*describe offence in respect of which search is to be made*]

are to be found in the following place or premises

[*describe place or premises to be searched*]:

This is, therefore, to authorize you to enter the said place or premises between the hours of [*as the justice may direct*] and to search for and seize the said things and to report thereon as soon as practicable but within a period not exceeding seven days after the execution of the warrant to the clerk of the court for the [*territorial division in which the warrant is intended for execution*].

Issued at [*time*] on the [*day*] of [*month*] A.D. [*year*], at [*place*].

_____
A Judge of the Provincial Court in and for
the Province of [*specify province*].

To the Occupant: This search warrant was issued by telephone or other means of telecommunication. If you wish to know the basis on which this warrant was issued, you may apply to the clerk of the court for the territorial division in which the warrant was executed, at [*address*], to obtain a copy of the information on oath.

You may obtain from the clerk of the court a copy of the report filed by the peace officer who executed this warrant. That report will indicate the things, if any, that were seized and the location where they are being held.

FORM 6

(Sections 493, 508 and 512)

SUMMONS TO A PERSON CHARGED WITH AN OFFENCE

Canada,

Province of ....,

(territorial division).

To A.B., of ...., *(occupation)*:

Whereas you have this day been charged before me that (*set out briefly the offence in respect of which the accused is charged*);

This is therefore to command you, in Her Majesty's name:

(*a*) to attend court on ...., the .... day of .... A.D. ...., at .... o'clock in the .... noon, at .... or before any justice for the said (*territorial division*) who is there, and to attend thereafter as required by the court, in order to be dealt with according to law; and

(*b*) to appear on ...., the .... day of .... A.D. ...., at .... o'clock in the .... noon, at ...., for the purposes of the *Identification of Criminals Act*. (*Ignore, if not filled in*).

You are warned that failure without lawful excuse to attend court in accordance with this summons is an offence under subsection 145(4) of the *Criminal Code*.

Subsection 145(4) of the *Criminal Code* states as follows:

"(4) Every one who is served with a summons and who fails, without lawful excuse, the proof of which lies on him, to appear at a time and place stated therein, if any, for the purposes of the *Identification of Criminals Act* or to attend court in accordance therewith, is guilty of

(*a*) an indictable offence and is liable to imprisonment for a term not exceeding two years; or

(*b*) an offence punishable on summary conviction."

Section 510 of the *Criminal Code* states as follows:

"**510.** Where an accused who is required by a summons to appear at a time and place stated therein for the purposes of the *Identification of Criminals Act* does not appear at that time and place, a justice may issue a warrant for the arrest of the accused for the offence with which he is charged."

Dated this .... day of ...., A.D. ...., at ....

_____
A Justice of the Peace in and for

_____ or Judge

FORM 7

(Sections 475, 493, 597, 800 and 803)

WARRANT FOR ARREST

Canada,

Province of ....,

(*territorial division*).

To the peace officers in the said (*territorial division*):

This warrant is issued for the arrest of A.B., of ...., (*occupation*), hereinafter called the accused.

Whereas the accused has been charged that (*set out briefly the offence in respect of which the accused is charged*);

And whereas:*

(*a*) there are reasonable grounds to believe that it is necessary in the public interest to issue this warrant for the arrest of the accused [507(4), 512(1)];

(*b*) the accused failed to attend court in accordance with the summons served on him [512(2)];

(*c*) (an appearance notice *or* a promise to appear *or* a recognizance entered into before an officer in charge) was confirmed and the accused failed to attend court in accordance therewith [512(2)];

(*d*) it appears that a summons cannot be served because the accused is evading service [512(2)];

(*e*) the accused was ordered to be present at the hearing of an application for a review of an order made by a justice and did not attend the hearing [520(5), 521(5)];

(*f*) there are reasonable grounds to believe that the accused has contravened or is about to contravene the (promise to appear *or* undertaking *or* recognizance) on which he was released [524(1), 525(5), 679(6)];

(*g*) there are reasonable grounds to believe that the accused has since his release from custody on (a promise to appear *or* an undertaking *or* a recognizance) committed an indictable offence [524(1), 525(5), 679(6)];

(*h*) the accused was required by (an appearance notice *or* a promise to appear *or* a recognizance entered into before an officer in charge *or* a summons) to attend at a time and place stated therein for the purposes of the *Identification of Criminals Act* and did not appear at that time and place [502, 510];

(*i*) an indictment has been found against the accused and the accused has not appeared or remained in attendance before the court for his trial [597];

(*j*) **

(Form 7 continues on next page.)

This is, therefore, to command you, in Her Majesty's name, forthwith to arrest the said accused and to bring him before (*state court, judge or justice*), to be dealt with according to law.

(*Add where applicable*) Whereas there are reasonable grounds to believe that the accused is or will be present in (*here describe dwelling-house*);

This warrant is also issued to authorize you to enter the dwelling-house for the purpose of arresting or apprehending the accused, subject to the condition that you may not enter the dwelling-house unless you have, immediately before entering the dwelling-house, reasonable grounds to believe that the person to be arrested or apprehended is present in the dwelling-house.

Dated this .... day of .... A.D. ...., at ....

....
Judge, Clerk of the Court,
Provincial Court Judge *or* Justice

* *Initial applicable recital.*

** *For any case not covered by recitals (a) to (i), insert recital in the words of the statute authorizing the warrant.*

FORM 9

(Section 493)

APPEARANCE NOTICE ISSUED BY A PEACE OFFICER TO A PERSON NOT YET CHARGED WITH AN OFFENCE

Canada, Province of ...., *(territorial division)*.

To A.B., of ...., *(occupation)*:

You are alleged to have committed *(set out substance of offence)*.

1. You are required to attend court on .... day, the .... day of .... A.D. ...., at .... o'clock in the .... noon, in courtroom No. ...., at .... court, in the municipality of ...., and to attend thereafter as required by the court, in order to be dealt with according to law.

2. You are also required to appear on .... day, the .... day of .... A.D. ...., at .... o'clock in the .... noon, at .... *(police station)*, *(address)*, for the purposes of the *Identification of Criminals Act. (Ignore if not filled in.)*

You are warned that failure to attend court in accordance with this appearance notice is an offence under subsection 145(5) of the *Criminal Code*.

Subsections 145(5) and (6) of the *Criminal Code* state as follows:

"(5) Every person who is named in an appearance notice or promise to appear, or in a recognizance entered into before an officer in charge or another peace officer, that has been confirmed by a justice under section 508 and who fails, without lawful excuse, the proof of which lies on the person, to appear at the time and place stated therein, if any, for the purposes of the *Identification of Criminals Act* or to attend court in accordance therewith, is guilty of

(*a*) an indictable offence and liable to imprisonment for a term not exceeding two years; or

(*b*) an offence punishable on summary conviction.

(6) For the purposes of subsection (5), it is not a lawful excuse that an appearance notice, promise to appear or recognizance states defectively the substance of the alleged offence."

Section 502 of the *Criminal Code* states as follows:

"**502.** Where an accused who is required by an appearance notice or promise to appear or by a recognizance entered into before an officer in charge or another peace officer to appear at a time and place stated therein for the purposes of the *Identification of Criminals Act* does not appear at that time and place, a justice may, where the appearance notice, promise to appear or recognizance has been confirmed by a justice under section 508, issue a warrant for the arrest of the accused for the offence with which the accused is charged."

Issued at .... a.m./p.m. this .... day of .... A.D. ...., at ....

....
(Signature of peace officer)

....
(Signature of accused)

FORM 10

(Section 493)

PROMISE TO APPEAR

Canada, Province of ...., *(territorial division)*.

I, A.B., of ...., *(occupation)*, understand that it is alleged that I have committed *(set out substance of offence)*.

In order that I may be released from custody,

1. I promise to attend court on .... day, the .... day of .... A.D. ...., at .... o'clock in the .... noon, in courtroom No. ...., at .... court, in the municipality of ...., and to attend thereafter as required by the court, in order to be dealt with according to law.

2. I also promise to appear on .... day, the .... day of .... A.D. ...., at .... o'clock in the .... noon, at .... *(police station)*, *(address)*, for the purposes of the *Identification of Criminals Act*. *(Ignore if not filled in.)*

I understand that failure without lawful excuse to attend court in accordance with this promise to appear is an offence under subsection 145(5) of the *Criminal Code*.

Subsections 145(5) and (6) of the *Criminal Code* state as follows:

"(5) Every person who is named in an appearance notice or promise to appear, or in a recognizance entered into before an officer in charge or another peace officer, that has been confirmed by a justice under section 508 and who fails, without lawful excuse, the proof of which lies on the person, to appear at the time and place stated therein, if any, for the purposes of the *Identification of Criminals Act* or to attend court in accordance therewith, is guilty of

(*a*) an indictable offence and liable to imprisonment for a term not exceeding two years; or

(*b*) an offence punishable on summary conviction.

(6) For the purposes of subsection (5), it is not a lawful excuse that an appearance notice, promise to appear or recognizance states defectively the substance of the alleged offence."

Section 502 of the *Criminal Code* states as follows:

"**502.** Where an accused who is required by an appearance notice or promise to appear or by a recognizance entered into before an officer in charge or another peace officer to appear at a time and place stated therein for the purposes of the *Identification of Criminals Act* does not appear at that time and place, a justice may, where the appearance notice, promise to appear or recognizance has been confirmed by a justice under section 508, issue a warrant for the arrest of the accused for the offence with which the accused is charged."

Dated this .... day of .... A.D. ...., at ....

....

(Signature of accused)

FORM 11

(Section 493)

RECOGNIZANCE ENTERED INTO BEFORE AN
OFFICER IN CHARGE OR OTHER PEACE OFFICER

Canada, Province of ...., *(territorial division)*.

I, A.B., of ...., *(occupation)*, understand that it is alleged that I have committed (*set out substance of offence*).

In order that I may be released from custody, I hereby acknowledge that I owe $ (*not exceeding $500*) to Her Majesty the Queen to be levied on my real and personal property if I fail to attend court as hereinafter required.

(or, for a person not ordinarily resident in the province in which the person is in custody or within two hundred kilometres of the place in which the person is in custody)

In order that I may be released from custody, I hereby acknowledge that I owe $ (*not exceeding $500*) to Her Majesty the Queen and deposit herewith (*money or other valuable security not exceeding in amount or value $500*) to be forfeited if I fail to attend court as hereinafter required.

1. I acknowledge that I am required to attend court on .... day, the .... day of .... A.D. ...., at .... o'clock in the .... noon, in courtroom No. ...., at .... court, in the municipality of ...., and to attend thereafter as required by the court, in order to be dealt with according to law.

2. I acknowledge that I am also required to appear on .... day, the .... day of .... A.D. ...., at .... o'clock in the .... noon, at .... (*police station*), (*address*), for the purposes of the *Identification of Criminals Act*. (*Ignore if not filled in.*)

I understand that failure without lawful excuse to attend court in accordance with this recognizance to appear is an offence under subsection 145(5) of the *Criminal Code*.

Subsections 145(5) and (6) of the *Criminal Code* state as follows:

"(5) Every person who is named in an appearance notice or promise to appear, or in a recognizance entered into before an officer in charge or another peace officer, that has been confirmed by a justice under section 508 and who fails, without lawful excuse, the proof of which lies on the person, to appear at the time and place stated therein, if any, for the purposes of the *Identification of Criminals Act* or to attend court in accordance therewith, is guilty of

(*a*) an indictable offence and liable to imprisonment for a term not exceeding two years; or

(*b*) an offence punishable on summary conviction.

(6) For the purposes of subsection (5), it is not a lawful excuse that an appearance notice, promise to appear or recognizance states defectively the substance of the alleged offence."

Section 502 of the *Criminal Code* states as follows:

"**502.** Where an accused who is required by an appearance notice or promise to appear or by a recognizance entered into before an officer in charge or another peace officer to appear at a time and place stated therein for the purposes of the *Identification of Criminals Act* does not appear at that time and place, a justice may, where the appearance notice, promise to appear or recognizance has been confirmed by a justice under section 508, issue a warrant for the arrest of the accused for the offence with which the accused is charged."

Dated this .... day of .... A.D. ...., at ....

....
(Signature of accused)

FORM 11.1

(Sections 493, 499 and 503)

UNDERTAKING GIVEN TO A PEACE OFFICER OR AN OFFICER IN CHARGE

Canada, Province of ...., (*territorial division*).

I, A.B., of ...., (*occupation*), understand that it is alleged that I have committed (*set out substance of the offence*).

In order that I may be released from custody by way of (a promise to appear *or* a recognizance), I undertake to (*insert any conditions that are directed*):

(*a*) remain within (*designated territorial jurisdiction*);

(*b*) notify (*name of peace officer or other person designated*) of any change in my address, employment or occupation;

(*c*) abstain from communicating, directly or indirectly, with (*identification of victim, witness or other person*) or from going to (*name or description of place*) except in accordance with the following conditions: (*as the peace officer or other person designated specifies*);

(*d*) deposit my passport with (*name of peace officer or other person designated*);

(*e*) to abstain from possessing a firearm and to surrender to (*name of peace officer or other person designated*) any firearm in my possession and any authorization, licence or registration certificate or other document enabling the acquisition or possession of a firearm;

(*f*) report at (*state times*) to (*name of peace officer or other person designated*);

(*g*) to abstain from

(i) the consumption of alcohol or other intoxicating substances, or

(ii) the consumption of drugs except in accordance with a medical prescription; and

(*h*) comply with any other conditions that the peace officer or officer in charge considers necessary to ensure the safety and security of any victim of or witness to the offence.

I understand that I am not required to give an undertaking to abide by the conditions specified above, but that if I do not, I may be kept in custody and brought before a justice so that the prosecutor may be given a reasonable opportunity to show cause why I should not be released on giving an undertaking without conditions.

I understand that if I give an undertaking to abide by the conditions specified above, then I may apply, at any time before I appear, or when I appear, before a justice pursuant to (a promise to appear *or* a recognizance entered into before an officer in charge or another peace officer), to have this undertaking vacated or varied and that my application will be considered as if I were before a justice pursuant to section 515 of the *Criminal Code*.

I also understand that this undertaking remains in effect until it is vacated or varied.

I also understand that failure without lawful excuse to abide by any of the conditions specified above is an offence under subsection 145(5.1) of the *Criminal Code*.

Subsection 145(5.1) of the *Criminal Code* states as follows:

"(5.1) Every person who, without lawful excuse, the proof of which lies on the person, fails to comply with any condition of an undertaking entered into pursuant to subsection 499(2) or 503(2.1)

(*a*) is guilty of an indictable offence and is liable to imprisonment for a term not exceeding two years; or

(*b*) is guilty of an offence punishable on summary conviction."

Dated this .... day of .... A.D. ...., at ....

....

(*Signature of accused*)

FORM 12

(Sections 493 and 679)

UNDERTAKING GIVEN TO A JUSTICE OR A JUDGE

Canada,

Province of ....,

(territorial division).

I, A.B., of ...., *(occupation)*, understand that I have been charged that *(set out briefly the offence in respect of which accused is charged)*.

In order that I may be released from custody, I undertake to attend court on .... day, the .... day of .... A.D. ...., and to attend after that as required by the court in order to be dealt with according to law *(or, where date and place of appearance before court are not known at the time undertaking is given, to attend at the time and place fixed by the court and after that as required by the court in order to be dealt with according to law)*.

(and, where applicable)

I also undertake to *(insert any conditions that are directed)*

(a) report at *(state times)* to *(name of peace officer or other person designated)*;

(b) remain within *(designated territorial jurisdiction)*;

(c) notify *(name of peace officer or other person designated)* of any change in my address, employment or occupation;

(d) abstain from communicating, directly or indirectly, with *(identification of victim, witness or other person)* except in accordance with the following conditions: *(as the justice or judge specifies)*;

(e) deposit my passport *(as the justice or judge directs)*; and

(f) *(any other reasonable conditions)*.

I understand that failure without lawful excuse to attend court in accordance with this undertaking is an offence under subsection 145(2) of the *Criminal Code*.

Subsections 145(2) and (3) of the *Criminal Code* as follows:

"(2) Every one who,

(a) being at large on his undertaking or recognizance given to or entered into before a justice or judge, fails, without lawful excuse, the proof of which lies on him, to attend court in accordance with the undertaking or recognizance, or

(b) having appeared before a court, justice or judge, fails, without lawful excuse, the proof of which lies on him, to attend court as thereafter required by the court, justice or judge,

or to surrender himself in accordance with an order of the court, justice or judge, as the case may be, is guilty of an indictable offence and liable to imprisonment for a term not exceeding two years or is guilty of an offence punishable on summary conviction.

(3) Every person who is at large on an undertaking or recognizance given to or entered into before a justice or judge and is bound to comply with a condition of that undertaking or recognizance, and every person who is bound to comply with a direction under subsection 515(12) or 522(2.1) or an order under subsection 516(2), and who fails, without lawful excuse, the proof of which lies on them, to comply with the condition, direction or order is guilty of

(a) an indictable offence and liable to imprisonment for a term not exceeding two years; or

(b) an offence punishable on summary conviction."

Dated this .... day of .... A.D. ...., at ....

....
(Signature of accused)

FORM 16

(Section 699)

SUBPOENA TO A WITNESS

Canada,

Province of ....,

(*territorial division*).

To E.F., of ...., (*occupation*);

Whereas A.B. has been charged that (*state offence as in the information*), and it has been made to appear that you are likely to give material evidence for (the prosecution *or* the defence);

This is therefore to command you to attend before (*set out court or justice*), on .... the .... day of .... A.D. ...., at .... o'clock in the .... noon at .... to give evidence concerning the said charge.*

**Where a witness is required to produce anything, add the following*:

and to bring with you anything in your possession or under your control that relates to the said charge, and more particularly the following: (*specify any documents, objects or other things required*).

Dated this .... day of .... A.D. ...., at ....

....

A Judge, Justice *or* Clerk of the court

(*Seal, if required*)

FORM 21

(Sections 570 and 806)

WARRANT OF COMMITTAL ON CONVICTION

Canada,

Province of ....,

(territorial division).

To the peace officers in *(territorial division)* and to the keeper of *(prison)* at ....:

Whereas *(name)*, in this Form called the offender, was, on the .... day of .... 20......, convicted by *(name of judge and court)* of having committed the following offence(s) and it was adjudged that the offender be sentenced as follows:

Offence	Sentence	Remarks
(state offence of which offender was convicted)	*(state term of imprisonment for the offence and, in case of imprisonment for default of payment of fine, so indicate together with the amount of it and applicable costs and whether payable immediately or within a time fixed)*	*(state the amount of time spent in custody before sentencing, the term of imprisonment that would have been imposed before any credit was granted under subsection 719(3) or (3.1), the amount of time credited, if any, and whether the sentence is consecutive or concurrent, and specify consecutive to or concurrent with what other sentence)*

1. ....

2. ....

3. ....

4. ....

You are hereby commanded, in Her Majesty's name, to arrest the offender if it is necessary to do so in order to take the offender into custody, and to take and convey him or her safely to *(prison)* at .... and deliver him or her to its keeper, who is hereby commanded to receive the accused into custody and to imprison him or her there for the term(s) of his or her imprisonment, unless, if a term of imprisonment was imposed only in default of payment of a fine or costs, those amounts and the costs and charges of the committal and of conveying the offender to that prison are paid sooner, and this is a sufficient warrant for so doing.

Dated this .... day of .... 20........, at ....

....

Clerk of the Court, Justice, Judge *or* Provincial Court Judge

FORM 32

(Sections 493, 550, 679, 706, 707, 810, 810.1 and 817)

RECOGNIZANCE

Canada,

Province of ....,

(*territorial division*).

Be it remembered that on this day the persons named in the following schedule personally came before me and severally acknowledged themselves to owe to Her Majesty the Queen the several amounts set opposite their respective names, namely,

Name	Address	Occupation	Amount
A.B.			
C.D.			
E.F.			

to be made and levied of their several goods and chattels, lands and tenements, respectively, to the use of Her Majesty the Queen, if the said A.B. fails in any of the conditions hereunder written.

Taken and acknowledged before me on the .... day of .... A.D. ...., at ....

....
Judge, Clerk of the Court, Provincial Court Judge *or* Justice

1. Whereas the said ...., hereinafter called the accused, has been charged that (*set out the offence in respect of which the accused has been charged*);

Now, therefore, the condition of this recognizance is that if the accused attends court on .... day, the .... day of .... A.D. ...., at .... o'clock in the .... noon and attends thereafter as required by the court in order to be dealt with according to law (*or, where date and place of appearance before court are not known at the time recognizance is entered into* if the accused attends at the time and place fixed by the court and attends thereafter as required by the court in order to be dealt with according to law) [515, 520, 521, 522, 523, 524, 525, 680];

And further, if the accused (*insert in Schedule of Conditions any additional conditions that are directed*),

the said recognizance is void, otherwise it stands in full force and effect.

2. Whereas the said ...., hereinafter called the appellant, is an appellant against his conviction (*or* against his sentence) in respect of the following charge (*set out the offence for which the appellant was convicted*) [679, 680];

Now, therefore, the condition of this recognizance is that if the appellant attends as required by the court in order to be dealt with according to law;

And further, if the appellant (*insert in Schedule of Conditions any additional conditions that are directed*),

the said recognizance is void, otherwise it stands in full force and effect.

3. Whereas the said ...., hereinafter called the appellant, is an appellant against his conviction (*or* against his sentence *or* against an order *or* by way of stated case) in respect of the following matter (*set out offence, subject-matter of order or question of law*) [816, 831, 832, 834];

Now, therefore, the condition of this recognizance is that if the appellant appears personally at the sittings of the appeal court at which the appeal is to be heard;

And further, if the appellant (*insert in Schedule of Conditions any additional conditions that are directed*),

the said recognizance is void, otherwise it stands in full force and effect.

4. Whereas the said ...., hereinafter called the appellant, is an appellant against an order of dismissal (*or* against sentence) in respect of the following charge (*set out the name of the defendant and the offence, subject-matter of order or question of law*) [817, 831, 832, 834];

Now, therefore, the condition of this recognizance is that if the appellant appears personally or by counsel at the sittings of the appeal court at which the appeal is to be heard the said recognizance is void, otherwise it stands in full force and effect.

5. Whereas the said ...., hereinafter called the accused, was ordered to stand trial on a charge that (*set out the offence in respect of which the accused has been charged*);

And whereas A.B. appeared as a witness on the preliminary inquiry into the said charge [550, 706, 707];

Now, therefore, the condition of this recognizance is that if the said A.B. appears at the time and place fixed for the trial of the accused to give evidence on the indictment that is found against the accused, the said recognizance is void, otherwise it stands in full force and effect.

6. The condition of the above written recognizance is that if A.B. keeps the peace and is of good behaviour for the term of .... commencing on ...., the said recognizance is void, otherwise it stands in full force and effect [810 and 810.1].

7. Whereas a warrant was issued under section 462.32 or a restraint order was made under subsection 462.33(3) of the *Criminal Code* in relation to any property (*set out a description of the property and its location*);

Now, therefore, the condition of this recognizance is that A.B. shall not do or cause anything to be done that would result, directly or indirectly, in the disappearance, dissipation or reduction in value of the property or otherwise affect the property so that all or a part thereof could not be subject to an order of forfeiture under section 462.37 or 462.38 of the *Criminal Code* ior any other provision of the *Criminal Code* ior any other Act of Parliament [462.34].

Schedule of Conditions

(*a*) reports at (*state times*) to (*name of peace officer or other person designated*);

(*b*) remains within (*designated territorial jurisdiction*);

(*c*) notifies (*name of peace officer or other person designated*) of any change in his address, employment or occupation;

(*d*) abstains from communicating, directly or indirectly, with (*identification of victim, witness or other person*) except in accordance with the following conditions: (*as the justice or judge specifies*);

(*e*) deposits his passport (*as the justice or judge directs*); and

(*f*) (*any other reasonable conditions*).

(Form 32 continues on next page.)

Note: Section 763 and subsections 764(1) to (3) of the *Criminal Code* state as follows:

"**763.** Where a person is bound by recognizance to appear before a court, justice or provincial court judge for any purpose and the session or sittings of that court or the proceedings are adjourned or an order is made changing the place of trial, that person and his sureties continue to be bound by the recognizance in like manner as if it had been entered into with relation to the resumed proceedings or the trial at the time and place at which the proceedings are ordered to be resumed or the trial is ordered to be held.

764. (1) Where an accused is bound by recognizance to appear for trial, his arraignment or conviction does not discharge the recognizance, but it continues to bind him and his sureties, if any, for his appearance until he is discharged or sentenced, as the case may be.

(2) Notwithstanding subsection (1), the court, justice or provincial court judge may commit an accused to prison or may require him to furnish new or additional sureties for his appearance until he is discharged or sentenced, as the case may be.

(3) The sureties of an accused who is bound by recognizance to appear for trial are discharged if he is committed to prison pursuant to subsection (2)."

FORM 46

(Section 732.1)

PROBATION ORDER

Canada,

Province of ....,

(territorial division).

Whereas on the .... day of .... at ...., A.B., hereinafter called the offender, (pleaded guilty to *or* was tried under (*here insert Part XIX, XX or XXVII, as the case may be*) of the *Criminal Code* and was (*here insert convicted or found guilty, as the case may be*) on the charge that (*here state the offence to which the offender pleaded guilty or for which the offender was convicted or found guilty, as the case may be*);

And whereas on the .... day of .... the court adjudged*

*Use whichever of the following forms of disposition is applicable:

(*a*) that the offender be discharged on the following conditions:

(*b*) that the passing of sentence on the offender be suspended and that the said offender be released on the following conditions:

(*c*) that the offender forfeit and pay the sum of .... dollars to be applied according to law and in default of payment of the said sum without delay (*or within a time fixed, if any*), be imprisoned in the (*prison*) at .... for the term of .... unless the said sum and charges of the committal and of conveying the said offender to the said prison are sooner paid, and in addition thereto, that the said offender comply with the following conditions:

(*d*) that the offender be imprisoned in the (*prison*) at .... for the term of .... and, in addition thereto, that the said offender comply with the following conditions:

(*e*) that following the expiration of the offender's conditional sentence order related to this or another offence, that the said offender comply with the following conditions:

(*f*) that following the expiration of the offender's sentence of imprisonment related to another offence, that the said offender comply with the following conditions:

(*g*) when the offender is ordered to serve the sentence of imprisonment intermittently, that the said offender comply with the following conditions when not in confinement:

Now therefore the said offender shall, for the period of .... from the date of this order (*or, where paragraph (d), (e) or (f) is applicable*, the date of expiration of the offender's sentence of imprisonment or conditional sentence order) comply with the following conditions, namely, that the said offender shall keep the peace and be of good behaviour, appear before the court when required to do so by the court and notify the court or probation officer in advance of any change of name or address and promptly notify the court or probation officer of any change of employment or occupation, and, in addition,

(*here state any additional conditions prescribed pursuant to subsection 732.1(3) of the Criminal Code*).

Dated this .... day of .... A.D. ...., at ....

....

Clerk of the Court, Justice *or* Provincial Court Judge

Form / *Formule* 1
APPLICATION
DEMANDE

ONTARIO COURT OF JUSTICE
COUR DE JUSTICE DE L'ONTARIO

(Rule 2.1, *Criminal Rules of the Ontario Court of Justice*)
(Règle 2.1, Règles de procédure en matière criminelle de la Cour de justice de l'Ontario)

Court File No. (if known)
N° du dossier de la cour (s'il est connu)

Region / *Région*

BETWEEN: / *ENTRE*

HER MAJESTY THE QUEEN / *SA MAJESTÉ LA REINE*

- and / *et -*

(defendant(s) / *défendeur(s)*)

1. **APPLICATION HEARING DATE AND LOCATION**
   DATE ET LIEU DE L'AUDIENCE SUR LA DEMANDE

   Application hearing date:
   Date de l'audience sur la demande _____

   Time _____
   Heure

   Courtroom number: _____
   Numéro de la salle d'audience

   Court address: _____
   Adresse de la Cour _____

2. **LIST CHARGES**
   LISTE DES ACCUSATIONS

Charge Information / *Renseignements sur les accusations*			
Description of Charge *Description de l'accusation*	**Sect. No.** *Article n°*	**Next Court Date** *Prochaine date d'audience*	**Type of Appearance (e.g. trial date, set date, pre-trial meeting, etc.)** *Type de comparution (p. ex., date de procès, établissement d'une date, conférence préparatoire au procès, etc.)*

3. **NAME OF APPLICANT** _____
   NOM DE L'AUTEUR DE LA DEMANDE

4. **CHECK ONE OF THE TWO BOXES BELOW:**
   COCHEZ LA CASE QUI CONVIENT CI-DESSOUS

   ☐   I am appearing in person. My address, fax or email for service is as follows:
   Je comparais en personne. Mon adresse, mon numéro de télécopieur ou mon adresse électronique aux fins de signification sont les suivants :

   _____
   _____
   _____

   ☐   I have a legal representative who will be appearing. The address, fax or email for service of my legal representative is as follows:
   J'ai un représentant juridique qui sera présent. L'adresse, le numéro de télécopieur ou l'adresse électronique de mon représentant juridique aux fins de signification sont les suivants :

   _____
   _____
   _____

COR-OCJ-1 (rev. 04/12) CSD

APPLICATION / *DEMANDE*

(Rule 2.1, Criminal Rules of the Ontario Court of Justice) / (Règle 2.1, Règles de procédure en matière criminelle de la Cour de justice de l'Ontario)

PAGE 2

5.   CONCISE STATEMENT OF THE SUBJECT OF APPLICATION
BRÈVE DÉCLARATION DE L'OBJET DE LA DEMANDE

(Briefly state why you are bringing the Application. For example, "This is an application for an order adjourning the trial"; "This is an application for an order requiring the Crown to disclose specified documents"; or "This is an application for an order staying the charge for delay.")

(Expliquez brièvement pourquoi vous déposez la demande. Par exemple : « Il s'agit d'une demande d'ordonnance d'ajournement du procès. », « Il s'agit d'une demande d'ordonnance exigeant de la Couronne qu'elle divulgue les documents précisés. », ou « Il s'agit d'une demande d'ordonnance d'annulation de l'accusation pour cause de retard. »)

_____

_____

6.   GROUNDS TO BE ARGUED IN SUPPORT OF THE APPLICATION
MOTIFS QUI SERONT INVOQUÉS À L'APPUI DE LA DEMANDE

(Briefly list the grounds you rely on in support of this Application. For example, "I require an adjournment because I am scheduled to have a medical operation the day the trial is scheduled to start"; "The disclosure provided by the Crown does not include the police notes taken at the scene"; or "There has been unreasonable delay since the laying of the charge that has caused me prejudice.")

(Énumérez brièvement les motifs que vous invoquez à l'appui de la demande. Par exemple : « J'ai besoin d'un ajournement parce que je dois subir une intervention médicale le jour prévu pour le début du procès. », « Les documents divulgués par la Couronne ne contiennent pas les notes de la police prises sur les lieux. » ou « Un retard excessif a suivi le dépôt des accusations qui m'a causé un préjudice. »)

_____

_____

7.   DETAILED STATEMENT OF THE SPECIFIC FACTUAL BASIS FOR THE APPLICATION
DÉCLARATION DÉTAILLÉE DES FAITS PRÉCIS SUR LESQUELS SE FONDE LA DEMANDE

_____

_____

_____

_____

8.   INDICATE BELOW OTHER MATERIALS OR EVIDENCE YOU WILL RELY ON IN THE APPLICATION
INDIQUEZ CI-DESSOUS D'AUTRES DOCUMENTS OU PREUVES QUE VOUS ALLEZ INVOQUER DANS LA DEMANDE

☐   Transcripts   (Transcripts required to determine the application must be filed with this application.)
     Transcriptions   (Les transcriptions exigées pour prendre une décision sur la demande doivent être déposées avec la demande.)

☐   Brief statement of legal argument
     Bref exposé des arguments juridiques

☐   Affidavit(s)   (List below) _____
     Affidavits   (Énumérez ci-dessous)

_____

☐   Case law or legislation   (Relevant passages should be indicated on materials. Well-known precedents do not need to be filed. Only materials that will be referred to in submissions to the Court should be filed.)
     Jurisprudence ou lois.   (Les passages pertinents doivent être indiqués dans les documents. Les arrêts bien connus ne doivent pas être déposés. Il ne faut déposer que les documents qui seront mentionnés dans les observations au tribunal.)

☐   Agreed statement of facts
     Exposé conjoint des faits

☐   Oral testimony   (List witnesses to be called at hearing of application) _____
     Témoignage oral   (Liste des témoins qui seront appelés à témoigner à l'audience sur la demande)

_____

☐   Other   (Please specify) _____
     Autre   (Veuillez préciser)

_____   _____
              (Date)   Signature of Applicant or Legal Representative / *Signature de l'auteur de la*
                                                 demande ou de son représentant juridique

To: _____
À :   (Name of Respondent or legal representative / *Nom de l'intimé ou de son représentant juridique*)

_____
      (Address/fax/email for service / *Adresse, numéro de télécopie ou adresse électronique aux fins de signification*)

NOTE: Rule 2.1 requires that the application be served on all opposing parties and on any other affected parties.
NOTA : La règle 2.1 exige que la demande soit signifiée à toutes les parties adverses et aux autres parties concernées.

COR-OCJ-1 (rev. 04/12) CSD

Form / *Formule* 2
RESPONSE
RÉPONSE

ONTARIO COURT OF JUSTICE
COUR DE JUSTICE DE L'ONTARIO

(Rule 2.2, *Criminal Rules of the Ontario Court of Justice*)
(Règle 2.2, Règles de procédure en matière criminelle de la
Cour de justice de l'Ontario)

_____
Region / *Région*

Court File No. (if known)
N° du dossier de la cour (s'il est connu)

BETWEEN: / *ENTRE*

HER MAJESTY THE QUEEN / *SA MAJESTÉ LA REINE*

- and / *et* **-**

_____
(defendant(s) / *défendeur(s)*)

1. **NAME OF RESPONDENT**
   NOM DE LA PERSONNE INTIMÉE

   _____

2. **CHECK ONE OF THE TWO BOXES BELOW**
   COCHEZ LA CASE QUI CONVIENT CI-DESSOUS

   ☐ I am appearing in person. My address, fax or email for service is as follows:
   Je comparais en personne. Mon adresse, mon numéro de télécopieur ou mon adresse électronique aux fins de signification sont les suivants :

   _____

   ☐ I have a legal representative who will be appearing. The address, fax or email for service of my legal representative is as follows:
   J'ai un représentant juridique qui sera présent. L'adresse, le numéro de télécopieur ou l'adresse électronique de mon représentant juridique aux fins de signification sont les suivants :

   _____

3. **CONCISE STATEMENT OF REASONS FOR RESPONDING**
   BRÈVE DÉCLARATION DES MOTIFS DE LA RÉPONSE

   (Briefly state why you are opposing the Application. For example, "The Applicant has not provided any medical evidence about pending surgery"; "The Crown disclosure is complete"; or "The length of time is not unreasonable, the Applicant has acquiesced to any delay, and there has been no prejudice flowing from the time to trial.")
   (Expliquez brièvement pourquoi vous vous opposez à la demande. Par exemple : « L'auteur de la demande n'a pas produit de preuve médicale au sujet de son intervention chirurgicale imminente. », « La Couronne a divulgué tous les documents qu'elle pouvait. », « Le temps écoulé n'est pas excessif. L'auteur de la demande a accepté n'importe quel retard et le temps écoulé jusqu'au procès ne lui a causé aucun préjudice. »)

   _____
   _____

4. **RESPONSE TO THE APPLICANT'S GROUNDS TO BE ARGUED IN SUPPORT OF APPLICATION (#6 on application)**
   RÉPONSE AUX MOTIFS DE L'AUTEUR DE LA DEMANDE QUI SERONT INVOQUÉS À L'APPUI DE LA DEMANDE (point 6 de la demande)

   _____
   _____
   _____

5. **DETAILED STATEMENT OF SPECIFIC FACTUAL BASIS FOR OPPOSING APPLICATION**
   DÉCLARATION DÉTAILLÉE DES FAITS PRÉCIS SUR LESQUELS SE FONDE L'OPPOSITION À LA DEMANDE

   _____
   _____
   _____

COR-OCJ-2 (rev. 04/12) CSD

RESPONSE
RÉPONSE
(Rule 2.2, *Criminal Rules of the Ontario Court of Justice*)
(Règle 2.2, Règles de procédure en matière criminelle de la Cour de justice de l'Ontario)
PAGE 2

6. **INDICATE BELOW OTHER MATERIALS OR EVIDENCE YOU WILL RELY ON IN RESPONSE TO THE APPLICATION**
INDIQUEZ CI-DESSOUS D'AUTRES DOCUMENTS OU PREUVES QUE VOUS ALLEZ INVOQUER EN RÉPONSE À LA DEMANDE

☐ Brief statement of legal argument
Bref exposé des arguments juridiques

☐ Affidavit(s)   (List below)
Affidavits   *(Énumérez ci-dessous)*

_____

_____

_____

_____

_____

_____

☐ Case law or legislation   (Relevant passages should be indicated on materials. Well-known precedents do not need to be filed. Only materials that will be referred to in submissions to the Court should be filed.)
Jurisprudence ou lois. (Les passages pertinents doivent être indiqués dans les documents. Les arrêts bien connus ne doivent pas être déposés. Il ne faut déposer que les documents qui seront mentionnés dans les observations au tribunal.)

☐ Agreed statement of facts
Exposé conjoint des faits

☐ Oral testimony   (List witnesses to be called at hearing of application)
Témoignage oral   (Liste des témoins qui seront appelés à témoigner à l'audience sur la demande)

_____

_____

_____

_____

_____

_____

_____

☐ Other   (Please specify)
Autre   (Veuillez préciser)

_____

_____

_____

_____

_____

_____   _____
(Date)   Signature of Respondent or Legal Representative / *Signature de l'intimé ou de son représentant juridique*

To: _____
À :   (Name of Applicant or legal representative / *Nom de l'auteur de la demande ou de son représentant juridique*)

_____

(Address/fax/email for service / *Adresse, numéro de télécopie ou adresse électronique aux fins de signification*)

NOTE: Rule 2.2 requires that a response to an application be served on the applicant and on any other affected parties.
NOTA : La règle 2.2 exige qu'une réponse à une demande soit signifiée à l'auteur de la demande et aux autres parties concernées.

COR-OCJ-2 (rev. 04/12) CSD

Form / *Formule* 3
CONSENT
CONSENTEMENT

ONTARIO COURT OF JUSTICE
COUR DE JUSTICE DE L'ONTARIO

(Rule 2.7, *Criminal Rules of the Ontario Court of Justice*)
(Règle 2.7, Règles de procédure en matière criminelle de la Cour de justice de l'Ontario)

Court File No. (if known)
N° du dossier de la cour (s'il est connu)

_____
Region / *Région*

BETWEEN: / *ENTRE*

HER MAJESTY THE QUEEN / *SA MAJESTÉ LA REINE*

- and / *et -*

_____
(defendant(s) / *défendeur(s))*

The Applicant _____ and the Respondent _____
L'auteur de la demande *et l'intimé*

consent to the granting of the Application as follows:
consentent à ce que la demande soit acceptée, comme suit :

_____   _____
(Date)   (Date)

_____   _____
(Signature of Applicant's licensed legal representative / *Signature du représentant juridique titulaire d'un permis de l'auteur de la demande)*   (Signature of Respondent's licensed legal representative / *Signature du représentant juridique titulaire d'un permis de l'intimé)*

_____   _____
(Name (please print) / *Nom (en caractères d'imprimerie))*   (Name (please print) / *Nom (en caractères d'imprimerie))*

_____   _____
(Address / *Adresse)*   (Address / *Adresse)*

_____   _____
(Telephone no. / *N° de téléphone)*   (Telephone no. / *N° de téléphone)*

FOR JUDICIAL USE ONLY / *RÉSERVÉ AUX MAGISTRATS*

Date _____

☐   Order to go as requested: _____
Ordonnance rendue telle que demandée

☐   Application to be heard in Court: _____
Demande sera entendue devant le tribunal

NOTE: Rule 2.7(3) states:

(3)   An application in which a party is not represented by counsel or by a licensed paralegal may be dealt with on consent if

   (a)   a party files an application consent in Form 3;

   (b)   the self-represented party appears before the Court; and

   (c)   the Court is satisfied that the party understand the nature of the consent and the consequences of giving it.

La disposition (3) de la Règle 2.7 stipule ce qui suit :

(3)   Une requête pour laquelle une partie n'est pas représentée par un avocat ou par un parajuriste titulaire d'un permis peut être traitée sur consentement si les conditions suivantes sont réunies :

   a)   une partie dépose son consentement rédigé selon le formulaire 3;

   b)   la partie autoreprésentée comparaît devant le tribunal;

   c)   le tribunal est convaincu que la partie comprend la nature du consentement et les conséquences d'un tel consentement.

COR-OCJ-1 (rev. 04/12) CSD

FORM A

NOTICE OF APPEAL FOR INMATE APPEAL

COURT OF APPEAL FOR ONTARIO

To: The Registrar

Name of appellant

Place of trial

Name of court[1]

Name of judge

Offence(s) of which convicted[2]

Plea at trial

Sentence imposed

Date of conviction

Date of imposition of sentence

Name and address of place at which appellant is in custody

I, the above-named appellant, hereby give notice that I desire to appeal to the Court of Appeal against my[3]

on the grounds hereinafter set forth in this notice.

I desire to present my case and argument, whether it be for leave to appeal[4] or by way of appeal where leave is not necessary,[5]

    (*a*) in person; or

    (*b*) in writing.[6]

(Form A continues on next page.)

If a new trial is ordered and you have a right to trial by jury do you wish trial by jury?

Dated this   day of   , 20

Signed[7] [*Appellant*] _____

Numbered instructions set out below refer to corresponding numbers on notice.

INSTRUCTIONS

1. Ontario Court (General Division) or Ontario Court (Provincial Division).

2. E.g. theft, forgery

3. If you wish to appeal against conviction, you must write the word "conviction". If you wish to appeal against sentence, you must write the word "sentence". If you wish to appeal both conviction and sentence, you must write the words "conviction and sentence". If you are convicted of more than one offence and wish to appeal against some only of the convictions or sentences, you must state clearly the convictions or sentences against which you wish to appeal.

4. See item #1 in the Notes set out below.

5. Stroke out either (*a*) or (*b*).

6. If you desire to submit your case and argument in writing you may deliver your written argument with this notice of appeal or you may deliver your written argument within fourteen days after receipt by you of the report of the trial judge which will be sent to you later.

7. This notice must be signed by the appellant. If the appellant cannot read or write he or she must affix his or her mark in the presence of a witness. The name and address of the witness must be given.

NOTES

1. (1) If your appeal against conviction involves a question of law alone you have a right of appeal.

   (2) If your appeal against conviction is upon any ground other than a question of law then you have no right of appeal unless leave is granted by the Court of Appeal.

   (3) You have no right of appeal against sentence unless leave to appeal is granted by the Court of Appeal and your notice of appeal includes an application for leave to appeal.

2. (1) Whether your appeal is from conviction, sentence or both, this notice must be served within thirty days after the date of the sentence(s).

   (2) If this notice is served beyond that time then you must apply for an extension of time by completing the application set out below.

   (3) If you are in custody, this notice of appeal must be served by delivering it to the senior official of the institution in which you are confined.

APPLICATION FOR EXTENSION OF TIME

I hereby apply for an extension of time within which I may launch my appeal, upon the following grounds: (here state the reasons for delay)

Signed _____   Date _____

The Appellant, (strike out inapplicable provisions)

(*a*) appeals against his or her conviction upon grounds involving a question of law alone;

(*b*) applies for leave to appeal his or her conviction upon grounds involving a question of fact alone or a question of mixed law and fact, and if leave be granted, hereby appeals against the conviction;

(*c*) applies for leave to appeal against sentence, and if leave is granted, hereby appeals against the sentence.

GROUNDS OF APPEAL

These must be filled in before the notice is sent to the Registrar. The appellant must here set out the grounds or reasons why he or she alleges the conviction should be quashed or the sentence reduced. If one of the grounds set out is "misdirection to the jury" by the judge, particulars of the alleged misdirection must be set out in this notice.

FORM B

NOTICE OF APPEAL OR APPLICATION FOR LEAVE TO APPEAL

COURT OF APPEAL FOR ONTARIO

BETWEEN:

HER MAJESTY THE QUEEN

Respondent

and

A. B.

Appellant

NOTICE OF APPEAL

PARTICULARS OF CONVICTION

1. Place of conviction[1]

2. Name of judge

3. Offence(s)[2] of which accused convicted

4. Section(s) of Criminal Code under which accused convicted

5. Plea at trial

6. Length of trial

7. Sentence imposed

8. Date of conviction

9. Date of sentence

10. If accused in custody, place of incarceration

The appellant, (use applicable provisions)

(*a*) appeals against his or her conviction upon grounds involving a question of law alone;

(*b*) applies for leave to appeal his or her conviction upon grounds involving a question of fact alone or a question of mixed law and fact, and if leave be granted hereby appeals against the conviction; or

(*c*) applies for leave to appeal against sentence, and if leave be granted hereby appeals against the sentence.

The grounds for appeal are

The relief sought is

The appellant's address for service is

The appellant's address[3] is

Dated this   day of   , 20

[Name, address and telephone number of appellant's solicitor or, where none, the appellant]

To: The Registrar

Numbered notes set out below refer to corresponding numbers on notice.

Note 1.
Where the appeal is from the summary conviction appeal court, in addition to the matters specified in paragraphs 1 to 10 the Notice of Appeal must also specify the name of the judge of the appeal court, the date of the judgment of the appeal court and the result of the summary conviction Appeal.

Note 2.
The Notice of Appeal must refer to all offences under appeal.

Note 3.
These rules provide for service upon the appellant of certain material at the address provided in the Notice of Appeal. If the appellant changes address then the appellant must notify the Registrar.

References

Legislation and Rules

Bill C-45, *An Act to amend the Criminal Code (criminal liability of organizations)*, 2nd Sess., 37th Parl., 2003.

British North America Act, 30 & 31 Vict., c. 3 (U.K.).

Canada Evidence Act, R.S.C. 1985, c. C-5.

Canadian Bill of Rights, S.C. 1960, c. 44.

Canadian Charter of Rights and Freedoms, part I of the *Constitution Act, 1982*, R.S.C. 1985, app. II, no. 44.

Canadian Human Rights Act, R.S.C. 1985, c. H-6.

Citizen's Arrest and Self-defence Act, S.C. 2012, c. 9.

Constitution Act, 1867 (U.K.), 30 & 31 Vict., c. 3.

Constitution Act, 1982, R.S.C. 1985, app. II, no. 44.

Controlled Drugs and Substances Act, S.C. 1996, c. 19.

Corrections and Conditional Release Act, S.C. 1992, c. 20.

Crimes Against Humanity and War Crimes Act, S.C. 2000, c. 24.

Criminal Appeal Rules, S.I./93-169.

Criminal Code, 1892, S.C. 1982, 55-56 Vict., c. 29.

Criminal Code, R.S.C. 1985, c. C-46, as amended.

Criminal Proceedings Rules for the Superior Court of Justice (Ontario), S.I./2012-7.

Criminal Records Act, R.S.C. 1985, c. C-47.

Criminal Rules of the Ontario Court of Justice, S.I./2012-30.

DNA Identification Act, S.C. 1998, c. 37.

Highway Traffic Act, R.S.O. 1990, c. H.8.

Human Rights Code, R.S.B.C. 1996, c. 210.

Human Rights Code, R.S.O. 1990, c. H.19.

Identification of Criminals Act, R.S.C. 1985, c. I-1.

Income Tax Act, R.S.C. 1985, c. 1 (5th Supp.), as amended.

Juvenile Delinquents Act, S.C. 1908, c. 40, repealed.

National Defence Act, R.S.C. 1985, c. N-5.

Ontario Water Resources Commission Act, The, R.S.O. 1970, c. 332.

Provincial Offences Act, R.S.O. 1990, c. P.33.

Provincial Offences Procedures Act, R.S.A. 2000, c. P-34.

Rules of Professional Conduct, Law Society of Upper Canada, http://www.lsuc.on.ca/with.aspx?id=671.

Rules of the Ontario Court of Justice in Criminal Proceedings, S.I./97-133 [Repealed, S.I./2012-30, s. 6].

Summary Proceedings Act, R.S.N.S. 1989, c. 450.

Young Offenders Act, R.S.C. 1985, c. Y-1, repealed.

Youth Criminal Justice Act, S.C. 2002, c. 1.

Publications

Daubney Report. David Daubney, *Taking Responsibility: Report of the Standing Committee on Justice and Solicitor General on its review of sentencing, conditional release and related aspects of corrections* (Ottawa: Ministry of Supply and Services, 1988).

Legal Aid Ontario website: http://www.legalaid.on.ca.

Martin's Annual Criminal Code. Edward L. Greenspan, Marc Rosenberg, and Marie Henein (Toronto: Canada Law Book, 2013).

Record Suspension Guide: Step-by-Step Instructions and Application Forms, Parole Board of Canada, March 2012, http://pbc-clcc.gc.ca/prdons/pardoninstr-eng.pdf.

Youth Justice Renewal Initiative, 1998; http://www.justice.gc.ca/eng/pi/yj-jj/about-apropos/about-apropos.html.

Case Law

A.G. (Nova Scotia) v. MacIntyre, [1982] 1 S.C.R. 175, 132 D.L.R. (3d) 385, 65 C.C.C. (2d) 129.

A.M.J., R. v., (1999), 137 C.C.C. (3d) 213 (B.C.C.A.).

Agawa and Mallett, R. v., (1975), 28 C.C.C. (2d) 379 (Ont. C.A.).

Ash-Temple Co., R. v., (1949), 93 C.C.C. 267 (Ont. C.A.).

Askov, R. v., [1990] 2 S.C.R. 1199.

B.C. Motor Vehicle Act, Re, [1985] 2 S.C.R. 486.

Babcock, R. v., (1989), 31 O.A.C. 354 (C.A.).

Bachman, R. v., [1979] 6 W.W.R. 468 (B.C.C.A.).

Balderstone, R. v., (1983), 8 C.C.C. (3d) 532 (Man. C.A.), leave to appeal to the S.C.C. refused.

Beaudry, R. v., 2007 SCC 5, [2007] 1 S.C.R. 190.

Bedford v. Canada, 2010 ONSC 4264.

Bedford, Canada (Attorney General) v., 2012 ONCA 186.

Biniaris, R. v., 2000 SCC 15, [2000] 1 S.C.R. 381.

Boucher v. The Queen, [1955] S.C.R. 16.

Burke, R. v., [2002] 2 S.C.R. 857.

Butler, R. v., [1992] 1 S.C.R. 452.

Cameron, R. v., (1991), 2 O.R. (3d) 633, 64 C.C.C. (3d) 96 (C.A.).

Canadian Dredge & Dock Co. v. The Queen, [1985] 1 S.C.R. 662.

Chow, R. v., [2005] 1 S.C.R. 384.

Christensen, R. v., (1995), 100 Man. R. (2d) 25 (C.A.).

Collins, R. v., [1987] 1 S.C.R. 265, (1987), 33 C.C.C. (3d) 1.

Creighton, R. v., [1993] 3 S.C.R. 3, (1993), 83 C.C.C. (3d) 346.

Curtis, R. v., (1998), 123 C.C.C. (3d) 178 (Ont. C.A.).

Daviault, R. v., [1994] 3 S.C.R. 3.

Deutsch, R. v., [1986] 2 S.C.R. 2.

Ertel, R. v., (1987), 35 C.C.C. (3d) 398 (Ont. C.A.), leave to appeal to the S.C.C. refused.

Evans, R. v., [1996] 1 S.C.R. 8, 104 C.C.C. (3d) 23.

Fane Robinson Ltd., R. v., [1941] 3 D.L.R. 409 (Alta. C.A.).

Gladue, R. v., [1999] 1 S.C.R. 688.

Golden, R. v., 2001 SCC 83, [2001] 3 S.C.R. 679, 159 C.C.C. (3d) 449.

Gougeon, R. v., R. v. Haesler, R. v. Gray (1980), 55 C.C.C. (2d) 218 (Ont. C.A.), leave to appeal to the S.C.C. refused 35 N.R. 83n.

Grant, R. v., 2009 SCC 32, [2009] 2 S.C.R. 353.

Gruenke, R. v., [1991] 3 S.C.R. 263.

Guimond, R. v., [1979] 1 S.C.R. 960.

Hall, R. v., [2002] 3 S.C.R. 309.

Hibbert, R. v., (1995), 99 C.C.C. (3d) 193.

Hufsky, R. v., [1990] 1 S.C.R. 1257, 56 C.C.C. (3d) 22.

Hundal, R. v., [1993] 1 S.C.R. 867.

Hunter et al. v. Southam Inc., [1984] 2 S.C.R. 145, 14 C.C.C. (3d) 97.

Kendall and McKay, R. v., (1987), 35 C.C.C. (3d) 105 (Ont. C.A.).

Khan, R. v., [2001] 3 S.C.R. 823, 2001 SCC 86.

Lagiorgia v. Canada, [1987] 3 F.C. 28; leave to appeal to S.C.C. refused (1988), 43 C.C.C. (3d) vi.

Latimer, R. v., 2001 SCC 1, [2001] 1 S.C.R. 3.

Lennard's Carrying Co. v. Asiatic Petroleum Co., [1915] A.C. 705.

Lerke, R. v., (1986) 24 C.C.C (3d) 129, 25 D.L.R. (4th) 403 (Alta. C.A.).

Logan, R. v., [1990] 2 S.C.R. 731, 58 C.C.C. (3d) 391.

Mann, R. v., [2004] 3 S.C.R. 59, 185 C.C.C. (3d) 225.

McNamara (No. 1), R. v., (1981), 56 C.C.C. (2d) 193 (Ont. C.A.).

Morgentaler, Smoling and Scott, R. v., [1988] 1 S.C.R. 30.

Morin, R. v., [1992] 3 S.C.R. 286.

Parks, R. v., [1992] 2 S.C.R. 871.

Perka v. The Queen, [1984] 2 S.C.R. 232.

Pontes, R. v., [1995] 3 S.C.R. 44.

Pottle, R. v., (1979), 49 C.C.C. (2d) 113 (Nfld. C.A.).

Proulx, R. v., [2000] 1 S.C.R. 61.

Quiring and Kuipers, R. v., (1974), 19 C.C.C. (2d) 337 (Sask. C.A.).

Rhône (The) v. The Peter A.B. Widener, [1993] 1 S.C.R. 497.

Rose, R. v., [1998] 3 S.C.R. 262.

Ruzic, R. v., [2001] 1 S.C.R. 687, 153 C.C.C. (3d) 1.

S.A.B., R. v., 2003 SCC 60, [2003] 2 S.C.R. 678.

Saint-Laurent, R. v., (1993), 90 C.C.C. (3d) 291 (Que. C.A.).

Sansregret v. The Queen, [1985] 1 S.C.R. 570, 18 C.C.C.
    (3d) 223.

Sault Ste. Marie, R. v., [1978] 2 S.C.R. 1299.

Stinchcombe, R. v., [1991] 3 S.C.R. 326.

Stone, R. v., [1999] 2 S.C.R. 290.

Swain, R. v., [1991] 1 S.C.R. 993, 63 C.C.C (3d) 481.

Taillefer, R. v.; R. v. Duguay, [2003] 3 S.C.R. 307.

Therens, R. v., [1985] 1 S.C.R. 613.

Thornton, R. v., (1991), 1 O.R. (3d) 480 (Ont. C.A.); aff'd.
    1993 CanLII 95 (SCC), [1993] 2 S.C.R. 445.

Torbiak and Gillis, R. v., (1978), 40 C.C.C. (2d) 193 (Ont. C.A.).

Toronto Star Newspapers Ltd. v. Canada, [2010] 1 S.C.R. 721.

Tse, R. v., [2012] 1 S.C.R. 531.

Whitfield, R. v., [1970] S.C.R. 46.

Wills, R. v., (1992), 70 C.C.C. (3d) 529 (Ont. C.A.).

Yebes, R. v., [1987] 2 S.C.R. 168.

Glossary

A

abetting encouraging the principal offender to commit the offence, knowing that an offence is being committed

absolute discharge a sentence where there has been a finding of guilt made against the offender, but where no conviction is registered

absolute jurisdiction a court's exclusive authority to hear a case

absolute liability a regulatory offence (non-criminal) that has no fault element—the Crown need only prove the *actus reus* of the offence and the accused may not raise any defence as to his intention

accessory after the fact a person who, knowing that an offence has been committed, offers assistance to the offender for the purpose of helping him to escape detention or capture by the police

actus reus Latin term that is often translated as "the guilty act"; it involves the physical elements of a criminal offence

adjudication the process that leads to the making of a legal decision

admissibility refers to whether or not a particular piece of evidence is capable of being used at trial

adult sentences sentences that are available for offenders over the age of 18 under the *Criminal Code* and other federal statutes

aggravating circumstances circumstances surrounding the commission of an offence that increase the culpability associated with the offence

aggravating factors circumstances surrounding the commission of an offence that increase the penalty associated with the offence

aiding helping or assisting the principal offender to commit the offence, knowing that an offence is being committed

alibi generally, evidence of innocence—usually that the accused was somewhere else when the crime was committed; the word "alibi" derives from the Latin term for "elsewhere"

alternative measures various options outside the traditional criminal justice system that are available for dealing with offenders

appeal book a book that contains all of the documents that are necessary for the hearing of an appeal by an appellate court

application similar to a motion, it is a hearing that usually concerns a procedural issue before a final decision is reached in the case

appreciate to have an awareness and understanding of the consequences of one's actions

arbitrary detention action in which the police improperly and unlawfully stop and hold a person in their custody for even a few minutes

arraignment the formal reading of the charge in court; the arraignment signifies the start of a criminal trial

arrest warrant a court order directed to the police in a certain geographical area to arrest an accused and bring him or her before the court to answer a criminal charge *autrefois acquit* a special plea that is made by a person charged with a criminal offence where the person has previously been acquitted or found not guilty in respect of the charge and thus cannot be tried again for the same offence

autrefois convict a special plea that is made by a person charged with a criminal offence where the person has previously been convicted or found guilty in respect of the charge and thus cannot be tried again for the same offence

B

bench warrant a type of arrest warrant issued by a justice when an accused person does not appear in criminal court as required

beyond mere preparation a legal test applied by a judge to determine whether the accused has taken enough significant steps toward the commission of an offence to be found guilty of an attempt

block fee a pre-arranged amount that will be paid to the lawyer for providing specified legal services to the client

book of authorities a book for use at trial by the parties and the court containing all authorities, including cases and legislation that will be relied upon at trial

C

case management supervision by the court of a legal case as it proceeds through the justice system; the concept of case management has existed for years in civil cases, but is a relatively recent phenomenon in criminal cases

causation part of the *actus reus* of some criminal offences where the Crown is required to prove that the actions or behaviour of the accused resulted in or caused a specified consequence

challenge for cause the ability of the Crown and the accused to challenge a prospective juror's impartiality

civil law the body of law in the Canadian legal system that is non-criminal; the term may also be used to describe world legal systems that are based on foundations other than British common law; most countries in Europe have civil law systems, as does the province of Quebec in its provincial law

colour of right a person honestly believes that they have a legal right to the property in question

compellable witness a witness who can be lawfully required to give evidence; a compellable witness can be forced to give evidence

competent witness a witness who is lawfully capable of giving evidence; a competent witness may give evidence

concurrent jurisdiction the *actus reus* has taken place in more than one location, and courts in either location may have jurisdiction to hear the case; an accused may only be tried in one jurisdiction

concurrent sentence a sentence in which the time that is actually spent in custody is determined by the longest sentence, and the sentences are served at the same time

conditional discharge a sentence similar to an absolute discharge except that it takes effect only after the offender has satisfied specified court-imposed conditions

consecutive sentence a sentence in which the time that is actually spent in custody is the sum of all sentences, and the sentences are served one after another

conspiracy a serious indictable offence in which two or more persons make an agreement to commit an offence and intend to commit the planned offence

contingency fee an agreement between a lawyer and client that legal fees will be payable and based on a future event occurring; normally, a contingency fee is payable upon successful completion of a matter and is calculated as a percentage of any moneys recovered by the lawyer

contract law the body of law that deals with legally enforceable agreements made between parties that spell out their rights and obligations in relation to each other in a particular transaction

correctness a standard of review that permits an appellate court to substitute its decision for the decision of a lower court when, in its opinion, the decision of the lower court is incorrect or wrong

counselling instructing, recruiting, or advising a person to commit a criminal offence, knowing that the person is likely to commit the offence

counts consecutively numbered paragraphs in an Information or Indictment that set out the charges against an accused person

criminal law body of law that deals with wrongs or harm caused to society as a whole that is prosecuted by the state or government rather than the person who is harmed by the wrongdoing

criminal liability liability for committing a criminal act

criminal procedure the broad body of law that governs the legal route that must be taken as a criminal charge is laid and makes its way through the court system to completion

cross-examination principle of the adversarial system in which one side in a legal proceeding is given an opportunity to question the witnesses for the opposing party in order to challenge their evidence and the entire case

D

dead time credit for the period of time that an offender spends in pretrial custody

denunciation a principle of sentencing that focuses on denouncing or condemning criminal behaviour

deterrence a principle of sentencing that focuses on deterring or discouraging criminal behaviour

direct examination initial questioning of a witness that is conducted by the party who called the witness to provide evidence in the proceeding; also called an examination-in-chief

directed verdict of acquittal a motion to the court by the accused for an acquittal immediately following the completion of the Crown's case when there has not been any evidence upon which a reasonable jury, properly instructed, could convict the accused; sometimes referred to as a non-suit

directing mind the person within a corporation who has the power to exercise decision-making authority on matters of corporate policy

disbursements out-of-pocket expenses incurred by a lawyer on behalf of a client

discovery procedural devices that occur before trial where a party is able to obtain evidence from an adverse party: in civil law, any party can discover any adverse party; in criminal law, only the accused may have discovery rights

diversion redirection of a criminal charge from prosecution to an alternative program that often focuses on rehabilitation

docket a record of time spent working on a client matter

due diligence a defence to a strict liability offence in which the accused attempts to establish that he or she took every reasonable precaution to avoid committing a regulatory offence

duplicitous count a count that contains more than a single transaction

E

election of the accused for indictable offences not listed in s. 469 or 553, the accused has a choice as to the level of court in which they want to be tried

endorsement a justice shows approval of a document by signing his or her name on it, indicating agreement

error of law an error in the interpretation or application of law; an error of law is understood by contrasting it with an error of fact, which is an error in the resolution of the facts in issue

exclusionary remedy power given to the courts under s. 24 of the Charter to prevent the admission of wrongfully obtained evidence at an accused person's trial

exculpatory evidence that relieves of blame or liability

exigent circumstances an urgent situation

extrajudicial measures various options outside the traditional criminal justice system that are available for dealing with offenders

F

federal law-making power the authority given by the Constitution to the federal government to make laws in certain areas—criminal law is made only by the federal government

federal state a country in which the constitution provides for more than one level of government—Canada is a federal state

focus hearing an informal meeting between a judge, Crown, and defence to facilitate a more efficient preliminary inquiry; a new feature of the *Criminal Rules of the Ontario Court of Justice*

G-H

general intent a basic level of *mens rea* in which the Crown must prove that the accused had the intent to commit the *actus reus* of the offence

grounds for appeal basis upon which an appeal can be commenced and be successful

hybrid or Crown option offences offences that may be prosecuted as either summary conviction offences or indictable offences, at the choice or election of the Crown

I

identification theory the theory that establishes *mens rea* in a corporation by reference to the directing mind

inchoate offence an offence in which the *mens rea* is present but the *actus reus* may not be complete

inculpatory evidence that is incriminating

indictable offences offences that are the more serious offences in the *Criminal Code* and that follow the indictable procedure in the Code

Indictment a document signed by a Crown attorney that replaces an Information when a criminal matter is before the Superior Court of Justice

informant a person who swears an Information, usually a police officer

Information a sworn document that commences the prosecution of a criminal offence

infringement of rights action by governments or their agents that violates a right granted under the *Charter of Rights and Freedoms*

innocent agent a person who helps the principal offender commit the offence, without realizing that an offence is being committed

intermittent sentence a jail sentence that is served in small blocks of time instead of all at once

intoxication to have an impaired consciousness of one's actions due to the use of alcohol or drugs

intra vires a Latin term meaning that a law has been made within the authority of the law-making body

J-K

joint submission a sentencing submission put forth to the court that has been agreed to by both the Crown and defence

judicare a government-funded program that provides free legal services to those who meet financial eligibility requirements

judicial measures the manner in which offenders are traditionally dealt with by the criminal justice system

jurisdiction the legal authority for government to pass laws in certain areas or the power of the courts to make legal decisions and judgments; the power or authority of a court to hear a case—without jurisdiction, the court cannot deal with the matter

jury panel/jury array these terms are used interchangeably and refer to the large pool from which a jury is selected

justice model of criminal justice a model of criminal justice that focuses on the protection of the public and the rights of the person charged with an offence

know to be merely aware of one's actions

L

leave to appeal where permission to appeal is a prerequisite to hearing the appeal; the purpose is to establish a threshold that must be met before an appeal can be heard by an appellate court

legalese language that uses obscure legal terms and that is difficult to understand without legal training

lesser and included offence an offence that includes all the elements of a less serious offence

limitation period a period of time in which a legal action, including the laying of a summary conviction charge, must be taken or the power to take the action is lost forever

line-up to establish the identity of a suspect, police gather a number of people with a similar appearance, line them up side-by-side, and then ask the victim of the crime to pick out the perpetrator of the offence

litigation privilege a form of privilege that applies to communications between a lawyer and third parties where the dominant purpose of the communication is pending or actual litigation

M

mens rea Latin term that is commonly translated as "the guilty mind"; it involves the mental or fault elements of a criminal offence

mental disorder a disease of the mind that legally makes a person incapable of appreciating the nature or quality of his or her act, or of knowing it is wrong

mistrial a trial that has been terminated before reaching its conclusion because of an irregularity

mitigating factors circumstances surrounding the commission of an offence that reduce the penalty associated with the offence

N

no force or effect a law that is struck down by the courts is said to be of no force or effect because it is inoperable

notwithstanding clause a rarely used controversial provision in the *Charter of Rights and Freedoms* that allows the federal government or a provincial legislature to override certain portions of the Charter

nullity a nullity is that which is legally void and has no legal validity

O

objective *mens rea* proving criminal intention by determining what a reasonable person would have had in his or her mind

objective test a legal test that focuses on the actions and beliefs of a hypothetical reasonable person; includes a consideration of reasonableness

omission a type of *actus reus* in which the accused person fails to do something that he is legally required to do

onus of proof the prosecutor in a criminal case or the plaintiff in a civil case has the burden or onus to present enough evidence to win their case beyond a reasonable doubt or on the balance of probabilities, respectively

order a decision or direction made or given by the court

P

panel of judges appeals in the higher courts are often heard by more than one judge; the judges form a panel

pardon a special plea where the commission of a criminal offence and the relevant penalty are forgiven, usually by a head of state or by an act of Parliament

parole the release of an offender from custody before the sentence has been fully completed, subject to various conditions

particulars specific details supporting a more general statement or proposition; in criminal law, an application for particulars is normally a request for a detailed itemization of a count in an Information

party to the offence anyone who helps, encourages, advises, or protects the principal offender may also be a party to the offence and can be charged with that offence even though they did not actually commit it

peace bond a court order that requires a person to keep the peace and be of good behaviour for a specified period of time; it is not a conviction or a finding of guilt

penal negligence a type of *mens rea* in which an objective standard is applied to determine the mental element of some offences

peremptory challenge the ability of the Crown and the accused to reject a potential juror without further explanation or reason

plea agreement an arrangement between the prosecution and the defence in which the accused agrees to plead guilty to the charge in exchange for a lesser penalty or to plead guilty to a lesser charge; the justice must agree to the arrangement before it can be put into place

preferred indictment a special indictment (sometimes referred to as a direct indictment) that is signed by the Attorney General that sends an indictable offence directly to trial without a preliminary inquiry

pretrial detention the period of time that a person who has been charged with an offence spends in custody without being released while awaiting trial

prima facie Latin for "at first appearance" or "on the face of it": during the presentation of their evidence at trial, the Crown must prove enough facts beyond a reasonable doubt that the accused will be convicted unless he or she successfully raises a proper defence

principal offender the person who actually commits the offence

private law the body of law that deals with relationships between individuals or individuals and businesses—contract law is an example

privilege a rule that requires certain communications to be kept confidential and private

probation a sentence that permits an offender to live in the community but under supervision and subject to various conditions

procedural law the body of law that sets out the rules for a case that is making its way through the court to completion; in criminal law, it begins with the police investigation and the laying of the charge and goes through to the end of the trial

provincial offences offences created by provincial legislatures to enforce certain regulatory laws that are within their constitutional law-making authority; they are not criminal offences

public law body of law that deals with the relationship between the government and individuals or businesses—criminal law is an example

Q

quash nullify or cancel

quasi-criminal offences offences created to enforce regulatory laws—they are not criminal offences but they have a number of the features of criminal law; provincial offences are an example

R

real and substantial connection a legal test that is applied to determine whether a Canadian court may take geographical jurisdiction in a case

reasonable doubt very high standard of proof that the Crown must meet to prove the guilt of the accused person

reasonable person test an objective test for *mens rea* in which the court does not look at what was in the mind of the actual accused person before the court, but rather at what an ordinary person of normal capabilities, in the same circumstances as the accused, would have understood to be the risk of his or her actions

reasonableness a standard of review that permits an appellate court to substitute its decision for the decision of a lower court only when the decision of the lower court is unreasonable

rebuttal evidence evidence that contradicts or refutes earlier evidence

recklessness a type of *mens rea* in which the accused fully understands the risk of harm associated with his behaviour or actions and engages in the behaviour despite the risk

record suspension an order granted by the Parole Board of Canada that permits a qualifying offender to have a criminal record separated and kept apart from other criminal records; formerly called a pardon

re-examination a second questioning of a witness that is conducted by the party who called the witness to provide evidence in the proceeding; a re-examination will follow a cross-examination

reparations a principle of sentencing that focuses on repairing the harm done by the offender to the victim or to society as a whole

representative any director, partner, employee, member, agent, or contractor of an organization

restitution a sentence that requires the offender to compensate the victim for any loss or injury arising out of the commission of the offence

retainer (agreement) a written agreement or contract that sets out the rights and obligations of the lawyer and client

retainer (deposit) a deposit paid by a client before legal services have been provided by a lawyer

retainer (engagement) the engagement by a client of a lawyer to provide specified legal services

S

seizure confiscation of evidence by police

senior officer a representative who plays an important role in the establishment of an organization's policies, or is responsible for managing an important aspect of an organization's activities

service legal delivery of a court document according to court rules

set-date an early appearance in court to set a trial date in a case

severance separation of one matter or issue into two or more with each being decided on its own without regard for the other(s)

show cause hearing another term for bail hearing

single transaction rule a rule requiring that each count in an Information or Indictment can only refer to a single transaction

solicitor–client privilege a form of privilege that applies to communications between a lawyer and his or her client

specific intent a *mens rea* that has two levels in that the Crown must prove that the accused had the intent to perform the *actus reus* for a specific purpose or ulterior motive

standard of proof the legal level of proof that must be established in a court case before the case may be won; the standard of proof in a criminal case is beyond a reasonable doubt and in a non-criminal case it is the lower standard of the balance of probabilities

standard of review the manner in which an appellate court will evaluate the decision of a lower court

stare decisis the legal principle used in the common law by which the lower courts must follow the decisions, or precedents, set by the higher courts when the facts of a case are generally the same

stay of proceedings a court ruling to stop or suspend legal proceedings

strict liability a regulatory offence (non-criminal) that requires the Crown to prove only the *actus reus* and not the *mens rea* of the offence—the accused may raise the defence of due diligence

striking down a law power given to the courts under the *Charter of Rights and Freedoms* to make a law inoperable because the law violates the Charter

subjective *mens rea* determining criminal intention by looking at what was actually in the mind of the accused before the court

subjective test a legal test that focuses on the actions and beliefs of the person in issue; does not include a consideration of reasonableness

submission in general, the act of making a presentation or an assertion; can also be used to mean "closing argument"

subpoena a document that compels a witness to attend court; in civil proceedings the document is often called a summons (under the *Criminal Code*, however, a summons is a document that compels the accused to attend court)

substantive law the part of an area of law that defines the rights and responsibilities in that area of law; in criminal law, it is the part of the law that deals with the creation of criminal offences, the defences that may apply, and the penalties for breaking the law

summary conviction offences offences that are the least serious offences in the *Criminal Code* and that follow the summary conviction procedure in the Code

summons a court order commanding a person to appear in court on a specific date and time to answer a criminal charge against him or her

super summary conviction offences summary conviction offences that carry a higher maximum imprisonment penalty than the general penalty of six months

supreme statute a statute with which all other statutes must comply; the Constitution is a supreme statute

surety a person who agrees to supervise the accused while he or she is out on bail and ensure that the accused attends court and obeys any conditions placed on him or her; the promise to supervise is backed by a promise and an ability to pay the bail amount if the accused does not attend court or comply with conditions

surrebuttal evidence evidence that contradicts or refutes rebuttal evidence; it is essentially a rebuttal to a rebuttal

suspended sentence a sentence where the sentencing court suspends or holds in abeyance the passing of a sentence on an offender

T

tort law the body of law that deals with harm caused to a person by another for which the injured person may sue the wrongdoer for monetary compensation for the harm caused

transcript a word-for-word, written record of everything said in court; it is prepared by a court reporter

trial *de novo* a form of appeal where the appellate court holds a new trial without any regard to the first trial; the appeal essentially takes the form of a completely new trial, as if the previous trial had not occurred

trial book a book for use at trial by a legal representative where all papers and documents relating to the proceeding are organized in an easy-to-use and easy-to-find way

trier of fact person or persons who must determine the credible facts in a case; this can be a jury, or if there is no jury, the judge who hears the evidence

trier of law the judge who determines the law that applies to the facts of a case and who, in a trial with a jury, instructs the jury on the application of the law

U–V

ultra vires a Latin term meaning that a law has been made outside the authority of the law-making body

voir dire a mini trial or trial within a trial that is designed to determine the admissibility of evidence

voluntariness in all criminal and quasi-criminal prosecutions, a statement made by a person charged with an offence is not admissible as evidence against that person unless the Crown proves beyond a reasonable doubt that it was made voluntarily

W–Y

welfare model of criminal justice a model of criminal justice that focuses on the welfare and well-being of the offender

wilful blindness a type of *mens rea* in which the accused person intentionally closes his eyes to obvious criminal actions in an attempt to claim that he did not know that the actions were criminal

without prejudice communications a form of privilege that extends to communications concerning settlement discussions

wrongfully obtained evidence evidence that is obtained as a result of a violation of a person's rights under the *Charter of Rights and Freedoms*

youth justice court the court that has exclusive jurisdiction over persons under the age of 18 who have been charged with a criminal or other federal offence

Index